D1564355

HISTORICAL WRITINGS

Classics of British Historical Literature

JOHN CLIVE, EDITOR

Lord Bolingbroke

———

Historical Writings

EDITED AND WITH AN INTRODUCTION BY
ISAAC KRAMNICK

The University of Chicago Press
CHICAGO AND LONDON

The University of Chicago Press, Chicago 60637
The University of Chicago Press, Ltd., London
© 1972 by the University of Chicago
All rights reserved
Published 1972
Printed in the United States of America
International Standard Book Number: 0–226–06345–3 (clothbound)
Library of Congress Catalog Card Number: 72–75608

Contents

Series Editor's Preface		vii
Editor's Introduction		xi
I.	Letters on the Study and Use of History	
	Letter 1	3
	Letter 2	7
	Letter 3	23
	Letter 4	49
	Letter 5	61
	Letter 6	81
	Letter 8	99
II.	Remarks on the History of England	
	Letter 1	153
	Letter 2	163
	Letter 4	177
	Letter 5	182
	Letter 6	188
	Letter 7	193
	Letter 8	201
	Letter 9	209
	Letter 10	215
	Letter 11	221
	Letter 12	229
	Letter 13	238
	Letter 14	245
	Letter 15	254
	Letter 16	264
	Letter 17	275

CONTENTS

Letter 18	281
Letter 19	291
Letter 20	299
Letter 21	309
Letter 22	320
Letter 23	330
Index	341

Series Editor's Preface

This series of reprints has one major purpose: to put into the hands of students and other interested readers outstanding—and sometimes neglected—works dealing with British history which have either gone out of print or are obtainable only at a forbiddingly high price.

The phrase Classics of British Historical Literature requires some explanation, in view of the fact that the two companion series published by the University of Chicago Press are entitled Classic European Historians and Classic American Historians. Why, then, introduce the word *literature* into the title of this series?

One reason is obvious. History, if it is to live beyond its own generation, must be memorably written. The greatest British historians—Clarendon, Gibbon, Hume, Carlyle, Macaulay—survive today, not merely because they contribute to the cumulative historical knowledge about their subjects, but because they were masters of style and literary artists as well. And even historians of the second rank, if they deserve to survive, are able to do so only because they can still be read with pleasure. To emphasize this truth at the present time, when much eminently solid and worthy academic history suffers from being almost totally unreadable, seems worth doing.

The other reason for including the word *literature* in the title of the series has to do with its scope. To read history is to learn about the past. But if, in trying to learn about the British past, one were to restrict oneself to the reading of formal works of history, one would miss a great deal. Often a historical novel, a sociological inquiry, or an account of events and institutions couched in semifictional form teaches us just as much about the past as does the "history" that calls itself by that name. And, frequently, these "informal" historical works turn out to be less well known than their merit deserves. By calling this series Classics of British Historical Literature it will be possible to include such books without doing violence to the usual nomenclature.

Along with Churchill, Bolingbroke is the outstanding example in modern British history of the statesman and politician who was, at the same time, a historian. The conjunction brings to mind at once the question of the extent of political party bias in the resultant product, and that is indeed one of the questions that must be raised in any consideration of Bolingbroke. But the latter was, of course, a philosopher of history as well as a historian. In most discussions of the intellectual history of the eighteenth century he figures as the author of the aphorism that history is philosophy teaching by examples. Actually, as a glance at letter 2 of the *Letters on the Study and Use of History* will reveal, Bolingbroke does not take credit for this aphorism himself, but remarks that he has read it somewhere or other, probably in Dionysius of Halicarnassus. Furthermore, this single sentence hardly does justice to the complexity and subtlety of Bolingbroke's historical thought, admirably illuminated by Professor Kramnick in his introduction to this volume.

Professor Kramnick places Bolingbroke between two traditions—the didactic historiography of classical humanism and the skeptical historiography of the Enlightenment. Both of these traditions appear and intermingle in his writings, which demonstrate the tensions that result from attempting to sustain the moral mission of history in an age that tended to doubt the worth of all such missions. But that is not the end of Bolingbroke's complexity as a writer of history. He was a partisan himself, a leader of the opposition against Walpole's "Robinocracy" in the 1730s. But, as Professor Kramnick shows, far from launching a series of missiles clearly marked "Tory" at Walpole, he attacked him with the very Whiggish weapons of the myth of the common law and the ancient and immemorial constitution.

As a philosopher of history no less than as a practicing historian, Bolingbroke resists simple labeling. On the one hand, he developed an economic interpretation of history, useful to him for his fierce onslaught on Walpole and the plutocracy. On the other, he could not wholly divest himself of his humanist moralism which ascribed historical change to the thoughts and actions of great individuals.

As Professor Kramnick presents him, then, Bolingbroke the historian must be seen from different angles in order to be fully understood. But in whatever role the reader encounters him, he is always a pleasure to read—thanks to his mordant style, his elegant wit, and the effortless brilliance of anything he wrote.

JOHN CLIVE

Editor's Introduction

Bolingbroke's Life and Career

The Tory party has provided England in each of the past three centuries with, among other things, a statesman who could write. Bolingbroke wrote no novels, though he did try poetry; Churchill wrote one novel and a great deal of history. Disraeli, no mean novelist, wrote no history. Bolingbroke was more than a historian, however; he was a political and philosophical essayist who drew such wits as Pope, Swift, and Gay to his circle in opposition to Walpole. By the end of the century, however, Burke could ask, "Who now reads Bolingbroke, whoever read him through?"[1] John Adams felt obliged, several years later, to answer Burke. Writing to Jefferson in 1813, he commented, "I have read him through more than five times in my life." Morever, what he read there pleased him. "There is nothing so profound, correct, and perfect on the subject of government in the English or any other language," Adams exclaimed. Jefferson himself recommended that Bolingbroke's writings be in the library of every well-read gentleman.[2] Of all Bolingbroke's

1. Edmund Burke, *Reflections on the Revolution in France* (New York, 1955), p. 101.

2. Quoted in Zoltan Haraszti, *John Adams and the Prophets of Progress* (Cambridge, Mass., 1952), p. 54; Julian Boyd, ed., *The Papers of Thomas Jefferson* (Princeton, 1950), 1:374 (Jefferson to Skipworth, "A Virginia Gentleman's Library").

works, the one most widely read in the nineteenth century was, interestingly enough, *Letters on the Study and Use of History*. The essay that Chesterfield had advised his son "almost to get by heart" went through more foreign editions in the next century and a half than anything else written by the Tory statesman.[3] But before we turn to an analysis of his historical writings, some comments are in order on Bolingbroke the public figure.

Bolingbroke was often read less for his powers of persuasion than for his social and political position. In looking at a Bolingbroke essay, the eighteenth- and nineteenth-century reader confronted one of the most important and controversial figures in English public life during the period that spanned the Glorious Revolution and the reign of George III. From his entrance into Parliament in 1700 his rise to fame was meteoric;[4] by 1711, for example, he was one of Queen Anne's secretaries of state. Convinced that the long war with Louis XIV had enriched Whig financial circles while impoverishing the gentry, Bolingbroke, aided by Swift, sought an end to hostilities. This effort culminated in Bolingbroke's greatest achievement, his negotiation of the Treaty of Utrecht in April 1713. The Tory government which brought the peace came to an abrupt end, however, in 1714. Harley resigned as Anne's first minister, and she, remembering Bolingbroke's rakish past, refused to name him as Harley's replacement. She gave the staff instead to Shrewsbury, a Hanoverian, who in turn was replaced by Townshend. Anne died in August 1714, and on 18 September George I landed in England. Fearing Whig reprisals against the former Tory government, Bolingbroke fled the country on 26 March 1715 and joined the forces of the Stuart Pretender in Paris.

Bolingbroke spent the next ten years in exile. These were the years during which he turned to the study of history and philosophy, met and was befriended by Voltaire and Montesquieu, wrote his first essays, and became one of the important intermediaries of French and English ideas in the early Enlighten-

---

3. P. D. Stanhope, Earl of Chesterfield, *Letters to His Son* (London, 1744), 1:213; G. Barber, "A Bibliography of Henry St. John, Viscount Bolingbroke" (Ph.D. diss., Oxford, 1963).

4. See the bibliographic note at the end of this essay for sources on Bolingbroke's career.

ment. At his Château, La Source, and in Paris at Le Club de L'Entresol, the exiled English nobleman gathered around him a coterie of learned men from whom he could learn much and to whom he was willing and able to impart much. When he returned to England in 1725, his friends hardly knew him, for in France he had become a philosopher, quite above "trifling" in politics. Pope, impressed with the new Bolingbroke, wrote to Swift: "Lord Bolingbroke is the most improved mind since you saw him, that was ever improved without shifting into a new body or being."[5]

But Bolingbroke preferred to continue in political life. Walpole had seen to it that he could never reenter the House of Lords or hold public office, so he turned to journalism as a platform from which to attack Walpole's Whig ministry. His weekly newspaper, *The Craftsman,* waged constant warfare on Walpole for the next ten years. In its pages appeared two of Bolingbroke's most important works: the *Remarks on the History of England,* which came out in weekly installments in 1730–31, and the *Dissertation Upon Parties,* which appeared in 1734.

Bolingbroke returned to France in 1735, remaining there until 1738. It was during these years that he wrote the *Letters on the Study and Use of History.* Returning to England in 1738, he was received back into the opposition circles now formed around Frederick, the Prince of Wales. It was for Frederick that he wrote in 1739 (though did not publish until 1749) his most famous essay, *The Idea of a Patriot King.* The Commons and the nobility had failed to rescue the country from Walpole and the new order of financial capitalism ushered in by the Whigs and their Bank of England. The only hope for returning England to its original principles was that the next monarch, Frederick, might be a Patriot King, "a sort of standing miracle, so rarely seen." Even this was not to be, however; for Frederick, the darling of the opposition, soon died. Convinced that the English had outlived their greatness and that, like the Romans, they too would be eaten away by the internal disease of corruption, Bolingbroke returned once again to France where he resumed his philosophical and historical writings.

5. Whitwell Elwin and W. J. Courthope, eds., *The Works of Alexander Pope* (London, 1871–88), 3:58.

He returned to England, this time to stay, after Walpole's fall from power in 1742. Political life after Walpole was still not to Bolingbroke's taste. He was convinced that the state of public life had not improved, and that the Pelhams were no better than Walpole. Venality, corruption, and factionalism were as prevalent then, he held, as they had been in 1710 or 1734. Compounding his disappointment was personal chagrin at his treatment by Pitt and the old Patriots. "Some who leaned upon me as their crutch in their days of lameness, have laid me by as a useless implement," he lamented.[6]

In December of 1751 Bolingbroke died. His poet friend Mallet published his remaining works in the course of the next three years. Literary and intellectual England was shocked by the *Letters on the Study and Use of History,* published for the first time in 1752, and by the *Philosophical Fragments,* published in 1754. Horace Walpole's comments are typical of the general reaction:

> It is comical to see how he is given up here, since the last of his writings . . . have been published. While he betrayed and abused every man who trusted him, or who had forgiven him, or to whom he was obliged, he was a hero, a patriot, and a philosopher; and the greatest genius of the age; the moment his craftsmen against Moses and St. Paul etc. were published, we have discovered that he was the worst man, and the worst writer in the world.[7]

To Samuel Johnson these posthumous works marked Bolingbroke "a scoundrel and a coward," a scoundrel "for charging a blunderbuss against religion and morality" and a coward because "he had not the resolution to fire it off himself"[8] and had left it to be published after his death. No less than thirteen pamphlets appeared in the three years after 1752 attacking Bolingbroke's *Letters on the Study and Use of History.*[9] One appeared in its defense, albeit of towering import, for in 1753 *A Defense*

---

6. G. H. Rose, ed., *The Marchmont Papers* (London, 1831), 2:360.
7. Horace Walpole, *Letters to Sir Horace Mann,* 2 vols. (London, 1833), 2:86.
8. James Boswell, *Life of Johnson,* 5 vols. (London, 1889), 1:218.
9. See G. H. Nadel, "Bolingbroke's Letters on History," *Journal of the History of Ideas,* October–December 1962, vol. 23, no. 4.

of the Late Lord Bolingbroke's Letters on the Study and Use of History was offered by Voltaire. Bolinbroke's controversial life and career had come to this—upon his death, men debated his views on history.

The Utility of Example: Bolingbroke the Humanist Historian

Bolingbroke's historical writings bridge two great and con-tradictory traditions of historical scholarship. He is, on the one hand, one of the last great humanist historians concerned with didactic history as a source of exemplary moral behavior. On the other hand, he is an early figure in the development of Enlighten-ment historiography, with its skeptical attitude to the validity and utility of history. It is not surprising, then, that Bolingbroke's writings on history present two distinct faces. In the one there is a positive attitude to history, a conviction of its practical value to teach and instruct; in the other there is a suspiciousness of history and an eagerness to discredit it. While the tone of one is positive, unreflective, anecdotal, and practical, that of the other is critical, scholarly, skeptical, and negative. These different orientations to history do not represent stages in the development of a changing historical attitude. They are simultaneous expressions of his views on history, found side by side in the *Letters on the Study and Use of History.* This obviously creates problems. Consistent adherence to both positions is impossible. It is difficult for his-tory to instruct if, at the same time, it is unreliable. As we shall see, however, Bolingbroke does try to reconcile the two posi-tions in a humanist revision of Bayle's pyrrhonism.

However, Bolingbroke did not see history only from the per-spective of a historian. He was before all else a politician, and as such very much aware of the importance of history as ammuni-tion to be used in political battle. In addition, then, to Boling-broke the humanist historian and Bolingbroke the Enlighten-ment historian, we shall have to look at Bolingbroke the parti-san historian. An analysis of Bolingbroke's historical method must begin, however, with his vision of history's moral mission.

From antiquity to the eighteenth century, history served in large part as a medium of moral instruction. Its purpose was primarily conceived as providing examples and lessons from the past for the education of the public in general and of rulers in particular. Historical events were described and studied, not in terms of their intrinsic meaning or their importance as historical phenomena, but in terms of their relevance for moral and political education. This "exemplary theory of history," as Nadel calls it,[10] suffered first the assault of the philosophes who questioned the reliability and the utility of history, and then finally succumbed in the nineteenth century to the positivist heirs of the Enlightenment. In the nineteenth century the study of historical events was shorn of its didactic role and became an academic discipline concerned only with the pursuit and validation of facts. Ranke rings the death knell for moralizing history in his vision of the historian as one whose job it is "simply to show how things really were." "To history," he writes in 1824, "has been attributed the office to judge the past and to instruct the present to make its future useful; at such high functions this present attempt does not aim—it merely wants to show how things really were."[11]

Bolingbroke held no such lowly view of the historian's craft. The function of history, according to him, was to "make men better and wiser," to train them in "private and public virtue." The humanist Bolingbroke saw history's mission as a noble one. It was, he quotes Dionysius of Halicarnassus, "philosophy teaching by example."[12] It is by this aphorism that Bolingbroke's "exemplary theory of history" is usually remembered.[13] It is most appropriate that this central tenet of his humanist historiographic orientation should have been borrowed from antiquity;

10. G. H. Nadel, "Philosophy of History before Historicism," in *Studies in the Philosophy of History,* ed. G. H. Nadel (New York, 1965).

11. Quoted in G. H. Nadel, "Philosophy of History before Historicism," p. 73.

12. *Letters on the Study and Use of History,* in *The Works of Lord Bolingbroke,* 4 vols. (Philadelphia, 1841), 2:177 (hereafter referred to as *Letters*).

13. See Leslie Stephen, *History of English Thought in the Eighteenth Century,* 2 vols. (New York, 1962); Herbert Butterfield, *The Englishman and His History* (Cambridge, 1944); idem, *The Statecraft of Machiavelli* (New York, 1962); J. G. A. Pocock, *The Ancient Constitution and the Feudal Law: A Study of English Historical Thought in the Seventeenth Century* (Cambridge, 1957); D. C. Douglas, *English Scholars* (London, 1939); Nadel, "Philosophy of History."

for the roots of his attitude to history in this phase of his argument are firmly embedded in the writings of the classical historians.

Nadel has eloquently described the rich didactic tradition that can be found in the historical writings of Polybius, Cicero, Dionysius, Diodorus Siculus, Lucian of Samosata, and Tacitus. These writers shared the conviction that history served a very practical function, relating the past experiences of others as examples to influence the behavior of posterity. The attitude is best expressed in Polybius's very practical and political justification of the writing and reading of history. "The soundest education and training for a life of active politics is the study of history, and . . . the surest and indeed the only method of learning how to bear the vicissitudes of fortune is to recall the calamities of others."[14] This justification of the study of history is shared by Bolingbroke, who wrote near the end of the long hegemony of the "exemplary theory." Addressing the young and future leaders of England, Bolingbroke implores them "to be useful to society, and to promote the happiness of mankind," to serve the republic and not their private ambition. To better serve this public they must study history. Bolingbroke quotes Polybius to make his point.

> "I have recorded these things," says Polybius, after giving an account of the defeat of Regulus, "that they who read these commentaries may be rendered better by them; for all men have two ways of improvement, one arising from their own experience, and one from the experience of others. . . . " Polybius goes on and concludes, "that since the first of these ways exposes us to great labor and peril, whilst the second works the same good effect, and is attended by no evil circumstances, every one ought to take for granted that the study of history is the best school where he can learn how to conduct himself in all the situations of life."[15]

In seeing history in terms of its didactic value, Bolingbroke was part of a tradition that had long outlived antiquity. During and after the Renaissance, the "exemplary theory" dominated

14. Quoted in Nadel, "Philosophy of History," p. 53.
15. *Letters,* 2:184, 221.

the humanist attitude. In England in the middle of the sixteenth century it can be found in the *Mirror for Magistrates*. This series of verse narratives describes the downfall of various magnates in English history. The premise is self-evident. The good prince in Renaissance England should hold up to the present the mirror of the past and draw from it lessons for good government.[16] This humanist conception of history was equally at home in France. In 1670 Père Le Moyne described history as "a sustained account of things that are true, outstanding, and of public import, written . . . for the instruction of princes and their subjects, and for the edification of the commonality as a whole." Fénelon was of the same mind: "History is very important; it is history that gives us great examples, and makes even the vices of the wicked serve for the instruction of the good."[17] The English and the French humanist traditions meet in the writings of Rapin de Thoyras, the exiled French Huguenot who wrote one of the eighteenth century's most popular English histories. Bolingbroke used Rapin's history frequently and liberally in his own writings and in his *Craftsman,* as we shall see. But Bolingbroke shared more than Rapin's reading of the English past. He also shared the Frenchman's general views on history. In 1689 Rapin compiled an abridgment "of what has been written on the manner of writing history by the greatest men of the first and later ages." The message was clear. "Romance only pleases, history instructs; this is the essential difference between them, this [the latter] having no other end than the instructing of the publick." The historian ought "to think of nothing but of being useful, by ruling the hearts and minds of men by the instruction he gives them."[18]

Four themes emerge from this humanist tradition of historical writing and deserve special attention. First, it is clear that history

16. For an interesting discussion on the *Mirror* see Butterfield, *The Englishman and His History,* pp. 15–20.

17. L. P. LeMoyne, *De l'histoire* (Paris, 1670), pp. 76–77; François de Salignac de La Mothe-Fénelon, "Lettre à l'Académie," in *Ouevres choisies* (Paris, 1848–51), 6:636.

18. Paul de Rapin Thoyras, *The Modest Critick: Or Remarks Upon the Most Eminent Historians, Ancient, and Modern. With Useful Cautions and Instructions, as well for Writing, as Reading History* (London, 1689), pp. 29–30.

as education and instruction is intended primarily for rulers and men of action. This is as explicit in the writings of Polybius and other stoics like Cicero, as it is in the Tudor *Mirror for Magistrates,* or in Machiavelli's writings. Statesmen, generals, and other practical men of leadership can deal better with the crises of power, it is assumed, if they have before them the example of others from the past who have faced similar problems. Bolingbroke shares this elitist orientation of humanist historiography. The *Letters on the Study and Use of History* were written for Baron Hyde, viscount Cornbury, a descendant of the great Clarendon. The end of letter 5 and the beginning of letter 6 make it quite clear that the care of states is not given to the multitude, but that men like Hyde "are called to it in a particular manner by their rank." The obligations one has to public service increase "in proportion to the ranks we hold, and the other circumstances of birth." The study of history, then, Bolingbroke informs Hyde, "has an immediate relation to the great duty and business of your life," governing. Genius and birth may qualify one to govern, but practical knowledge is required to do it well. Observation and experience will provide some of this; the rest "must be collected from the study of history."[19] James Burgh, the influential radical publicist, shared Bolingbroke's conviction that Britain's governors, more than most people, needed the guidance of history. In an ingenious and perceptive aside he suggests that

> history is the great instructor for all ranks in life, but especially the highest. For these who are besieged and blocked up by triple guards of flatterers, whose chief care and great interest it is above all things to prevent the approach of truth, in history may see characters as great or greater than their own, treated with the utmost plainness.[20]

A second feature of the exemplary theory of history is its assumption of a uniform and consistent human nature. If the example of how men in the past have acted is to be relevant for posterity, then men in all ages must be alike. Not only must the situations with which they deal be recurring and similar, but their

19. *Letters,* 2:237–38.
20. James Burgh, *The Dignity of Human Nature* (London, 1754), p. 129.

responses must be prompted by the same basic human feelings, motives, and attitudes.

Combined in this humanist historical tradition, then, are notions of historical recurrence and of the constancy of human nature. Polybius writes of "the mental transference of similar circumstances to our own times that gives us the means of forming presentiments of what is about to happen,"[21] while Machiavelli, the Renaissance humanist, describes the cyclical path of history forming repeating patterns. Machiavelli adds that all peoples throughout history share the same desires and passions; one must study the past, then, and imitate the conduct of great men.[22] Here Bolingbroke was, as in so many other areas of his thought, in agreement with Machiavelli. He wrote in letter 3:

> There are certain general principles, and rules of life and conduct, which always must be true, because they are conformable to the invariable nature of things. He who studies history . . . will soon distinguish and collect them, and by doing so will soon form to himself a general system of ethics and politics on the surest foundations, on the trial of these principles and rules in all ages, and on the confirmation of them by universal experience.[23]

The conservative thrust of this view of history should be apparent. The uniform norms, the natural laws of human conduct, are found not in nature but writ large in history. The shading off of humanist history into Tory history illustrated by Bolingbroke is equally evident in Hume, who writes: "Mankind are so much the same, in all times and places, that history informs us of nothing new or strange in this particular. Its chief use is only to discover the constant and universal principles of human nature."[24]

The Tory quality of exemplary history in the eighteenth century is further illustrated by its disdain for philosophy and its

21. Quoted in Nadel, "Philosophy of History," p. 57.
22. Nicolo Machiavelli, *Discourses on Titus Livius* (New York: Modern Library Edition, 1950), p. 216; also Butterfield, *Statecraft of Machiavelli*, p. 25.
23. *Letters*, 2:193.
24. Quoted in C. L. Becker, *The Heavenly City of the Eighteenth-Century Philosophers* (New Haven, 1960), p. 95.

juxtaposition of history as a source of prudential and experiential teachings with the abstract, ahistorical, speculative wisdom derived from philosophers and learned men.[25] This skeptical aspect of exemplary history is its third distinguishing feature. Once again, the continuity of the tradition is striking, for this attitude is found in antiquity as well as in Bolingbroke. Nadel skillfully traces the dialectic of precept and example out of which the disciplines of philosophy and history grew in antiquity. The study of history, he contends, came less from the Greek philosophers than from developments begun by rhetoricians like Isocrates, whose theory of education contrasted "learning from the experience of the past to learning, as with Plato, from philosophy." In the Roman era the dialectic consists of the useful, the teaching by example on the one hand, and the useless, the instruction by precept or principle (praeceptum), on the other. The latter smacked too much of the Greek schools. A central assumption of Roman rhetoric and oratory was the discovery of virtue and wisdom through example. For Quintilian the contrast was a simple one: "If the Greeks are strong on precepts, the Romans are stronger on examples, which is a far greater thing."[26]

Given this perspective, Plato and Greek philosophy emerge as the nemesis of exemplary historians. Polybius puts it this way: "Plato tells us that human affairs will then go well when either philosophers become kings or kings study philosophy, and I would say it will be well with history either when men of action undertake to write history . . . or regard training in actual affairs as necessary for writing history."[27] (XII, 28, 1–5.) Bacon returned to this theme. One learns not from the precepts of traditional philosophers, he writes, but from the historians. "Aristotle's and Plato's moral doctrines are admired by many; but Tacitus utters observations on morals that are much truer to life

25. For a general discussion of this tradition in English political and social thought see Isaac Kramnick, "The Skeptical Tradition in English Political Thought: From Temple to Burke," *Studies on Burke and His Times*, Winter, 1970.

26. Quoted in Nadel, "Philosophy of History," pp. 52, 55. It should be apparent that this part of the introduction is very much in debt to Nadel's excellent article.

27. Ibid., p. 57.

. . . the poets and writers of histories are the best doctors of this knowledge."[28] Bacon had learned well the teachings of his admired Machiavelli; so had Bolingbroke. Bolingbroke, however, combined his humanist disdain for the impracticality of Greek philosophizing with a healthy dose of eighteenth-century skepticism about abstract speculation which he derived from the epistemological writings of Locke. His *Philosophical Fragments* contain long invectives against the imaginative fantasies of metaphysical speculators. The power of mind is limited, and men must adjust themselves to their restricted capacities. This theme appears in letter 2 of the *Letters on the Study and Use of History.* Bolingbroke writes there of the ancient dichotomy between precept and example, but now with Locke on his mind. Note, too, the Enlightenment theme of independence used at the end of the argument, to make the case against precept even stronger.

> Such is the imperfection of human understanding, such is the frail temper of our minds, that abstract or general propositions, though ever so true, appear obscure or doubtful to us very often, till they are explained by examples; and that the wisest lessons in favor of virtue go but a little way to convince the judgement, and determine the will, unless they are enforced by the same means; and we are obliged to apply to ourselves what we see happen to other men. Instructions by precept have the further disadvantage of coming on the authority of others, and frequently require a long deduction of reasoning. . . . When examples are pointed out to us, there is a kind of appeal, with which we are flattered, made to our senses, as well as our understandings. The instruction comes then upon our own authority; we frame the precept after our own experience, and yield to fact when we resist speculation.[29]

Bolingbroke returned to this theme in letter 5. Studying the "experience of other men and other ages with our own" is, he writes, a much better approach to first principles than the "abstract speculations of ethics" or "those ideas, those increated essences, a Platonist would say, which no human creature can reach in practice."[30] This is, in part, what Bolingbroke means

28. Francis Bacon, "Temporis Partus Masculus," in *The Works of Francis Bacon,* ed. Spedding, Ellis, and Heath (Boston, 1863), 7:31.
29. *Letters,* 2:178.
30. Ibid., 2:222.

when he describes history as philosophy teaching by example. History, in fact, replaces philosophy as a guide to life, virtue, and public duty. "Thus history becomes what she ought to be, and what she has been sometimes called, 'magistra vitae,' the mistress, like philosophy, of human life."[31]

One final aspect of exemplary history remains to be discussed. Such history invades not only the preserve of philosophy, but also that of religion. Christianity has always offered as an inducement to virtuous and moral behavior the prospect of everlasting glory in the afterlife. Vindication for good and evil comes with the sanction of judgment day. Exemplary history substitutes the esteem and reputation of posterity for these divine rewards and punishments. Pre-Christian humanists like Diodorus and Seneca contended that the wicked were moved to good "out of fear of everlasting opprobrium." According to Nadel, Tacitus held the historian responsible for checking vice by threatening to perpetuate its memory in the annals of history.[32] A mighty sword of righteousness is wielded by the vindictive historian! Later humanists made the same substitution. Boulainvilliers wrote: "L'histoire a deux faces, elle nous montre le bien pour l'imiter et le vice pour le détester." Rapin asked: "What can we imagine finer than history which can do justice to virtue by perpetuating the memory of noble actions?"[33] Bolingbroke was not above using this argument to recommend his craft. In letter 3, he depicts the power of the historian, not unlike God's, to give to some "the charms of a bright and lasting reputation" and to others "the terror of being delivered over as criminals to all posterity."[34]

This may well be the fundamental theme of exemplary history, for in its secularized version it serves the same moral end as Christian teachings, the encouragement of good and the discouragement of evil. This is the moral foundation to learning by example from the past. The *Letters on the Study and Use of History* are an excellent embodiment of that tradition in their

---

31. Ibid., 2:223.
32. Nadel, "Philosophy of History," p. 60.
33. Quoted in Renée Simon, *Henry de Boulainvilliers* (Paris, 1941), p. 203; Rapin, *The Modest Critick*, p. 2.
34. *Letters*, 2:191.

oft repeated call for men, especially statesmen, to study history in order to become better, wiser, and more virtuous. Studying history will not only make better men, but, even more importantly for Bolingbroke, it will produce better citizens, citizens who seek the public good over private ambition. The works of Sallust, Livy, Tully, and Tacitus, Bolingbroke writes, are "a school of private *and* public virtue." Historians teach and inculcate "the general principles of virtue, and the general rules of wisdom and good policy. . . . Whilst they narrate as historians, they hint often as philosophers."[35] For Bolingbroke, the historian has replaced the priest and the philosopher as moral and political mentor.

With such an exalted conception of the historian's mission, it is hardly surprising that Bolingbroke attacked writers on history whom he labeled antiquarians. The humanist historical tradition saw the pursuit of historical fact as an objective always secondary to the primary one of drawing lessons from the past. But this did not prevent zealous chroniclers and historians from obsessively compiling and recording the factual trivia of the past. Many writers on the past in the sixteenth and seventeenth centuries neglected the primary didactic role of humanist history in the pursuit of the secondary concern, the facts. Dates, battles, marriages, and deaths became for many the stuff of history in what was very much a proto-positivist conception of the art. Bolingbroke turned on this historical positivism in the name of the humanist vision of a moralizing history.

Several modern writers have singled out Bolingbroke's attack on historical chroniclers and antiquarians as the heart of his importance as a writer on historical method. J. G. A. Pocock deals with this at some length in *The Ancient Constitution and the Feudal Law: A Study of English Historical Thought in the Seventeenth Century*. But it is really D. C. Douglas's *English Scholars* that makes this case. Douglas's books deals with the remarkable collection of historical scholars and antiquarians that included Dugdale, Hickes, Wanley, Brady, Wharton, Rymer, Atwood, and many others who contributed so much to a knowledge of English medieval history. Their research flourished from

35. Ibid., 2:177, 183, 221, 227, 229. Italics mine.

the Restoration in 1660 until about 1730 and the appearance of the arch-villain Bolingbroke. The *Letters on the Study and Use of History,* Douglas argues, mark the end of this great age of historical scholarship.

> By the middle of the eighteenth century the leaders of English taste had come to profess a hatred of the past and a disdain for those who explored it. Bolingbroke saw fit to express a thorough contempt for the whole business of these learned lives, "for all the systems of chronology and history that we owe to the immense labours of a Scaliger, a Bochart, an Ussher, or even a Marsham."[36]

Bolingbroke had little hatred of the past, but Douglas is certainly right in noting his antipathy to his, Douglas's, beloved band of medieval scholars. In explaining the antipathy, Douglas falls back on characterizing Bolingbroke and other critics of the antiquarians as mere literary men incapable and therefore disdainful of scholarship. He charges further that Bolingbroke is more concerned with elegance than accuracy, and that, unable to match the erudition of a Dugdale, Bolingbroke ridicules it.[37] Douglas is closer to the mark in suggesting, as does Pocock, that Bolingbroke demanded generalizations and not random accumulation of facts. The real explanation of Bolingbroke's dislike for Douglas's collection of scholars, however, is Bolingbroke's rejection of the amoral quality of their research, which they pursued as an end in itself, unmindful of history's responsibility for moral teaching.

But Bolingbroke was by no means the first historian to criticize the positivist heresy of the antiquarian. Once again, the tradition is rich in commonly shared convictions. Even, for example, before the great age of English historical scholarship traced by Douglas, the author of the *Mirror for Magistrates* cautioned that tales of past princes must teach lessons, and that

> They be unworthy the name of chroniclers that leave these cleane out of their registers.[38]

French writers had as much to complain about as Bolingbroke.

36. Douglas, *English Scholars,* p. 356.
37. Ibid., pp. 360, 366.
38. Quoted in Butterfield, *The Englishman and His History,* p. 15.

Brumfitt describes seventeenth-century French histories as either
laden with erudition or painstaking descriptions of the battlefield
and court.[39] No surprise, then, that Fénelon should curse "the
dry and sad maker of annals, who knows no other order than that
of chronology." Far more important, he wrote, "was to observe
the changes in the nation as a whole than to relate particular
facts." Boulainvilliers is equally distressed by history concerned
only with "the names of princes, of their ministers, of their
generals, and of their mistresses." Fontenelle agreed: "To
amass in the head fact upon fact, retain dates exactly, fill oneself
with the spirit of wars, treaties of peace, marriages, genealogies
—that is what is called knowing history. . . . I had as soon a man
acquired exactly the history of all the clocks of Paris."[40] Among
eighteenth-century writers, Grimm would add, much like Bolingbroke, that "history must be written by philosophers, whatever our pedants say." Diderot's comments on Voltaire's history
will do as an excellent French critique of the positivist antiquarian:

> Other historians relate facts to inform us of facts. You relate
> them to excite in our hearts an intense hatred of lying, ignorance,
> hypocrisy, superstition, tyranny; and this anger remains even
> after the memory of the facts has disappeared.[41]

Despite its similarity to other humanist critiques of historians
preoccupied with scholarship, Bolingbroke's merits special attention because it is by far the most sustained and devastating
assault. As early as 1724 he had written to Pope from France that
"it was hard to find historians more interested in ideas of the
spirit, than in facts of the memory."[42] Several years later he
wrote to his Tory comrade Windham, "In whatever I write that
is historical, I will be neither apologist, panegyrist, nor satirist,
and besides, I shall touch very lightly marches, battles, sieges,
encampments, and that inferior detail of history, for such I think

39. J. H. Brumfitt, *Voltaire Historian* (Oxford, 1958), pp. 2–3.
40. Fénelon, "Lettre à l'Académie," 6:639–40; Boulainvilliers quoted in Simon, *Henry de Boulainvilliers*, p. 173; Fontenelle, *Oeuvres* (Paris, 1790), 5:433.
41. Grimm and Diderot quoted in Becker, *The Heavenly City*, pp. 91–92.
42. Philippe-Henri, Comte de Grimoard, ed., *Lettres historiques, politiques, philosophiques et particulières de Henri Saint-John Vicomte Bolingbroke, depuis 1710 jusqu'en 1736*, 3 vols. (Paris, 1808), 2:232.

it."[43] We shall see that he never kept the first resolve. The latter conviction he stuck to and developed in great detail in the *Letters on the Study and Use of History*. The failure of the chroniclers and antiquarians, he writes, is their irrelevance in training men to virtue. Their history lacks "a philosophical spirit and manner." It is too concerned with particular events and thus provides no generalizations and lessons that can be learned and that can serve as models for action. Their histories, far from making men wiser or better citizens, only leave them "prating pedants." Much more important than the vast learning of these scholars is the practical knowledge of how to conduct one's private and public life which true history teaches. History must be "of use towards our improvement in wisdom and virtue." If it is not, it is a worthless "gazette of antiquity, or a dry register of useless anecdotes."[44]

His most devastating response to the antiquarians is really the suggestion in letter 6 that Hyde need only study English history since the fifteenth century. It is an outright repudiation of all their work by the simple act of ignoring it. Douglas is right, then, if this is what he means by Bolingbroke's hatred of the past. No future governor, Bolingbroke suggests, need look beyond the Tudors for inspiration and guidance. In the fifteenth century all the basic changes occurred that affected life and governance in eighteenth-century England. To be useful to the present day the statesman needed only modern examples. To be knowledgeable about the more remote past was a useless affectation.

Bolingbroke may well have gone too far in this attack on the gazetteers and pedants, for in suggesting that only modern history was useful for the study of England's leaders he undermined the basic humanist convictions about the utility of the past and the uniformity of human nature over time. These confusions cannot be explained away. They exist. To understand them one must remember that Bolingbroke was more than simply a humanist historian, he was also a philosophe skeptical about his-

43. William Coxe, *Memoirs of the Life and Administration of Sir Robert Walpole, Containing Correspondence and Original Papers of the Period*, 3 vols. (London, 1798), 2:337.
44. *Letters*, 2:174, 177, 191.

torical truth, and a partisan interested in party and cause. In turning to these other dimensions of his historical method one may better understand the seeming aberration of his advice to Hyde.

On Pyrrhonism and Doubt:
Bolingbroke the Enlightenment Historian

More than Bolingbroke's slight of medieval history has led Douglas and others to read him as disdainful of history. While praising history as the school for statesmen, Bolingbroke, in seeming contradiction, is very much an important figure in the Enlightenment school of historical skepticism. Bolingbroke the humanist historian desperately tried to come to terms with the disconcerting evidence proffered by the skeptics. By inclination he was one of them; he was a philosophe. He shared their worship of Bacon and Locke, especially the Locke of *The Essay on Human Understanding*. Like most of the philosophes he was a deist and a radical empiricist. Like them he attacked the clergy and the church, and found the Christian Middle Ages irrelevant and embarrassing. But he was, on the other hand, incapable of utter doubt; in the end he turned on Bayle. He had to salvage something of history's value, if only to maintain one basic aspect of his partisan appeal, his claim that history's lessons rquired that England repudiate Walpole's Whig reign.

Humanist history was doomed not by the pseudo-positivism of seventeenth-century antiquarian scholarship nor by the full-blown nineteenth-century positivist history as enshrined in the university. Its demise came more immediately from the Enlightenment's conviction that history was a collection of fables revealing only the ignorance and criminal disposition of pre-Enlightenment men and ages. A truly revolutionary change had come over many European intellectuals who, perhaps for the first time, repudiated the cult of antiquity, so basic a component of the Western mind. The battle of the ancients and the moderns was symptomatic, if not of a repudiation of the past and history, then at least of a growing indifference to them. In explaining this reorientation to history, some, like Douglas, have suggested that it must be read as simply a rejection of one large chunk of the past, the Christian Era. There is a great deal of truth to this. Voltaire, after all, despite his dictum on history and crime, does, in his *Essai sur les moeurs,* find much of worth in Periclean Athens and Augustan Rome. Much like Douglas's reading of Bolingbroke, dismissal by the philosophes of the more immediate past (medieval) is often read as rejecting the past itself. A second explanation closely akin to this relates the new attitude toward history to broader political and ideological currents. Just as the philosophes opposed Christianity and priests, so they opposed custom, tradition, and precedent as guides to thought and belief;[45] thus, the argument goes, they were led to dispense with the past, either as rationalists or as modernizing bourgeois. Once again, there is much truth in this. But by no means will it account for a Bolingbroke, for example, who was clearly a social and political traditionalist. Anyone who has read the philosophes closely, for that matter, knows the problems raised in labeling them as progressive or liberal, let alone radical. Conservatives could, and often did, share their skeptical attitude to history. "We must consider," said Dr. Johnson, "how very little history there is; I mean real authentic history. . . . All the coloring, all the philosophy of history is conjecture."[46] What united the conservatives, Johnson and Bolingbroke, with the more iconoclastic Bayle and Voltaire in this common suspicion of history was their skepticism. Cartesian doubt and Lockean empiricism had led to this.

> If, now, men turned their backs on the past, it was because they thought it something evanescent, Protean, something impossible to grasp and retain, something inherently and inveterately deceptive. People no longer trusted those who professed to understand and interpret it. Those who pretended to do so deceived either themselves or their readers. A sort of landslide had taken place, and in its track, in what remained after its passage, nothing was to be seen for certain but what immediately confronted the eye, that is to say the "here and now"—in other words the present.[47]

45. See Pocock, *The Ancient Constitution,* for this reading.
46. Quoted in Douglas, *English Scholars,* p. 358.
47. Paul Hazard, *The European Mind: The Critical Years (1680–1715)* (New Haven, 1953), p. 30.

It is this intellectual tradition of skepticism at the heart of the Enlightenment's attitude to history, which informs the second perspective found in Bolingbroke's historical method. The home of this historical skepticism is, of course, France. Its roots run at least as far back as Descartes, who not only had questioned all traditional authority, but had, in particular, doubted that one could be a better man simply because he knew Greek or Roman history. Truth was a matter not of history, but of internal doubt and questioning. Skepticism towards history emerged full blown, however, in the school of seventeenth-century libertines and free-thinkers. La Mothe le Vayer's *Du peu de certitude qu'il y a dans l'histoire* and Saint-Evremond's *Réflexions sur les divers génies du peuple romain* agree on the untrustworthiness of most historical writing. Far from giving facts, history, they claimed, simply consists of the various interpretations offered by interested parties. History produced no truths; it offered only myth, falsehood, and self-serving party and personal gloss. The first victim of historical skepticism was the prestigious and value-laden history of Greece and Rome. The antique world kept no accurate records, its chronology and periodization were fanciful and absurd, the freethinkers charged. Saint-Evremond wrote that ancient history was nothing more than a series of fairy tales, written by people concerned only with identifying their heritage and past with fictitious connections to favored gods. To study this history as received truth was thus merely to compound and repeat the original errors and falsehoods. Fontenelle, the champion of the moderns, ridiculed Greek history as a collection of mere "dreams and fantastic imaginings." "A nation's early history," he wrote, "is in reality nothing but a phantasmagoria, a string of childish tales."[48] Like Bolingbroke, however, Fontenelle could not quite free himself from humanist history. He, too, suggests that the only profitable history from which one can learn is modern history, where it is hoped the level of fantasy is diminished.

The second pillar of history attacked by the skeptics was God's

---

48. Quoted in Hazard, p. 51. This discussion of the libertines and the free-thinkers is derived in part from the excellent treatment of the two groups in Hazard, *The European Mind,* pt. 1, chap. 2, and Brumfitt, *Voltaire Historian,* chap. 2.

history as found in his Bible. Chronologists, mathematicians, and logicians slowly pecked away at the biblical stories, until what was once considered the sure and factual tale of ancient history became a confused and apparently ludicrous source of truth. The most significant piece of biblical skepticism appeared in 1678 from the pen of a Catholic priest, Richard Simon. His *Histoire critique du Vieux Testament* is a ruthlessly critical philological reading of the Bible which concludes that the text has been altered and modified to such an extent that it presents almost insurmountable chronological and interpretive problems. To be sure, the priest in him insisted that those who continued, or altered, or even those who changed God's words were still inspired by God. But no amount of disclaimer could hide his central finding—that this allegedly impeccable source of historical truth was in fact fitted together by many different hands and redone so often that it was impossible to know the original wording and meaning.[49] What powerful ammunition Simon's work would be for later, less priestly critics like Bolingbroke and Voltaire! As far as they were concerned, he had totally undermined the historical authority of the Scriptures.

The various strains that made up the school of historical skepticism came together in the writings of Pierre Bayle. Any received doctrine, any assumed truth, whatever be its source, history or Scripture, was false, he assumed, unless it met the test of the individual's power of reasoning. His dictionary purported to tell of man's historical record. What it related was a summary of his errors, his crimes, and his follies. History was, even into the modern era, a set of fables invented by greed-filled and ignorant imaginations. All history dwelt on lies and myths. Bayle's is the ultimate skepticism, for he doubts whether truth might ever be attained. The *Dictionnaire historique et critique* not only finds all previous written history distorted and misrepresented, but its final message is historical pyrrhonism. Future histories will be no more accurate, no more truthful, Bayle predicts. One can, in fact, never possess historical truth. Such is the limited power of man's faculties, such is the impossibility of resurrecting the past, and such is man's enduring ignorance and

49. For a good discussion of Simon see Hazard, *The European Mind,* pt. 2, chap. 3.

incredulity that "certainty can be affirmed of nothing, that nothing can be known beyond all doubt."[50] Historical skepticism had come to this, a total and unqualified historical negativism.

Bolingbroke's historical writings are perhaps the best English example of the historical skepticism which ushered in the French Enlightenment.[51] A rationalist indifference to the past and a generally skeptical posture to the possibility of attaining historical knowledge are woven into the fabric of the *Letters on the Study and Use of History.* The foundation for this skepticism was laid years earlier during Bolingbroke's exile in France.

From 1715 to 1725 the young English lord had immersed himself in the study of history and historiography. His correspondence with Pope and Swift during this period often comments on his readings in Polybius, Thucydides, Tacitus, Diodorus, and Machiavelli, or on his general concern with Roman and Greek history. In 1724 he described to Pope his intention to write a history of modern Europe since the sixteenth century. These plans are almost an outline sketch of the last two-thirds of the *Letters.* Bolingbroke even did historical research for his friends during his years in exile. When Stanhope visited France in 1719, he told Bolingbroke of the plan to change the composition of the House of Lords. He would be much obliged, Stanhope told the statesman turned student of history, if Bolingbroke could get him some material on how the senate of Rome had been selected.[52]

But Bolingbroke's historical research was not entirely haphazard or amateurish. It was given direction by the two intellectual mentors of this period in his life, the Abbé Pierre Joseph Alary and Levesque de Pouilly, and also by his association with the Parisian learned society, Le Club de L'Entresol.[53] Bolingbroke learned most of his ancient history from Alary, one of

50. Hazard, *The European Mind,* p. 109.
51. See Pocock, *The Ancient Constitution,* pp. 238–39.
52. Grimoard, ed., *Lettres historiques,* 1:453; 2:163, 232; for the Stanhope incident see ibid., 2:6.
53. For details of these French intellectual connections see Grimoard, ed., *Lettres historiques;* E. R. Briggs, "The Political Academies of France in the Early Eighteenth Century with Special Reference to the Club de l'Entresol, and to Its Founder, the Abbé Pierre-Joseph Alary" (Ph.D. diss., Cambridge University, 1931); D. J. Fletcher, "The Intellectual Relations of Lord Bolingbroke with France" (M.A. thesis, University College of Wales, 1953).

the most learned men in France. From Pouilly and the members of L'Entresol he derived the historical skepticism and pyrrhonism then so voguish in the clandestine freethinking circles of France. Pouilly's was the dominant intellectual influence on Bolingbroke during these years at La Source. It was because of him, Bolingbroke claims, that he became interested in physics, deism, and the uncertainty of history. So close were the two that when Bolingbroke returned to England he took Pouilly with him. Pouilly, the author of "L'Incertitude de l'histoire des quatre premiers siècles de Rome," a paper presented to the Académie des Inscriptions et Belles-Lettres, transmitted to Bolingbroke a permanent suspicion of historical authenticity.[54] The doubts were quite evident even during these years. Some fifteen years before the writing of the *Letters,* in July 1719, Bolingbroke wrote to Alary:

> The little that I have read in my youth of ancient history has left me with the conviction that it is impossible to have any positive knowledge of events of that time; the historical and chronological systems which the learned debate for us with so much confidence and show are based only on special pleadings. If we had the books of which the Greeks have only left the titles and some fragments, we would realize how uncertain, vague, and contradictory the traditions of two or three countries are. Each one seeks to attribute to itself the honors of antiquity, the birth of gods, and the invention of arts, which consequently make it ridiculous to work on the little pieces of information that we have.[55] [Translated from the French]

Virtually all the themes stressed by the French school of historical skepticism are here in Bolingbroke's letter of 1719. Several years later, while still in France, he returned to this doubt and uncertainty in some letters to an English acquaintance, the Newtonian physicist Brooks Taylor.

> Upon this occasion, I'll tell you that I have very near done, for my whole life, with all inquiries into remote antiquity. My intention was to see the foundations of those historical and chronological systems which have been erected with so much learned pain in our western world. . . . When Varro fixed the

54. Fletcher, "The Intellectual Relations," p. 59.
55. Grimoard, ed., *Lettres historiques,* 2:21.

famous epoch (as Censorenius says he did), this learned Roman could hardly have any better reason for doing so, than the desire of including the foundation of his city within that period; from which, the fabulous age being ended, the historical age began.

I have gone through all that I proposed to myself, in the way of studying, wherein I was when you gave us your good company. I never intended to do more than to examine, as well as I was able, the foundations on which those sermons of chronology and ancient history, which obtain in our western world, are built. . . . I have done this, and I have no more desire to pursue this study than I have to be proficient in judicial astrology. Who can resolve to build with great cost and pain, when he finds, how deep soever he digs, nothing but loose sand?[56]

I have quoted from Bolingbroke's correspondence at some length because it provides important new evidence in a rather old debate, the dispute over Bolingbroke's influence on Voltaire. Several commentators have argued that Voltaire's early views were very much molded by Bolingbroke.[57] In 1723 Voltaire was, to be sure, dazzled by milord Bolingbroke, in whom he found *"toute l'érudition de son pays, et toute la politesse du nôtre."* Moreover, *"il sait l'histoire des anciens Égyptiens comme celle d'Angleterre."*[58] As their deism has much in common, so also there is much in Voltaire's histories that could have had its origin in Bolingbroke, most noticeably the attacks on biblical history, on Moses, St. Paul, and the Jews in general. Voltaire, like Bolingbroke, is also reluctant completely to give up history as a moralizing and didactic force.[59] This alleged chain of influence has been seriously challenged, however, by Norman Torrey, who goes so far as to label it fictitious.[60] He takes his stand on publication dates. Bolingbroke's *Letters* were published in

56. Brooks Taylor, *Contemplatio Philosophica* (London, 1793), p. 126.
57. J. C. Collins, *Voltaire, Montesquieu and Rousseau in England* (London, 1908); A. S. Hurn, *Voltaire et Bolingbroke* (Paris, 1915); Leslie Stephen, *History of English Thought*, 1:151; T. Besterman, ed., *Voltaire's Correspondence* (Geneva, 1953), 1:245–48.
58. Voltaire, *Oeuvres*, ed. Moland, 52 vols. (Paris, 1877–85), 33:84.
59. Brumfitt, *Voltaire Historian*, passim, esp. p. 96.
60. N. L. Torrey, "Bolingbroke and Voltaire: A Fictitious Influence," *Publications of the Modern Language Association* 42 (1927):788–97; idem, *Voltaire and the English Deists* (New Haven, 1930).

1752. Voltaire read them and wrote his *Défense de milord Bolingbroke* in the same year. Obviously, Torrey argues, this was some time after Voltaire had much to learn as a historian. J. H. Brumfitt and George Nadel have, in turn, easily disposed of Torrey's objection.[61] Brumfitt tentatively suggests that an earlier edition of the *Letters* may have existed, and Nadel conclusively shows that not only were the *Letters* written in the mid-1730s, but six or seven copies of the manuscript were printed by Pope, any one of which could have fallen into Voltaire's hands or passed to him through word of mouth via Voltaire's or Bolingbroke's extensive Anglo-French connections. We can now add that even this link through an early manuscript of the *Letters* is not crucial in establishing the possible influence of Bolingbroke on Voltaire's attitudes to history. In those very years when they first met and the errant English lord so enchanted Voltaire, Bolingbroke was in fact deeply involved in historical study and already very much the historical skeptic.

The extent of this skepticism would shock Englishmen, as we have seen, when the *Letters on the Study and Use of History* were finally published after Bolingbroke's death. A people convinced of the importance and continuity of history, convinced that their liberties were handed down from their ancestors in the historical past, used to thinking in terms of tradition and precedent, were bound to be deeply shocked by Bolingbroke's savage assault on history. It may well have been necessary, as Pocock contends, for Bolingbroke to spend so many of his formative intellectual years in France that he might be able to emancipate himself from the customary English common law mentality and its instinctive deference to a believed past.[62] In the *Letters* Bolingbroke the skeptic informs the traditionalist English that a nation's past is no more than a "thread of dark and uncertain tradition." Any nation's early history consists of "fanciful preludes." The great national scholars "have dealt and deal in fables at least as much as our poets." Ancient history, he continues, is based on nothing more substantial than "broken, perplexed, and doubtful scraps of

61. Brumfitt, *Voltaire Historian,* pp. 42–45; Nadel, "Bolingbroke's Letters on History," passim.
62. See the argument in Pocock, *The Ancient Constitution,* p. 241.

tradition." The ancients wrote pleasing fables which they passed off as history, relating things they had never heard nor seen.[63] Most shocking of all in the *Letters,* at least in terms of the numerous pamphlets and the comments of Walpole and Johnson that it elicited, was Bolingbroke's attack on biblical history. How can one believe these books as history, he asks, when, to begin with, they are written by the Jews, "a superstitious and lying people." Simon is enlisted to make the point that the scriptures are "broken, and confused, full of additions, interpolations, and transpositions, made we neither know when, nor by whom." The genealogy, geography, and chronology found in the Bible, Bolingbroke maintains, are inaccurate and pure fancy. Names and events are mentioned there without any description of the relationship between events; yet these "imperfect and dark accounts" of Moses have been used by rabbis and priests to continue the false story of early history. Bolingbroke's language was not the kind to endear him to his pious readers. It was, after all, hardly usual to find a former minister of state and peer of the realm write:

> One is tempted to think, that the patriarch [Noah] was still drunk; and that no man in his senses could hold such language, or pass such a sentence. Certain it is, that no writer but a Jew could impute to the economy of Divine Providence the accomplishment of such a prediction, nor make the Supreme Being the executor of such a curse.[64]

Ancient and biblical histories are unfit, then, for any reasonable man to believe, for they are mere fables. Ought men to conclude from this that all history, even that written in modern times, is uncertain, that "the very best is nothing better than a probable tale, artfully contrived, and plausibly told," but not to be believed? Ought men, in short, to follow Bayle into "this sort of Pyrrhonism?"[65] In Bolingbroke's effort to answer this question we come to the critical juncture in his discussion of historical method. As he deals with Bayle, he vainly tries to reconcile his skepticism with his humanist faith in the exemplary value of history. He begins the answer by repeating his doubts.

63. *Letters,* 2:196, 199.
64. Ibid., 2:201, 204, 209.
65. Ibid., 2:213.

In all ages history has been "purposely and systematically falsified," and the greatest perpetrators of this falsification have been religious authorities. He suggests that the "lying spirit" which pervades history has been contributed to mostly, after the priesthood, by national or party sympathizers. As a result, history is imperfect and corrupt. But once again he asks, must one join Bayle in pyrrhonism in this flight from credulity? The answer is definitive and clear—no. Although all history, past and present, contains some lies and mistakes, one should not cease trying as best he can to come closer to historical truth. The way this can be done is to set doubtful account against doubtful account and let the modicum of truth emerge on its own power. A degree of truthfulness may be the best one can hope for, but proper discernment and discrimination, as well as judicious choice among competing historical accounts, will allow the more probable historical truth to emerge. Bolingbroke offers the marketplace of competing historical description as the way to find historical truth, much like Mill's later marketplace of ideas. But why the need for such a tortured naysaying to Bayle? The reason should be clear—how else can the moral mission of history be salvaged?

> History must have a certain degree of probability and authenticity, or the examples we find in it would not carry a force sufficient to make due impressions on our minds, nor to illustrate nor to strengthen the precepts of philosophy and the rules of good policy.[66]

The reconciliation of his two perspectives on history is complete. History is uncertain, to be sure; the best histories are defective, and most give false explanations. But one must transcend skepticism, with its childish delight in finding historical error and inaccuracy. According to the synthesis Bolingbroke has worked out, one is obliged to examine and compare historical authority, prefer some, and not reject all. In doing this one is bound to have a less than perfect history, but one will at least have history, and thus posterity will be instructed by the example of former ages.

Bolingbroke had dealt with these problems raised in the *Let-*

66. Ibid., 2:219.

ters on the Study and Use of History many years earlier in *The Substance of Some Letters to M. de Pouilly.* This essay, while not included in this volume because of its primarily philosophical character, does deal in passing, however, with historical incredulity. The solution offered in 1720 was much like, if not even better stated than, that of the *Letters.* This, too, is important evidence that the extent of Bolingbroke's concern with history while exiled in France was such that it could easily have influenced the young Voltaire. As in the later *Letters,* Bolingbroke makes clear in this early essay his sympathies with historical pyrrhonism. History is so full of fraud that it ought basically to be doubted, he recommends. The reason for this falsification, he contends, is that originally and for a long time the keepers of records were priests. "They were to keep up the credit of ancient lies, and to invent as many new ones, as were necessary to propagate the same fraud. By these means, and on these motives, the whole of history was corrupted."[67] But Bolingbroke will not let his cynicism preclude all belief in the past. He derives a justification for the value and relevance of history from his broader epistemological convictions. It must be granted that one cannot have certain knowledge of a fact which he has not witnessed himself, but "high probability must stand often in lieu of certainty, or we must be, every moment, at a loss how to inform our opinions and to regulate our conduct." One can attain a "degree of probability which is little distant from evident truth." He even offers in this essay of 1720 a set of rules with which to test history:

> An historical fact, which contains nothing that contradicts general experience, and our own observation, has already the appearance of probability; and if it be supported by the testimony of proper witnesses, it acquires all the appearances of truth; that is, it becomes really probable in the highest degree. . . . The degree of assent, which we give to history, may be settled, in proportion to the number, characters, and circumstances of the original witnesses.[68]

These rules, a curiously naïve marriage of Bayle to Hume's later

67. *Substance of Some Letters to M. de Pouilly,* in *The Works of Lord Bolingbroke,* 2:490.
68. Ibid., 2:467, 487.

writings, provide less than adequate guidelines. No wonder, then, that Bolingbroke saw no reason to offer even such general suggestions when he wrote the *Letters*. By then he needed no specific rules to make the case for the utility of history and the error of Bayle. All that was needed in 1736 to make the case for history, he was convinced, was its usefulness in recommending to the English that they oppose Walpole.

History and Partisanship: Bolingbroke the English Historian

History, Croce tells us, is always "contemporary history." However remote the events described may be, "history," he writes, "in reality refers to present needs and present situations wherein these events vibrate."[69] E. H. Carr goes so far as to suggest that good history requires that the historian's vision of the past be informed by concern with and insights into problems of his own age.[70] This is certainly the case with Bolingbroke's history. It is so shaped by concern with England in the 1730s that it is veritably partisan history. History, which is philosophy teaching by example, has one clear message—statesmen ought to be wary of Walpole; good policy requires a repudiation of the Whig rule of political corruption and financial capitalism. The probable historical truths that withstand Bolingbroke's skepticism point to a fundamental lesson—English history is one long endorsement of the Opposition. All the doubt and uncertainty so evident in the general methodological discussion of history vanish when Bolingbroke turns his hand to actually writing history. He produces exemplary history with a vengeance.

In his weekly *Craftsman* he often used historical satire in his campaign against Walpole. Countless essays were directed against corrupt and despotic ministers who could be used for thinly disguised comparisons with Walpole. The two most often enlisted were Cardinal Wolsey and James I's minister, Buckingham, with due emphasis placed on their obscure birth and low education and on the exorbitant wealth that they acquired in office and that enabled them to raise families of parts, to build

69. Benedetto Croce, *History as the Story of Liberty* (London, 1941), p. 19.
70. E. H. Carr, *What Is History?* (New York, 1961), pp. 42–44.

palaces, and to offend the nobility. If, on the other hand, a disguise for criticism of Walpole's corrupt financial dealings in the house of Commons was needed, the career of the Earl of Danby was used.

One particular example of such partisan historical satire deserves special mention. For three consecutive Saturdays, Bolingbroke sustained a critique of Pericles, who, it was clear to all, was Walpole. Pericles was described as subverting the Athenian constitution and destroying Athens. He protected corrupt men and distributed bribes and jobs in the assembly. He fostered luxury with public money. Bolingbroke even extended the comparison to include Pericles' corrupting the Athenian assembly with a species of secret service money, and of refusing to allow anyone to look at the books of his administration. Meanwhile, poets and wits warned the *polis* against Pericles, but the warnings were never heeded. This history might not have impressed the Abbé Alary, but if nothing else, it helps to illustrate the nature of the political dialogue in Augustan England. One week later there appeared in Walpole's *London Journal* and *Daily Courant* a defense of Pericles![71]

It was also in *The Craftsman,* in 1730 and 1731, that the twenty-four essays appeared that would later be published as Bolingbroke's *Remarks on the History of England.* Bolingbroke began this long discussion of English history by citing Machiavelli's plea that nations and governments return to their first principles in order to maintain their health and prolong their lives. The purpose of the essays, Bolingbroke suggested, was to help revive the spirit of liberty and recall the minds of men to the true notions of the British Constitution. In Bolingbroke's history, the dynamics were provided by the interplay of two "spirits," one of liberty and one of faction. The former embodied the national interest, while the latter embodied individual and partisan interest. Bolingbroke saw the development of English history as a manichaean struggle between these good and evil forces. The spirit of liberty was represented in the mixed constitution whose parts were so balanced that no one part depended

---

71. *The Craftsman,* nos. 324, 325, 326 (16, 23, and 30 September 1732); *The London Journal* no. 693 (7 October 1732); *Daily Courant* (10 October 1732).

on the others, while the spirit of faction was embodied in any threat against this ideal constitutional structure.

The spirit of liberty first emerged, he contended, in England's Saxon past, and it persisted through the Middle Ages, unaffected by the Norman Conquest. From the Conquest to the Civil War, various monarchs and their reigns gave substance to one spirit or the other. The evil monarchs who gave succor to the ever-lurking spirit of faction included Richard II, Henry VI, Henry VII, and, of course, James I and Charles I. The patrons of the spirit of liberty included Edward III and Henry V. Henry VIII began as a partisan of liberty, but under the evil influence of his corrupt and upstart minister, Wolsey, he developed into the most evil of all England's monarchs. The greatest of all patrons of liberty was, of course, Elizabeth.

The intent of the *Remarks* is overtly partisan, as its entrance into the world in the form of weekly essays in *The Craftsman* attests. There are countless allusions to Walpole in its references to corrupt and scheming ministers seeking to end the independence of Parliament and upset the balance of the constitution, the essence of liberty. In addition, the *Remarks* had one most significant repercussion; they touched off a debate that raged for five years in the party press and pamphlet literature, in which Walpole and Bolingbroke refought the historiographical battles of the seventeenth century. In the course of this debate Bolingbroke contradicts most of his later advice to Hyde. He delves deep into the English past, far beyond the sixteenth century, to find historical lessons of relevance for today's statesman. Bolingbroke the partisan historian, moreover, is by no means the skeptic indifferent to the past or critical of precedent and custom. Far from being the rationalist historian schooled in the French tradition, he turns out to be one of the "pedants of nation" and "tools of party" that he himself would warn against in his *Letters*.[72]

Behind the Walpole-Bolingbroke debate in the 1730s lay the late seventeenth-century controversy on the nature of English history. In this controversy, described in J. G. A. Pocock's masterful study, Dr. Brady answered the Whig notions of an im-

72. *Letters*, 2:215.

memorial constitution found in William Petyt, William Atwood, and the *Argumentum Anti-Normanicum.* Brady wrote that William I had completely altered English law and government by importing feudal tenures. Brady was ruthlessly single-minded and, encouraged by his royalist partisanship, he abandoned the ingrained image of the ancient constitution and embraced the new, more accurate feudal history of Sir Henry Spelman and Sir William Dugdale.[73] He denied Petyt's claim that a class of freeholders maintaining continuity with Anglo-Saxon society had survived the Conquest. In Brady's writings the entire medieval population was depicted as consisting of tenants in military service to some higher lord, with the chain of tenure leading ultimately to the grand suzerain, the king. In such a totally feudal society there could be no freeholders. Before Edward I's reign in the late thirteenth century, Brady wrote, no commoner sat on the king's feudal council. The council then comprised only the king's tenants-in-chief—the bishops, earls, and barons. As did Spelman, Brady asserted that the Commons evolved gradually from lesser tenants into freeholding knights through the commutation of their feudal obligations. Magna Charta, for Brady, was merely a demand for relaxation of feudal service and a call to the more powerful barons to implement feudal privileges of council and advice; it represented no appeal to any older, pre-feudal ancient law.

Such was Brady's history, offered "to teach the people loyalty and obedience and frustrate the designs of the seditious."[74] No omnipotent Parliament and elective Crown could threaten the Stuarts if the claim that the ancient constitution had accorded power to Parliament was erroneous. During the years of the Exclusion crisis, Brady's scholarship was at the service of Filmer's position. It maintained the omnipotence of the Crown and the subjugation to it of the law, liberties, and Commons of England.

The Royalist cause of Filmer and Brady was rejected in 1688. It has been traditionally assumed that with this defeat the influence of Brady's history also declined. Brady had to wait, it is

73. For Spelman see Pocock, *The Ancient Constitution,* pp. 92–115; for the antiquarian circle in general see Douglas, *English Scholars,* passim.
74. Quoted in Pocock, *The Ancient Constitution,* p. 194.

usually held, for the romantic historians of the nineteenth century to justify his early and perceptive insights into the real nature of the English Middle Ages.[75] A study of the political press in the Augustan period indicates, however, that Brady's scholarship did not have to wait so long for its revival. Dr. Brady found important disciples only a half-century after his eclipse, and what is more startling, his champions were the spokesmen for the most successful of the Whig beneficiaries of 1688, Robert Walpole. His newspapers, the *London Journal* and the *Daily Gazetteer*, revived Brady's history in the early 1730s in their battle with Bolingbroke and his press. The dynamics of Augustan politics led Walpole to embrace the theories of the Tory Brady, because Bolingbroke made partisan use of the Whig common-law myth of an ancient and immemorial constitution. Brady's scholarship was made respectable long before the nineteenth century, and it was a Whig government that took this step so crucial for future students of English history.[76]

Bolingbroke, in his *Remarks on the History of England* and *A Dissertation upon Parties,* revived the seventeenth-century common-law and Whig notions of an ancient constitution with immemorial free institutions that Brady had repudiated. In the *Remarks* Bolingbroke's prose on the continuity of English freedom was no less exalted than that of any seventeenth-century Whig. He found the roots of English freedom in the original British and Saxon constitutions. In the latter, he wrote, the "supreme power centered in the Witenagemot, composed of the king, the lords, and the Saxon freemen, that original sketch of a British Parliament." The people had had great power in the democratic Saxon commonwealth, "and these principles prevailed through all subsequent changes." As for William the Conqueror, "neither he nor they [his two sons] could destroy the old Constitution."[77] Not only could they not extinguish the old spirit of liberty; they were, in fact, inspired and seized by it themselves. For Bolingbroke, Magna Carta represented a mile-

75. See ibid., pp. 209, 226, 231; Butterfield, *The Englishman and His History,* p. 78; Douglas, *English Scholars,* pp. 355–69.

76. I have discussed this entire incident in much greater detail in "Augustan Politics and English Historiography," *History and Theory* 6 (1967):33–56.

77. *Remarks on the History of England* in *The Works of Lord Bolingbroke,* 1:317–19.

stone in the people's watchful protection of the spirit of liberty, a victory for the continuity of Saxon freedoms. The Middle Ages, in Bolingbroke's history, was a stage upon which the people continually defended the spirit of freedom against kings, barons, and clergy. Some kings were good and furthered these free institutions, while others opposed them; the total freedom varied according to the political developments of each reign.

Bolingbroke's Harringtonian perception of the rise of the Commons under the Tudors and his general preference for the Elizabethan Age and its balance—which Harrington did not share—did not interfere with his belief in immemorial popular freedom residing in a representative body of commoners. To be sure, Henry VII's actions had given the Commons great power, but only such as it had enjoyed formerly. Tudor constitutional arrangements returned the English "to the principles of government which had prevailed amongst our Saxon ancestors."[78] Although the power of the Commons had declined under the Norman and subsequent dynasties, it was never extinct; under the Tudors it was merely revitalized in full Saxon measure.

Week after week during the five years after the original publication of the *Remarks,* Bolingbroke's *Craftsman* defended the theory of the ancient constitution against Brady's history appearing weekly in Walpole's newspaper. The history of Walpole's publicists was, *The Craftsman* suggested, a "novel and pernicious doctrine, first advanced by the Tories, and since adopted by our modern Whigs, that liberty is not our ancient inheritance but only an acquisition since the Revolution."[79] The Revolution, *The Craftsman* contended, was merely a renewal of the ancient spirit of liberty; it did not mark the end of centuries of tyranny and slavery. In using these arguments, the Tory Bolingbroke and his *Craftsman* saw themselves firmly in the tradition of such great Whig patriots as Petyt, Sidney, and Tyrell, in contrast to a "set of men who call themselves the advocates of a Whig ministry, defend those prerogative principles, and lick up the spittle of such slavish writers as Brady and his followers."[80]

Much more than this was at stake, of course. Behind the entire

78. Ibid., 1:36.
79. *The Craftsman,* no. 256 (29 May 1731).
80. Ibid., no. 467 (14 June 1735).

historical debate lay the political strife of the 1730s. Boling-broke's use of Whig history served obvious partisan purposes. How better to attack Walpole than with traditional Whig con-ceptions of the past! The present corrupt age, Bolingbroke main-tained, was one of slavery compared to the great freedoms of the past. In both the *Remarks on the History of England* and *A Dissertation upon Parties,* Bolingbroke concluded that the an-cient English were freemen: "In all their ages, Britain hath been the Temple, as it were, of liberty."[81] But this glorious and continuous tradition of freedom was once again threatened, as it had been in the seventeenth century by the Stuarts. In 1730 the English were not free. The Revolution, which had sought to restore the ancient constitution and its freedoms, was betrayed by the new political and economic world of Robert Walpole. Despotism was reducing the English to slavery, and the longing for the freedoms of old England could be met only by a Machiavellian *ricorso,* a return to the first principles of the ancient constitution. Annual parliaments, a militia, and the ex-clusion of placemen were steps toward a freer past and were associated with an old England which was everywhere being replaced by new and disturbing innovations. Bolingbroke had learned well the lesson of the seventeenth-century common law-yers and the Whigs of the Exclusion crisis. To the English polit-ical mind, a most effective way to combat a contemporary evil was to use a historical argument that contrasted present slavery and lack of freedom with an idyllic image of a free past. Boling-broke was a Whig historian because his opposition to Walpole and to the new England over which Walpole presided made him one.

If opposing Walpole made Bolingbroke a Whig historian, then Bolingbroke's charges, cloaked in the theory of the ancient constitution, made Walpole's press Tory historians. In the de-sire to prove that Walpole's administration and post-Revolu-tionary Whiggery in general had enlarged the degree of English freedom, it was necessary for ministerial writers to destroy Bol-ingbroke's picture of a free past and to replace it with Dr. Brady's description of English history.

81. *A Dissertation upon Parties,* in *The Works of Lord Bolingbroke,* 2:108.

Leaving aside now the debate with Walpole's press on the nature of the English Middle Ages, we ought to note that it was also clear to Bolingbroke that the past was a source of historical lessons in areas other than those of constitutional practice and domestic politics, which were at issue in that debate. Letter 8 of the *Letters on the Study and Use of History,* for example, is devoted primarily to the history of England's foreign relations. Here, too, there is an overriding lesson for modern statesmen, one which Bolingbroke charges that Walpole has, of course, not learned. History teaches that the balance of power is the cardinal prescription for England's dealings with the outside world.

> 'Tis not the Emperor, nor France, nor Spain, nor this nor t'other Potentate, to whom we must keep up a perpetual opposition, or grant a constant assistance; power will always be fluctuating amongst the princes of Europe and wherever the present flow of it appears, there is our enemy, there the proper object of our fears.[82]

England's proper role was that of the "balancer" seeking to maintain the equilibrium upon which its safety depended, "to hinder it from being destroyed, by preventing too much power from falling into one scale." Her primary interest was to guarantee that no single power emerged on the continent, for "if a superior power gives the law to the continent, I apprehend that it will give it to us, too, in some great degree." One of the criteria by which Bolingbroke judged the English monarchs was their faithful adherence to the balance of power. Elizabeth stood highest; Cromwell and the Stuarts stood near the bottom because of their alliances with the superior powers of Spain and France.[83]

In adhering to the principle of the balance of power, Bolingbroke projected onto the international sphere the preoccupation with balance and limitations on power which characterized his image of the English constitution. The very terminology of the domestic equilibrium could be transferred to the international. Like the three branches of government, the ruling houses of Europe had fairly well-defined limits of influence and control.

82. *The Craftsman,* no. 27 (6 March 1727).
83. *Letters,* 2:249 ff.

If one power transcended its limits, the others banded together to defeat it or discourage its effort. Bolingbroke saw both constitutional and international politics in terms that postulated rival independent powers who were still interdependent enough to check a single power's claims to hegemony. We have come full circle with this, for Bolingbroke's beloved exemplar in the writing of history, Polybius, had made this same identification of the balance of power in domestic and international politics:

> For when any branch of it, swelling beyond its bounds, becomes ambitious, and aims at unwarrantable power, it is manifest that no one of them being, as I have said, absolute, but the designs of each subject to the contradiction and control of the other two, no one can run into any excess of power or arrogance; but all three must remain in the terms prescribed by the constitution, either by being defeated in their attempts to exceed them, or, by being prevented, through the fear of the other two, from attempting it.[84]

How fitting that these two historians, one writing at the beginning and the other at the end of the long tradition of humanist historiography, should find history teaching the same lesson.

Economics and Historical Change: Bolingbroke's Philosophy of History

Up to this point our concern has been Bolingbroke's historical method, his methodological convictions and his practice of writing history. We must now ask if Bolingbroke had a philosophy of history as well. Does he, for example, see causal or explanatory patterns in the unfolding of history? Does he see forces or movements at work that give meaning to historical change? He does, most emphatically, see the function of history as providing generalizations and explanations. His major criticism of the antiquarians, after all, was their failure to generalize from their accumulation of facts. If men were to learn from history, they had to lift their eyes from their facts and seek causal explanation. "Naked facts," he writes in the *Letters,* "without the causes

---

84. Edward Spelman, ed., *A Fragment out of The Sixth Book of Polybius* (London, 1743), p. 91.

that produced them . . . are not sufficient to characterize actions or counsels." In letter 2 he reminded Hyde that historical events were not produced by accident or chance; they have "causes, immediate or remote."[85] This advance from seeing history as the accumulation of unrelated data and facts to a concern with explanation and generalization is what both Trevor-Roper and J. G. A. Pocock see as the achievement of Enlightenment history.[86] Out of this develops inquiry into social history. The dull chronicles of important events are replaced by histories of society, generalizations about and explanations of social change. Narrative and chronological history are replaced by sociological history, the quest for the inner dynamics of society that account for its general character and explain its development and change. In France this is the achievement of Montesquieu and Voltaire; in England, of Gibbon.[87] But important credit must also be given to Bolingbroke in this turning of history to generalizations about society.

In this area of his thought, Bolingbroke once again showed two important tendencies. He vacillated between a humanist philosophy of history that emphasized morality and voluntarism as the energy of social change, and a materialist philosophy of history which stressed the structural aspects of society, the social and economic components, as basic in explaining historical development. Bolingbroke's most original contribution is his emphasis on the economic factor in history. But, as we shall see, here, too, he could not free himself from his humanist heritage.

The central tenet of the humanist philosophy of history is the importance of personality, human nature, and great men in history. It is a voluntaristic conception which sees certain individuals able to intervene self-consciously in history by their own free choice and to leave their imprint for posterity. The roots of this attitude lie deep in the humanist past when classical historians depicted their communities as founded and forever

85. *Letters,* 2:186, 228.
86. H. R. Trevor-Roper, "The Historical Philosophy of the Enlightenment," *Studies on Voltaire and the Eighteenth Century* 24/27 (1963):1675 ff.; Pocock, *The Ancient Constitution,* pp. 185–90.
87. See Trevor-Roper, "The Historical Philosophy."

molded by the great lawgivers, Solon, Lycurgus, or Romulus. Bolingbroke's histories often smack of this humanist belief in the role of personality; he is, for example, constantly singling out individuals for their important historical contributions, most often and most dramatically his own favorite, good Queen Elizabeth. His constant concern with corruption and his use of Roman examples can be read as passing judgment on the evil inclinations of human nature, which, if only men were regenerate, would lead to a healthy body politic. On the other hand, Bolingbroke was also a neo-Harringtonian who sometimes repudiated the voluntarism of humanist history and offered a deterministic philosophy of history, emphasizing social structure and, in particular, economics.[88]

I have argued elsewhere that Bolingbroke's entire corpus of writings must be read in terms of his central conviction that economic activity shapes social and political life.[89] The opposition to Walpole had at its ideological core the belief that financial capitalism, represented by the stock market, the national debt, and the Bank of England, lay behind Walpole's Whig rule and also explained the general decline and corruption sensed in English public life by people like Bolingbroke, Swift, Pope, and Gay. This conviction that economic change was the primal historical force is found writ large in Bolingbroke's writings. One need go no further, however, than the *Letters on the Study and Use of History* to find it. Part II of letter 6 describes the decisive change given to English history by the shifts in property-owning under the Tudors. But the full flavor of Bolingbroke's economic determinism is best seen in the last paragraphs of letter 2. Who could have known, he asks, that the Revolution of 1688 would lead to a new ordering of the revenue and a new method of public finance, such that forty years later the entire constitution stood threatened, and all English liberties seemed in danger of extinction? Partisan exaggeration, to be sure, but the nature of the explanation is clear enough. The alleged sorry state of Eng-

88. See my *Bolingbroke and His Circle: The Politics of Nostalgia in the Age of Walpole* (Cambridge, Mass., 1968); and J. G. A. Pocock, "Machiavelli, Harrington and English Political Ideologies in the Eighteenth Century," *William and Mary Quarterly* 22 (October 1965).

89. Kramnick, *Bolingbroke and His Circle*, passim.

land under Walpole in the 1730s is not a result of a wicked prime minister's evil passions, nor is it due to some general decline among the English. Its origin was structurally determined and material. "The creation of the funds, the establishment of great corporations, the trafficking in paper, the arts of jobbing," these were the "causes, immediate and remote." But even this, alas, is not the last word; he is still of two minds.

The conflicting tendencies of Bolingbroke's views on historical change can be illustrated most graphically by juxtaposing his writings and Machiavelli's. Machiavelli's philosophy of history is a paradigmatic example of the humanist explanation of historical change, with its emphasis on great men and the qualities of human nature as responsible for political change in states. In most areas of his thought, Bolingbroke, as we have seen, closely followed Machiavelli; but he did not accept all of Machiavelli's teachings. He could see no value in factions, as Machiavelli had, for example; nor did he share the Florentine's negative views on landed gentlemen. But the most significant area in which Bolingbroke's thought differs from Machiavelli's is in the explanation of historical change, specifically the decline and regeneration that preoccupied them both. Machiavelli saw the roots of decline inherent in human nature and its inevitable tendency, shared with all things, to degenerate, unless periodically rejuvenated.[90] Bolingbroke, however, like Harrington, thought change a product, not of some invariable human nature, but of the social and economic structure of society. In his *Remarks,* his *Letters,* his *Dissertation upon Parties,* even in his *Craftsman,* Bolingbroke diagnosed the corruption of Walpole's England not in terms of man's spirit, but in the structural terms of his condition. In this respect he differed from Machiavelli in all his writings except his last, the *Patriot King.* For in this, his most famous work, Bolingbroke abandoned Harrington's economic determinism and accepted the humanism of Machiavelli.

The freedom of a constitution, Bolingbroke wrote in the *Patriot King,* rests on two foundations: the "orders" of the community (the "different classes and assemblies of men, with different powers and privileges") and the "spirit and character

90. Machiavelli, *Discourses,* book 1, chaps. 2, 4.

1

of the people."[91] The Patriot King who seeks to reform a corrupt
people in order to reestablish a free constitution will not alter
the powers and privileges of the orders and classes, for this would
cause too great a shock to the body politic; and, moreover, it
would be impossible in a corrupt commonwealth. His methods
must be moral, not political. The reforming Patriot King must
be a humanist prince who influences by his moral example, and
not a political reformer who deals with classes, powers, and
privileges.

Bolingbroke's Patriot King is Machiavelli's Prince, whose
virtuous moral example will return the body politic to its lost
liberty and true principles. He is "the most powerful of all reformers" who can renew the spirit of liberty in people's minds.
"Under him they [his people] will not only cease to do evil, but
learn to do well." Overnight "a new people will seem to arise
with a new King." The moral example of this humanist prince
is all that is required to restore the political and social balance
of class and privilege which had been corrupted and destroyed
over the past half-century.

> As soon as a Patriot King is raised to the throne, the panacea is
> applied; the spirit of the constitution revives of course; and, as
> fast as it revives, the orders and form of the constitution are
> restored to their primitive integrity.[92]

In this, the statement of his cause that would most be remembered by posterity, Bolingbroke abandoned his Harringtonian
insight into the structural changes in English history—that
change in the balance and nature of property was the root of
hateful corruption. Like Machiavelli, Bolingbroke, in the *Patriot King,* regards change and degeneration as inevitable in all
systems, regardless of their structural uniqueness.

> Absolute stability is not to be expected in anything human. . . .
> The best instituted governments, like the best constituted animal
> bodies, carry in them the seeds of their destruction: and, though
> they grow and improve for a time, they will soon tend visibly
> to their dissolution.[93]

91. *The Idea of a Patriot King,* in *The Works of Lord Bolingbroke,* 2:393.
92. Ibid., 2:396.
93. Ibid., 2:397.

Bolingbroke's prescription for regeneration in the *Patriot King* assumed a degeneration caused by a decline in virtue; he assumed a moral cause rather than the structural cause he had himself diagnosed so well elsewhere. Convinced of the prospects for moral reform through an exemplary Patriot King, Bolingbroke devoted the last pages of his essay to a minute description of the desirable private and public character of this king. He outlined his proper education, upbringing, and social dealings, all of which were designed to make him a "great and good man." Bolingbroke's retreat into humanism was complete when he offered a "mirror for princes," an "education for a Christian Prince," a "book for governors."[94] In all his other writings he had attributed historical change, in this case the rise of corruption and the passing of the ideal order, to social and economic causes; yet here, in the *Patriot King,* he suggests that the only way to reestablish the ideal order is by the moral example and theatrical deportment of a humanist prince.

Once again, this time in his philosophy of history, Bolingbroke could not shed the humanist ideal and give himself completely to the more modern tendency of his thought. This may well have been because he was himself so much the very model of the humanist prince—scholar, statesman, historian, philosopher, patron and friend of poets, and, but for Anne's decision on her deathbed, his people's first minister.

Further Reading

A large number of books on Bolingbroke's life exists. The most exhaustive, but far from definitive, is Walter Sichel's *Bolingbroke and His Times,* 2 vols. (London, 1901–2). The most recent and most reliable is H. Dickinson's *Bolingbroke* (London, 1970). Various aspects of Bolingbroke's thought have been treated in several recent books. S. W. Jackman's *Man of Mercury* (London, 1965) is both biographical and a survey of his thought. Jeffrey Hart's *Viscount Bolingbroke: Tory Humanist* (London, 1966) and Harvey Mansfield, Jr.'s *Statesmanship*

---

94. See Felix Gilbert, "The Humanist Concept of the Prince and the Prince of Machiavelli," *Journal of Modern History* 2 (December 1939).

and Party Government (Chicago, 1965) are very readable and both have very definite points of view, albeit opposite ones. Two books that deal primarily with his political and constitutional thought are my *Bolingbroke and His Circle: The Politics of Nostalgia in the Age of Walpole* (Cambridge, Mass., 1968) and Kurt Kluxen, *Das Problem der Politischen Opposition* (Freiburg, 1956).

The best and most available source of Bolingbroke's own works is the 1841 Philadelphia edition. Harvard University's Houghton Rare Book Library does contain one of the original six or seven manuscript copies of the *Letters on the Study and Use of History* that Bolingbroke had circulated to close friends in 1736. Issues of *The Craftsman* were published in bound editions in 1730 and again in 1736. The original essays for the *Remarks on the History of England* may be seen there.

Surprisingly little has been written on Bolingbroke the historian. In 1938 Trevelyan published letters 6–8 of the *Letters* under the title of *Bolingbroke's Defense of the Treaty of Utrecht.* He omitted the first five letters, convinced that the general discussion of history found there was of little value. Some discussion of Bolingbroke's writings on history can be found in D. C. Douglas, *English Scholars* (London, 1939); Herbert Butterfield, *The Englishman and His History* (Cambridge, 1944); J. H. Brumfitt, *Voltaire Historian* (Oxford, 1958); J. G. A. Pocock, *The Ancient Constitution and the Feudal Law: A Study of English Historical Thought in the Seventeenth Century* (Cambridge, 1957); G. H. Nadel, "Philosophy of History before Historicism," in *Studies in the Philosophy of History,* ed. Nadel (New York, 1965); G. H. Nadel, "Bolingbroke's *Letters on History,*" *Journal of the History of Ideas* October–December 1962, vol. 23, no. 4; Leo Braudy, *Narrative Form in History and Fiction* (Princeton, 1970); and my "Augustan Politics and English Historiography," *History and Theory* 6 (1967).

ISAAC KRAMNICK

I
Letters on the
Study and Use
of History

Letter 1

Chantelou in Touraine, Nov. 6, 1735.
My Lord: I have considered formerly, with a good deal of attention, the subject on which you command me to communicate my thoughts to you: and I practised in those days, as much as business and pleasure allowed me time to do, the rules that seemed to me necessary to be observed in the study of history. They were very different from those which writers on the same subject have recommended, and which are commonly practised. But I confess to your lordship, that this neither gave me then, nor has given me since, any distrust of them. I do not affect singularity. On the contrary, I think that a due deference is to be paid to received opinions, and that a due compliance with received customs is to be held; though both the one and the other should be, what they often are, absurd or ridiculous. But this servitude is outward only, and abridges in no sort the liberty of private judgment. The obligations of submitting to it likewise, even outwardly, extend no further than to those opinions and customs which cannot be opposed, or from which we cannot deviate without doing hurt, or giving offence to society. In all these cases our speculations ought to be free: in all other cases, our practice may be so. Without any regard, therefore, to the opinion and practice even of the learned world, I am very willing to tell you mine. But, as it is hard to recover a thread of thought long ago laid aside, and impossible to prove some things, and explain others, without the assistance of many books which I

3

have not here, your lordship must be content with such an imperfect sketch, as I am able to send you at present in this letter. The motives that carry men to the study of history are deficient. Some intend, if such as they may be said to study, nothing more than amusement, and read the life of Aristides or Phocion, of Epaminondas or Scipio, Alexander or Cæsar, just as they play a game at cards, or as they would read the story of the seven champions.

Others there are, whose motive to this study is nothing better, and who have the further disadvantage of becoming a nuisance very often to society, in proportion to the progress they make. The former do not improve their reading to any good purpose; the latter pervert it to a very bad one, and grow in impertinence as they increase in learning. I think I have known most of the first kind in England, and most of the last in France. The persons I mean are those who read to talk, to shine in conversation, and to impose in company; who having few ideas to vend of their own growth, store their minds with crude unruminated facts and sentences; and hope to supply, by bare memory, the want of imagination and judgment.

But these are in the two lowest forms. The next I shall mention are in one a little higher; in the form of those who grow neither wiser nor better by study themselves, but who enable others to study with greater ease, and to purposes more useful; who make fair copies of foul manuscripts, give the signification of hard words, and take a great deal of other grammatical pains. The obligation to these men would be great indeed, if they were in general able to do any thing better, and submitted to this drudgery for the sake of the public: as some of them, it must be owned with gratitude, have done, but not later, I think, than about the time of the resurrection of letters. When works of importance are pressing, generals themselves may take up the pick-axe and the spade; but in the ordinary course of things, when that pressing necessity is over, such tools are left in the hands destined to use them—the hands of common soldiers and peasants. I approve, therefore, very much the devotion of a studious man at Christ-church, who was overheard in his oratory entering into a detail with God, as devout persons are apt to do, and, amongst other particular thanksgivings, acknowledging the

4

divine goodness in furnishing the world with makers of dictionaries! These men court fame, as well as their betters, by such means as God has given them to acquire it: and Littleton exerted all the genius he had, when he made a dictionary, though Stephens did not. They deserve encouragement, however, while they continue to compile, and neither affect wit, nor presume to reason.

There is a fourth class, of much less use than these, but of much greater name. Men of the first rank in learning, and to whom the whole tribe of scholars bow with reverence. A man must be as indifferent as I am to common censure or approbation, to avow a thorough contempt for the whole business of these learned lives; for all the researches into antiquity, for all the systems of chronology and history, that we owe to the immense labors of a Scaliger, a Bochart, a Petavius, an Usher, and even a Marsham. The same materials are common to them all; but these materials are few, and there is a moral impossibility that they should ever have more. They have combined these into every form that can be given to them: they have supposed, they have guessed, they have joined disjointed passages of different authors, and broken traditions of uncertain originals, of various people, and of centuries remote from one another as well as from ours. In short, that they might leave no liberty untaken, even a wild fantastical similitude of sounds has served to prop up a system. As the materials they have are few, so are the very best, and such as pass for authenic, extremely precarious; as some of these learned persons themselves confess.

Julius Africanus, Eusebius, and George the monk, opened the principal sources of all this science; but they corrupted the waters. Their point of view was to make profane history and chronology agree with sacred; though the latter chronology is very far from being established with the clearness and certainty necessary to make it a rule. For this purpose, the ancient monuments, that these writers conveyed to posterity, were digested by them according to the system they were to maintain: and none of these monuments were delivered down in their original form, and genuine purity. The Dynasties of Manetho, for instance, are broken to pieces by Eusebius, and such fragments of them as suited his design, are stuck into his work. We have, we know, no more of them. The Codex Alexandrinus we owe to George the monk. We have no other authority for it; and one cannot see without amazement such a man as Sir John Marsham undervaluing this authority in one page, and building his system upon it in the next. He seems even by the lightness of his expressions, if I remember well, for it is long since I looked into his canon, not to be much concerned what foundation his system had, so he showed his skill in forming one, and in reducing the immense antiquity of the Egyptians within the limits of the Hebraic calculation. In short, my lord, all these systems are so many enchanted castles; they appear to be something, they are nothing but appearances: like them too, dissolve the charm, and they vanish from the sight. To dissolve the charm, we must begin at the beginning of them: the expression may be odd, but it is significant. We must examine scrupulously and indifferently the foundations on which they lean: and when we find these either faintly probable, or grossly improbable, it would be foolish to expect any thing better in the superstructure. This science is one of those that are "a limine salutandæ." To do thus much may be necessary, that grave authority may not impose on our ignorance: to do more, would be to assist this very authority in imposing false science upon us. I had rather take the Darius whom Alexander conquered, for the son of Hystaspes, and make as many anachronisms as a Jewish chronologer, than sacrifice half my life to collect all the learned lumber that fills the head of an antiquary.

Letter 2

Concerning the
True Use and Advantages
of the Study
of History

Let me say something of history, in general, before I descend into the consideration of particular parts of it, or of the various methods of study, or of the different views of those that apply themselves to it, as I had begun to do in my former letter.

The love of history seems inseparable from human nature, because it seems inseparable from self-love. The same principle in this instance carries us forward and backward, to future and to past ages. We imagine that the things, which affect us, must affect posterity: this sentiment runs through mankind, from Cæsar down to the parish-clerk in Pope's Miscellany. We are fond of preserving, as far as it is in our frail power, the memory of our own adventures, of those of our own time, and of those that preceded it. Rude heaps of stones have been raised, and ruder hymns have been composed, for this purpose, by nations who had not yet the use of arts and letters. To go no farther back, the triumphs of Odin were celebrated in runic songs, and the feats of our British ancestors were recorded in those of their bards. The savages of America have the same custom at this day: and long historical ballads of their huntings and their wars are sung at all their festivals. There is no need of saying how this passion grows, among civilised nations, in proportion to the means of gratifying it: but let us observe that the same principle of nature directs us as strongly, and more generally as well as more early, to indulge our own curiosity, instead of preparing to gratify that of others. The child hearkens with delight to the

tales of his nurse: he learns to read, and he devours with eagerness fabulous legends and novels: in riper years he applies himself to history, or to that which he takes for history, to authorised
romance: and, even in age, the desire of knowing what has
happened to other men, yields to the desire alone of relating
what has happened to ourselves. Thus history, true or false,
speaks to our passions always. What pity is it, my lord, that
even the best should speak to our understandings so seldom?
That it does so, we have none to blame but ourselves. Nature
has done her part. She has opened this study to every man
who can read and think: and what she has made the most
agreeable, reason can make the most useful, application of our
minds. But if we consult our reason, we shall be far from following the examples of our fellow-creatures, in this as in most
other cases, who are so proud of being rational. We shall neither
read to soothe our indolence, nor to gratify our vanity: as
little shall we content ourselves to drudge like grammarians
and critics, that others may be able to study with greater ease
and profit, like philosophers and statesmen; as little shall we
affect the slender merit of becoming great scholars at the expense
of groping all our lives in the dark mazes of antiquity. All
these mistake the true drift of study, and the true use of history.
Nature gave us curiosity to excite the industry of our minds;
but she never intended it should be made the principal, much
less the sole object of their application. The true and proper
object of this application is a constant improvement in private
and in public virtue. An application to any study that tends
neither directly nor indirectly to make us better men and better
citizens, is at best but a specious and ingenious sort of idleness,
to use an expression of Tillotson: and the knowledge we acquire
by it is a creditable kind of ignorance, nothing more. This
creditable kind of ignorance is, in my opinion, the whole benefit
which the generality of men, even of the most learned, reap
from the study of history: and yet the study of history seems to
me, of all other, the most proper to train us up to private and
public virtue.

Your lordship may very well be ready by this time, and after
so much bold censure on my part, to ask me, what then is the
true use of history? in what respects may it serve to make us

better and wiser? and what method is to be pursued in the study
of it, for attaining these great ends? I will answer you by quoting
what I have read some where or other, in Dionysius Halicarn
[assus], I think, that history is philosophy teaching by examples.
We need but to cast our eyes on the world, and we shall see the
daily force of example: we need but to turn them inward, and
we shall soon discover why example has this force. "Pauci
prudentia," says Tacitus, "honesta abdeterioribus, utilia ab noxiis
discernunt: plures aliorum eventis docentur." Such is the imperfection of human understanding, such is the frail temper of
our minds, that abstract or general propositions, though ever so
true, appear obscure or doubtful to us very often, till they are
explained by examples; and that the wisest lessons in favor of
virtue go but a little way to convince the judgment, and determine the will, unless they are enforced by the same means; and
we are obliged to apply to ourselves what we see happen to
other men. Instructions by precept have the further disadvantage of coming on the authority of others, and frequently require
a long deduction of reasoning. "Homines amplius oculis, quam
auribus, credunt: longum iter est per præcepta, breve et efficax
per exempla." The reason of this judgment, which I quote from
one of Seneca's epistles in confirmation of my own opinion,
rests, I think, on this; that when examples are pointed out to us,
there is a kind of appeal, with which we are flattered, made to
our senses, as well as our understandings. The instruction comes
then upon our own authority: we frame the precept after our
own experience, and yield to fact when we resist speculation.
But this is not the only advantage of instruction by example; for
example appeals not to our understanding alone, but to our passions likewise. Example assuages these, or animates them; sets
passion on the side of judgment, and makes the whole man of a
piece; which is more than the strongest reasoning and the clearest
demonstration can do: and thus forming habits by repetition,
example secures the observance of those precepts which example
insinuated. Is it not Pliny, my lord, who says, that the gentlest,
he should have added the most effectual, way of commanding, is
by example? "Mitius jubetur exemplo." The harshest orders are
softened by example, and tyranny itself becomes persuasive.
What pity it is that so few princes have learned this way of com-

manding! But again: the force of examples is not confined to those alone, that pass immediately under our sight: the examples, that memory suggests, have the same effect in their degree, and a habit of recalling them will soon produce the habit of imitating them. In the same epistle, from whence I cited a passage just now, Seneca says that Cleanthes had never become so perfect a copy of Zeno, if he had not passed his life with him; that Plato, Aristotle, and the other philosophers of that school, profited more by the example, than by the discourse of Socrates. [But here, by the way, Seneca mistook; for Socrates died two years according to some, and four years according to others, before the birth of Aristotle: and his mistake might come from the inaccuracy of those who collected for him; as Erasmus observes, after Quintilian, in his judgment on Seneca.] But be this, which was scarce worth a parenthesis, as it will; he adds that Metrodorus, Hermachus, and Polyænus, men of great note, were formed by living under the same roof with Epicurus, not by frequenting his school. These are instances of the force of immediate example. But your lordship knows that the citizens of Rome placed the images of their ancestors in the vestibules of their houses; so that, whenever they went in or out, these venerable bustoes met their eyes, and recalled the glorious actions of the dead, to fire the living, to excite them to imitate and even to emulate their great forefathers. The success answered the design. The virtue of one generation was transfused, by the magic of example, into several: and a spirit of heroism was maintained through many ages of that commonwealth. Now these are so many instances of the force of remote example; and from all these instances we may conclude, that examples of both kinds are necessary.

The school of example, my lord, is the world: and the masters of this school are history and experience. I am far from contending that the former is preferable to the latter. I think upon the whole otherwise: but this I say, that the former is absolutely necessary to prepare us for the latter, and to accompany us whilst we are under the discipline of the latter, that is, through the whole course of our lives. No doubt some few men may be quoted, to whom nature gave what art and industry can give to no man. But such examples will prove nothing against me, because I admit that the study of history, without experience, is insufficient, but assert, that experience itself is so without genius. Genius is preferable to the other two; but I would wish to find the three together: for how great soever a genius may be, and how much soever he may acquire new light and heat, as he proceeds in his rapid course, certain it is that he will never shine with the full lustre, nor shed the full influence he is capable of, unless to his own experience he adds the experience of other men and other ages. Genius, without the improvement, at least of experience, is what comets once were thought to be, a blazing meteor, irregular in his course, and dangerous in his approach; of no use to any system, and able to destroy any. Mere sons of earth, if they have experience without any knowledge of the history of the world, are but half scholars in the science of mankind. And if they are conversant in history without experience, they are worse than ignorant; they are pedants, always incapable, sometimes meddling and presuming. The man, who has all three, is an honor to his country, and a public blessing: and such, I trust, your lordship will be in this century, as your great-grandfather[1] was in the last.

I have insisted a little longer on this head, and have made these distinctions the rather, because though I attribute a great deal more than many will be ready to allow, to the study of history, yet I would not willingly even seem to fall into the ridicule of ascribing it to such extravagant effects, as several have done from Tully down to Casaubon, La Mothe le Vayer, and other modern pedants. When Tully informs us, in the second book of his Tusculan disputations, that the first Scipio Africanus had always in his hands the works of Xenophon, he advances nothing but what is probable and reasonable. To say nothing of the retreat of the ten thousand, nor of other parts of Xenophon's writings; the images of virtue, represented in that admirable picture the Cyropædia, were proper to entertain a soul that was fraught with virtue, and Cyrus was worthy to be imitated by Scipio. So Selim emulated Cæsar, whose commentaries were translated for his use against the customs of the Turks; so Cæsar emulated Alexander; and Alexander, Achilles.

1. Earl of Clarendon.

There is nothing ridiculous here, except the use that is made of this passage by those who quote it. But what the same Tully says, in the fourth book of his academical disputations, concerning Lucullus, seems to me very extraordinary. "In Asiam factus imperator venit; cum esset Roma profectus rei militaris rudis;" [one would be ready to ascribe so sudden a change, and so vast an improvement, to nothing less than knowledge infused by inspiration, if we were not assured in the same place that they were effected by very natural means, by such as it is in every man's power to employ] "partim percontando a peritis, partim in rebus gestis legendis." Lucullus, according to this account, verified the reproach on the Roman nobility, which Sallust puts into the mouth of Marius. But as I discover the passion of Marius, and his prejudices to the patricians, in one case; so I discover, methinks, the cunning of Tully, and his partiality to himself, in the other. Lucullus, after he had been chosen consul, obtained by intrigue the government of Cilicia, and so put himself into a situation of commanding the Roman army against Mithridates: Tully had the same government afterwards, and though he had no Mithridates, nor any other enemy of consequence, opposed to him; though all his military feats consisted in surprising and pillaging a parcel of highlanders and wild Cilicians; yet he assumed the airs of a conqueror, and described his actions in so pompous a style, that the account becomes burlesque. He laughs, indeed, in one of his letters to Atticus, at his generaliship; but if we turn to those he wrote to Cœlius Rufus, and to Cato, upon this occasion, or to those wherein he expresses to Atticus his resentment against Cato for not proposing in his favor the honors usually decreed to conquerors, we may see how vanity turned his head, and how impudently he insisted on obtaining a triumph. Is it any strain now to suppose, that he meant to insinuate, in the passage I have quoted about Lucullus, that the difference between him and the former governor of Cilicia, even in a military merit, arose from the different conjuncture alone; and that Lucullus could not have done in Cilicia, at that time, more than he himself did? Cicero had read and questioned at least as much Lucullus, and would therefore have appeared as great a captain if he had had as great a prince as Mithridates to encounter. But the truth is that Lucullus was made a great captain by theory, or the study of history, alone, no more than Ferdinand of Spain and Alphonsus of Naples were cured of desperate distempers by reading Livy and Quintus Curtius; a silly tale, which Bodin, Amyot, and others have picked up and propagated. Lucullus had served in his youth against the Marsi, probably in other wars, and Sylla took early notice of him: he went into the east with this general and had a great share in his confidence. He commanded in several expeditions. It was he who restored the Colophonians to their liberty, and who punished the revolt of the people of Mytelene. Thus we see that Lucullus was formed by experience, as well as study, and by an experience gained in those very countries, where he gathered so many laurels afterwards in fighting against the same enemy. The late Duke of Marlborough never read Xenophon, most certainly, nor the relation perhaps of any modern wars; but he served in his youth under Monsieur de Turenne, and I have heard that he was taken notice of, in those early days, by that great man. He afterwards commanded in an expedition to Ireland, served a campaign or two, if I mistake not, under king William in Flanders: and, besides these occasions, had none of gaining experience in war, till he came to the head of our armies in one thousand seven hundred and two, and triumphed not over Asiatic troops, but over the veteran armies of France. The Roman had on his side genius and experience cultivated by study: the Briton had genius improved by experience, and no more. The first therefore is not an example of what study can do alone; but the latter is an example of what genius and experience can do without study. They can do so much, to be sure, when the first is given in a superior degree. But such examples are very rare; and when they happen it will be still true, that they would have had fewer blemishes, and would have come nearer to the perfection of private and public virtue, in all the arts of peace and achievements of war, if the views of such men had been enlarged, and their sentiments ennobled, by acquiring that cast of thought, and that temper of mind, which will grow up and become habitual in every man who applies himself early to the study of history, as to the study of philosophy, with the intention of being wiser and better, without the affectation of being more learned.

The temper of the mind is formed and a certain turn given to our ways of thinking; in a word, the seeds of that moral character which cannot wholly alter the natural character, but may correct the evil and improve the good that is in it, or do the very contrary, are sown betimes, and much sooner than is commonly supposed. It is equally certain, that we shall gather or not gather experience, be the better or the worse for this experience, when we come into the world and mingle amongst mankind, according to the temper of mind, and the turn of thought, that we have acquired beforehand, and bring along with us. They will tincture all our future acquisitions; so that the very same experience which secures the judgment of one man, or excites him to virtue, shall lead another into error, or plunge him into vice. From hence, it follows, that the study of history has in this respect a double advantage. If experience alone can make us perfect in our parts, experience cannot begin to teach them till we are actually on the stage: whereas, by a previous application to this study, we con them over at least before we appear there: we are not quite unprepared; we learn our parts sooner, and we learn them better.

Let me explain what I mean by an example. There is scarce any folly or vice more epidemical among the sons of men, than that ridiculous and hurtful vanity by which the people of each country are apt to prefer themselves to those of every other; and to make their own customs, and manners, and opinions, the standards of right and wrong, of true and false. The Chinese mandarins were strangely surprised, and almost incredulous, when the Jesuits showed them how small a figure their empire made in the general map of the world. The Samojedes wondered much at the Czar of Muscovy for not living among them: and the Hottentot, who returned from Europe, stripped himself naked as soon as he came home, put on his bracelets of guts and garbage, and grew stinking and lousy as fast as he could. Now nothing can contribute more to prevent us from being tainted with this vanity, than to accustom ourselves early to contemplate the different nations of the earth, in that vast map which history spreads before us, in their rise and their fall, in their barbarous and civilised states, in the likeness and unlikeness of them all to one another, and of each to itself. By frequently renewing

14

this prospect to the mind, the Mexican with his cap and coat of feathers, sacrificing a human victim to his god, will not appear more savage to our eyes than the Spaniard with a hat on his head, and a gonilla round his neck, sacrificing whole nations to his ambition, his avarice, and even the wantonness of his cruelty. I might show, by a multitude of other examples, how history prepares us for experience, and guides us in it: and many of these would be both curious and important. I might likewise bring several other instances, wherein history serves to purge the mind of those national partialities and prejudices that we are apt to contract in our education, and that experience for the most part rather confirms than removes: because it is for the most part confined, like our education. But I apprehend growing too prolix, and shall therefore conclude this head by observing, that though an early and proper application to the study of history will contribute extremely to keep our minds free from a ridiculous partiality in favor of our own country, and a vicious prejudice against others; yet the same study will create in us a preference of affection to our own country. There is a story told of Abgarus. He brought several beasts taken in different places to Rome, they say, and let them loose before Augustus: every beast ran immediately to that part of the circus where a parcel of earth taken from his native soil had been laid. "Credat Judæus Apella." This tale might pass on Josephus; for in him, I believe, I read it: but surely the love of our country is a lesson of reason, not an institution of nature. Education and habit, obligation and interest, attach us to it, not instinct. It is however so necessary to be cultivated, and the prosperity of all societies, as well as the grandeur of some, depends upon it so much, that orators by their eloquence, and poets by their enthusiasm, have endeavored to work up this precept of morality into a principle of passion. But the examples which we find in history, improved by the lively descriptions, and the just applauses or censures of historians, will have a much better and more permanent effect than declamation or song, or the dry ethics of mere philosophy. In fine, to converse with historians is to keep good company: many of them were excellent men, and those who were not such, have taken care, however, to appear such in their writings. It must be, therefore, of great use to prepare ourselves by this conversation for that of the world; and to receive our first impressions, and to acquire our first habits, in a scene where images of virtue and vice are continually represented to us in the colors that belong properly to them, before we enter on another scene, where virtue and vice are too often confounded, and what belongs to one is ascribed to the other.

Besides the advantage of beginning our acquaintance with mankind sooner, and of bringing with us into the world, and the business of it, such a cast of thought and such a temper of mind, as will enable us to make a better use of our experience; there is this further advantage in the study of history, that the improvement we make by it extends to more objects, and is made at the expense of other men: whereas that improvement, which is the effect of our own experience, is confined to fewer objects, and is made at our own expense. To state the account fairly, therefore, between these two improvements, though the latter be the more valuable, yet allowance being made on one side for the much greater number of examples that history presents to us, and deduction being made on the other of the price we often pay for our experience, the value of the former will rise in proportion. "I have recorded these things," says Polybius, after giving an account of the defeat of Regulus, "that they who read these commentaries may be rendered better by them; for all men have two ways of improvement, one arising from their own experience, and one from the experience of others. Evidentior quidem illa est, quæ per propria ducit infortunia at tutior illa, quæ per aliena." I use Casaubon's translation. Polybius goes on, and concludes, "that since the first of these ways exposes us to great labor and peril, whilst the second works the same good effect, and is attended by no evil circumstance, every one ought to take for granted that the study of history is the best school where he can learn how to conduct himself in all the situations of life." Regulus had seen at Rome many examples of magnanimity, of frugality, of the contempt of riches, and of other virtues; and these virtues he practised. But he had not learned, nor had opportunity of learning another lesson, which the examples recorded in history inculcate frequently, the lesson of moderation. An insatiable thirst of military fame, an unconfined ambition of extending their empire, an extravagant confidence in their own courage and force, an insolent contempt of their enemies, and an impetuous overbearing spirit with which they pursued all their enterprises, composed in his days the distinguishing character of a Roman. Whatever the senate and people resolved, to the members of that commonwealth appeared both practicable and just. Neither difficulties nor dangers could check them; and their sages had not yet discovered, that virtues in excess degenerate into vices. Notwithstanding the beautiful rant which Horace puts into his mouth, I make no doubt that Regulus learned at Carthage those lessons of moderation which he had not learned at Rome: but he learned them by experience, and the fruits of this experience came too late, and cost too dear; for they cost the total defeat of the Roman army, the prolongation of a calamitous war which might have been finished by a glorious peace, the loss of liberty to thousands of Roman citizens, and to Regulus himself the loss of life in the midst of torments, if we are entirely to credit what is perhaps exaggeration in the Roman authors.

There is another advantage, worthy our observation, that belongs to the study of history; and that I shall mention here, not only because of the importance of it, but because it leads me immediately to speak of the nature of the improvement we ought to have in our view, and of the method in which it seems to me that this improvement ought to be pursued: two particulars from which your lordship may think perhaps that I digress too long. The advantage I mean consists in this, that the examples which history presents to us, both of men and of events, are generally complete: the whole example is before us, and consequently the whole lesson, or sometimes the various lessons, which philosophy proposes to teach us by this example. For first, as to men; we see them at their whole length in history, and we see them generally there through a medium less partial at least than that of experience: for I imagine that a whig or a tory, whilst those parties subsisted, would have condemned in Saturninus the spirit of faction which he applauded in his own tribunes, and would have applauded in Drusus the spirit of moderation which he despised in those of the contrary party, and which he suspected and hated in those of his own party. The villain who has imposed on mankind by his power or cunning, and whom experience could not unmask for a time, is unmasked at length: and the honest man, who has been misunderstood or defamed, is justified before his story ends. Or if this does not happen, if the villain dies with his mask on, in the midst of applause, and honor, and wealth, and power, and if the honest man dies under the same load of calumny and disgrace under which he lived, driven perhaps into exile, and exposed to want; yet we see historical justice executed, the name of one branded with infamy, and that of the other celebrated with panegyric to succeeding ages. "Præcipuum munus annalium reor, ne virtutes sileantur; utque pravis dictis factisque ex posteritate et infamia metus sit." Thus, according to Tacitus, and according to truth, from which his judgments seldom deviate, the principal duty of history is to erect a tribunal, like that among the Egyptians, mentioned by Diodorus Siculus, where men and princes themselves were tried, and condemned or acquitted, after their deaths; where those who had not been punished for their crimes, and those who had not been honored for their virtues, received a just retribution. The sentence is pronounced in one case, as it was in the other, too late to correct or recompense; but it is pronounced in time to render these examples of general instruction to mankind. Thus Cicero, that I may quote one instance out of thousands, and that I may do justice to the general character of that great man, whose particular failing I have censured so freely; Cicero, I say, was abandoned by Octavius, and massacred by Antony. But let any man read this fragment of Aurelius Fuscus, and choose which he would wish to have been, the orator, or the triumvir? "Quoad humanum genus incolume manserit, quamdiu usus literis, honor summæ eloquentiæ pretium erit, quamdiu rerum natura aut fortuna steterit, aut memoria duraverit, admirabile posteris vigebis ingenium, et uno proscriptus seculo, proscribes Antonium omnibus."

Thus again, as to events that stand recorded in history; we see them all, we see them as they followed one another, or as they produced one another, causes or effects, immediate or remote. We are cast back, as it were, into former ages: we live with the men who lived before us, and we inhabit countries that we never saw. Place is enlarged, and time prolonged, in this manner; so that the man who applies himself early to the study of history, may acquire in a few years, and before he sets his foot abroad in the world, not only a more extended knowledge of mankind, but the experience of more centuries than any of the patriarchs saw. The events we are witnesses of, in the course of the longest life, appear to us very often original, unprepared, single, and unrelative, if I may use such an expression for want of a better English; in French I would say isolés: they appear such very often, are called accidents, and looked on as the effects of chance; a word, by the way, which is in constant use, and has frequently no determinate meaning. We get over the present difficulty, we improve the momentary advantage, as well as we can, and we look no farther. Experience can carry us no farther; for experience can go a very little way back in discovering causes: and effects are not the objects of experience till they happen. From hence many errors in judgment, and by consequence in conduct, necessarily arise. And here too lies the difference we are speaking of between history and experience. The advantage on the side of the former is double. In ancient history, as we have said already, the examples are complete, which are incomplete in the course of experience. The beginning, the progression, and the end appear, not of particular reigns, much less of particular enterprises, or systems of policy alone, but of governments, of nations, of empires, and of all the various systems that have succeeded one another in the course of their duration. In modern history, the examples may be, and sometimes are, incomplete; but they have this advantage when they are so, that they serve to render complete the examples of our own time. Experience is doubly defective; we are born too late to see the beginning, and we die too soon to see the end of many things. History supplies both these defects. Modern history shows the causes, when experience presents the effects alone: and ancient history enables us to guess at the effects, when experience presents the causes alone. Let me explain my meaning by two examples of these kinds; one past, the other actually present.

When the revolution of one thousand six hundred and eighty-eight happened, few men then alive, I suppose, went farther in their search after the causes of it, than the extravagant attempt of king James against the religion and liberty of his people. His former conduct, and the passages of king Charles the

Second's reign might rankle still at the hearts of some men, but could not be set to account among the causes of his deposition; since he had succeeded, notwithstanding them, peaceably to the throne: and the nation in general, even many of those who would haxe excluded him from it, were desirous, or at least willing, that he should continue in it. Now this example, thus stated, affords, no doubt, much good instruction to the kings, and people of Britain. But this instruction is not entire, because the example thus stated, and confined to the experience of that age, is imperfect. King James's mal-administration rendered a revolution necessary and practicable; but his mal-administration, as well as all his preceding conduct, was caused by his bigot attachment to popery, and to the principles of arbitrary government, from which no warning could divert him. His bigot attachment to these was caused by the exile of the royal family; this exile was caused by the usurpation of Cromwell: and Cromwell's usurpation was the effect of a former rebellion, begun not without reason on account of liberty, but without any valid pretence on account of religion. During this exile, our princes caught the taint of popery and foreign politics. We made them unfit to govern us, and after that were forced to recall them that they might rescue us out of anarchy. It was necessary therefore, your lordship sees, at the revolution, and it is more so now, to go back in history, at least as far as I have mentioned, and perhaps farther, even to the beginning of king James the First's reign, to render this event a complete example, and to develope all the wise, honest, and salutary precepts, with which it is pregnant, both to king and subject.

The other example shall be taken from what has succeeded the revolution. Few men at that time looked forward enough to foresee the necessary consequences of the new constitution of the revenue, that was soon afterwards formed; nor of the method of funding that immediately took place; which, absurd as they are, have continued ever since, till it is become scarce possible to alter them. Few people, I say, foresaw how the creation of funds, and the multiplication of taxes, would increase yearly the power of the crown, and bring our liberties by a natural and necessary progression, into more real, though less apparent danger, than they were in before the revolution. The excessive ill husbandry practised from the very beginning of king William's reign, and which laid the foundations of all we feel and all we fear, was not the effect of ignorance, mistakes, or what we call chance, but of design and scheme in those who had the sway at that time. I am not so uncharitable, however, as to believe that they intended to bring upon their country all the mischiefs that we, who came after them, experience and apprehend. No, they saw the measures, they took singly, and unrelatively, or relatively alone to some immediate object. The notion of attaching men to the new government, by tempting them to embark their fortunes on the same bottom, was a reason of state to some: the notion of creating a new, that is, a moneyed interest, in opposition to the landed interest or as a balance to it, and of acquiring a superior influence in the city of London at least by the establishment of great corporations, was a reason of party to others: and I make no doubt that the opportunity of amassing immense estates by the management of funds, by trafficking in paper, and by all the arts of jobbing, was a reason of private interest to those who supported and improved this scheme of iniquity, if not to those who devised it. They looked no farther. Nay, we who came after them, and have long tasted the bitter fruits of the corruption they planted, were far from taking such an alarm at our distress and our danger, as they deserved; till the most remote and fatal effects of causes, laid by the last generation, was very near becoming an object of experience in this. Your lordship, I am sure, sees at once how much a due reflection on the passages of former times, as they stand recorded in the history of our own, and of other countries, would have deterred a free people from trusting the sole management of so great a revenue, and the sole nomination of those legions of officers employed in it, to their chief magistrate. There remained indeed no pretence for doing so, when once a salary was settled on the prince, and the public revenue was no longer in any sense his revenue, nor the public expense his expense. Give me leave to add, that it would have been, and would be still, more decent with regard to the prince, and less repugnant if not more conformable to the principles and practice too of our government, to take this power and influence from the prince, or to share it with him; than to exclude men from the privilege of representing their fellow-subjects who would choose them in parliament, purely because they are employed and trusted by the prince.

Your lordship sees, not only how much a due reflection upon the experience of other ages and countries would have pointed out national corruption, as the natural and necessary consequence of investing the crown with the management of so great a revenue; but also the loss of liberty, as the natural and necessary consequence of national corruption.

These two examples explain sufficiently what they are intended to explain. It only remains therefore upon this head, to observe the difference between the two manners in which history supplies the defects of our own experience. It shows us causes as in fact they were laid, with their immediate effects: and it enables us to guess at future events. It can do no more, in the nature of things. My Lord Bacon, in his second book of the Advancement of Learning, having in his mind, I suppose, what Philo and Josephus asserted of Moses, affirms divine history to have this prerogative, that the narration may be before the fact as well as after. But since the ages of prophecy, as well as miracles, are past, we must content ourselves to guess at what will be, by what has been: we have no other means in our power, and history furnishes us with these. How we are to improve, and apply these means, as well as how we are to acquire them, shall be deduced more particularly in another letter.

Letter 3

An Objection against the Utility of History Removed

An Objection against the Utility of History Removed

Were these letters to fall into the hands of some ingenious persons who adorn the age we live in, your lordship's correspondent would be joked upon for his project of improving men in virtue and wisdom by the study of history. The general characters of men, it would be said, are determined by their natural constitutions, as their particular actions are by immediate objects. Many very conversant in history would be cited, who have proved ill men, or bad politicians; and a long roll would be produced of others, who have arrived at a great pitch of private, and public virtue, without any assistance of this kind. Something has been said already to anticipate this objection; but, since I have heard several persons affirm such propositions with great confidence, a loud laugh, or a silent sneer at the pedants who presumed to think otherwise; I will spend a few paragraphs, with your lordship's leave, to show that such affirmations, for to affirm amongst these fine men is to reason, either prove too much, or prove nothing.

If our general characters were determined absolutely, as they are certainly influenced, by our constitutions, and if our particular actions were so by immediate objects; all instruction by precept, as well as example, and all endeavors to form the moral character by education, would be unnecessary. Even the little care that is taken, and surely it is impossible to take less, in the

23

57903

training up our youth, would be too much. But the truth is widely different from this representation of it; for, what is vice, and what is virtue? I speak of them in a large and philosophical sense. The former is, I think, no more than the excess, abuse, and misapplication of appetites, desires, and passions, natural and innocent, nay useful and necessary. The latter consists in the moderation and government, in the use and application of these appetites, desires, and passions, according to the rules of reason, and therefore often in opposition to their own blind impulse.

What now is education? that part, that principle and most neglected part of it, I mean, which tends to form the moral character? It is, I think, an institution designed to lead men from their tender years, by precept and example, by argument and authority, to the practice, and to the habit of practising these rules. The stronger our appetites, desires, and passions are, the harder indeed is the task of education: but when these efforts of education are proportioned to this strength, although our keenest appetites and desires, and our ruling passions cannot be reduced to a quiet and uniform submission, yet, are not their excesses assuaged? are not their abuses and misapplications, in some degree, diverted or checked? Though the pilot cannot lay the storm, cannot he carry the ship, by his art, better through it, and often prevent the wreck that would always happen, without him? If Alexander who loved wine, and was naturally choleric, had been bred under the severity of Roman discipline, it is probable he would neither have made a bonfire of Persepolis for his whore, nor have killed his friend. If Scipio, who was naturally given to women, for which anecdote we have, if I mistake not, the authority of Polybius, as well as some verses of Nævius preserved by A. Gellius, had been educated by Olympius at the court of Philip, it is improbable that he would have restored the beautiful Spaniard. In short, if the renowned Socrates had not corrected nature by art, this first apostle of the Gentiles had been a very profligate fellow, by his own confession; for he was inclined to all the vices Zopyrus imputed to him, as they say, on the observation of his physiognomy.

With him, therefore, who denies the effects of education, it would be in vain to dispute; and with him who admits them, there can be dispute, concerning that share which I ascribe to the

24

study of history, in forming our moral characters, and making us better men. The very persons who pretend that inclinations cannot be restrained, nor habits corrected, against our natural bent, would be the first perhaps to prove, in certain cases, the contrary. A fortune at court, or the favors of a lady, have prevailed on many to conceal, and they could not conceal without restraining, which is one step towards correcting, the vices they were by nature addicted to the most. Shall we imagine now, that the beauty of virtue and the deformity of vice, the charms of a bright and lasting reputation, the terror of being delivered over as criminals to all posterity, the real benefit arising from a conscientious discharge of the duty we owe to others, which benefit fortune can neither hinder nor take away, and the reasonableness of conforming ourselves to the designs of God manifested in the constitution of the human nature; shall we imagine, I say, that àll these are not able to acquire the same power over those who are continually called upon to a contemplation of them, and they who apply themselves to the study of history are so called upon, as other motives, mean and sordid in comparison of these, can usurp on other men?

The False and True Aims of Those Who Study It

That the study of history, far from making us wiser, and more useful citizens, as well as better men, may be of no advantage whatsoever; that it may serve to render us mere antiquaries and scholars; or that it may help to make us forward coxcombs, and prating pedants, I have already allowed. But this is not the fault of history: and to convince us that it is not, we need only contrast the true use of history with the use that is made of it by such men as these. We ought always to keep in mind, that history is philosophy teaching by examples how to conduct ourselves in all the situations of private and public life; that therefore we must apply ourselves to it in a philosophical spirit and manner; that we must rise from particular to general knowledge, and that we must fit ourselves for the society and business of mankind by accustoming our minds to reflect and meditate on the characters we find described, and the course of events we find related there. Particular examples may be of use sometimes in particular cases; but the application of them is dangerous. It must be done with the utmost circumspection, or it will be seldom done with success. And yet one would think that this was the principal use of the study of history, by what has been written on the subject. I know not whether Machiavel himself is quite free from defect on this account: he seems to carry the use and application of particular examples sometimes too far. Marius and Catulus passed the Alps, met, and defeated the Cimbri beyond the frontiers of Italy. Is it safe to conclude from hence, that whenever one people is invaded by another, the invaded ought to meet and fight the invaders at a distance from their frontiers? Machiavel's countryman, Guicciardin, was aware of the danger that might arise from such an application of examples. Peter of Medicis had involved himself in great difficulties, when those wars and calamities began which Lewis Sforza first drew and entailed on Italy, by flattering the ambition of Charles the Eighth in order to gratify his own, and calling the French into that country. Peter owed his distress to his folly in departing from the general tenor of conduct his father Laurence had held, and hoped to relieve himself by imitating his father's example in one particular instance. At a time when the wars with the pope and king of Naples had reduced Laurence to circumstances of great danger, he took the resolution of going to Ferdinand, and of treating in person with that prince. The resolution appears in history imprudent and almost desperate: were we informed of the secret reasons on which this great man acted, it would appear very possible a wise and safe measure. It succeeded, and Laurence brought back with him public peace, and private security. As soon as the French troops entered the dominions of Florence, Peter was struck with a panic terror, went to Charles the Eighth, put the port of Leghorn, the fortresses of Pisa, and all the keys of the country, into this prince's hands; whereby he disarmed the Florentine commonwealth, and ruined himself. He was deprived of his authority, and driven out of the city, by the just indignation of the magistrates, and people: and in the treaty which they made afterwards with the king of France, it was stipulated, that Peter should not remain within an hundred miles of the state, nor his brothers within the same distance of the city of Florence. On this occasion Guicciardin observes, how dangerous it is to govern ourselves by particular examples; since to have the same success, we must have the same prudence, and the same fortune; and since the example must not only answer the case before us in general, but in every minute circumstance. This is the sense of that admirable historian, and these are his words— "é senza dubio molta pericoloso il governarsi con gl' esempi, se non concorrono, non solo in generale, ma in tutti i particulari, le medesime ragioni; se le cose non sono regolate con la medesima prudenza, et se oltre a tutti li altri fondamenti, non, v'ha la parte sua la medesima fortuna." An observation that Boileau makes, and a rule he lays down in speaking of translations, will properly find their place here, and serve to explain still better what I would establish.

> To translate servilely into modern language an ancient author phrase by phrase, and word by word, is preposterous: nothing can be more unlike the original than such a copy. It is not to show, it is to disguise the author: and he who has known him only in this dress, would not know him in his own. A good writer, instead of taking this inglorious and unprofitable task upon him, will *jouster contre l'original,* rather imitate than translate, and rather emulate than imitate; he will transfuse the sense and spirit of the original into his own work, and will endeavor to write as the ancient author would have written, had he written in the same language.

Now, to improve by examples is to improve by imitation. We must catch the spirit, if we can, and conform ourselves to the reason of them; but we must not affect to translate servilely into our conduct, if your lordship will allow me the expression, the particular conduct of those good and great men, whose images history sets before us. Codrus and the Decii devoted themselves to death: one, because an oracle had foretold that the army whose general was killed would be victorious; the others in compliance with a superstition that bore great analogy to a ceremony practised in the old Egyptian church, and added afterwards, as many others of the same origin were, to the ritual of the Israelites. These are examples of great magnanimity, to be sure, and of magnanimity employed in the most worthy cause. In the early days of the Athenian and Roman government, when the credit of oracles and all kinds of superstition prevailed, when heaven was piously thought to delight in blood, and even human blood was shed under wild notions of atonement, propitiation, purgation, expiation, and satisfaction; they who set such examples as these, acted an heroical and a rational part too. But if a general should act the same part now, and, in order to secure his victory, get killed as fast as he could, he might pass for a hero, but, I am sure, he would pass for a madman. Even these examples, however, are of use: they excite us at least to venture our lives freely in the service of our country, by proposing to our imitation men who devoted themselves to certain death in the service of theirs. They show us what a turn of imagination can operate, and how the greatest trifle, nay the greatest absurdity, dressed up in the solemn airs of religion, can carry ardor and confidence, or the contrary sentiments, into the breasts of thousands.

These are certain general principles, and rules of life and conduct, which always must be true, because they are conformable to the invariable nature of things. He who studies history as he would study philosophy, will soon distinguish and collect them, and by doing so will soon form to himself a general system of ethics and politics on the surest foundations, on the trial of these principles and rules in all ages, and on the confirmation of them by universal experience. I said he will distinguish them; for once more I must say, that as to particular modes of actions, and measures of conduct, which the customs of different countries, the manners of different ages, and the circumstances of different conjunctures, have appropriated, as it were; it is always ridiculous, or imprudent and dangerous to employ them. But this is not all. By contemplating the vast variety of particular characters and events; by examining the strange combination of causes, different, remote, and seemingly opposite, that often concur in producing one effect; and the surprising fertility of one single and uniform cause in the producing of a multitude of effects, as different, as remote, and seemingly as opposite; by tracing carefully, as carefully as if the subject he considers were of personal and immediate concern to him, all the minute and sometimes scarce perceivable circumstances, either in the characters of actors, or in the course of actions, that history enables him to trace, and according to which the success of affairs, even the greatest, is mostly determined; by these, and such methods as these, for I might descend into a much greater detail, a man of parts may improve the study of history to its proper and principal use; he may sharpen the penetration, fix the attention of his mind, and strengthen his judgment; he may acquire the faculty and the habit of discerning quicker, and looking farther; and of exerting that flexibility, and steadiness, which are necessary to be joined in the conduct of all affairs that depend on the concurrence or opposition of other men.

Mr. Locke, I think, recommends the study of geometry even to those who have no design of being geometricians: and he gives a reason for it, that may be applied to the present case. Such persons may forget every problem that has been proposed, and every solution that they or others have given; but the habit of pursuing long trains of ideas will remain with them, and they will pierce through the mazes of sophism, and discover a latent truth, where persons who have not this habit will never find it.

In this manner the study of history will prepare us for action and observation. History is the ancient author: experience is the modern language. We form our taste on the first, we translate the sense and reason, we transfuse the spirit and force; but we imitate only the particular graces of the original; we imitate them according to the idiom of our own tongue, that is, we substitute often equivalents in the lieu of them, and are far from affecting to copy them servilely. To conclude, as experience is conversant about the present, and the present enables us to guess at the future; so history is conversant about the past, and by knowing the things that have been, we become better able to judge of the things that are.

This use, my lord, which I make the proper and principal use of the study of history, is not insisted on by those who have written concerning the method to be followed in this study: and since we propose different ends, we must of course take different ways. Few of their treatises have fallen into my hands: one, the method of Bodin, a man famous in his time, I remember to have read. I took it up with much expectation many years ago; I went through it, and remained extremely disappointed. He might have given almost any other title to his book as properly as that which stands before it. There are not many pages in it that relate any more to his subject than a tedious fifth chapter, wherein he accounts for the characters of nations according to their positions on the globe, and according to the influence of the stars; and assures his reader that nothing can be more necessary than such a disquisition; "ad universam historiarum cognitionem, et incorruptum earum judicium." In his method, we are to take first a general view of universal history, and chronology, in short abstracts, and then to study all particular histories and systems. Seneca speaks of men who spend their whole lives in learning how to act in life, "dum vitæ instrumenta conquirunt." I doubt that this method of Bodin would conduct us in the same, or as bad a way; would leave us no time for action, or would make us unfit for it. A huge common-place book, wherein all the remarkable sayings and facts that we find in history are to be registered, may enable a man to talk or write like Bodin, but will never make him a better man, nor enable him to promote, like an useful citizen, the security, the peace, the welfare, or the grandeur of the community to which he belongs. I shall proceed therefore to speak of a method that leads to such purposes as these directly and certainly, without any regard to the methods that have been prescribed by others.

I think then we must be on our guard against this very affectation of learning, and this very wantonness of curiosity, which the examples and precepts we commonly meet with are calculated to flatter and indulge. We must neither dwell too long in the dark, nor wander about till we lose our way in the light. We are too apt to carry systems of philosophy beyond all our ideas, and systems of history beyond all our memorials. The philosopher begins with reason, and ends with imagination. The historian inverts this order: he begins without memorials, and he sometimes ends with them. This silly custom is so prevalent among men of letters who apply themselves to the study of history, and has so much prejudice and so much authority on the side of it, that your lordship must give me leave to speak a little more particularly and plainly than I have done, in favor of common sense against an absurdity which is almost sanctified.

Of the History of the First Ages, with
Reflections on the State of Ancient History, Profane and Sacred

The nature of man, and the constant course of human affairs, render it impossible that the first ages of any new nation which forms itself, should afford authentic materials for history. We have none such concerning the originals of any of those nations that actually subsist. Shall we expect to find them concerning the originals of nations dispersed, or extinguished, two or three thousand years ago? If a thread of dark and uncertain traditions, therefore, is made, as it commonly is, the introduction to history, we should touch it lightly, and run swiftly over it, far from insisting on it, either as authors or readers. Such introductions are at best no more than fanciful preludes, that try the instruments, and precede the concert. He must be void of judgment, and taste, one would think, who can take the first for true history, or the last for true harmony. And yet so it has been, and so it is, not in Germany and Holland alone; but in Italy, in France, and in England, where genius has abounded, and taste has been long refined. Our great scholars have dealt and deal in fables at least as much as our poets, with this difference to the disadvantage of the former, to whom I may apply the remarks as justly as Seneca applied it to the dialecticians—"tristius inepti sunt. Illi ex professio lasciviunt; hi agere seipsos aliquid existimant." Learned men, in learned and inquisitive ages, who possessed many advantages that we have not, and among others that of being placed so many centuries nearer the original truths that are the objects of so much laborious search, despaired of finding them, and gave fair warning to posterity, if posterity would have taken it. The ancient geographers, as Plutarch says in the life of Theseus, when they laid down in their maps the little extent of sea and land that was known to them, left great spaces void. In some of these spaces they wrote, Here are sandy deserts, in others, Here are impassable marshes, Here is a chain of inhospitable mountains, or Here is a frozen ocean. Just so both he and other historians, when they related fabulous originals, were not wanting to set out the bounds beyond which there was neither history nor chronology. Censorinus has preserved the distinction of three eras established by Varro. This learned Roman anti-quary did not determine whether the first period had any begin-ning, but fixed the end of it at the first, that is, according to him, the Ogygian, deluge; which he placed, I think, some centuries more backward than Julius Africanus thought fit to place it afterwards. To this era of absolute darkness he supposed that a kind of twilight succeeded, from the Ogygian deluge to the Olympic era, and this he called the fabulous age. From this vulgar era when Coræbus was crowned victor, and long after the true era when these games were instituted by Iphitus, the Greeks pretend to be able to digest their history with some order, clearness, and certainty. Varro therefore looked on it as the break of day, or the beginning of the historical age. He might do so the rather, perhaps, because he included by it the date he likewise fixed, or, upon recollection, that the elder Cato had fixed, of the foundation of Rome within the period from which he supposed that historical truth was to be found. But yet most certain it is, that the history and chronology of the ages that follow are as confused and uncertain, as the history and chronology of those which immediately precede this era.

The State of Ancient Profane History

The Greeks did not begin to write in prose till Pherecides of Syros introduced the custom: and Cadmus Milesius was their first historian. Now these men flourished long after the true, or even the vulgar Olympic era; for Josephus affirms, and in this he has great probability on his side, that Cadmus Milesius, and Acusilaus Argivus, in a word, the oldest historians in Greece, were very little more ancient than the expedition of the Persians against the Greeks. As several centuries passed between the Olympic era and these first historians, there passed likewise several more between these and the first Greek chronologers. Timæus about the time of Ptolemy Philadelphus, and Eratos-thenes about that of Ptolemy Evergetes, seem first to have di-gested the events recorded by them, according to the Olympiads. Precedent writers mentioned sometimes the Olympiads; but this rule of reckoning was not brought into established use sooner. The rule could not serve to render history more clear and certain till it was followed: it was not followed till about five hundred years after the Olympic era. There remains therefore no pretence to place the beginning of the historical age so high as Varro placed it, by five hundred years.

Hellanicus indeed and others pretended to give the originals of cities and governments, and to deduce their narrations from great antiquity. Their works are lost, but we can judge how inconsiderable the loss is, by the writings of that age which remain, and by the report of those who had seen the others. For instance, Herodotus was cotemporary with Hellanicus. Herodotus was inquisitive enough in all conscience, and proposed to publish all he could learn of the antiquities of the Ionians, Lydians, Phrygians, Egyptians, Babylonians, Medes, and Persians: that is, of almost all the nations who were known in his time to exist. If he wrote Assyriacs, we have them not: but we are sure that this word was used proverbially to signify fabulous legends, soon after his time, and when the mode of publishing such relations and histories prevailed among the Greeks.

In the nine books we have, he goes back indeed almost to the Olympic era, without taking notice of it however; but he goes back only to tell an old woman's tale, of a king who lost his crown for showing his wife naked to his favorite; and from Candaules and Gyges he hastens, or rather he takes a great leap, down to Cyprus.

Something like a thread of history of the Medes and then of the Persians, to the flight of Xerxes, which happened in his own time, is carried on. The events of his own time are related with an air of history. But all accounts of the Greeks as well as the Persians, which precede these, and all the accounts which he gives occasionally of other nations, were drawn up most manifestly on broken, perplexed, and doubtful scraps of tradition. He had neither original records, nor any authentic memorials to guide him, and yet these are the sole foundations of true history. Herodotus flourished, I think, little more than half a century, and Xenophon little more than a whole century, after the death of Cyrus: and yet how various and repugnant are the relations made by these two historians, of the birth, life, and death of this prince? If more histories had come down from these ages to ours, the uncertainity and inutility of them all would be but the more manifest. We should find that Acusilaus rejected the traditions of Hesiod, that Hellanicus contradicted Acusilaus, that Ephorus accused Hellanicus, that Timæus accused Ephorus, and all posterior writers Timæus. This is the report of Josephus. But, in order to show the ignorance and falsehood of all those writers through whom the traditions of profane antiquity came to the Greeks, I will quote to your lordship a much better authority than that of Josephus; the authority of one who had no prejudice to bias him, no particular cause to defend, nor system of ancient history to establish, and all the helps, as well as talents, necessary to make him a competent judge. The man I mean is Strabo.

Speaking of the Massagetæ in his eleventh book, he writes to this effect: that no author had given a true account of them, though several had written of the war that Cyrus waged against them; and that historians had found as little credit in what they had related concerning the affairs of the Persians, Medes, and Syrians: that this was due to their folly; for observing that those who wrote fables professedly were held in esteem, these men imagined they should render their writings more agreeable, if, under the appearance and pretence of true history, they related what they had neither seen nor heard from persons able to give them true information; and that accordingly their only aim had been to dress up pleasing and marvellous relations: that one may better give credit to Hesiod and Homer, when they talk of their heroes, nay, even to dramatic poets, than to Ctesias, Herodotus, Hellanicus, and their followers: that it is not safe to give credit even to the greatest part of the historians who wrote concerning Alexander; since they too, encouraged by the greater reputation of this conqueror, by the distance to which he carried his arms, and by the difficulty of disproving what they said of actions performed in regions so remote, were apt to deceive: that indeed when the Roman empire on one side, and the Parthian on the other, came to extend themselves, the truth of things grew to be better known.

You see, my lord, not only how late profane history began to be written by the Greeks, but how much later it began to be written with any regard to truth; and consequently what wretched materials the learned men, who arose after the age of Alexander, had to employ, when they attempted to form systems of ancient history and chronology. We have some remains of that laborious compiler Diodorus Siculus, but do we find in him any thread of ancient history, I mean, that which passed for ancient in his time? What complaints, on the contrary, does he not make of former historians? how frankly does he confess the little and uncertain light he had to follow in his researches? Yet Diodorus, as well as Plutarch, and others, had not only the older Greek historians, but the more modern antiquaries, who pretended to have searched into the records and registers of nations, even at that time renowned for their antiquity. Berosus, for instance, and Manetho, one a Babylonian and the other an Egyptian priest, had published the antiquities of their countries in the time of the Ptolemys. Berosus pretended to give the history of four hundred and eighty years. Pliny, if I remember right, for I say this on memory, speaks to this effect in the sixth book of his Natural History: and if it was so, these years were probably years of Nabonassar. Manetho began his history, God knows when, from the progress of Isis, or some other as well ascertained period. He followed the Egyptian tradition of dynastics of gods and demi-gods; and derived his anecdotes from the first Mercury, who had inscribed them in sacred characters, on antediluvian pillars, antediluvian at least according to our received chronology, from which the second Mercury had transcribed them, and inserted them into his works. We have not these antiquities; for the monk of Viterbo was soon detected: and if we had them, they would either add to our uncertainty, and increase the chaos of learning, or tell us nothing worth our knowledge. For thus I reason. Had they given particular and historical accounts conformable to the scriptures of the Jews, Josephus, Julius Africanus, and Eusebius would have made quite other extracts from their writings, and would have altered and contradicted them less. The accounts they gave, therefore, were repugnant to sacred writ, or they were defective: they would have established Pyrrhonism, or have balked our curiosity.

Of Sacred History

What memorials therefore remain to give us light into the originals of ancient nations, and the history of those ages, we commonly call the first ages? The Bible, it will be said; that is, the historical part of it in the Old Testament. But, my lord, even these divine books must be reputed insufficient to the purpose, by every candid and impartial man who considers either their authority as histories, or the matter they contain. For what are they? and how come they to us? At the time when Alexander carried his arms into Asia, a people of Syria, till then unknown, became known to the Greeks: this people had been slaves to the Egyptians, Assyrians, Medes, and Persians, as the several empires prevailed: ten parts in twelve of them had been transplanted by ancient conquerors, and melted down and lost in the east, several ages before the establishment of the empire that Alexander destroyed: the other two parts had been carried captive to Babylon a little before the same era. This captivity was not indeed perpetual, like the other; but it lasted so long, and such circumstances, whatever they were, accompanied it, that the captives forgot their country, and even their language, the Hebrew dialect at least and character: and a few of them only could be wrought upon, by the zeal of some particular men, to return home, when the indulgence of the Persian monarchs gave them leave to rebuild their city and to repeople their ancient patrimony. Even this remnant of the nation did not continue long entire. Another great transmigration followed; and the Jews, that settled under the protection of the Ptolemys, forgot their language in Egypt, as the forefathers of these Jews had forgot theirs in Chaldea. More attached however to their religion in Egypt, for reasons easy to be deduced from the new institutions that prevailed after the captivity among them, than their ancestors had been in Chaldea, a version of their sacred writings was made into Greek at Alexandria, not long after the canon of these scriptures had been finished at Jerusalem; for many years could not intervene between the death of Simon the Just, by whom this canon was finished, if he died during the reign of Ptolemy Soter, and the beginning of this famous translation under Ptolemy Philadelphus. The Hellenist Jews reported as many marvellous things to authorise, and even to sanctify this translation, as the other Jews had reported about Esdras who began, and Simon the Just who finished, the canon of their scriptures. These holy romances slid into tradition, and tradition became history: the fathers of our Christian church did not disdain to employ them. St. Jerome, for instance, laughed at the story of the seventy-two elders, whose translations were found to be, upon comparison, word for word the same, though made separately, and by men who had no communication with one another. But the same St. Jerome, in the same place, quotes Aristeas, one of the guard of Ptolemy Philadelphus, as a real personage.

The account pretended to be written by this Aristeas, of all that passed relating to the translation, was enough for his purpose. This he retained, and he rejected only the more improbable circumstances, which had been added to the tale, and which laid it open to most suspicion. In this he showed great prudence; and better judgment, than that zealous, but weak apologist Justin, who believed the whole story himself, and endeavored to impose it on mankind.

Thus you see, my lord, that when we consider these books barely as histories, delivered to us on the faith of a superstitious people, among whom the custom and art of pious lying prevailed remarkably, we may be allowed to doubt whether greater credit is to be given to what they tell us concerning the original, compiled in their own country and as it were out of the sight of the rest of the world; than we know, with such a certainty as no scholar presumes to deny, that we ought to give to what they tell us concerning the copy?

The Hellenist Jews were extremely pleased, no doubt, to have their scriptures in a language they understood, and that might spread the fame of their antiquity, and do honor to their nation, among their masters the Greeks. But yet we do not find that the authority of these books prevailed, or that even they were much known among the pagan world. The reason of this cannot be, that the Greeks admired nothing that was not of their own growth, "sua tantum mirantur": for, on the contrary, they were inquisitive and credulous in the highest degree, and they collected and published at least as many idle traditions of other nations, as they propagated of their own. Josephus pretended that Theopompus, a disciple of Isocrates being about to insert in his history some things he had taken out of holy writ, the poor man became troubled in mind for several days: and that having prayed to God, during an intermission of his illness, to reveal to him the cause of it, he learned in his sleep that this attempt was the cause; upon which he quitted the design and was cured. If Josephus had been a little more consistent than he is very often, such a story as this would not have been told by one, who was fond, as Jews and Christians in general have been, to create an opinion that the Gentiles took not their history alone, but their philosophy and all their valuable knowledge, from the Jews. Notwithstanding this story, therefore, which is told in the fifteenth book of the Jewish antiquities, and means nothing, or means to show that the divine providence would not suffer anecdotes of sacred to be mingled with profane history; the practice of Josephus himself, and of all those who have had the same design in view, has been to confirm the former by the latter, and at any rate to suppose an appearance at least of conformity between them. We are told Hecateus Abderita, for there were two of that name, wrote a history favorable to the Jews: and, not to multiply instances, though I might easily do it, even Alexander Polyhistor is called in. He is quoted by Josephus, and praised by Eusebius as a man of parts and great variety of learning. His testimony, about the deluge and tower of Babel, is produced by St. Cyril in his first book against Julian: and Justin the apologist and martyr, in his exhortation to the Greeks, makes use of the same authority, among those that mention Moses as a leader and prince of the Jews. Though this Polyhistor, if I remember right what I think I have met with in Suidas, spoke only of a woman he called Moso, "cujus scriptum est lex Hebræorum." Had the Greek historians been conformable to the sacred, I cannot see that their authority, which was not cotemporary, would have been of any weight. They might have copied Moses, and so they did Ctesias. But even this was not the case: whatever use a particular writer here and there might make occasionally of the scriptures, certain it is that the Jews continued to be as much despised, and their history to be as generally neglected, nay almost as generally unknown, for a long time at least after the version was made at Alexandria, as they had been before. Apion, an Egyptian, a man of much erudition, appeared in the world some centuries afterwards. He wrote, among other antiquities, those of his own country: and as he was obliged to speak very often of the Jews, he spoke of them in a manner neither much to their honor, nor to that of their histories. He wrote purposely against them: and Josephus attempted afterwards, but Apion was then dead, to refute him. Apion passed, I know, for a vain and noisy pedant; but he passed likewise for a curious, a laborious, and a learned antiquary. If he was cabalistical, or superstitious, Josephus was at least as much so as he: and if he flattered Caligula, Josephus introduced himself to the court of Nero and the favor of Poppæa, by no very honorable means, under the protection of Aliturus a player, and a Jew; to say nothing of his applying to Vespasian the prophecies concerning the Messiah, nor of his accompanying Titus to the siege of Jerusalem.

In short, my lord, the Jewish history never obtained any credit in the world, till Christianity was established. The foundations of this system being laid partly in these histories, and in the prophecies joined to them or inserted in them, Christianity has reflected back upon them an authority which they had not before, and this authority has prevailed wherever Christianity has spread. Both Jews and Christians hold the same books in great veneration, whilst each condemns the other for not understanding, or for abusing them. But I apprehend that the zeal of both has done much hurt, by endeavoring to extend their authority much farther than is necessary for the support perhaps of Judaism, but to be sure of Christianity. I explain myself, that I may offend no pious ear.

Simon, in the preface of his critical history of the Old Testament, cites a divine of the faculty of Paris, who held that the inspirations of the authors of those books, which the church receives as the word of God, should be extended no farther than to matters purely of doctrine, or to such as have a near and necessary relation to these; and that whenever these authors wrote on other subjects, such as Egyptian, Assyrian, or other history, they had no more of the divine assistance than any other persons of piety. This notion of inspirations that came occasionally, that illuminated the minds and guided the hands of the sacred penmen while they were writing one page, and restrained their influence while the same authors were writing another, may be cavilled against: and what is there that may not? But surely it deserves to be treated with respect, since it tends to establish a distinction between the legal, doctrinal, or prophetical parts of the Bible, and the historical: without which distinction it is impossible to establish the first, as evidently and solidly as the interests of religion require: at least it appears impossible to me, after having examined and considered, as well as I am able, all the trials of this kind that have been made by subtile as well as learned men. The Old is said to be the foundation of the New, and so it is in one sense: the system of religion contained in the latter, refers to the system of religion contained in the former, and supposes the truth of it. But the authority on which we receive the books of the New Testament, is so far from being founded on the authority of the Old Testament, that it is quite independent on it; the New being proved, gives authority to the Old, but borrows none from it; and gives this authority to the particular parts only. Christ came to fulfil the prophecies; but not to consecrate all the written, any more than the oral, traditions of the Jews. We must believe these traditions as far as they relate to Christianity, as far as Christianity refers to them, or supposes them necessary; but we can be under no obligation to believe them any farther, since without Christianity we should be under no obligation to believe them at all.

It hath been said by Abbadie, and others, "That the accidents which have happened to alter the texts of the Bible, and to disfigure, if I may say so, the Scriptures in many respects, could not have been prevented without a perpetual standing miracle, and that a perpetual standing miracle is not in the order of Providence." Now I can by no means subscribe to this opinion. It seems evident to my reason that the very contrary must be true; if we suppose that God acts towards men according to the moral fitness of things: and if we suppose that he acts arbitrarily, we can form no opinion at all. I think that these accidents would not have happened, or that the Scriptures would have been preserved entirely in their genuine purity notwithstanding these accidents, if they had been entirely dictated by the Holy Ghost: and the proof of this probable proposition, according to our clearest and most distinct ideas of wisdom and moral fitness, is obvious and easy. But these Scriptures are not so come down to us: they are come down broken and confused, full of additions, interpolations, and transpositions, made we neither know when, nor by whom; and such, in short, as never appeared on the face of any other book, on whose authority men have agreed to rely.

This being so, my lord, what hypothesis shall we follow? Shall we adhere to some such distinction as I have mentioned? Shall we say, for instance, that the Scriptures were written originally by the authors to whom they are vulgarly ascribed, but that these authors wrote nothing by inspiration, except the legal, the doctrinal, and the prophetical parts, and that in every other respect their authority is purely human, and therefore fallible? Or shall we say that these histories are nothing more than compilations of old traditions, and abridgments of old records, made in later times, as they appear to every one who reads them without prepossession, and with attention? Shall we add, that which ever of these probabilities be true, we may believe, consistently with either, notwithstanding the decision of any divines, who know no more than you or I, or any other man, of the order of Providence, that all those parts and passages of the Old Testament, which contain prophecies, or matters of law or doctrine, and which were from the first of such importance in the designs of Providence to all future generations, and even to the whole race of mankind, have been from the first the peculiar care of Providence? Shall we insist that such particular parts and passages, which are plainly marked out and sufficiently confirmed by the system of the Christian revelation, and by the completion of the prophecies, have been preserved from corruption by ways impenetrable to us, amidst all the changes and chances to which the books wherein they are recorded have been exposed; and that neither original writers, nor later compilers, have been suffered to make any essential alterations, such as would have falsified the law of God and the principles of the Jewish and Christian religions, in any of these divine fundamental truths? Upon such hypotheses, we may assert without scruple, that the genealogies and histories of the Old Testament are in no respect sufficient foundations for a chronology from the beginning of time, nor for universal history. But then the same hypotheses will secure the infallibility of scripture authority as far as religion is concerned. Faith and reason may be reconciled a little better than they commonly are. I may deny that the Old Testament is transmitted to us under all the conditions of an authentic history, and yet be at liberty to maintain that the passages in it which establish original sin, which seem favorable to the doctrine of the Trinity, which foretell the coming of the Messiah, and all others of similar kind, are come down to us as they were originally dictated by the Holy Ghost.

In attributing the whole credibility of the Old Testament to the authority of the New, and in limiting the authenticity of the Jewish Scriptures to those parts alone that concern law, doctrine, and prophecy, by which their chronology and the far greatest part of their history are excluded, I will venture to assure your lordship that I do not assume so much, as is assumed in every hypothesis that affixes the divine seal of inspiration to the whole canon; that rests the whole proof on Jewish veracity; and that pretends to account particularly and positively for the descent of these ancient writings in their present state.

Another reason, for which I have insisted the rather on the distinction so often mentioned, is this. I think we may find very good foundation for it even in the Bible: and though this be a point very little attended to, and much disguised, it would not be hard to show, upon great inducements of probability, that the law and the history were far from being blended together as they now stand in the Pentateuch, even from the time of Moses down to that of Esdras. But the principal and decisive reason for separating in such manner the legal, doctrinal, and prophetical parts, from the historical, is the necessity of having some rule to go by: and, I protest, I know of none that is yet agreed upon. I content myself, therefore, to fix my opinion concerning the authority of the Old Testament in this manner, and carry it thus far only. We must do so, or we must enter into that labyrinth of dispute and contradiction, wherein even the most orthodox Jews and Christians have wandered so many ages, and still wander. It is strange, but it is true; not only the Jews differ from the Christians, but Jews and Christians both differ among themselves, concerning almost every point that is necessary to be certainly known and agreed upon, in order to establish the authority of books which both have received already as authentic and sacred. So that whoever takes the pains to read what learned men have written on this subject, will find that they leave the matter as doubtful as they took it up. Who were the authors of these Scriptures, when they were published, how they were composed and preserved, or renewed, to use a remarkable expression of the famous Huet in his Demonstration; in fine, how they were lost during the captivity, and how they were retrieved after it, are all matters of controversy to this day.

It would be easy for me to descend into a greater detail, and to convince your lordship of what I have been saying in general by an induction of particulars, even without any other help than that of a few notes which I took when I applied myself to this examination, and which now lie before me. But such a digression would carry me too far: and I fear that you will think I have said already more than enough upon this part of my subject. I go on, therefore, to observe to your lordship, that if the history of the Old Testament was as exact and authentic, as the ignorance and impudence of some rabbies have made them assert that it is; if we could believe with them that Moses wrote every syllable in the Pentateuch as it now stands, or that all the Psalms were written by David: nay, if we could believe, with Philo and Josephus, that Moses wrote the account of his own death and sepulchre, and made a sort of funeral panegyric on himself, as we find them in the last chapter of Deuteronomy; yet still would I venture to assert, that he who expects to find a system of chronology, or a thread of history, or sufficient materials for either, in the books of the Old Testament, expects to find what the authors of these books, whoever they were, never intended. They are extracts of genealogies, not genealogies: extracts of histories, not histories. The Jews themselves allow their genealogies to be very imperfect, and produce examples of omissions and errors in them, which denote sufficiently that these genealogies are extracts, wherein every generation in the course of descent is not mentioned. I have read somewhere, perhaps in the works of St. Jerome, that this father justifies the opinion of those who think it impossible to fix any certain chronology on that of the Bible: and this opinion will be justified still better, to the understanding of every man who considers how grossly the Jews blunder whenever they meddle with chronology; for this plain reason, because their Scriptures are imperfect in this respect, and because they rely on their oral, to rectify and supply their written, traditions: that is, they rely on traditions compiled long after the canon of their Scriptures, but deemed by them of equal antiquity and authority. Thus, for instance, Daniel and Simon the Just, according to them, were members at the same time of the great synagogue which began and finished the canon of the Old Testament, under the presidency of Esdras. This Esdras was the prophet Malachi. Darius the son of Hystaspes was Artaxerxes Longimanus; he was Ahasuerus, and he was the same Darius whom Alexander conquered. This may serve as a sample of Jewish chronology, formed on their Scriptures which afford insufficient lights, and on their traditions which afford false lights. We are indeed more correct, and come nearer to the truth in these instances, perhaps in some others, because we make use of profane chronology to help us. But profane chronology is itself so modern, so precarious, that this help does not reach to the greatest part of that time to which sacred chronology extends; that when it begins to help, it begins to perplex us too; and finally, that even with this help we should not have had so much as the appearance of a complete chronological system, and the same may be said of universal history, if learned men had not proceeded very wisely, on one uniform maxim, from the first ages of Christianity, when a custom of sanctifying profane learning, as well as profane rites, which the Jews had imprudently laid aside, was taken up by the Christians. The maxim I mean is this, that profane authority be admitted without scruple or doubt, whenever it says, or whenever it can be made to say, if not "totidem verbis," yet "totidem syllabis," or "totidem literis," at least, or whenever it can be made by any interpretation to mean, what confirms, or supplies in a constant manner, the holy writ; and that the same authority be rejected, when nothing of this kind can be done, but the contradiction or inconsistency remains irreconcilable. Such a liberty as this would not be allowed in any other case; because it supposes the very thing that is to be proved. But we see it taken, very properly to be sure, in favor of sacred and infallible writing, when they are compared with others.

In order to perceive with the utmost evidence, that the scope and design of the author or authors of the Pentateuch, and of the other books of the Old Testament, answer as little the purpose of antiquaries, in history, as in chronology, it will be sufficient briefly to call to mind the sum of what they relate, from the creation of the world to the establishment of the Persian empire. If the antediluvian world continued one thousand six hundred and fifty-six years, and if the vocation of Abraham is to be placed four hundred and twenty-six years below the deluge, these twenty centuries make almost two-thirds of the period mentioned: and the whole history of them is comprised in eleven short chapters of Genesis; which is certainly the most compendious extract that ever was made. If we examine the contents of these chapters, do we find anything like an universal history, or so much as an abridgment of it? Adam and Eve were created, they broke the commandment of God, they were driven out of the garden of Eden, one of their sons killed his brother, but their race soon multiplied and peopled the earth. What geography now have we, what history of this antediluvian world? Why, none. The sons of God, it is said, lay with the daughters of men, and begot giants, and God drowned all the inhabitants of the earth, except one family. After this we read that the earth was repeopled; but these children of one family were divided into several languages, even whilst they lived together, spoke the same language, and were employed in the same work. Out of one of the countries into which they dispersed themselves, Chaldea, God called Abraham sometime afterwards, with magnificent promises, and conducted him to a country called Canaan. Did this author, my lord, intend an universal history? Certainly not. The tenth chapter of Genesis names indeed some of the generations descending from the sons of Noah, some of the cities founded, and some of the countries planted by them. But what are bare names, naked of circumstances, without descriptions of countries, or relations of events? They furnish matter only for guess and dispute; and even the similitude of them, which is often used as a clue to lead us to the discovery of historical truth, has notoriously contributed to propagate error, and to increase the perplexity of ancient tradition. These imperfect and dark accounts have not furnished matter for guess and dispute alone; but a much worse use has been made of them by Jewish rabbies, Christian fathers, and Mahometan doctors, in their profane extensions of this part of the Mosaic history. The creation of the first man is described by some, as if, Preadamites, they had assisted at it. They talk of his beauty as if they had seen him, of his gigantic

size as if they had measured him, and of his prodigious knowledge as if they had conversed with him. They point out the very
spot where Eve laid her head the first time he enjoyed her. They
have minutes of the whole conversation between this mother of
mankind, who damned her children before she bore them, and
the serpent. Some are positive that Cain quarreled with Abel
about a point of doctrine, and others affirm that the dispute rose
about a girl. A great deal of such stuff may be easily collected
about Enoch, about Noah, and about the sons of Noah; but I
waive any farther mention of such impertinences as Bonzes or
Talapoins would almost blush to relate. Upon the whole matter, if we may guess at the design of an author by the contents
of his book, the design of Moses, or of the author of the history
ascribed to him, in this part of it, was to inform the people of
Israel of their descent from Noah by Sem, and of Noah's from
Adam by Seth; to illustrate their original; to establish their
claim to the land of Canaan, and to justify all the cruelties committed by Joshua in the conquest of the Canaanites, in whom,
says Bochart, "the prophecy of Noah was completed, when
they were subdued by the Israelites, who had been so long slaves
to the Egyptians."

Allow me to make, as I go along, a short reflection or two on
this prophecy, and the completion of it, as they stand recorded
in the Pentateuch, out of many that might be made. The terms
of the prophecy then are not very clear: and the curse pronounced
in it contradicts all our notions of order and of justice. One is
tempted to think, that the patriarch was still drunk; and that no
man in his senses could hold such language, or pass such a sentence. Certain it is, that no writer but a Jew could impute to
the economy of Divine Providence the accomplishment of such
a prediction, nor make the Supreme Being the executor of such
a curse.

Ham alone offended; Canaan was innocent; for the Hebrew
and other doctors who would make the son an accomplice with
his father, affirm not only without, but against the express authority of the text. Canaan was however alone cursed: and he
became, according to his grandfather's prophecy, "a servant of
servants"; that is, the vilest and worst of slaves (for I take these
words in sense, if not the most natural, the most favorable to

46

the prophecy, and the least absurd) to Sem, though not to Japhet, when the Israelites conquered Palestine; to one of his uncles, not to his brethren. Will it be said—it has been said—that where we read Canaan we are to understand Ham, whose brethren Sem and Japhet were? At this rate, we shall never know what we read: as these critics never care what they say. Will it be said—this has been said too—that Ham was punished in his posterity, when Canaan was cursed, and his descendants were exterminated? But who does not see that the curse, and the punishment, in this case, fell on Canaan and his posterity, exclusively of the rest of the posterity of Ham; and were therefore the curse and punishment of the son, not of the father, properly? The descendants of Mesraim, another of his sons, were the Egyptians: and they were so far from being servants of servants to their cousins the Semites, that these were servants of servants to them, during more than fourscore years. Why the posterity of Canaan was to be deemed an accursed race, it is easy to account; and I have mentioned it just now. But it is not so easy to account, why the posterity of the righteous Sem, that great example of filial reverence, became slaves to another branch of the family of Ham.

It would not be worth while to lengthen this tedious letter, by setting down any more of the contents of the history of the Bible. Your lordship may please to call the substance of it to your mind, and your native candor and love of truth will oblige you then to confess, that these sacred books do not aim, in any part of them, at any thing like universal chronology and history. They contain a very imperfect account of the Israelites themselves; of their settlement in the land of promise, of which, by the way, they never had entire, and scarce ever peaceable possession; of their divisions, apostasies, repentances, relapses, triumphs, and defeats, under the occasional government of their judges, and under that of their kings; of the Galilean and Samaritan captivities, into which they were carried by the kings of Assyria, and of that which was brought on the remnant of this people when the kingdom of Judah was destroyed by those princes who governed the empire founded on the union of Nineveh and Babylon.

These things are all related, your lordship knows, in a very summary and confused manner: and we learn so little of other nations by these accounts, that if we did not borrow some light from the traditions of other nations, we should scarce understand them. One particular observation, and but one, I will make, to show what knowledge in the history of mankind, and in the computation of time, may be expected from these books. The Assyrians were their neighbors, powerful neighbors, with whom they had much and long to do. Of this empire, therefore, if of any thing, we might hope to find some satisfactory accounts. What do we find? The Scripture takes no notice of any Assyrian kingdom, till just before the time when profane history makes that empire to end. Then we hear of Phul, of Teglath-Phalasser, who was perhaps the same person, and of Salmanaser, who took Samaria in the twelfth of the era of Nabonasser, that is, twelve years after the Assyrian empire was no more. Senacherib succeeds to him, and Asserhaddon to Senacherib. What shall we say to this apparent contrariety? If the silence of the Bible creates a strong presumption against the first, may not the silence of profane authority create some against the second Assyrian monarchs? The pains that are taken to persuade, that there is room enough between Sardanapalus and Cyrus for the second, will not resolve the difficulty. Something much more plausible may be said, but even this will be hypothetical, and liable to great contradiction. So that upon the whole matter, the Scriptures are so far from giving us light into general history, that they increase the obscurity even of those parts to which they have the nearest relation. We have therefore neither in profane nor in sacred authors such authentic, clear, distinct, and full accounts of the originals of ancient nations, and of the great events of those ages that are commonly called the first ages, as deserve to go by the name of history, or as afford sufficient materials for chronology and history.

I might now proceed to observe to your lordship how this has happened, not only by the necessary consequences of human nature, and the ordinary course of human affairs, but by the policy, artifice, corruption, and folly of mankind. But this would be to heap digression upon digression, and to presume too much on your patience. I shall therefore content myself to apply these reflections on the state of ancient history to the study of history, and to the method to be observed in it; as soon as your lordship has rested yourself a little after reading, and I after writing so long a letter.

Letter 4

That There Is in History Sufficient Authenticity to
Render It Useful, notwithstanding All
Objections to the Contrary

Whether the letter I now begin to write will be long or short,
I know not: but I find my memory is refreshed, my imagination
warmed, and matter flows in so fast upon me, that I have not
time to press it close. Since therefore you have provoked me to
write, you must be content to take what follows.

I have observed already that we are apt naturally to apply to
ourselves what has happened to other men, and that examples
take their force from hence; as well those which history, as those
which experience, offers to our reflection. What we do not believe to have happened, therefore, we shall not thus apply: and
for want of the same application, such examples will not have
the same effect. Ancient history, such ancient history as I have
described, is quite unfit therefore in this respect to answer the
ends that every reasonable man should propose to himself in this
study; because such ancient history will never gain sufficient
credit with any reasonable man. A tale well told, or a comedy or
a tragedy well wrought up, may have a momentary effect upon
the mind, by heating the imagination, surprising the judgment,
and affecting strongly the passions. The Athenians are said to
have been transported into a kind of martial phrensy by the
representation of a tragedy of Æschylus, and to have marched

under this influence from the theatre to the plains of Marathon. These momentary impressions might be arranged, for aught I know, in such manner as to contribute a little, by frequent repetitions of them, towards maintaining a kind of habitual contempt of folly, detestation of vice, and admiration of virtue in well-policed commonwealths. But then these impressions cannot be made, nor this little effect be wrought, unless the fables bear an appearance of truth. When they bear this appearance, reason connives at the innocent fraud of imagination; reason dispenses, in favor of probability, with those strict rules of criticism that she has established to try the truth of fact: but, after all, she receives these fables as fables; and as such only she permits imagination to make the most of them. If they pretended to be history, they would be soon subjected to another and more severe examination. What may have happened, is the matter of an ingenious fable: what has happened, is that of an authentic history: the impressions which one or the other makes are in proportion. When imagination grows lawless and wild, rambles out of the precincts of nature, and tells of heroes and giants, fairies and enchanters, of events and of phenomena repugnant to universal experience, to our clearest and most distinct ideas, and to all the known laws of nature, reason does not connive a moment; but, far from receiving such narrations as historical, she rejects them as unworthy to be placed even among the fabulous. Such narrations therefore cannot make the slightest momentary impressions on a mind fraught with knowledge, and void of superstition. Imposed by authority, and assisted by artifice, the delusion hardly prevails over common sense; blind ignorance almost sees, and rash superstition hesitates: nothing less than enthusiasm and phrensy can give credit to such histories, or apply such examples. Don Quixote believed; but even Sancho doubted.

What I have said will not be much controverted by any man who has read Amadis of Gaul, or has examined our ancient traditions without prepossession. The truth is, the principal difference between them seems to be this. In Amadis of Gaul, we have a thread of absurdities that are invented without any regard to probability, and that lay no claim to belief: ancient traditions are a heap of fables, under which some particular truths, inscrutable, and therefore useless to mankind, may lie concealed; which have a just pretence to nothing more, and yet impose themselves upon us, and become, under the venerable name of ancient history, the foundations of modern fables, the materials with which so many systems of fancy have been erected.

But now, as men are apt to carry their judgments into extremes, there are some that will be ready to insist that all history is fabulous, and that the very best is nothing better than a probable tale, artfully contrived, and plausibly told, wherein truth and falsehood are indistinguishably blended together. All the instances, and all the common-place arguments, that Bayle and others have employed to establish this sort of Pyrrhonism, will be quoted: and from thence it will be concluded, that if the pretended histories of the first ages, and of the originals of nations, be too improbable and too ill vouched to procure any degree of belief, those histories that have been written later, that carry a greater air of probability, and that boast even cotemporary authority, are at least insufficient to gain that degree of firm belief, which is necessary to render the study of them useful to mankind. But here that happens which often happens: the premises are true, and the conclusion is false; because a general axiom is established precariously on a certain number of partial observations. This matter is of consequence; for it tends to ascertain the degrees of assent that we may have to history.

I agree, then, that history has been purposely and systematically falsified in all ages, and that partiality and prejudice have occasioned both voluntary and involuntary errors, even in the best. Let me say without offence, my lord, since I may say it with truth and am able to prove it, that ecclesiastical authority has led the way to this corruption in all ages, and all religions. How monstrous were the absurdities that the priesthood imposed on the ignorance and superstition of mankind in the Pagan world, concerning the originals of religions and governments, their institutions and rites, their laws and customs? What opportunities had they for such impositions, whilst the keeping the records and collecting the traditions was in so many nations the peculiar office of this order of men? A custom highly extolled by Josephus, but plainly liable to the grossest frauds, and even a temptation to them. If the foundations of Judaism and Christianity have been laid in truth, yet what numberless fables have been invented to raise, to embellish, and to support these structures, according to the interest and taste of the several architects? That the Jews have been guilty of this will be allowed: and, to the shame of Christians, if not of Christianity, the fathers of one church have no right to throw the first stone at the fathers of the other. Deliberate, systematical lying has been practised and encouraged from age to age; and among all the pious frauds that have been employed to maintain a reverence and zeal for their religion in the minds of men, this abuse of history has been one of the principal and most successful: an evident, an experimental proof, by the way, of what I have insisted upon so much, the aptitude and natural tendency of history to form our opinions, and to settle our habits. This righteous expedient was in so much use and repute in the Greek church, that one Metaphrastus wrote a treatise on the art of composing holy romances: the fact, if I remember right, is cited by Baillet, in his book of the lives of the saints. He and other learned men of the Roman church have thought it of service to their cause, since the resurrection of letters, to detect some impostures, and to depose, or to unniche, according to the French expression, now and then a reputed saint; but they seem in doing this to mean more than a sort of composition: they give up some fables that they may defend others with greater advantage, and they make truth serve as a stalking-horse to error. The same spirit that prevailed in the eastern church, prevailed in the western, and prevails still. A strong proof of it appeared lately in the country where I am. A sudden fury of devotion seized the people of Paris for a little priest,[1] undistinguished during his life, and dubbed a saint by the Jansenists after his death. Had the first minister been a Jansenist, the saint had been a saint still. All France had kept his festival: and since there are thousands of eye-witnesses ready to attest the truth of all the miracles supposed to have been wrought at his tomb, notwithstanding the discouragement which these zealots have met with from the government; we may assure ourselves, that these silly impostures would have been transmitted,

1. The Abbé Paris.

in all the solemn pomp of history, from the knaves of this age to the fools of the next.

This lying spirit has gone forth from ecclesiastical to other historians: and I might fill many pages with instances of extravagant fables that have been invented in several nations, to celebrate their antiquity, to ennoble their originals, and to make them appear illustrious in the arts of peace and the triumphs of war. When the brain is well heated, and devotion or vanity, the semblance of virtue or real vice, and, above all, disputes and contests, have inspired that complication of passions we term zeal, the effects are much the same, and history becomes very often a lying panegyric or a lying satire; for different nations or different parties in the same nation, belie one another without any respect for truth, as they murder one another without any regard to right or sense of humanity. Religious zeal may boast this horrid advantage over civil zeal, that the effects of it have been more sanguinary, and the malice more unrelenting. In another respect they are more alike, and keep a nearer proportion: different religions have not been quite so barbarous to one another as sects of the same religion; and, in like manner, nation has had better quarter from nation, than party from party. But in all these controversies, men have pushed their rage beyond their own and their adversaries' lives: they have endeavored to interest posterity in their quarrels, and by rendering history subservient to this wicked purpose, they have done their utmost to perpetuate scandal, and to immortalise their animosity. The heathen taxed the Jews even with idolatry; the Jews joined with the heathen to render Christianity odious: but the church, who beat them at their own weapons during these contests, has had this further triumph over them, as well as over the several sects that have arisen within her own pale; the works of those who have written against her have been destroyed, and whatever she advanced, to justify herself and to defame her adversaries, is preserved in her annals, and the writings of her doctors.

The charge of corrupting history, in the cause of religion, has been always committed to the most famous champions, and greatest saints of each church; and, if I was not more afraid of tiring, than of scandalising your lordship, I could quote to you examples of modern churchmen who have endeavored to justify foul language by the New Testament, and cruelty by the Old; nay, what is execrable beyond imagination, and what strikes horror into every mind that entertains due sentiments of the Supreme Being, God himself has been cited for rallying and insulting Adam after his fall. In other cases this charge belongs to the pedants of every nation, and the tools of every party. What accusations of idolatry and superstition have not been brought, and aggravated against Mahometans? Those wretched Christians who returned from those wars, so improperly called the holy wars, rumored these stories about the West; and you may find, in some of the old chroniclers and romance writers, as well as poets, the Saracens called Paynims; though surely they were much further off from any suspicion of polytheism, than those who called them by that name. When Mahomet the Second took Constantinople in the fifteenth century, the Mahometans began to be a little better, and but a little better known, than they had been before, to these parts of the world. But their religion, as well as their customs and manners, was strangely misrepresented by the Greek refugees that fled from the Turks: and the terror and hatred which this people had inspired by the rapidity of their conquests, and by their ferocity, made all these misrepresentations universally pass for truths. Many such instances may be collected from Maraccio's refutation of the Koran, and Relandus has published a very valuable treatise on purpose to refute these calumnies, and to justify the Mahometans. Does not this example incline your lordship to think, that the heathens and the Arians, and other heretics, would not appear quite so absurd in their opinions, nor so abominable in their practice, as the orthodox Christians have represented them; if some Relandus could arise, with the materials necessary to their justification in his hands? He who reflects on the circumstances that attended letters, from the time when Constantine instead of uniting the characters of emperor and sovereign pontiff in himself when he became Christian, as they were united in him and all the other emperors in the Pagan system of government, gave so much independent wealth and power to the clergy, and the means of acquiring so much more: he who carries these reflections on through all the latter empire, and through those

54

ages of ignorance and superstition, wherein it was hard to say which was greatest, the tyranny of the clergy or the servility of the laity: he who considers the extreme severity, for instance of the laws made by Theodosius in order to stifle every writing that the orthodox clergy, that is, the clergy then in fashion disliked; or the character and influence of such a priest as Gregory called the great, who proclaimed war to all heathen learning in order to promote Christian verity; and flattered Brunehault, and abetted Phocas: he who considers all these things, I say, will not be at a loss to find the reasons why history, both that which was written before, and a great part of that which has been written since the Christian era, is come to us so imperfect and so corrupt.

When the imperfection is due to a total want of memorials, either because none were originally written, or because they have been lost by devastations of countries, extirpations of people, and other accidents in a long course of time; or because zeal, malice, and policy have joined their endeavors to destroy them purposely; we must be content to remain in our ignorance, and there is no great harm in that. Secure from being deceived, I can submit to be uninformed. But when there is not a total want of memorials, when some have been lost or destroyed, and others have been preserved and propagated, then we are in danger of being deceived: and therefore he must be very implicit indeed who receives for true the history of any religion or nation, and much more that of any sect or party, without having the means of confronting it with some other history. A reasonable man will not be thus implicit. He will not establish the truth of history on single, but on concurrent testimony. If there be none such, he will doubt absolutely: if there be a little such, he will proportion his assent or dissent accordingly. A small gleam of light, borrowed from foreign anecdotes, serves often to discover a whole system of falsehood: and even they who corrupt history frequently betray themselves by their ignorance or inadvertency. Examples whereof I could easily produce. Upon the whole matter, in all these cases we cannot be deceived essentially, unless we please; and therefore there is no reason to establish Pyrrhonism, that we may avoid the ridicule of credulity.

In all other cases, there is less reason still to do so; for when histories and historical memorials abound, even those that are false serve to the discovery of the truth. Inspired by different passions, and contrived for opposite purposes, they contradict; and contradicting, they convict one another. Criticism separates the ore from the dross, and extracts from various authors a series of true history, which could not have been found entire in any one of them, and will command our assent, when it is formed with judgment, and represented with candor. If this may be done, as it has been done sometimes, with the help of authors who wrote on purpose to deceive; how much more easily, and more effectually may it be done, with the help of those who paid a greater regard to truth? In a multitude of writers there will be always some, either incapable of gross prevarication from the fear of being discovered, and of acquiring infamy whilst they seek for fame; or else attached to truth upon a nobler and surer principle. It is certain that these, even the last of them, are fallible. Bribed by some passion or other, the former may venture now and then to propagate a falsehood, or to disguise a truth; like the painter that drew in profile, as Lucian says, the picture of a prince that had but one eye. Montagne objects to the memorials of Du Bellay, that though the gross of the facts be truly related, yet these authors turned every thing they mentioned to the advantage of their master, and mentioned nothing which could not be so turned. The old fellow's words are worth quoting. "De contourner le jugement des évenemens souvent contre raison à notre avantage, et d'obmettre tout ce qu'il y a de chatouilleux en la vie de leur maistre, ils en font mestier." These, and such as these, deviate occasionally and voluntarily from truth; but even they who are attached to it the most religiously may slide sometimes into involuntary error. In matters of history we prefer very justly cotemporary authority; and yet cotemporary authors are the most liable to be warped from the straight rule of truth, in writing on subjects which have affected them strongly, "et quorum pars magna fuerunt." I am so persuaded of this from what I have felt in myself, and observed in others, that if life and health enough fall to my share, and I am able to finish what I meditate, a kind of history, from the late queen's accession to the throne, to the peace of Utrecht, there will be no materials that I shall examine more scrupulously and severely, than those of the time when the events to be spoken of were in transaction. But though the writers of these two sorts, both of whom pay as much regard to truth as the various infirmities of our nature admit, are fallible; yet this fallibility will not be sufficient to give color to Pyrrhonism. Where their sincerity as to fact is doubtful, we strike out truth by the confrontation of different accounts: as we strike out sparks of fire by the collision of flints and steel. Where their judgments are suspicious of partiality, we may judge for ourselves; or adopt their judgments, after weighing them with certain grains of allowance. A little natural sagacity will proportion these grains according to the particular circumstances of the authors, or their general characters; for even these influence. Thus Montagne pretends, but he exaggerates a little, that Guicciardin no where ascribes any one action to a virtuous, but every one to a vicious principle. Something like this has been reproached to Tacitus: and, notwithstanding all the sprightly loose observations of Montagne in one of his essays, where he labors to prove the contrary, read Plutarch's comparisons in what languages you please, I am of Bodin's mind, you will perceive they were made by a Greek. In short, my lord, the favorable opportunities of corrupting history have been often interrupted, and are now over in so many countries, that truth penetrates even into those where lying continues still to be part of the policy ecclesiastical and civil; or where, to say the best we can say, truth is never suffered to appear, till she has passed through hands, out of which she seldom returns entire and undefiled.

But it is time I should conclude this head, under which I have touched some of those reasons that show the folly of endeavoring to establish universal Pyrrhonism in matters of history, because there are few histories without some lies, and none without some mistakes; and that prove the body of history which we possess, since ancient memorials have been so critically examined, and modern memorials have been so multiplied, to contain in it such a probable series of events, easily distinguishable from the improbable, as force the assent of every man who is in his senses, and are, therefore, sufficient to answer all the purposes of the study of history. I might have appealed, perhaps, without entering into the argument at all, to any man of candor, whether his doubts concerning the truth of history have hindered him from applying the examples he has met with in it, and from judging of the present, and sometimes of the future, by the past? Whether he has not been touched with reverence and admiration, at the virtue and wisdom of some men, and of some ages; and whether he has not felt indignation and contempt for others? Whether Epaminondas or Phocion, for instance, the Decii, or the Scipios, have not raised in his mind a flame of public spirit, and private virtue? and whether he has not shuddered with horror at the proscriptions of Marius and Sylla, at the treachery of Theodotus and Achillas, and at the consummate cruelty of an infant king? "Quis non contra Marii arma, et contra Syllæ proscriptionem concitatur? Quis non Theodoto, et Achillæ, et ipsi puero, non puerile auso facinus, infestus est?" If all this be a digression, therefore, your lordship will be so good as to excuse it.

Of the Method and Due Restrictions to Be Observed in the Study of It

What has been said concerning the multiplicity of histories, and of historical memorials, wherewith our libraries abound since the resurrection of letters happened, and the art of printing began, puts me in mind of another general rule, that ought to be observed by every man who intends to make a real improvement, and to become wiser as well as better, by the study of history. I hinted at this rule in a former letter, where I said that we should neither grope in the dark, nor wander in the light. History must have a certain degree of probability and authenticity, or the examples we find in it would not carry a force sufficient to make due impressions on our minds, nor to illustrate nor to strengthen the precepts of philosophy and the rules of good policy. But besides, when histories have this necessary authenticity and probability, there is much discernment to be employed in the choice and the use we make of them. Some are to be read, some are to be studied; and some may be neglected entirely, not only without detriment, but with advantage. Some are the proper objects of one man's curiosity, some of another's, and some of all men's; but all history is not an object of curiosity for any man. He who improperly, wantonly, and absurdly makes it so, indulges a sort of canine appetite: the curiosity of one, like the hunger of the other, devours ravenously and without distinction whatever falls in its way; but neither of them digests. They heap crudity upon crudity, and nourish and improve nothing but their distemper. Some such characters I have known, though it is not the most common extreme into which men are apt to fall. One of them I knew in this country. He joined, to a more than athletic strength of body, a prodigious memory; and to both a prodigious industry. He had read almost constantly twelve or fourteen hours a day, for five-and-twenty or thirty years; and had heaped together as much learning as could be crowded into a head. In the course of my acquaintance with him, I consulted with him once or twice, not oftener; for I found this mass of learning of as little use to me as to the owner. The man was communicative enough: but nothing was distinct in his mind. How could it be otherwise? he had never spared time to think, all was employed in reading. His reason had not the merit of common mechanism. When you press a watch or pull a clock, they answer your question with precision; for they repeat exactly the hour of the day, and tell you neither more nor less than you desire to know. But when you asked this man a question, he overwhelmed you with pouring forth all that the several terms or words of your question recalled to his memory: and if he omitted any thing, it was that very thing to which the sense of the whole question should have led him and confined him. To ask him a question, was to wind up a spring in his memory, that rattled on with vast rapidity, and confused noise, till the force of it was spent: and you went away with all the noise in your ears, stunned and uninformed. I never left him that I was not ready to say to him, "Dieu vous fasse la grace de devenir moins savant!" a wish that La Mothe le Vayer mentions upon some occasion or other, and that he would have done well to have applied himself upon many.

He who reads with discernment and choice, will acquire less learning, but more knowledge: and as this knowledge is collected with design, and cultivated with art and method, it will be at all times of immediate and ready use to himself and others.

> Thus useful arms in magazines we place,
> All rang'd in order; and disposed with grace:
> Nor thus alone the curious eye to please;
> But to be found, when need requires, with ease.

You remember the verses, my lord, in our friend's Essay on Criticism, which was the work of his childhood almost; but is such a monument of good sense and poetry as no other, that I know, has raised in his riper years.

He who reads without this discernment and choice, and, like Bodin's pupil, resolves to read all, will not have time, no, nor capacity neither, to do any thing else. He will not be able to think, without which it is impertinent to read; nor to act, without which it is impertinent to think. He will assemble materials with much pains, and purchase them at much expense, and have neither leisure nor skill to frame them into proper scantlings, or to prepare them for use. To what purpose should he husband his time, or learn architecture? he has no design to build. But then to what purpose all these quarries of stone, all these mountains of sand and lime, all these forests of oak and deal? "Magno impendio temporum, magna alienarum aurium molestia, laudatio hæc constat, O hominem literatum! Simus hoc titulo rusticiore contenti, O virum bonum!" We may add, and Seneca might have added in his own style, and according to the manners and characters of his own age, another title as rustic, and as little in fashion, "O virum sapientia sua simplicem, et simplicitate sua sapientem? O virum utilem sibi, suis, reipublicæ, et humano generi!" I have said perhaps already, but no matter, it cannot be repeated too often, that the drift of all philosophy, and of all political speculations, ought to be the making us better men, and better citizens. Those studies, which have no intention towards improving our moral characters, have no pretence to be styled philosophical. "Quis est enim," says Tully in his Offices, "qui nullis officii præceptis, tradendis, philosophum se audeat dicere?" Whatever political speculations, instead of preparing us to be useful to society, and to promote the happiness of mankind, are only systems for gratifying private ambition, and promoting private interests at the public expense; all such, I say, deserve to be burnt, and the authors of them to starve, like Machiavel, in a jail.

Letter 5

The Great Use of History, Properly So Called, As Distinguished from the Writings of Mere Annalists and Antiquaries

I remember my last letter ended abruptly, and a long interval has since passed: so that the thread I had then spun has slipt from me. I will try to recover it, and to pursue the task your lordship has obliged me to continue. Besides the pleasure of obeying your orders, it is likewise of some advantage to myself, to recollect my thoughts, and resume a study in which I was conversant formerly. For nothing can be more true than that saying of Solon reported by Plato, though censured by him, impertinently enough in one of his wild books of laws; "Assidue addiscens, ad senium venio." The truth is, the most knowing man, in the course of the longest life, will have always much to learn, and the wisest and best much to improve. This rule will hold in the knowledge and improvement to be acquired by the study of history; and therefore even he who has gone to this school in his youth, should not neglect it in his age. "I read in Livy," says Montagne, "what another man does not: and Plutarch read there what I do not." Just so the same man may read at fifty what he did not read in the same book at five and twenty: at least I have found it so, by my own experience, on many occasions.

By comparing, in this study, the experience of other men and other ages with our own, we improve both: we analyse, as it were, philosophy. We reduce all the abstract speculations of ethics, and all the general rules of human policy, to their first principles. With these advantages every man may, though few men do, advance daily towards those ideas, those increated essences a Platonist would say, which no human creature can reach in practice, but in the nearest approaches to which the perfection of our nature consists; because every approach of this kind renders a man better, and wiser, for himself, for his family, for the little community of his own country, and for the great community of the world. Be not surprised, my lord, at the order in which I place these objects. Whatever order divines and moralists, who contemplate the duties belonging to these objects, may place them in, this is the order they hold in nature: and I have always thought that we might lead ourselves and others to private virtue, more effectually by a due observation of this order, than by any of those sublime refinements that pervert it.

> Self-love but serves the virtuous mind to wake;
> As the small pebble stirs the peaceful lake.
> The centre mov'd, a circle straight succeeds;
> Another still, and still another spreads;
> Friend, parent, neighbor, first it will embrace,
> His country next, and next all human race.

So sings our friend Pope, my lord, and so I believe. So I shall prove too, if I mistake not, in an epistle I am about to write to him, in order to complete a set that were written some years ago.

A man of my age, who returns to the study of history, has no time to lose, because he has little to live: a man of your lordship's age has no time to lose, because he has much to do. For different reasons therefore the same rules will suit us. Neither of us must grope in the dark, neither of us must wander in the light. I have done the first formerly a good deal; "ne verba mihi darentur; ne aliquid esse, in hac recondita antiquitatis scientia, magni ac secreti boni judicaremus." If you take my word, you will throw none of your time away in the same manner: and I shall have the less regret for that which I have misspent, if I persuade you to hasten down from the broken traditions of antiquity, to the more entire as well as more authentic histories of ages more modern. In the study of these we shall find many a complete series of events, preceded by a deduction of their immediate and remote causes, related in their full extent, and accompanied with such a detail of circumstances, and characters, as may transport the attentive reader back to the very time, make him a party to the councils, and an actor in the whole scene of affairs. Such draughts as these, either found in history or extracted by our own application from it, and such alone, are truly useful. Thus history becomes what she ought to be, and what she has been sometimes called, "magistra vitæ," the mistress, like philosophy, of human life. If she is not this, she is at best "nuntia vetustatis," the gazette of antiquity, or a dry register of useless anecdotes. Suetonius says that Tiberius used to inquire of the grammarians, "quæ mater Hecubæ? quod Achilles nomen inter virgines fuisset? quid Syrenes cantare sint solitæ?" Seneca mentions certain Greek authors, who examined very accurately whether Anacreon loved wine or women best, whether Sappho was a common whore, with other points of equal importance; and I make no doubt but that a man, better acquainted than I have the honor to be with the learned persons of our own country, might find some who have discovered several anecdotes, concerning the giant Albion, concerning Samothes the son, or Brito the grandson of Japhet, and concerning Brutus who led a colony into our island after the siege of Troy, as the others repeopled it after the deluge. But ten millions of such anecdotes as these, though they were true; and complete authentic volumes of Egyptian or Chaldean, of Greek or Latin, of Gallic or British, of French or Saxon records, would be of no value in my sense because of no use towards our improvement in wisdom and virtue; if they contained nothing more than dynasties and genealogies, and a bare mention of remarkable events in the order of time, like journals, chronological tables, or dry and meagre annals.

I say the same of all those modern compositions in which we find rather the heads of history, than any thing that deserves to be called history. Their authors are either abridgers or compilers. The first do neither honor to themselves, nor good to mankind; for surely the abridger is in a form below the translator; and the book, at least the history, that wants to be abridged, does not deserve to be read. They have done anciently a great deal of hurt by substituting many a bad book in the place of a good one; and by giving occasion to men, who contented themselves with extracts and abridgments, to neglect, and through their neglect, to lose the invaluable originals: for which reason I curse Constantine Porphyrogenetes as heartily as I do Gregory. The second are of some use, as far as they contribute to preserve public acts, and dates, and the memory of great events. But they who are thus employed have seldom the means of knowing those private passages on which all public transactions depend, and as seldom the skill and the talents necessary to put what they do know well together: they cannot see the working of the mine, but their industry collects the matter that is thrown out. It is the business, or it should be so, of others to separate the pure ore from the dross, to stamp it into coin, and to enrich, not encumber mankind. When there are none sufficient to this task, there may be antiquaries, and there may be journalists or annalists, but there are no historians.

It is worth while to observe the progress that the Romans and the Greeks made towards history. The Romans had journalists or annalists from the very beginning of their state. In the sixth century, or very near it at soonest, they began to have antiquaries, and some attempts were made towards writing of history. I call these first historical productions attempts only or essays: and they were no more, neither among the Romans, nor among the Greeks. "Græci ipsi sic initio scriptitarunt ut noster Cato, ut Pictor, ut Piso." It is Antony, not the triumvir, my lord, but his grandfather the famous orator, who says this in the second book of Tully *De Oratore:* he adds afterwards, "Itaque qualis apud Græcos Pherecydes, Hellanicus, Acusilaus, aliique permulti, talis noster Cato, et Pictor, et Piso." I know that Antony speaks here strictly of defect of style and want of oratory. They were, "tantummodo narratores, non exornatores," as he expresses himself: but as they wanted style and skill to write in such a manner as might answer all the ends of history, so they wanted materials. Pherecydes wrote something about Iphigenia, and the festivals of Bacchus. Hellanicus was a poetical historian, and Acusilaus graved genealogies on plates of brass. Pictor, who is called by Livy "scriptorum antiquissimus," published, I think, some short annals of his own time. Neither he nor Piso could have sufficient materials for the history of Rome; nor Cato, I presume, even for the antiquities of Italy. The Romans, with the other people of that country, were then just rising out of barbarity, and growing acquainted with letters; for those that the Grecian colonies might bring into Sicily, and the southern parts of Italy, spread little, or lasted little, and made in the whole no figure. And whatever learning might have flourished among the ancient Etrurians, which was perhaps at most nothing better than augury, and divination, and superstitious rites, which were admired and cultivated in ignorant ages, even that was almost entirely worn out of memory. Pedants, who would impose all the traditions of the four first ages of Rome, for authentic history, have insisted much on certain annals, of which mention is made in the very place I have just now quoted. "Ab initio rerum Romanarum," says the same interlocutor, "usque ad P. Mucium pontificem maximum, res omnes singulorum annorum mandabat literis pontifex maximus, efferebatque in album, et proponebat tabulam domi, potestas ut esset populo cognoscendi; idemque etiam nunc annales maximi nominantur." But, my lord, be pleased to take notice, that the very distinction I make is made here between a bare annalist and a historian: "erat historia nihil aliud," in these early days, "nisi annalium confectio." Take notice likewise, by the way, that Livy, whose particular application it had been to search into this matter, affirms positively that the greatest part of all public and private monuments, among which he specifies these very annals, had been destroyed in the sack of Rome by the Gauls: and Plutarch cites Clodius for the same assertion, in the life of Numa Pompilius. Take notice, in the last place, of that which is more immediately to our present purpose. These annals could contain nothing more than short minutes or memorandums hung up in a table at the pontiff's house, like the rules of the game in the billiard-room, and much such history as we have in the epitomes prefixed to the books of Livy or of any other historian, in lapidary inscriptions, or in some modern almanacs. Materials for history they were no doubt, but scanty and insufficient; such as those ages could produce when writing and reading were accomplishments so uncommon, that the prætor was directed by law, "clavum pangere," to drive a nail into the door of a temple, that the number of years might be reckoned by the number of nails. Such in short as we have in monkish annalists, and other ancient chroniclers of nations now in being: but not such as can entitle the authors of them to be called historians, nor can enable others to write history in that fulness in which it must be written to become a lesson of ethics and politics. The truth is, nations, like men, have their infancy: and the few passages of that time, which they retain, are not such as deserved most to be remembered; but such as, being most proportioned to that age, made the strongest impressions on their minds. In those nations that preserve their dominion long, and grow up to manhood, the elegant as well as the necessary arts and sciences are improved to some degree of perfection; and history, that was at first intended only to record the names, or perhaps the general characters of some famous men, and to transmit in gross the remarkable events of every age to posterity, is raised to answer another, and a nobler end.

Greek and Roman Historians

Thus it happened among the Greeks, but much more among the Romans, notwithstanding the prejudices in favor of the former, even among the latter. I have sometimes thought that Virgil might have justly ascribed to his countrymen the praise of writing history better, as well as that of affording the noblest subjects for it, in those famous verses,[1] where the different excellences of the two nations are so finely touched: but he would have weakened perhaps by lengthening, and have flattened the climax. Open Herodotus, you are entertained by an agreeable story-teller, who meant to entertain, and nothing more. Read Thucydides or Xenophon, you are taught indeed as well as en-

---

1. Excudent alii spirantia mollius æra,
   Credo equidem: vivos ducent de marmore vultus;
   Orabunt causas melius: cœlique meatus
   Describent radio, et surgentia sidera dicent:
   Tu regere imperio populos, Romane, memento:
   Hæ tibi erunt artes; pacisque imponere morem,
   Parcere subjectis, et debellare superbos.

tertained: and the statesman or the general, the philosopher or the orator, speaks to you in every page. They wrote on subjects on which they were well informed, and they treated them fully: they maintained the dignity of history, and thought it beneath them to vamp up old traditions, like the writers of their age and country, and to be the trumpeters of a lying antiquity. The Cyropædia of Xenophon may be objected perhaps; but if he gave it for a romance, not a history, as he might for aught we can tell, it is out of the case: and if he gave it for a history, not a romance, I should prefer his authority to that of Herodotus, or any other of his countrymen. But however this might be, and whatever merit we may justly ascribe to these two writers, who were almost single in their kind, and who treated but small portions of history; certain it is in general, that the levity as well as loquacity of the Greeks made them incapable of keeping up to the true standard of history: and even Polybius and Dionysius of Halicarnassus must bow to the great Roman authors. Many principal men of that commonwealth wrote memorials of their own actions and their own times: Sylla, Cæsar, Labienus, Pollio, Augustus, and others. What writers of memorials, what compilers of the *materia historica* were these? What genius was necessary to finish up the pictures that such masters had sketched? Rome afforded men that were equal to the task. Let the remains, the precious remains, of Sallust, of Livy, and of Tacitus, witness this truth. When Tacitus wrote, even the appearances of virtue had been long proscribed, and taste was grown corrupt as well as manners. Yet history preserved her integrity and her lustre. She preserved them in the writings of some whom Tacitus mentions, in none perhaps more than his own; every line of which outweighs whole pages of such a rhetor as Famianus Strada. I single him out among the moderns, because he had the foolish presumption to censure Tacitus, and to write history himself: and your lordship will forgive this short excursion in honor of a favorite author.

What a school of private and public virtue had been opened to us at the resurrection of learning, if the latter historians of the Roman commonwealth, and the first of the succeeding monarchy, had come down to us entire? The few that are come down, though broken and imperfect, compose the best body of history that we have, nay the only body of ancient history that deserves to be an object of study. It fails us indeed most at that remarkable and fatal period, where our reasonable curiosity is raised the highest. Livy employed five and forty books to bring his history down to the end of the sixth century, and the breaking out of the third Punic war: but he employed ninety-five to bring it down from thence to the death of Drusus; that is, through the course of one hundred and twenty or thirty years. Apian, Dion Cassius, and others, nay even Plutarch included, make us but poor amends for what is lost of Livy. Among all the adventitious helps by which we endeavor to supply this loss in some degree, the best are those which we find scattered up and down in the works of Tully. His orations, particularly, and his letters, contain many curious anecdotes and instructive reflections, concerning the intrigues and machinations that were carried on against liberty, from Catiline's conspiracy to Cæsar's. The state of the government, the constitution and temper of the several parties, and the characters of the principal persons who figured at that time on the public stage, are to be seen there in a stronger and truer light than they would have appeared perhaps if he had written purposely on this subject, and even in those memorials which he somewhere promises Atticus to write. "Excudam aliquod Heraclidium opus, quod lateat in thesauris tuis." He would hardly have unmasked in such a work, as freely as in familiar occasional letters, Pompey, Cato, Brutus, nay himself; the four men of Rome, on whose praises he dwelt with the greatest complacency. The age in which Livy flourished abounded with such materials as these: they were fresh, they were authentic; it was easy to procure them, it was safe to employ them. How he did employ them in executing the second part of his design, we may judge by his execution of the first: and, I own to your lordship, I should be glad to exchange, if it were possible, what we have of this history for what we have not. Would you not be glad, my lord, to see, in one stupendous draught, the whole progress of that government from liberty to servitude? the whole series of causes and effects, apparent and real, public and private? those which all men saw, and all good men lamented and opposed at the time; and those which were so disguised to the prejudices, to the partialities of a divided people, and even to the corruption of mankind, that many did not, and that many could pretend they did not, discern them, till it was too late to resist them? I am sorry to say it, this part of the Roman story would be not only more curious and more authentic than the former, but of more immediate and more important application to the present state of Britain. But it is lost: the loss is irreparable, and your lordship will not blame me for deploring it.

Some Idea of a Complete History

They who set up for scepticism may not regret the loss of such a history: but this I will be bold to assert to them, that a history must be written on this plan, and must aim at least at these perfections, or it will answer sufficiently none of the intentions of history. That it will not answer sufficiently the intention I have insisted upon in these letters, that of instructing posterity by the example of former ages, is manifest: and I think it is as manifest, that a history cannot be said even to relate faithfully, and inform us truly that does not relate fully, and inform us of all that is necessary to make a true judgment concerning the matters contained in it. Naked facts, without the causes that produced them, and the circumstances that accompanied them, are not sufficient to characterise actions or counsels. The nice degrees of wisdom and of folly, of virtue and of vice, will not only be undiscoverable in them; but we must be very often unable to determine under which of these characters they fall in general. The sceptics I am speaking of are therefore guilty of this absurdity: the nearer a history comes to the true idea of history, the better it informs and the more it instructs us, the more worthy to be rejected it appears to them. I have said and allowed enough to content any reasonable man about the uncertainty of history. I have owned that the best are defective, and I will add in this place an observation which did not, I think, occur to me before. Conjecture is not always distinguished perhaps as it ought to be; so that an ingenious writer may sometimes do very innocently, what a malicious writer does very criminally as often as he dares, and as his malice requires it: he may account for events, after they have happened, by a system of causes and conduct that did not really produce them, though it might possibly or even probably have produced them. But this observation, like several others, becomes a reason for examining and comparing authorities, and for preferring some, not for rejecting all. Davila, a noble historian surely, and one whom I should not scruple to confess equal in many respects to Livy, as I should not scruple to prefer his countryman Guicciardin to Thucydides in every respect; Davila, my lord, was accused, from the first publication of his history, or at least was suspected, of too much refinement and subtlety, in developing the secret motives of actions, in laying the causes of events too deep, and deducing them often through a series of progression too complicated, and too artistly wrought. But yet the suspicious person who should reject this historian upon such general inducements as these, would have no grace to oppose his suspicions to the authority of the first duke of Epernon, who had been an actor, and a principal actor too, in many of the scenes that Davila recites. Girard, secretary to this duke, and no contemptible biographer, relates, that this history came down to the place where the old man resided in Gascony, a little before his death; that he read it to him, that the duke confirmed the truth of the narrations in it, and seemed only surprised by what means the author could be so well informed of the most secret councils and measures of those times.

Further Cautions to Be Observed in This Study, and the Regulation of It According to the Different Possessions and Situations of Men: Above All, the Use to Be Made of It (1) by Divines, and (2) by Those Who Are Called to the Service of Their Country

I have said enough on this head, and your lordship may be induced, perhaps, by what I have said, to think with me, that such histories as these, whether ancient or modern, deserve alone to be studied. Let us leave the credulous learned to write history without materials, or to study those who do so; to wrangle about ancient traditions, and to ring different changes on the same set of bells. Let us leave the sceptics, in modern as well as ancient history, to triumph in the notable discovery of the ides of one month mistaken for the calends of another, or in the various dates and contradictory circumstances which they find in weekly gazettes and monthly mercuries. Whilst they are thus employed, your lordship and I will proceed, if you please, to consider more closely, than we have yet done, the rule mentioned above; that, I mean, of using discernment and choice in the study of the most authentic history, that of not wandering in the light, which is as necessary as that of not groping in the dark.

Man is the subject of every history; and to know him well, we must see him and consider him, as history alone can present him to us, in every age, in every country, in every state, in life and in death. History, therefore, of all kinds, of civilised and uncivilised, of ancient and modern nations, in short, all history that descends to a sufficient detail of human actions and characters, is useful to bring us acquainted with our species, nay, with ourselves. To teach and to inculcate the general principles of virtue, and the general rules of wisdom and good policy, which result from such details of actions and characters, comes for the most part, and always should come, expressly and directly into the design of those who are capable of giving such details and, therefore, whilst they narrate as historians, they hint often as philosophers; they put into our hands, as it were, on every proper occasion, the end of a clue, that serves to remind us of searching, and to guide us in the search of that truth which the example before us either establishes or illustrates. If a writer neglects this part, we are able, however, to supply his neglect by our own attention and industry: and when he gives us a good history of Peruvians or Mexicans, of Chinese or Tartars, of Muscovites or Negroes, we may blame him, but we must blame ourselves much more, if we do not make it a good lesson of philosophy. This being the general use of history, it is not to be neglected. Every one may make it, who is able to read and reflect on what he reads, and every one who makes it will find in his degree, the benefit that arises from an early acquaintance contracted in this manner with mankind. We are not only passengers or sojourners in this world, but we are absolute strangers at the first step we make in it. Our guides are often ignorant, often unfaithful. By this map of the country, which history spreads before us, we may learn, if we please, to guide ourselves. In our journey through it, we are beset on every side. We are besieged, sometimes even in our strongest holds. Terrors and temptations, conducted by the passions of other men, assault us: and our own passions, that correspond with these, betray us. History is a collection of the journals of those who have travelled through the same country, and been exposed to the same accidents: and their good and their ill success are equally instructive. In this pursuit of knowledge an immense field is opened to us: general histories, sacred and profane; the histories of particular countries, particular events, particular orders, particular men; memorials, anecdotes, travels. But we must not ramble in this field without discernment or choice, nor even with these must we ramble too long.

As to the choice of authors, who have written on all these various subjects, so much has been said by learned men concerning all those that deserve attention, and their several characters are so well established, that it would be a sort of pedantic affectation to lead your lordship through so voluminous, and at the same time so easy, a detail. I pass it over therefore in order to observe, that as soon as we have taken this general view of mankind, and of the course of human affairs in different ages and different parts of the world, we ought to apply, and, the shortness of human life considered, to confine ourselves almost entirely in our study of history, to such histories as have an immediate relation to our professions, or to our rank and situation in the society to which we belong. Let me instance in the profession of divinity, as the noblest and the most important.

1. I have said so much concerning the share which divines of all religions have taken in the corruption of history, that I should have anathemas pronounced against me, no doubt, in the east and the west, by the dairo, the mufti, and the pope, if these letters were submitted to ecclesiastical censure; for surely, my lord, the clergy have a better title, than the sons of Apollo, to be called "genus irritabile vatum." What would it be, if I went about to show, how many of the Christian clergy abuse, by misrepresentation and false quotation, the history they can no longer corrupt? And yet this task would not be, even to me, an hard one. But as I mean to speak in this place of Christian divines

alone, so I mean to speak of such of them particularly as may be called divines without any sneer; of such of them, for some such I think there are, as believe themselves, and would have mankind believe; not for temporal but spiritual interest, not for the sake of the clergy, but for the sake of mankind. Now it has been long matter of astonishment to me, how such persons as these could take so much silly pains to establish mystery on metaphysics, revelation on philosophy, and matters of fact on abstract reasoning? A religion founded on the authority of a divine mission, confirmed by prophecies and miracles, appeals to facts: and the facts must be proved as all other facts that pass for authentic are proved; for faith so reasonable after this proof, is absurd before it. If they are thus proved, the religion will prevail without the assistance of so much profound reasoning: if they are not thus proved, the authority of it will sink in the world even with this assistance. The divines object in their disputes with atheists, and they object very justly, that these men require improper proofs; proofs that are not suited to the nature of the subject, and then cavil that such proofs are not furnished. But what then do they mean, to fall into the same absurdity themselves in their disputes with theists, and to din improper proofs in ears that are open to proper proofs? The matter is of great moment, my lord, and I make no excuse for the zeal which obliges me to dwell a little on it. A serious and honest application to the study of ecclesiastical history, and every part of profane history and chronology relative to it, is incumbent on such reverend persons as are here spoken of, on a double account: because history alone can furnish the proper proofs, that the religion they teach is of God; and because the unfair manner, in which these proofs have been and are called furnished, creates prejudices, and gives advantages against Christianity that require to be removed. No scholar will dare to deny, that false history, as well as sham miracles, has been employed to propagate Christianity formerly: and whoever examines the writers of our own age, will find the same abuse of history continued. Many and many instances of this abuse might be produced. It is grown into custom, writers copy one another, and the mistake that was committed, or the falsehood that was invented by one, is adopted by hundreds.

Abbadie says in his famous book, that the Gospel of St. Matthew is cited by Clemens, bishop of Rome, a disciple of the apostles; that Barnabas cites it in his epistle; that Ignatius and Polycarp receive it; and that the same fathers, that give testimony for Matthew, give it likewise for Mark. Nay your lordship will find, I believe, that the present bishop of London, in his third pastoral letter, speaks to the same effect. I will not trouble you nor myself with any more instances of the same kind. Let this, which occurred to me as I was writing, suffice. It may well suffice; for I presume the fact advanced by the minister and the bishop is a mistake. If the fathers of the first century do mention some passages that are agreeable to what we read in our evangelists, will it follow that these fathers had the same gospels before them? To say so is a manifest abuse of history, and quite inexcusable in writers that knew, or should have known, that these fathers made use of other gospels, wherein such passages might be contained, or they might be preserved in unwritten tradition. Besides which, I could almost venture to affirm that these fathers of the first century do not expressly name the gospels we have of Matthew, Mark, Luke, and John. To the two reasons that have been given why those who make divinity their profession, should study history, particularly ecclesiastical history, with an honest and serious application; in order to support Christianity against the attacks of unbelievers, and to remove the doubts and prejudices that the unfair proceedings of men of their own order have raised in minds candid but not implicit, willing to be informed but curious to examine; to these, I say, we may add another consideration that seems to me of no small importance. Writers of the Roman religion have attempted to show, that the text of the holy writ is on many accounts insufficient to be the sole criterion of orthodoxy: I apprehend too that they have shown it. Sure I am that experience, from the first promulgation of Christianity to this hour, shows abundantly with how much ease and success the most opposite, the most extravagant, nay, the most impious opinions, and the most contradictory faiths, may be founded on the same text; and plausibly defended by the same authority. Writers of the reformed religion have erected their batteries against tradition; and the only difficulty they had to encounter in this enterprise lay in levelling and pointing their cannon so as to avoid demolishing, in one common ruin, the traditions they retain, and those they reject. Each side has been employed to weaken the cause and explode the system of his adversary: and, whilst they have been so employed, they have jointly laid their axes to the root of Christianity: for thus men will be apt to reason upon what they have advanced. "If the text has not that authenticity, clearness, and precision which are necessary to establish it as a divine and a certain rule of faith and practice; and if the tradition of the church, from the first ages of it till the days of Luther and Calvin, has been corrupted itself, and has served to corrupt the faith and practice of Christians; there remains at this time no standard at all of Christianity. By consequence, either this religion was not originally of divine institution, or else God has not provided effectually for preserving the genuine purity of it, and the gates of hell have actually prevailed, in contradiction to his promise, against the church." The best effect of this reasoning that can be hoped for, is, that men should fall into theism, and subscribe to the first proposition; he must be worse than an atheist who can affirm the last. The dilemma is terrible, my lord. Party zeal and private interest have formed it: the common interest of Christianity is deeply concerned to solve it. Now, I presume, it can never be solved without a more accurate examination, not only of the Christian but of the Jewish system, than learned men have been hitherto impartial enough and sagacious enough to take, or honest enough to communicate. Whilst the authenticity and sense of the text of the bible remain as disputable, and whilst the tradition of the church remains as problematical, to say no worse, as the immense labors of the Christian divines in several communions have made them appear to be; Christianity may lean on the civil and ecclesiastical power, and be supported by the forcible influence of education: but the proper force of religion, that force which subdues the mind, and awes the conscience by conviction, will be wanting.

I had reason, therefore, to produce divinity, as one instance of those professions that require a particular application to the study of some particular parts of history; and since I have said so much on the subject in my zeal for Christianity, I will add this further. The resurrection of letters was a fatal period: the Christian system has been attacked, and wounded too, very se-

verely since that time. The defence has been better made indeed by modern divines, than it had been by ancient fathers and
apologists. The moderns have invented new methods of defence, and have abandoned some posts that were not tenable:
but still there are others, in defending which they lie under great
disadvantages. Such are various facts, piously believed in former times, but on which the truth of Christianity has been rested
very imprudently in more enlightened ages; because the falsity
of some, and the gross improbability of others are so evident,
that, instead of answering the purpose for which they were invented, they have rendered the whole tenor of ecclesiastical history and tradition precarious, ever since a strict but just application of the rules of criticism has been made to them. I touch
these things lightly; but if your lordship reflects upon them, you
will find reason perhaps to think as I do, that it is high time the
clergy in all Christian communions should join their forces, and
establish those historical facts, which are the foundations of the
whole system, on clear and unquestionable historical authority,
such as they require in all cases of moment from others; reject
candidly what cannot be thus established; and pursue their inquiries in the same spirit of truth through all the ages of the
church; without any regard to historians, fathers, or councils,
more than they are strictly entitled to on the face of what they
have transmitted to us, on their own consistency, and on the concurrence of other authority. Our pastors would be thus, I presume, much better employed than they generally are. Those of
the clergy who make religion merely a trade, who regard nothing
more than the subsistence it affords them, or in higher life the
wealth and power they enjoy by the means of it, may say to
themselves, that it will last their time, or that policy and reason
of state will preserve the form of a church when the spirit of religion is extinct. But those whom I mentioned above, those
who act for survival not temporal ends, and are desirous that
men should believe and practise the doctrines of Christianity, as
well as go to church and pay tithes, will feel and own the weight
of such considerations as these; and agree, that however the
people have been, and may be still amused, yet Christianity has
been in decay ever since the resurrection of letters; and that it
cannot be supported as it was supported before the era, nor by

any other way than that which I propose, and which a due application to the study of history, chronology, and criticism, would enable our divines to pursue, no doubt, with success.

I might instance, in other professions, the obligations men lie under of applying themselves to certain parts of history, and I can hardly forbear doing it in that of the law; in its nature the noblest and most beneficial to mankind, in its abuse and debasement the most sordid and the most pernicious. A lawyer now is nothing more, I speak of ninety-nine in a hundred at least, to use some of Tully's words, "nisi legulcius quidam cautus, et acutus præco actionum, cantor formularum, auceps syllabarum." But there have been lawyers that were orators, philosophers, historians: there have been Bacons and Clarendons, my lord. There will be none such any more, till, in some better age, true ambition or the love of fame prevails over avarice; and till men find leisure and encouragement to prepare themselves for the exercise of this profession, by climbing up to the "vantage ground," so my Lord Bacon calls it, of science; instead of grovelling all their lives below, in a mean but gainful application to all the little arts of chicane. Till this happen, the profession of the law will scarce deserve to be ranked among the learned professions: and whenever it happens, one of the vantage grounds, to which men must climb, is metaphysical, and the other historical knowledge. They must pry into the secret recesses of the human heart, and become well acquainted with the whole moral world, that they may discover the abstract reason of all laws: and they must trace the laws of particular states, especially of their own, from the first rough sketches to the more perfect draughts; from the first causes or occasions that produced them, through all the effects, good and bad, that they produced. But I am running insensibly into a subject, which would detain me too long from one that relates more immediately to your lordship, and with which I intend to conclude this long letter.

2. I pass from the consideration of those professions to which particular parts or kinds of history seem to belong: and I come to speak of the study of history, as a necessary means to prepare men for the discharge of that duty which they owe to their country, and which is common to all the members of every society that is constituted according to the rules of right reason,

and with a due regard to the common good. I have met, in St. Real's works, or some other French book, with a ridicule cast on private men who make history a political study, or who apply themselves in any manner to affairs of state. But the reflection is too general. In governments so arbitrary by their constitution, that the will of the prince is not only the supreme, but the sole law, it is so far from being a duty, that it may be dangerous, and must be impertinent in men, who are not called by the prince to the administration of public affairs, to concern themselves about it, or to fit themselves for it. The sole vocation there is the favor of the court; and whatever designation God makes by the talents he bestows, though it may serve, which it seldom ever does, to direct the choice of the prince, yet I presume that it cannot become a reason to particular men, or create a duty on them, to devote themselves to the public service. Look on the Turkish government. See a fellow taken, from rowing in a common passage-boat, by the caprice of the prince: see him invested next day with all the power the soldans took under the caliphs, or the mayors of the palace under the successors of Clovis: see a whole empire governed by the ignorance, inexperience, and arbitrary will of this tyrant, and a few other subordinate tyrants, as ignorant and unexperienced as himself. In France indeed, though an absolute government, things go a little better. Arts and sciences are encouraged, and here and there an example may be found of a man who has risen by some extraordinary talents, amidst innumerable examples of men who have arrived at the greatest honors and highest posts by no other merit than that of assiduous fawning, attendance, or of skill in some despicable puerile amusement: in training wasps, for instance, to take regular flights like hawks, and stoop at flies. The nobility of France, like the children of tribute among the ancient Saracens and modern Turks, are set apart for wars. They are bred to make love, to hunt, and to fight: and, if any of them should acquire knowledge superior to this, they would acquire that which might be prejudicial to themselves, but could not become beneficial to their country. The affairs of state are trusted to other hands. Some have risen to them by drudging long in business: some have been made ministers almost in the cradle: and the whole power of the government has been abandoned to others in the dotage of life. There is a monarchy, an absolute monarchy too, I mean that of China, wherein the administration of the government is carried on, under the direction of the prince, ever since the dominion of the Tartars has been established, by several classes of Mandarins, and according to the deliberation and advice of several orders of councils: the admission to which classes and orders depends on the abilities of the candidates, as their rise on them depends on the behavior they hold, and the improvements they make afterwards. Under such a government, it is neither impertinent nor ridiculous, in any of the subjects who are invited by their circumstances, or pushed to it by their talents, to make the history of their own and of other countries a political study, and to fit themselves by this and all other ways for the service of the public. It is not dangerous neither; or an honor, that outweighs the danger, attends it; since private men have a right by the ancient constitution of this government, as well as councils of state, to represent to the prince the abuses of his administration. But still men have not there the same occasion to concern themselves in the affairs of the state, as the nature of a free government gives to the members of it. In our own country, for in our own the forms of a free government at least are hitherto preserved, men are not only designed for the public service by the circumstances of their situation, and their talents, all which may happen in others: but they are designed to it by their birth in many cases, and in all cases they may dedicate themselves to this service, and take, in different degrees some share in it; whether they are called to it by the prince or no. In absolute governments, all public service is to the prince, and he nominates all those that serve the public. In free governments, there is a distinct and a principal service due to the state. Even the king, of such a limited monarchy as ours, is but the first servant of the people. Among his subjects, some are appointed by the constitution, and others are elected by the people, to carry on the exercise of the legislative power jointly with him, and to control the executive power independently on him. Thus your lordship is born a member of that order of men, in whom a third part of the supreme power of the government resides: and your right to the exercise of the power belonging to this order not being yet opened, you are chosen into another body of men, who have different power and a different constitution, but who possess another third part of the supreme legislative authority, for as long a time as the commission or trust delegated to them by the people lasts. Freemen, who are neither born to the first, nor elected to the last, have a right however to complain, to represent, to petition, and, I add, even to do more in cases of the utmost extremity. For sure there cannot be a greater absurdity, than to affirm, that the people have a remedy in resistance, when their prince attempts to enslave them; but that they have none, when their representatives sell themselves and them.

The sum of what I have been saying is, that, in free governments, the public service is not confined to those whom the prince appoints to different posts in the administration under him; that there the care of the state is the care of multitudes; that many are called to it in a particular manner by their rank, and by other circumstances of their situation; and that even those whom the prince appoints are not only answerable to him, but, like him, and before him, to the nation, for their behavior in their several posts. It can never be impertinent nor ridiculous therefore in such a country, whatever it might be in the abbot of St. Real's, which was Savoy I think; or in Peru, under the Incas, where, Garcilasso de la Vega says, it was lawful for none but the nobility to study—for men of all degrees to instruct themselves in those affairs wherein they may be actors, or judges of those that act, or controllers of those that judge. On the contrary, it is incumbent on every man to instruct himself, as well as the means and opportunities he has permit, concerning the nature and interests of the government, and those rights and duties that belong to him, or to his superiors, or to his inferiors. This in general; but in particular it is certain that the obligations under which we lie to serve our country increase, in proportion to the ranks we hold, and the other circumstances of birth, fortune, and situation that call us to this service; and, above all, to the talents which God has given us to perform it.

It is in this view, that I shall address to your lordship whatever I have further to say on the study of history.

Letter 6

From What Period Modern History Is Peculiarly Useful to the Service of Our Country

Since then you are, my lord, by your birth, by the nature of our government, and by the talents God has given you, attached for life to the service of your country; since genius alone cannot enable you to go through this service with honor to yourself and advantage to your country, whether you support or whether you oppose the administrations that arise; since a great stock of knowledge, acquired betimes and continually improved, is necessary to this end; and since one part of this stock must be collected from the study of history, as the other part is to be gained by observation and experience; I come now to speak to your lordship of such history as has an immediate relation to the great duty and business of your life, and of the method to be observed in this study. The notes I have by me, which were of some little use thus far, serve me no farther, and I have no books to consult. No matter; I shall be able to explain my thoughts without their assistance, and less liable to be tedious. I hope to be as full and as exact on memory alone, as the manner in which I shall treat the subject requires me to be.

I say, then, that however closely affairs are linked together in the progression of governments, and how much soever events that follow are dependent on those that precede, the whole connection diminishes to sight as the chain lengthens; till at last it seems to be broken, and the links that are continued from that point bear no proportion nor any similitude to the former. I would not be understood to speak only of those great changes that are wrought by a concurrence of extraordinary events: for instance, the expulsion of one nation, the destruction of one government, and the establishment of another: but even of those that are wrought in the same governments and among the same people, slowly and almost imperceptibly, by the necessary effects of time, and flux condition of human affairs. When such changes as these happen in several states about the same time, and consequently affect other states by their vicinity, and by many different relations which they frequently bear to one another; then is one of those periods formed, at which the chain spoken of is so broken as to have little or no real or visible connection with that which we see continue. A new situation, different from the former, begets new interests in the same proportion of difference; not in this or that particular state alone, but in all those that are concerned by vicinity or other relations, as I said just now, in one general system of policy. New interests beget new maxims of government, and new methods of conduct. These, in their turns, beget new manners, new habits, new customs. The longer this new constitution of affairs continues, the more will this difference increase: and although some analogy may remain long between what preceded and what succeeds such a period, yet will this analogy soon become an object of mere curiosity, not of profitable inquiry. Such a period therefore is, in the true sense of the words, an epocha or an era, a point of time at which you stop, or from which you reckon forward. I say forward; because we are not to study in the present case, as chronologers compute, backward. Should we persist to carry our researches much higher, and to push them even to some other period of the same kind, we should misemploy our time; the causes then laid having spent themselves, the series of effects derived from them being over, and our concern in both consequently at an end. But a new system of causes and effects, that subsists in our time, and whereof our conduct is to be a part, arising at the last period, and all that passes in our time being dependent on what has passed since that period, or being immediately relative to it, we are extremely concerned to be well informed about all these passages. To be entirely ignorant about the ages that precede this era would be shameful. Nay, some indulgence may be had to a temperate curiosity in the review of them. But to be learned about them is a ridiculous affectation in any man who means to be useful to the present age. Down to this era let us read history: from this era, and down to our time, let us study it.

The end of the fifteenth century seems to be just such a period as I have been describing, for those who live in the eighteenth, and who inhabit the western parts of Europe. A little before, or a little after this point of time, all those events happened, and all those revolutions began, that have produced so vast a change in the manners, customs, and interests of particular nations, and in the whole policy, ecclesiastical and civil, of these parts of the world. I must descend here into some detail, not of histories, collections, or memorials; for all these are well enough known: and though the contents are in the heads of few, the books are in the hands of many. But instead of showing your lordship where to look, I shall contribute more to your entertainment and instruction, by marking out, as well as my memory will serve me to do it, what you are to look for, and by furnishing a kind of clue to your studies. I shall give, according to custom, the first place to religion.

A View of the Ecclesiastical Government of Europe from the Beginning of the Sixteenth Century

Observe then, my lord, that the demolition of the papal throne was not attempted with success till the beginning of the sixteenth century. If you are curious to cast your eyes back, you will find Berenger in the eleventh, who was soon silenced; Arnoldus in the same, who was soon hanged; Valdo in the twelfth, and our Wickliff in the fourteenth, as well as others perhaps whom I do not recollect. Sometimes the doctrines of the church were alone attacked; and sometimes the doctrine, the discipline, and the usurpations of the pope. But little fires, kindled in corners of a dark world, were soon stifled by that great abettor of Christian unity, the hangman. When they spread and blazed out, as in the case of the Albigeois and of the Hussites, armies were raised to extinguish them by torrents of blood; and such saints as Dominic, with the crucifix in their hands, instigated the troops to the utmost barbarity. Your lordship will find that the church of Rome was maintained by such charitable and salutary means, among others, till the period spoken of; and you will be curious, I am sure, to inquire how this period came to be more fatal to her than any former conjuncture. A multitude of circumstances, which you will easily trace in the histories of the fifteenth and sixteenth centuries, to go no further back, concurred to bring about this great event: and a multitude of others, as easy to be traced, concurred to hinder the demolition from becoming total, and to prop the tottering fabric. Among these circumstances, there is one less complicated and more obvious than others, which was of principal and universal influence. The art of printing had been invented about forty or fifty years before the period we fix: from that time, the resurrection of letters hastened on apace; and at this period they had made great progress, and were cultivated with great application. Mahomet the Second drove them out of the east into the west; and the popes proved worse politicians than the mufties in this respect. Nicholas the Fifth encouraged learning and learned men. Sixtus the Fourth was, if I mistake not, a great collector of books at least: and Leo the Tenth was the patron of every art and science. The magicians themselves broke the charm by which they had bound mankind for so many ages: and the adventure of that knighterrant, who, thinking himself happy in the arms of a celestial nymph, found that he was the miserable slave of an infernal bag, was in some sort renewed. As soon as the means of acquiring and spreading information grew common, it is no wonder that a system was unravelled, which could not have been woven with success in any ages, but those of gross ignorance, and credulous superstition. I might point out to your lordship many other immediate causes, some general like this that I have mentioned, and some particular. The great schism, for instance, that ended in the beginning of the fifteenth century, and in the council of Constance, had occasioned prodigious scandal. Two or three vicars of Christ, two or three infallible heads of the church roaming about the world at a time, furnished matter of ridicule as well as scandal: and whilst they appealed, for so they did in effect, to the laity, and reproached and excommunicated one another, they taught the world what to think of the institution, as well as exercise of the papal authority. The same lesson was taught by the council of Pisa, that preceded, and by that of Basle, that followed the council of Constance. The horrid crimes of Alexander the Sixth, the saucy ambition of Julius the Second, the immense profusion and scandalous exactions of Leo the Tenth; all these events and characters, following in a continued series from the beginning of one century, provided the way for the revolution that happened in the beginning of the next. The state of Germany, the state of England, and that of the North, were particular causes in these several countries, of this revolution. Such were many remarkable events that happened about the same time, and a little before it, in these and in other nations; and such were likewise the characters of many of the princes of that age, some of whom favored the reformation, like the elector of Saxony, on a principle of conscience; and most of whom favored it, just as others opposed it, on a principle of interest. This your lordship will discover manifestly to have been the case; and the sole difference you will find between Henry the Eighth and Francis the First, one of whom separated from the pope, as the other adhered to him, is this: Henry the Eighth divided, with the secular clergy and his people, the spoil of the pope, and his satellites, the monks; Francis the First divided, with the pope, the spoil of his clergy, secular and regular, and of his people. With the same impartial eye that your lordship surveys the abuses of religion, and the corruptions of the church as well as court of Rome, which brought on the reformation at this period; you will observe the characters and conduct of those who began, who propagated, and who favored the reformation: and from your observation of these, as well as of the unsystematical manner in which it was carried on at the same time in various places, and of the want of concert, nay even of charity, among the reformers, you will learn what to think of the several religions that unite in their opposition to the Roman, and yet hate one another most heartily; what to think of the several sects that have sprouted, like suckers, from the same great roots; and what the true principles are of protestant ecclesiastical policy. This policy had no being till Luther made his establishment in Germany; till Zwinglius began another in Switzerland, which Calvin carried on, and, like Americus Vesputius who followed Christopher Columbus, robbed the first adventurer of his honor; and till the reformation in our country was perfected under Edward the Sixth and Elizabeth. Even popish ecclesiastical policy is no longer the same since that era. His holiness is no longer at the head of the whole western church: and to keep the part that adheres to him, he is obliged to loosen their chains, and to lighten his yoke. The spirit and pretensions of his court are the same, but not the power. He governs by expedient and management more, and by authority less. His decrees and his briefs are in danger of being refused, explained away, or evaded, unless he negotiates their acceptance before he gives them, governs in concert with his flock, and feeds his sheep according to their humor and interest. In short, his excommunications, that made the greatest emperors tremble, are despised by the lowest members of his own communion; and the remaining attachment to him has been, from this era, rather a political expedient to preserve an appearance of unity, than a principle of conscience; whatever some bigotted princes may have thought, whatever ambitious prelates and hireling scribblers may have taught, and whatever a people, worked up to enthusiasm by fanatical preachers, may have acted. Proofs of this would be easy to draw, not only from the conduct of such princes as Ferdinand the First and Maximilian the Second, who could scarce be esteemed papists though they continued in the pope's communion; but even from that of princes who persecuted their protestant subjects with great violence. Enough has been said, I think, to show your lordship how little need there is of going up higher than the beginning of the sixteenth century in the study of history, to acquire all the knowledge necessary at this time in ecclesiastical policy, or in civil policy as far as it is relative to this. Historical monuments of this sort are in every man's hand, the facts are sufficiently verified, and the entire scenes lie open to our observation: even that scene of solemn refined banter exhibited in the council of Trent, imposes on no man who reads Paolo, as well as Pallavicini, and the letters of Vargas.

A View of the Civil Government of Europe in the Beginning of the Sixteenth Century

In France

A very little higher need we go, to observe those great changes in the civil constitutions of the principal nations of Europe, in the partition of power among them, and by consequence in the whole system of European policy, which have operated so strongly for more than two centuries, and which operate still. I will not affront the memory of our Henry the Seventh so much as to compare him to Louis the Eleventh: and yet I perceive some resemblance between them; which would perhaps appear greater, if Philip of Commines had written the history of Henry as well as that of Louis; or if my Lord Bacon had written that of Louis as well as that of Henry. This prince came to the crown of England a little before the close of the fifteenth century: and Louis began his reign in France about twenty years sooner. These reigns make remarkable periods in the histories of both nations. To reduce the power, privileges, and possessions of the nobility, and to increase the wealth and authority of the crown, was the principal object of both. In this their success was so great, that the constitutions of the two governments have had, since that time, more resemblance, in name and in form than in reality, to the constitutions that prevailed before. Louis the Eleventh was the first, say the French, "qui mit les rois hors de page." The independency of the nobility had rendered the state of his predecessors very dependent, and their power precarious. They were the sovereigns of great vassals; but these vassals were so powerful that one of them was sometimes able, and two or three of them always, to give law to the sovereign. Before Louis came to the crown, the English had been driven out of their possessions in France, by the poor character of Henry the Sixth, the domestic troubles of his reign, and the defection of the house of Burgundy from this alliance, much more than by the ability of Charles the Seventh, who seems to have been neither a greater hero nor a greater politician than Henry the Sixth; and even than by the vigor and union of the French nobility in his service.

After Louis came to the crown, Edward the Fourth made a show of carrying the war again into France; but he soon returned home and your lordship will not be at a loss to find much better reasons for his doing so, in the situation of his affairs and the characters of his allies, than those which Philip of Commines draws from the artifice of Louis, from his good cheer, and his pensions. Now from this time our pretensions on France were in effect given up: and Charles the Bold, the last prince of the house of Burgundy, being killed, Louis had no vassal able to molest him. He re-united the Dutchy of Burgundy and Artois to his crown, he acquired Provence by gift, and his son Brittany by marriage: and thus France grew, in the course of a few years, into that great and compact body which we behold at this time. The history of France before his period is, like that of Germany, a complicated history of several states and several interests; sometimes concurring like members of the same monarchy, and sometimes warring on one another. Since this period, the history of France is the history of one state under a more uniform and orderly government; the history of a monarchy wherein the prince is possessor of some, as well as lord of all the great fieffes: and, the authority of many tyrants centering in one, though the people are not become more free, yet the whole system of domestic policy is entirely changed. Peace at home is better secured, and the nation grown fitter to carry war abroad. The governors of great provinces and of strong fortresses have opposed their king, and taken arms against his authority and commission since that time: but yet there is no more resemblance between the authority and pretensions of these governors, or the nature and occasions of these disputes, and the authority and pretensions of the vassals of the crown in former days, or the nature and occasions of their disputes with the prince and with one another, than there is between the ancient and the present peers of France. In a word, the constitution is so altered, that any knowledge we can acquire about it in the history that precedes this period, will serve to little purpose in our study of the history that follows it, and to less purpose still in assisting us to judge of what passes in the present age. The kings of France since that time, more masters at home, have been able to exert themselves more abroad: and they began to do so immediately; for Charles the Eighth, son and successor of Louis the Eleventh, formed great designs of foreign conquests, though they were disappointed by his inability, by the levity of the nation, and by other causes. Louis the Twelfth and Francis the First, but especially Francis, meddled deep in the affairs of Europe: and though the superior genius of Ferdinand called the Catholic, and the star of Charles the Fifth prevailed against them, yet the efforts they made show sufficiently how the strength and importance of this monarchy were increased in their time. From whence we may date likewise the rivalship of the house of France, for we may reckon that of Valois and that of Bourbon as one upon this occasion, and the house of Austria; that continues at this day, and that has cost so much blood and so much treasure in the course of it.

In England

Though the power and influence of the nobility sunk in the great change that began under Henry the Seventh in England, as they did in that which began under Louis the Eleventh in France; yet the new constitutions that these changes produced were very different. In France the lords alone lost, the king alone gained; the clergy held their possessions and their immunities, and the people remained in a state of mitigated slavery. But in England the people gained as well as the crown. The commons had already a share in the legislature; so that the power and influence of the lords being broke by Henry the Seventh, and the property of the commons increasing by the sale that his son made of church-lands, the power of the latter increased of course by this change in a constitution, the forms whereof were favorable to them. The union of the roses put an end to the civil wars of York and Lancaster, that had succeeded those we commonly call the barons' wars, and the humor of warring in France, that had lasted near four hundred years under the Normans and Plantagenets, for plunder as well as conquest, was spent. Our temple of Janus was shut by Henry the Seventh. We neither laid waste our own nor other countries any longer: and wise laws and a wise government changed insensibly the manners, and gave a new turn to the spirit of our people. We were no longer the freebooters we had been. Our nation maintained her reputation in arms whenever the public interest or the public authority required it; but war ceased to be, what it had been, our principal and almost our sole profession. The arts of peace prevailed among us. We became husband-men, manufacturers, and merchants, and we emulated neighboring nations in literature. It is from this time that we ought to study the history of our country, my lord, with the utmost application. We are not much concerned to know with critical accuracy what were the ancient forms of our parliaments, concerning which, however, there is little room for dispute from the reign of Henry the Third at least; nor in short the whole system of our civil constitution before Henry the Seventh, and of our ecclesiastical constitution before Henry the Eighth. But he who has not studied and acquired a thorough knowledge of them both, from these periods down to the present time, in all the variety of events by which they have been affected, will be very unfit to judge or take care of either. Just as little are we concerned to know, in any nice detail, what the conduct of our princes, relatively to our neighbors on the continent, was before this period, and at a time when the partition of power and a multitude of other circumstances rendered the whole political system of Europe so vastly different from that which has existed since. But he who has not traced this conduct from the period we fix, down to the present age, wants a principal part of the knowledge that every English minister of state should have. Ignorance in the respects here spoken of is the less pardonable, because we have more, and more authentic, means of information concerning this, than concerning any other period. Anecdotes enow to glut the curiosity of some persons, and to silence all the captious cavils of others, will never be furnished by any portion of history; nor indeed can they according to the nature and course of human affairs: but he who is content to read and observe, like a senator and a statesman, will find in our own and in foreign historians as much information as he wants, concerning the affairs of our island, her fortune at home and her conduct abroad, from the fifteenth century to the eighteenth. I refer to foreign historians as well as to our own, for this series of our own history; not only because it is reasonable to see in what manner the historians of other countries have related the transactions wherein we have

been concerned, and what judgment they have made of our conduct, domestic and foreign, but for another reason likewise. Our
nation has furnished as ample and as important matter, good
and bad, for history, as any nation under the sun: and yet we
must yield the palm in writing history most certainly to the
Italians and to the French, and, I fear, even to the Germans.
The only two pieces of history we have, in any respect to be
compared with the ancient, are, the reign of Henry the Seventh
by my lord Bacon, and the history of our civil wars in the last
century by your noble ancestor my lord chancellor Clarendon.
But we have no general history to be compared with some of
other countries: neither have we, which I lament much more,
particular histories, except the two I have mentioned, nor writers
of memorials, nor collectors of monuments and anecdotes, to
vie in number or in merit with those that foreign nations can
boast; from Commines, Guicciardin, Du Bellay, Paola, Davila,
Thuanus, and a multitude of others, down through the whole
period that I propose to your lordship. But although this be
true, to our shame; yet it is true likewise that we want no necessary means of information. They lie open to our industry and
our discernment. Foreign writers are for the most part scarce
worth reading when they speak of our domestic affairs; nor
are our English writers for the most part of greater value
when they speak of foreign affairs. In this mutual defect, the
writers of other countries are, I think, more excusable than ours:
for the nature of our government, the political principles in which
we are bred, our distinct interests as islanders, and the complicated various interests and humors of our parties, all these are
so peculiar to ourselves, and so different from the notions, manners, and habits of other nations, that it is not wonderful they
should be puzzled, or should fall into error, when they undertake
to give relations of events that result from all these, or to pass
any judgment upon them. But as these historians are mutually
defective, so they mutually supply each other's defects. We
must compare them therefore, make use of our discernment,
and draw our conclusions from both. If we proceed in this
manner, we have an ample fund of history in our power, from
whence to collect sufficient authentic information; and we must
proceed in this manner, even with our own historians of different

religions, sects, and parties, or run the risk of being misled by domestic ignorance and prejudice in this case, as well as by foreign ignorance and prejudice in the other.

In Spain and the Empire

Spain figured little in Europe till the latter part of the fifteenth century; till Castile and Arragon were united by the marriage of Ferdinand and Isabella; till the total expulsion of the Moors, and till the discovery of the West Indies. After this, not only Spain took a new form, and grew into immense power; but, the heir of Ferdinand and Isabella being heir likewise of the houses of Burgundy and Austria, such an extent of dominion accrued to him by all these successions, and such an addition of rank and authority by his election to the empire, as no prince had been master of in Europe from the days of Charles the Great. It is proper to observe here how the policy of the Germans altered in the choice of an emperor; because the effects of this alteration have been great. When Rodolphus of Hapsburg was chose in the year one thousand two hundred and seventy, or about that time, the poverty and the low estate of this prince, who had been marshal of the court to a king of Bohemia, was an inducement to elect him. The disorderly and lawless state of the empire made the princes of it in those days unwilling to have a more powerful head. But a contrary maxim took place at this era. Charles the Fifth and Francis the First, the two most powerful princes of Europe, were the sole candidates; for the elector of Saxony, who is said to have declined, was rather unable to stand in competition with them: and Charles was chosen by the unanimous suffrages of the electoral college, if I mistake not. Another Charles, Charles the Fourth, who was made emperor illegally enough on the deposition of Louis of Bavaria, and about one hundred and fifty years before, seems to me to have contributed doubly to establish this maxim; by the wise constitutions that he procured to pass, that united the empire in a more orderly form and better system of government; and by alienating the imperial revenues to such a degree, that they were no longer sufficient to support an emperor who had not great revenues of his own. The same maxim and other circumstances have concurred to keep the empire in this family ever since, as it had been often before; and this family having large dominions in the empire, and larger pretensions, as well as dominions, out of it, the other states of Europe, France, Spain and England particularly, have been more concerned since this period in the affairs of Germany, than they were before it: and by consequence the history of Germany, from the beginning of the sixteenth century, is of importance, and a necessary part of that knowledge which your lordship desires to acquire.

The Dutch commonwealth was not formed till near a century later. But as soon as it was formed, nay even whilst it was forming, these provinces, that were lost to observation among the many that composed the dominions of Burgundy and Austria, became so considerable a part of the political system of Europe, that their history must be studied by every man who would inform himself of this system.

Soon after this state had taken being, others of a more ancient original began to mingle in those disputes and wars, those councils, negotiations, and treaties, that are to be the principal objects of your lordship's application in the study of history. That of the northern crowns deserves your attention little, before the last century. Till the election of Frederic the First to the crown of Denmark, and till that wonderful revolution which the first Gustavus brought about in Sweden, it is nothing more than a confused rhapsody of events, in which the great kingdoms and states of Europe neither had any concern, nor took any part. From the time I have mentioned, the northern crowns have turned their counsels and their arms often southwards, and Sweden particularly, with prodigious effect.

To what purpose should I trouble your lordship with the mention of histories of other nations? They are either such as have no relation to the knowledge you would acquire, like that of the Poles, the Muscovites, or the Turks; or they are such as, having an occasional or a secondary relation to it, fall of course into your scheme; like the history of Italy for instance, which is sometimes a part of that of France, sometimes of that of Spain, and sometimes of that of Germany. The thread of history that you are to keep, is that of the nations who are and must always be concerned in the same scenes of action with your own. These are the principal nations of the west. Things that have no immediate relation to your own country, or to them, are either too remote, or too minute, to employ much of your time: and their history and your own is, for all your purposes, the whole history of Europe.

The two great powers, that of France and that of Austria, being formed, and a rivalship established by consequence between them; it began to be the interest of their neighbors to oppose the strongest and most enterprising of the two, and to be the ally and friend of the weakest. From hence arose the notion of a balance of power in Europe, on the equal poise of which the safety and tranquility of all must depend. To destroy the equality of this balance has been the aim of each of these rivals in his turn: and to hinder it from being destroyed, by preventing too much power from falling into one scale, has been the principle of all the wise councils of Europe, relatively to France and to the house of Austria, through the whole period that began at the era we have fixed, and subsists at this hour. To make a careful and just observation, therefore, of the rise and decline of these powers, in the two last centuries, and in the present; of the projects which their ambition formed; of the means they employed to carry these projects on with success; of the means employed by others to defeat them; of the issue of all these endeavors in war and in negotiation; and particularly, to bring your observations home to your own country and your own use, of the conduct that England held, to her honor or dishonor, to her advantage or disadvantage, in every one of the numerous and important conjunctures that happened—ought to be the principal subject of your lordship's attention in reading and reflecting on this part of modern history.

Now to this purpose you will find it of great use, my lord, when you have a general plan of the history in your mind, to go over the whole again in another method; which I propose to be this. Divide the entire period into such particular periods as the general course of affairs will mark out to you sufficiently, by the rise of new conjunctures, of different schemes of conduct, and of different theatres of action. Examine this period of history as you would examine a tragedy or a comedy; that is, take first the idea or a general notion of the whole, and after that examine every act and every scene apart. Consider them in themselves, and consider them relatively to one another. Read this history as you would that of any ancient period; but study it afterwards, as it would not be worth your while to study the other; nay as you could not have in your power the means of studying the other, if the study was really worth your while. The former part of this period abounds in great historians: and the latter part is so modern, that even tradition is authentic enough to supply the want of good history, if we are curious to inquire, and if we hearken to the living with the same impartiality and freedom of judgment as we read the dead; and he that does one, will do the other. The whole period abounds in memorials, in collections of public acts and monuments, of private letters, and of treaties. All these must come into your plan of study, my lord: many may not be read through, but all to be consulted and compared. They must not lead you, I think, to your inquiries, but your inquiries must lead you to them. By joining history and that which we call the *materia historica* together in this manner, and by drawing your information from both, your lordship will acquire not only that knowledge, which many have in some degree, of the great transactions that have passed, and the great events that have happened in Europe during this period, and of their immediate and obvious causes and consequences; but your lordship will acquire a much superior knowledge, and such a one as very few men possess almost in any degree, a knowledge of the true political system of Europe during this time. You will see it in its primitive principles, in the constitutions of governments, the situations of countries, their national and true interests, the characters and the religion of people, and other permanent circumstances. You will trace it through all its fluctuations, and observe how the objects vary seldom, but the means perpetually, according to the different characters of princes and of those who govern; the different abilities of those who serve; the course of accidents, and a multitude of other irregular and contingent circumstances.

The particular periods into which the whole period should be divided, in my opinion, are these. (1) From the fifteenth to the end of the sixteenth century. (2) From thence to the Pyrenean treaty. (3) From thence down to the present time.

Your lordship will find this division as apt and as proper, relatively to the particular histories of England, France, Spain, and Germany, the principal nations concerned, as it is relatively to the general history of Europe.

The death of queen Elizabeth, and the accession of king James the First, made a vast alteration in the government of our nation at home, and in her conduct abroad, about the end of the first of these periods. The wars that religion occasioned, and ambition fomented in France, through the reigns of Francis the Second, Charles the Ninth, Henry the Third, and a part of Henry the Fourth, ended: and the furies of the league were crushed by this great prince, about the same time. Phillip the Second of Spain marks this period likewise by his death, and by the exhausted condition in which he left the monarchy he governed: which took the lead no longer in disturbing the peace of mankind, but acted a second part in abetting the bigotry and ambition of Ferdinand the Second and the Third. The thirty years war that devasted Germany did not begin till the eighteenth year of the seventeenth century, but the seeds of it were sowing some time before, and even at the end of the sixteenth. Ferdinand the First and Maximilian had shown much lenity and moderation in the disputes and troubles that arose on account of religion. Under Rodolphus and Matthias, as the succession of their cousin Ferdinand approached, the fires that were covered began to smoke and to sparkle: and if the war did not begin with this century, the preparation for it, and the expectation of it did.

The second period ends in one thousand six hundred and sixty, the year of the restoration of Charles the Second to the throne of England; when our civil wars, and all the disorders which Cromwell's usurpation had produced, were over; and therefore a remarkable point of time, with respect to our country. It is no less remarkable with respect to Germany, Spain, and France.

As to Germany; the ambitious projects of the German branch of Austria had been entirely defeated, the peace of the empire had been restored, and almost a new constitution formed, or an old one revived, by the treaties of Westphalia; nay the imperial eagle was not only fallen, but her wings were clipped.

As to Spain; the Spanish branch was fallen as low twelve years afterwards, that is, in the year one thousand six hundred and sixty. Philip the Second left his successors a ruined monarchy. He left them something worse; he left them his example and his principles of government, founded in ambition, in pride, in ignorance, in bigotry, and all the pedantry of state. I have read somewhere or other, that the war of the Low Countries alone cost him, by his own confession, five hundred and sixty-four millions, a prodigious sum in what species soever he reckoned. Philip the Third and Philip the Fourth followed his example and his principles of government, at home and abroad. At home, there was much form, but no good order, no economy, nor wisdom of policy in the state. The church continued to devour the state, and that monster the inquisition to dispeople the country, even more than perpetual war, and all the numerous colonies that Spain had sent to the West Indies: for your lordship will find that Philip the Third drove more than nine hundred thousand Moriscoes out of his dominions by one edict, with such circumstances of inhumanity in the execution of it, as Spaniards alone could exercise, and that tribunal, who had provoked this unhappy race to revolt, could alone approve. Abroad, the conduct of these princes was directed by the same wild spirit of ambition: rash in undertaking though slow to execute, and obstinate in pursuing though unable to succeed, they opened a new sluice to let out the little life and vigor that remained in their monarchy. Philip the Second is said to have been piqued against his uncle Ferdinand, for refusing to yield the empire to him on the abdication of Charles the Fifth. Certain it is, that as much as he loved to disturb the peace of mankind, and to meddle in every quarrel that had the appearance of supporting the Roman and oppressing every other church, he meddled little in the affairs of Germany. But, Ferdinand and Maximilian dead, and the offspring of Maximilian extinct, the kings of Spain espoused the interests of the other branch of their family, entertained remote views of ambition in favor of their own branch, even on that side, and made all the enterprises of Ferdinand of Gratz, both before and after his elevation to the empire, the common cause of the house of Austria. What completed their ruin was this: they knew not how to lose, nor when to yield. They acknowledged the independence of the Dutch commonwealth, and became the allies of their ancient subjects at the treaty of Munster; but they would not forego their usurped claim on Portugal, and they persisted to carry on singly the war against France. Thus they were reduced to such a lowness of power as can hardly be parallelled in any other case: and Philip the Fourth was obliged at last to conclude a peace, on terms repugnant to his inclination, to that of his people, to the interest of Spain, and to that of all Europe, in the Pyrenean treaty.

As to France, this era of the entire fall of the Spanish power is likewise that from which we may reckon that France grew as formidable, as we have seen her, to her neighbors, in power and pretensions. Henry the Fourth meditated great designs, and prepared to act a great part in Europe in the very beginning of this period, when Ravaillac stabbed him. His designs died with him, and are rather guessed at than known; for surely those which his historian Perefixe and the compilers of Sully's memorials ascribe to him, of a Christian commonwealth divided into fifteen states, and of a senate to decide all differences, and to maintain this new constitution of Europe, are too chimerical to have been really his: but his general design of abasing the house of Austria, and establishing the superior power in that of Bourbon, was taken up, about twenty years after his death, by Richelieu, and was pursued by him and by Mazarin with so much ability and success, that it was effected entirely by the treaties of Westphalia and by the Pyrenean treaty; that is, at the end of the second of those periods I have presumed to propose to your lordship.

When the third, in which we now are, will end, and what circumstances will mark the end of it, I know not; but this I know, that the great events and revolutions, which have happened in the course of it, interest us still more nearly than those of the two precedent periods. I intended to have drawn up an elenchus or summary of the three, but I doubted, on further reflection, whether my memory would enable me to do it with exactness enough: and I saw that, if I was able to do it, the deduction would be immeasurably long. Something of this kind, however, it may be reasonable to attempt, in speaking of the last period: which may hereafter occasion a further trouble to your lordship.

But to give some breathing time, I will postpone it at present, and am in the meanwhile,

My lord, yours, &c.

Letter 8

The scales of the balance of power will never be exactly poised, nor in the precise point of equality either discernible or necessary to be discerned. It is sufficient in this, as in other human affairs, that the deviation be not too great. Some there will always be. A constant attention to these deviations is therefore necessary. When they are little, their increase may be easily prevented by early care and the precautions that good policy suggests. But when they become great for want of this care and these precautions, or by the force of unforeseen events, more vigor is to be exerted, and greater efforts to be made. But even in such cases, much reflection is necessary on all the circumstances that form the conjuncture; lest, by attacking with ill success, the deviation be confirmed, and the power that is deemed already exorbitant become more so; and lest, by attacking with good success, whilst one scale is pillaged, too much weight of power be thrown into the other. In such cases, he who has considered, in the histories of former ages, the strange revolutions that time produces, and the perpetual flux and reflux of public as well as private fortunes, of kingdoms and states as well as of those who govern or are governed in them, will incline to think, that if the scales can be brought back by a war, nearly, though not exactly, to the point they were at before this great deviation from it, the rest may be left to accidents, and to the use that good policy is able to make of them.

The first section of this letter has been omitted.

When Charles the Fifth was at the height of his power, and in the zenith of his glory, when a king of France and a pope were at once his prisoners; it must be allowed, that, his situation and that of his neighbors compared, they had as much at least to fear from him and from the house of Austria, as the neighbors of Louis the Fourteenth had to fear from him and from the house of Bourbon, when, after all his other success, one of his grand-children was placed on the Spanish throne. And yet among all the conditions of the several leagues against Charles the Fifth, I do not remember that it was ever stipulated, that "no peace should be made with him as long as he continued to be emperor and king of Spain; nor as long as any Austrian prince continued capable of uniting on his head the imperial and Spanish crowns."

If your lordship makes the application, you will find that the difference of some circumstances does not hinder this example from being very apposite and strong to the present purpose. Charles the Fifth was emperor and king of Spain; but neither was Louis the Fourteenth king of Spain, nor Philip the Fifth king of France. That had happened in one instance, which it was apprehended might happen in the other. It had happened, and it was reasonably to be apprehended that it might happen again, and that the Imperial and Spanish crowns might continue, not only in the same family, but on the same heads; for measures were taken to secure the succession of both to Philip the son of Charles. We do not find however that any confederacy was formed, any engagement taken, nor any war made, to remove or prevent this great evil. The princes and states of Europe contented themselves to oppose the designs of Charles the Fifth, and to check the growth of his power occasionally, and as interest invited, or necessity forced them to do; not constantly. They did perhaps too little against him, and sometimes too much for him; but if they did too little of one kind, time and accident did the rest. Distinct dominions, and different pretensions, created contrary interests in the house of Austria: and on the abdication of Charles the Fifth, his brother succeeded, not his son, to the empire. The house of Austria divided into a German and a Spanish branch: and if the two branches came to have a mutual influence on one another, and frequently a common interest, it was not till one of them had fallen from grandeur, and till the other was rather aiming at it, than in possession of it. In short, Philip was excluded from the imperial throne by so natural a progression of causes and effects, arising not only in Germany but in his own family, that if a treaty had been made to exclude him from it in favor of Ferdinand, such a treaty might have been said very probably to have executed itself.

The precaution I have mentioned, and that was neglected in this case without any detriment to the common cause of Europe, was not neglected in the grand alliance of one thousand seven hundred and one. For in that, one of the ends proposed by the war is, to obtain an effectual security against the contingent union of the crowns of France and Spain. The will of Charles the Second provides against the same contingency: and this great principle, of preventing too much dominion and power from falling to the lot of either of the families of Bourbon or Austria, seemed to be agreed on all sides; since in the partition-treaty the same precaution was taken against a union of the Imperial and Spanish crowns. King William was enough piqued against France. His ancient prejudices were strong and well founded. He had been worsted in war, overreached in negotiation, and personally affronted by her. England and Holland were sufficiently alarmed and animated, and a party was not wanting even in our island, ready to approve any engagements he would have taken against France and Spain, and in favor of the house of Austria; though we were less concerned, by any national interest, than any other power that took part in the war, either then, or afterwards. But this prince was far from taking a part beyond that which the particular interest of England and Holland, and the general interest of Europe, necessarily required. Pique must have no more a place than affection, in deliberations of this kind. To have engaged to dethrone Philip, out of resentment to Louis the Fourteenth, would have been a resolution worthy of Charles the Twelfth, king of Sweden, who sacrificed his country, his people, and himself at last, to his revenge. To have engaged to conquer the Spanish monarchy for the house of Austria, or to go, in favor of that family, one step beyond those that were necessary to keep this house on a foot of rivalry with the other, would have been, as I have hinted, to act the part of a vassal, not of an ally. The former pawns his state, and ruins his subjects, for the interest of his superior lord, perhaps for his lord's humor, or his passion: the latter goes no further than his own interests carry him; nor makes war for those of another, nor even for his own, if they are remote and contingent, as if he fought *pro aris et focis*, for his religion, his liberty, and his property. Agreeably to these principles of good policy, we entered into the war that began on the death of Charles the Second: but we soon departed from them, as I shall have occasion to observe in considering the state of things, at this remarkable conjuncture, in a view of strength.

Let me recall here what I have said somewhere else. They who are in the sinking scale of the balance of power do not easily, nor soon, come off from the habitual prejudices of superiority over their neighbors, nor from the confidence that such prejudices inspire. From the year one thousand six hundred and sixty-seven, to the end of that century, France had been constantly in arms, and her arms had been successful. She had sustained a war, without any confederates, against the principal powers of Europe confederated against her, and had finished it with advantage on every side, just before the death of the king of Spain. She continued armed after the peace, by sea and land. She increased her forces, whilst other nations reduced theirs; and was ready to defend, or to invade her neighbors whilst, their confederacy being dissolved, they were in no condition to invade her, and in a bad one to defend themselves. Spain and France had now one common cause. The electors of Bavaria and Cologne supported it in Germany: the Duke of Savoy was an ally, the Duke of Mantua a vassal of the two crowns in Italy. In a word, appearances were formidable on that side: and if a distrust of strength, on the side of the confederacy, had induced England and Holland to compound with France for a partition of the Spanish succession, there seemed to be still greater reason for this distrust after the acceptation of the will, the peaceable and ready submission of the entire monarchy of Spain to Philip, and all the measures taken to secure him in this possession. Such appearances might well impose. They did so on many, and on none more than on the French themselves, who engaged with great confidence and spirit in the war; when they found it, as they might well expect it would be, unavoidable. The strength of France however, though great, was not so great as the French thought it, nor equal to the efforts they undertook to make. Their engagement, to maintain the Spanish monarchy entire under the dominion of Philip, exceeded their strength. Our engagement, to procure some outskirts of it for the house of Austria, was not in the same disproportion to our strength. If I speak positively on this occasion, yet I cannot be accused of presumption; because, how disputable soever these points might be when they were points of political speculation, they are such no longer, and the judgment I make is dictated to me by experience. France threw herself into the sinking scale, when she accepted the will. Her scale continued to sink during the whole course of the war, and might have been kept by the peace as low as the true interest of Europe required. What I remember to have heard the Duke of Marlborough say, before he went to take on him the command of the army in the Low Countries in one thousand seven hundred and two, proved true. The French misreckoned very much, if they made the same comparison between their troops and those of the enemies, as they had made in precedent wars. Those that had been opposed to them, in the last, were raw for the most part when it began, the British particularly: but they had been disciplined, if I may say so, by their defeats. They were grown to be veteran at the peace of Ryswic, and though many had been disbanded, yet they had been disbanded lately: so that even these were easily formed anew, and the spirit that had been raised continued in all. Supplies of men to recruit the armies were more abundant on the side of the confederacy, than on that of the two crowns: a necessary consequence of which it seemed to be, that those of the former would grow better, and those of the latter worse, in a long, extensive, and bloody war. I believe it proved so; and if my memory does not deceive me, the French were forced very early to send recruits to their armies, as they send slaves to their galleys. A comparison between those who were to direct the councils, and to conduct the armies on both sides, is a task it would become me little to undertake. The event showed, that if France had had her Condé, her Turenne, or her Luxemburg, to oppose to the confederates; the confederates might have opposed to her, with equal confidence, their Eugene of Savoy, their Marlborough, or their Starenberg. But there is one observation I cannot forbear to make. The alliances were concluded, the quotas were settled, and the season for taking the field approached, when king William died. The event could not fail to occasion some consternation on one side, and to give some hopes on the other; for, notwithstanding the ill success with which he made war generally, he was looked upon as the sole centre of union that could keep together the great confederacy then forming: and how much the French feared, from his life, had appeared a few years before, in the extravagant and indecent joy they expressed on a false report of his death. A short time showed how vain the fears of some, and the hopes of others were. By his death, the Duke of Marlborough was raised to the head of the army, and indeed of the confederacy: where he, a new, a private man, a subject, acquired by merit and by management a more deciding influence, than high birth, confirmed authority, and even the crown of Great Britain, had given to king William. Not only all the parts of that vast machine, the grand alliance, were kept more compact and entire; but a more rapid and vigorous motion was given to the whole: and, instead of languishing or disastrous campaigns, we saw every scene of the war full of action. All those wherein he appeared, and many of those wherein he was not then an actor, but abettor however of their action, were crowned with the most triumphant success. I take with pleasure this opportunity of doing justice to that great man, whose faults I knew, whose virtues I admired; and whose memory, as the greatest general and as the greatest minister that our country or perhaps any other has produced, I honor. But besides this, the observation I have made comes into my subject, since it serves to point out to your lordship the proof of what I said above, that France undertook too much, when she undertook to maintain the Spanish monarchy entire in the possession of Philip: and that we undertook no more than what was proportionable to our strength, when we undertook to weaken that monarchy by dismembering it, in the hands of a prince of the house of Bourbon, which we had been disabled by ill fortune and worse conduct to keep out of them. It may be said that the great success of the confederates against France proves that their generals were superior to hers, but not that their forces and their national strength were so; that with the same force with which she was beaten, she might have been victorious; that if she had been so, or if the success of the war had varied, or been less decisive against her in Germany, in the Low Countries, and in Italy, as it was in Spain, her strength would have appeared sufficient, and that of the confederacy insufficient. Many things may be urged to destroy this reasoning: I content myself with one. France could not long have made even the unsuccessful efforts she did make, if England and Holland had done what it is undeniable they had strength to do; if besides pillaging, I do not say conquering, the Spanish West Indies, they had hindered the French from going to the South Sea; as they did annually during the whole course of the war without the least molestation, and from whence they imported into France in that time as much silver and gold as the whole species of that kingdom amounted to. With this immense and constant supply of wealth France was reduced in effect to bankruptcy before the end of the war. How much sooner must she have been so, if this supply had been kept from her? The confession of France herself is on my side. She confessed her inability to support what she had undertaken, when she sued for peace as early as the year one thousand seven hundred and six. She made her utmost efforts to answer the expectation of the Spaniards, and to keep their monarchy entire. When experience had made it evident that this was beyond her power, she thought herself justified to the Spanish nation, in consenting to a partition, and was ready to conclude a peace with the allies on the principles of their grand alliance. But as France seemed to flatter herself, till experience made her desirous to abandon an enterprise that exceeded her strength; you will find, my lord, that her enemies began to flatter themselves in their turn, and to form designs and take engagements that exceeded theirs. Great Britain was drawn into these engagements little by little; for I do not remember any parliamentary declaration for continuing the war till Philip should be dethroned, before the year one thousand seven hundred and six: and then such a declaration was judged necessary to second the resolution of our ministers and our allies, in departing from the principle of the grand alliance, and in proposing not only the reduction of the French, but the conquest of the Spanish monarchy, as the objects of the war. This new plan had taken place, and we had begun to act upon it, two years before, when the treaty with Portugal was concluded, and the archduke Charles, now emperor, was sent into Portugal first, and into Catalonia afterwards, and was acknowledged and supported as king of Spain.

When your lordship peruses the anecdotes of the times here spoken of, and considers the course and event of the great war which broke out on the death of the king of Spain, Charles the Second, and was ended by the treaties of Utrecht and Radstat; you will find, that in order to form a true judgment on the whole, you must consider very attentively the great change made by the new plan that I have mentioned; and compare it with the plan of the grand alliance, relatively to the general interest of Europe, and the particular interest of your own country. It will not, because it cannot, be denied, that all the ends of the grand alliance might have been obtained by a peace in one thousand seven hundred and six. I need not recall the events of that, and the precedent years of the war. Not only the arms of France had been defeated on every side, but the inward state of that kingdom was already more exhausted than it had ever been. She went on indeed, but she staggered and reeled under the burden of the war. Our condition, I speak of Great Britain, was not quite so bad: but the charge of the war increased annually upon us. It was evident that this charge must continue to increase, and it was no less evident that our nation was unable to bear it without falling soon into such distress, and contracting such debts, as we have seen and felt, and still feel. The Dutch neither restrained their trade, nor overloaded it with taxes. They soon altered the proportion of their quotas, and were deficient even after this alteration in them. But, however, it must be allowed, that they exerted their whole strength; and they and we paid the whole charge of the war. Since therefore by such efforts as could not be continued any longer, without oppressing and impoverishing these nations to a degree that no interest except that of their very being, nor any engagement of assisting an alliance *totis viribus* can require, France was reduced, and all the ends of the war were become attainable; it will be worth

your lordship's while to consider, why the true use was not made
of the success of the confederates against France and Spain,
and why a peace was not concluded in the fifth year of the war.
When your lordship considers this, you will compare in your
thoughts what the state of Europe would have been, and that of
your own country might have been, if the plan of the grand
alliance had been pursued; with the possible as well as certain,
the contingent as well as necessary, consequences of changing
this plan in the manner it was changed. You will be of opinion,
I think, and it seems to me, after more than twenty years of recollection, re-examination, and reflection, that impartial posterity
must be of the same opinion; you will be of opinion, I think,
that the war was wise and just before the change, because necessary to maintain that equality among the powers of Europe on
which the public peace and common prosperity depends: and
that it was unwise and unjust after this change, because unnecessary to this end, and directed to other and to contrary ends.
You will be guided by undeniable facts to discover, through all
the false colors which have been laid, and which deceived many
at the time, that the war, after this change, became a war of
passion, of ambition, of avarice, and of private interest; the private interest of particular persons and particular states; to which
the general interest of Europe was sacrificed so entirely, that if
the terms insisted on by the confederates has been granted, nay
if even those which France was reduced to grant, in one thousand seven hundred and ten, had been accepted, such a new
system of power would have been created as might have exposed
the balance of this power to deviations, and the peace of Europe
to troubles, not inferior to those that the war was designed, when
it began, to prevent. Whilst you observe this in general, you
will find particular occasion to lament the fate of Great Britain,
in the midst of triumphs that have been sounded so high. She
had triumphed indeed to the year one thousand seven hundred
and six inclusively: but what were her triumphs afterwards?
What was her success after she proceeded on the new plan? I
shall say something on that head immediately. Here let me
only say, that the glory of taking towns, and winning battles, is
to be measured by the utility that results from those victories.
Victories, that bring honor to the arms, may bring shame to the

councils, of a nation. To win a battle, to take a town, is the glory of a general, and of an army. Of this glory we had a very large share in the course of the war. But the glory of a nation is to proportion the end she proposes, to her interest and her strength; the means she employs, to the ends she proposes, and the vigor she exerts, to both. Of this glory, I apprehend, we have had very little to boast at any time, and particularly in the great conjuncture of which I am speaking. The reasons of ambition, avarice, and private interest, which engaged the princes and states of the confederacy to depart from the principles of the grand alliance, were no reasons for Great Britain. She neither expected nor desired any thing more than what she might have obtained by adhering to those principles. What hurried our nation, then, with so much spirit and ardor, into those of the new plan? Your lordship will answer this question to yourself, I believe, by the prejudices and rashness of party; by the influence that the first successes of the confederate arms gave to our ministers; and the popularity that they gave, if I may say so, to the war; by ancient and fresh resentments, which the unjust and violent usurpations, in short the whole conduct of Louis the Fourteenth for forty years together, his haughty treatment of other princes and states, and even the style of his court, had created; and, to mention no more, by a notion, groundless but prevalent, that he was and would be master as long as his grandson was king of Spain, and that there could be no effectual measure taken, though the grand alliance supposed that there might, to prevent a future union of the two monarchies, as long as a prince of the house of Bourbon sat on the Spanish throne. That such a notion should have prevailed, in the first confusion of thoughts which the death and will of Charles the Second produced, among the generality of men, who saw the fleets and armies of France take possession of all the parts of the Spanish monarchy, is not to be wondered at by those that consider how ill the generality of mankind are informed, how incapable they are of judging, and yet how ready to pronounce judgment; in fine, how inconsiderately they follow one another in any popular opinion which the heads of party broach, or to which the first appearances of things have given occasion. But, even at this time, the councils of England and Holland did not entertain this notion. They acted on quite another, as might be shown in many instances, if any other besides that of the grand alliance was necessary. When these councils therefore seemed to entertain this notion afterwards, and acted and took engagements to act upon it, we must conclude that they had other motives. They could not have these; for they knew, that as the Spaniards had been driven by the two treaties of partition to give their monarchy to a prince of the house of Bourbon, so they were driven into the arms of France by the war that we made to force a third upon them. If we acted rightly on the principles of the grand alliance, they acted rightly on those of the will: and if we could not avoid making an offensive war, at the expense of forming and maintaining a vast confederacy, they could not avoid purchasing the protection and assistance of France in a defensive war, and especially in the beginning of it, according to what I have somewhere observed already, by yielding to the authority and admitting the influence of that court in all the affairs of their government. Our ministers knew therefore, that if any inference was to be drawn from the first part of this notion, it was for shortening, not prolonging, the war; for delivering the Spaniards as soon as possible from habits of union and intimacy with France; not for continuing them under the same necessity, till by length of time these habits should be confirmed. As to the latter part of this notion, they knew that it was false, and silly. Garth, the best natured ingenious wild man I ever knew, might be in the right, when he said, in some of his poems

————An Austrian prince alone
Is fit to nod upon a Spanish throne.

The setting an Austrian prince upon it was, no doubt, the surest expedient to prevent a union of the two monarchies of France and Spain; just as setting a prince of the house of Bourbon on that throne was the surest expedient to prevent a union of the Imperial and Spanish crowns. But it was equally false to say, in either case, that this was the sole expedient. It would be no paradox, but a proposition easily proved, to advance, that if these unions had been effectually provided against, the general interest of Europe would have been little concerned whether

Philip or Charles had nodded at Madrid. It would be likewise
no paradox to say, that the contingency of uniting France and
Spain under the same prince appeared more remote, about the
middle of the last great war, when the dethronement of Philip
in favor of Charles was made a condition of peace *sine qua non*
than the contingency of a union of the Imperial and Spanish
crowns. Nay, I know not whether it would be a paradox to
affirm, that the expedient that was taken, and that was always
obvious to be taken, of excluding Philip and his race from the
succession of France, by creating an interest in all the other
princes of the blood, and by consequence a party in France itself, for their exclusion, whenever the case should happen, was
not in its nature more effectual than any that could have been
taken: and some must have been taken, not only to exclude
Charles from the empire whenever the case should happen that
happened soon, the death of his brother Joseph without issue
male, but his posterity likewise in all future vacancies of the imperial throne. The expedient that was taken against Philip at
the treaty of Utrecht, they who opposed the peace attempted to
ridicule; but some of them have had occasion since that time to
see, though the case has not happened, how effectual it would
have been if it had: and he, who should go about to ridicule it
after our experience, would only make himself ridiculous. Notwithstanding all this, he who transports himself back to that
time, must acknowledge, that the confederated powers in general
could not but be of Garth's mind, and think it more agreeable
to the common interest of Europe, that a branch of Austria, than
a branch of Bourbon, should gather the Spanish succession, and
that the maritime powers, as they are called impertinently enough
with respect to the superiority of Great Britain, might think it
was for their particular interest to have a prince, dependent for
some time at least on them, king of Spain, rather than a prince
whose dependence, as long as he stood in any, must be naturally
on France. I do not say, as some have done, a prince whose
family was an old ally, rather than a prince whose family was
an old enemy; because I lay no weight on the gratitude of
princes, and am as much persuaded that an Austrian king of
Spain would have made us returns of that sort in no other proportion than of his want of us, as I am that Philip and his race

will make no other returns of the same sort to France. If this affair had been entire, therefore, on the death of the king of Spain; if we had made no partition, nor he any will, the whole monarchy of Spain would have been the prize to be fought for: and our wishes, and such efforts as we were able to make, in the most unprovided condition imaginable, must have been on the side of Austria. But it was far from being entire. A prince of the house of Austria might have been on the spot, before the king of Spain died, to gather his succession; but instead of this, a prince of the house of Bourbon was there soon afterwards, and took possession of the whole monarchy, to which he had been called by the late king's will, and by the voice of the Spanish nation. The councils of England and Holland therefore preferred very wisely, by their engagements in the grand alliance, what was more practicable though less eligible, to what they deemed more eligible, but saw become by the course of events, if not absolutely impracticable, yet an enterprise of more length, more difficulty, and greater expense of blood and treasure, than these nations were able to bear; or than they ought to bear, when their security and that of the rest of Europe might be sufficiently provided for at a cheaper rate. If the confederates could not obtain, by the force of their arms, the ends of the war, laid down in the grand alliance, to what purpose would it be to stipulate for more? And if they were able to obtain these, it was evident that, whilst they dismembered the Spanish monarchy, they must reduce the power of France. This happened; the Low Countries were conquered; the French were driven out of Germany and Italy: and Louis the Fourteenth, who had so long and so lately set mankind at defiance, was reduced to sue for peace.

If it had been granted him in one thousand seven hundred and six, on what foot must it have been granted? The allies had already in their power all the states that were to compose the reasonable satisfaction for the emperor. I say, in their power; because though Naples and Sicily were not actually reduced at that time, yet the expulsion of the French out of Italy, and the disposition of the people of these kingdoms, considered, it was plain the allies might reduce them when they pleased. The confederate arms were superior till then in Spain, and several provinces acknowledged Charles the Third. If the rest had been yielded to him by treaty, all that the new plan required had been obtained. If the French would not yet have abandoned Philip, as we had found that the Castilians would not even when our army was at Madrid, all that the old plan, the plan of the grand alliance required, had been obtained; but still France and Spain had given nothing to purchase a peace, and they were in circumstances, not to expect it without purchasing it. They would have purchased it, my lord: and France, as well as Spain, would have contributed a larger share of the price, rather than continue the war, in her exhausted state. Such a treaty of peace would have been a third treaty of partition indeed, but vastly preferable to the two former. The great objection to the former was drawn from that considerable increase of dominion, which the crown of France, and not a branch of the house of Bourbon, acquired by them. I know what may be said speciously enough to persuade, that such an increase of dominion would not have augmented, but would rather have weakened the power of France, and what examples may be drawn from history to countenance such an opinion. I know likewise, that the compact figure of France, and the contiguity of all her provinces, make a very essential part of the force of her monarchy. Had the designs of Charles the Eighth, Louis the Twelfth, Francis the First, and Henry the Second, succeeded, the dominions of France, would have been more extensive, and I believe the strength of her monarchy would have been less. I have sometimes thought that even the loss of the battle of St. Quentin, which obliged Henry the Second to recall the Duke of Guise with his army out of Italy, was in this respect no unhappy event. But the reasoning which is good, I think, when applied to those times, will not hold when applied to ours, and to the case I consider here; the state of France, the state of her neighbors, and the whole constitution of Europe being so extremely different. The objection therefore to the two treaties of partition had a real weight. The power of France, deemed already exorbitant, would have been increased by this accession of dominion in the hands of Louis the Fourteenth: and the use he intended to make of it, by keeping Italy and Spain in awe, appears in the article that gave him the ports on the Tuscan coast, and the province of Guipuscoa. This king William might, and, I question not, did

LETTER 8

see; but that prince might think too, that for this very reason
Louis the Fourteenth would adhere, in all events, to the treaty
of partition: and that these consequences were more remote, and
would be less dangerous, than those of making no partition at
all. The partition, even the worst that might have been made,
by a treaty of peace in one thousand seven hundred and six,
would have been the very reverse of this. France would have
been weakened, and her enemies strengthened, by her concessions on the side of the Low Countries, of Germany and Savoy.
If a prince of her royal family had remained in possession of
Spain and the West Indies, no advantage would have accrued
to her by it, and effectual bars would have been opposed to an
union of the two monarchies. The house of Austria would have
had a reasonable satisfaction for that shadow of right, which a
former partition gave her. She had no other after the will of
Charles the Second: and this may be justly termed a shadow,
since England, Holland, and France could confer no real right
to the Spanish succession, nor to any part of it. She had declined acceding to that partition, before France departed from it,
and would have preferred the Italian provinces, without Spain
and the West Indies, to Spain and the West Indies without the
Italian provinces. The Italian provinces would have fallen to
her share by this partition. The particular demands of England
and Holland would have suffered no difficulty, and those that
we were obliged by treaty to make for others would have been
easy to adjust. Would not this have been enough, my lord, for
the public security, for the common interest, and for the glory of
our arms? To have humbled and reduced, in five campaigns, a
power that had disturbed and insulted Europe almost forty years;
to have restored, in so short a time, the balance of power in
Europe to a sufficient point of equality, after it had been more
than fifty years, that is from the treaty of Westphalia, in a grad-
ual deviation from this point; in short to have retrieved, in one
thousand seven hundred and six, a game that was become desperate at the beginning of the century. To have done all this,
before the war had exhausted our strength, was the utmost sure
that any man could desire who intended the public good alone:
and no honest reason ever was, nor ever will be given, why the
war was protracted any longer; why we neither made peace

113

after a short, vigorous, and successful war, nor put it entirely out of the power of France to continue at any rate a long one. I have said, and it is true, that this had been entirely out of her power, if we had given greater interruption to the commerce of Old and New Spain, and if we had hindered France from importing annually, from the year one thousand seven hundred and two, such immense treasures as she did import by the ships she sent, with the permission of Spain, to the South Sea. It has been advanced, and it is a common opinion, that we were restrained by the jealousy of the Dutch from making use of the liberty given by treaty to them and us, and which, without his imperial majesty's leave, since we entered into the war, we might have taken, of making conquests in the Spanish West Indies. Be it so. But to go to the South Seas, to trade there if we could, to pillage the West Indies without making conquests if we could not, and, whether we traded or whether we pillaged, to hinder the French from trading there; was a measure that would have given, one ought to think, no jealousy to the Dutch, who might, and it is to be supposed would, have taken their part in these expeditions; or if it had given them jealousy, what could they have replied when a British minister had told them, "That it little became them to find fault that we traded with or pillaged the Spaniards in the West Indies to the detriment of our common enemy, whilst we connived at them who traded with this enemy to his and their great advantage, against our remonstrances, and in violation of the condition upon which we had given the first augmentation of our forces in the Low Countries?" We might have pursued this measure notwithstanding any engagement that we took by the treaty with Portugal, if I remember that treaty right: but instead of this, we wasted our forces, and squandered millions after millions in supporting our alliance with this crown, and in pursuing the chimerical project which was made the object of this alliance. I call it chimerical, because it was equally so, to expect a revolution in favor of Charles the Third on the slender authority of such a trifler as the admiral of Castile; and, when this failed us, to hope to conquer Spain by the assistance of the Portuguese, and the revolt of the Catalans. Yet this was the foundation upon which the new plan of the war was built, and so many ruinous engagements were taken.

The particular motives of private men, as well as of princes and states, to protract the war, are partly known, and partly guessed, at this time. But whenever that time comes, and I am persuaded it will come, when their secret motives, their secret designs, and intrigues, can be laid open, I presume to say to your lordship that the most confused scene of iniquity, and folly, that it is possible to imagine, will appear. In the mean while, if your lordship considers only the treaty of barrier, as my lord Townshend signed it, without, nay in truth, against orders; for the Duke of Marlborough, though joint plenipotentiary, did not: if you consider the famous preliminaries of one thousand seven hundred and nine, which we made a mock-show of ratifying, though we knew that they would not be accepted; for so the Marquis of Torcy had told the pensionary before he left the Hague, as the said Marquis has assured me very often since that time: if you inquire into the anecdotes of Gertruydenberg, and if you consult other authenic papers that are extant, your lordship will see the policy of the new plan, I think, in this light. Though we had refused, before the war began, to enter into engagements for the conquest of Spain, yet as soon as it began, when the reason of things was still the same, for the success of our first campaign cannot be said to have altered it, we entered into these very engagements. By the treaty wherein we took these engagements first, Portugal was brought into the grand alliance; that is, she consented to employ her formidable forces against Philip, at the expense of England and Holland, provided we would debar ourselves from making any acquisitions, and the house of Austria promised, that she should acquire many important places in Spain, and an immense extent of country in America. By such bargains as this, the whole confederacy was formed, and held together. Such means were indeed effectual to multiply enemies to France and Spain; but a project so extensive and so difficult as to make many bargains of this kind necessary, and necessary for a great number of years, and for a very uncertain event, was a project into which, for this very reason, England and Holland should not have entered. It is worthy your observation, my lord, that these bad bargains would not have been continued, as they were almost to our immediate ruin, if the war had not been protracted under the pretended necessity of reducing the whole Spanish monarchy to the obedience of the house of Austria. Now, as no other confederate except Portugal was to receive his recompense by any dismemberment of dominions in Old or New Spain, the engagements we took to conquer this whole monarchy had no visible necessary cause, but the procuring the accession of this power, that was already neuter, to the grand alliance. This accession, as I have said before, served only to make us neglect immediate and certain advantages, for remote and uncertain hopes; and choose to attempt the conquest of the Spanish nation at our own vast expense, whom we might have starved, and by starving reduced both the French and them, at their expense.

I called the necessity of reducing the whole Spanish monarchy to the obedience of the house of Austria, a pretended necessity: and pretended it was, not real, without doubt. But I am apt to think your lordship may go further, and find some reasons to suspect, that the opinion itself of this necessity was not very real, in the minds of those who urged it: in the minds I would say of the able men among them; for that it was real in some of our zealous British politicians, I do them the justice to believe. Your lordship may find reasons to suspect perhaps, that this opinion was set up rather to occasion a diversion of the forces of France, and to furnish pretences for prolonging the war for other ends.

Before the year one thousand seven hundred and ten, the war was kept alive with alternate success in Spain; and it may be said, therefore, that the design of conquering this kingdom continued, as well as the hopes of succeeding. But why then did the States General refuse, in one thousand seven hundred and nine, to admit an article in the barrier treaty, by which they would have obliged themselves to procure the whole Spanish monarchy to the house of Austria, when that zealous politician my Lord Townshend pressed them to it? If their opinion of the necessity of carrying on the war, till this point could be obtained, was real; why did they risk the immense advantages given them with so much profuse generosity by this treaty, rather than consent to an engagement that was so conformable to their opinion?

After the year one thousand seven hundred and ten, it will not be said, I presume, that the war could be supported in Spain with any prospect of advantage on our side. We had sufficiently experienced how little dependence could be had on the vigor of the Portuguese; and how firmly the Spanish nation in general, the Castilians in particular, were attached to Philip. Our armies had been twice at Madrid, this prince had been twice driven from his capital, his rival had been there, none stirred in favor of the victorious, all wished and acted for the vanquished. In short, the falsehood of all those lures, by which we had been enticed to make war in Spain, had appeared sufficiently in one thousand seven hundred and six; but was so grossly evident in one thousand seven hundred and ten, that Mr. Craggs, who was sent towards the end of that year by Mr. Stanhope into England, on commissions which he executed with much good sense and much address, owned to me, that in Mr. Stanhope's opinion, and he was not apt to despond of success, especially in the execution of his own projects, nothing could be done more in Spain, the general attachment of the people to Philip, and their aversion to Charles considered: that armies of twenty or thirty thousand men might walk about that country till dooms day, so he expressed himself, without effect: that wherever they came, the people would submit to Charles the Third out of terror, and as soon as they were gone, proclaim Philip the Fifth again out of affection: that to conquer Spain required a great army; and to keep it, a greater.

Was it possible, after this, to think in good earnest of conquering Spain, and could they be in good earnest who continued to hold the same language, and to insist on the same measures? Could they be so in the following year, when the emperor Joseph died? Charles was become then the sole surviving male of the house of Austria, and succeeded to the empire as well as to all the hereditary dominions of that family. Could they be in earnest who maintained, even in this conjuncture, that "no peace could be safe, honorable, or lasting, so long as the kingdom of Spain and the West Indies remained in the possession of any branch of the house of Bourbon?" Did they mean that Charles should be emperor and king of Spain? In this project they would have had the allies against them. Did they mean to call the Duke of Savoy to the crown of Spain, or to bestow it on some other prince? In this project they would have had his imperial majesty against them. In either case the confederacy would have been broken: and how then would they have continued the war? Did they mean nothing, or did they mean something more than they owned, something more than to reduce the exorbitant power of France, and to force the whole Spanish monarchy out of the house of Bourbon?

Both these ends might have been obtained at Gertruydenberg. Why were they not obtained? Read the preliminaries of one thousand seven hundred and nine, which were made the foundation of this treaty. Inform yourself of what passed there, and observe what followed. Your lordship will remain astonished. I remain so every time I reflect upon them, though I saw these things at no very great distance, even whilst they were in transaction; and though I know most certainly that France lost, two years before, by the little skill and address of her principal minister[1], in answering overtures made during the siege of Lisle by a principal person among the allies, such an opportunity, and such a correspondence, as would have removed some of the obstacles that lay now in her way, have prevented others, and have procured her peace. An equivalent for the thirty-seventh article of the preliminaries, that is, for the cession of Spain and the West Indies, was the point to be discussed at Gertruydenberg. Naples and Sicily, or even Naples and Sardinia would have contented the French, at least they would have accepted them as the equivalent. Buys and Vanderdussen, who treated with them, reported this to the ministers of the allies: and it was upon this occasion that the Duke of Marlborough, as Buys himself told me, took immediately the lead, and congratulated the assembly on the near approach of a peace; said, that since the French were in this disposition, it was time to consider what further demands should be made upon them, according to the liberty reserved in the preliminaries; and exhorted all the ministers of the allies to adjust their several ulterior pretensions, and to prepare their demands.

This proceeding, and what followed, put me in mind of that of the Romans with the Carthaginians. The former were resolved to consent to no peace till Carthage was laid in ruins.

1. Chamillard.

They set a treaty however on foot, at the request of their old enemy, imposed some terms, and referred them to their generals for the rest. Their generals pursued the same method, and, by reserving still a right of making ulterior demands, they reduced the Carthaginians at last to the necessity of abandoning their city, or of continuing the war after they had given up their arms, their machines, and their fleet, in hopes of peace.

France saw the snare, and resolved to run any risk rather than to be caught in it. We continued to demand, under pretence of securing the cession of Spain and the West Indies, that Louis the Fourteenth should take on him to dethrone his grandson in the space of two months; and if he did not effect it in that time, that we should be at liberty to renew the war without restoring the places that were to be put into our hands according to the preliminaries; which were the most important places France possessed on the side of the Low Countries. Louis offered to abandon his grandson; and, if he could not prevail on him to resign, to furnish money to the allies, who might at the expense of France force him to evacuate Spain. The proposition made by the allies had an air of inhumanity: and the rest of mankind might be shocked to see the grandfather obliged to make war on his grandson. But Louis the Fourteenth had treated mankind with too much inhumanity in his prosperous days, to have any reason to complain even of this proposition. His people, indeed, who are apt to have great partiality for their kings, might pity his distress. This happened, and he found his account in it. Philip must have evacuated Spain, I think, notwithstanding his own obstinacy, the spirit of his queen, and the resolute attachment of the Spaniards, if his grandfather had insisted, and been in earnest to force him. But if this expedient was, as it was, odious, why did we prefer to continue the war against France and Spain, rather than accept the other? why did we neglect the opportunity of reducing, effectually and immediately, the exorbitant power of France, and of rendering the conquest of Spain practicable? both which might have been brought about, and consequently the avowed ends of the war might have been answered, by accepting the expedient that France offered. "France," it was said, "was not sincere: she meant nothing more than to amuse, and divide." This reason was given at the time; but some of those who gave it then, I have seen ashamed to insist on it since. France was not in a condition to act the part she had acted in former treaties: and her distress was no bad pledge of her sincerity on this occasion. But there was a better still. The strong places that she must have put into the hands of the allies, would have exposed her, on the least breach of faith, to see, not her frontier alone, but even the provinces that lie behind it, desolated: and prince Eugene might have had the satisfaction, it is said, I know not how truly, he desired, of marching with the torch in his hand to Versailles.

Your lordship will observe, that the conferences at Gertruydenberg ending in the manner they did, the inflexibility of the allies gave new life and spirit to the French and Spanish nations, distressed and exhausted as they were. The troops of the former withdrawn out of Spain, and the Spaniards left to defend themselves as they could, the Spaniards alone obliged us to retreat from Madrid, and defeated us in our retreat. But your lordship may think perhaps, as I do, that if Louis the Fourteenth had bound himself by a solemn treaty to abandon his grandson, had paid a subsidy to dethrone him, and had consented to acknowledge another king of Spain, the Spaniards would not have exerted the same zeal for Philip; the actions of Almenara and Saragossa might have been decisive, and those of Brihuega and Villa Viciosa would not have happened. After all these events, how could any reasonable man expect that a war should be supported with advantage in Spain, to which the court of Vienna had contributed nothing from the first, scarce bread to their archduke; which Portugal waged faintly and with deficient quotas; and which the Dutch had in a manner renounced, by neglecting to recruit their forces? How was Charles to be placed on the Spanish throne, or Philip at least to be driven out of it? By the success of the confederate arms in other parts. But what success, sufficient to this purpose, could we expect? This question may be answered best, by showing what success we had.

Portugal and Savoy did nothing before the death of the emperor Joseph; and declared in form, as soon as he was dead, that they would carry on the war no longer to set the crown of Spain on the head of Charles, since this would be to fight against the very principle they had fought for. The Rhine was a scene of inaction. The sole efforts, that were to bring about the great event of dethroning Philip, were those which the Duke of Marlborough was able to make. He took three towns in one thousand seven hundred and ten, Aire, Methune, and St. Venant: and one, Bouchain, in one thousand seven hundred and eleven. Now this conquest being in fact the only one the confederates made that year, Bouchain may be said properly and truly to have cost our nation very near seven millions sterling: for your lordship will find, I believe, that the charge of the war for that year amounted to no less. It is true that the Duke of Marlborough had proposed a very great project, by which incursions would have been made during the winter into France; the next campaign might have been opened early on our side; and several other great and obvious advantages might have been obtained: but the Dutch refused to contribute, even less than their proportion, for the queen had offered to take the deficiency on herself, to the expense of barracks and forage; and disappointed by their obstinacy the whole design.

We were then amused with visionary schemes of marching our whole army, in a year or two more, and after a town or two more were taken, directly to Paris, or at least in the heart of France. But was this so easy or so sure a game? The French expected we would play it. Their generals had visited the several posts they might take, when our army should enter France, to retard, to incommode, to distress us in our march, and even to make a decisive stand and to give us battle. I take what I say here from indisputable authority, that of the persons consulted and employed in preparing for this great distress. Had we been beaten, or had we been forced to retire towards our own frontier in the Low Countries, after penetrating into France, the hopes on which we protracted the war would have been disappointed, and, I think, the most sanguine, would have then repented refusing the offers made at Gertruydenberg. But if we had beaten the French, for it was scarcely lawful in those days of our presumption to suppose the contrary; would the whole monarchy of Spain have been our immediate and certain prize? Suppose, and I suppose it on good grounds, my lord, that the French had resolved to defend their country inch by inch, and that Louis the Fourteenth had determined to retire with his court to Lyons or elsewhere, and to defend the passage of the Loire, when he could no longer defend that of the Seine, rather than submit to the terms imposed on him: what should we have done in this case? Must we not have accepted such a peace as we had refused; or have protracted the war till we had conquered France first, in order to conquer Spain afterwards? Did we hope for revolutions in France? We had hoped for them in Spain: and we should have been bubbles of our hopes in both. That there was a spirit raised against the government of Louis the Fourteenth, in his court, nay, in his family, and that strange schemes of private ambition were formed and forming there, I cannot doubt: and some effects of this spirit produced perhaps the greatest mortifications that he suffered in the latter part of his reign.

A light instance of this spirit is all I will quote at this time. I supped, in the year one thousand seven hundred and fifteen, at a house in France, where two persons,[2] of no small figure, who had been in great company that night, arrived very late. The conversation turned on the events of the precedent war, and the negotiations of the late peace. In the process of the conversation one of them[3] broke loose, and said, directing his discourse to me, "Vous auriez pu nous écraser dans ce tems-là: pourquoi ne l'avez-vous pas fait?" I answered him coolly, "Par ce que dans ce tems-là nous n'avons plus craint vôtre puissance." This anecdote, too trivial for history, may find its place in a letter, and may serve to confirm what I have admitted, that there were persons even in France, who expected to find their private account in the distress of their country. But these persons were a few men of wild imaginations and strong passions, more enterprising than capable, and of more name than credit. In general the endeavors of Louis the Fourteenth, and the sacrifices he offered to make in order to obtain a peace, had attached his people more than ever to him: and if Louis had determined not to go any farther than he had offered at Gertruydenberg, in abandoning his grandson, the French nation would not have abandoned him.

But to resume what I have said or hinted already; the neces-

2. The Dukes de La Feuillade and Mortemar.
3. La Feuillade.

sary consequences of protracting the war in order to dethrone
Philip, from the year one thousand seven hundred and eleven
inclusively, could be no other than these: our design of penetrating into France might have been defeated, and have become
fatal to us by a reverse of fortune: our first success might not
have obliged the French to submit; and we might have had
France to conquer, after we had failed in our first attempt to
conquer Spain, and even in order to proceed to a second: the
French might have submitted, and the Spaniards not: and whilst
the former had been employed to force the latter, according to
the scheme of the allies; or whilst, the latter submitting likewise,
Philip had evacuated Spain, the high allies might have gone together by the ears about dividing the spoil, and disposing of the
crown of Spain. To these issues were things brought by protracting the war; by refusing to make peace, on the principles
of the grand alliance at worst, in one thousand seven hundred
and six; and by refusing to grant it, even on those of the new
plan, in one thousand seven hundred and ten. Such contingent
events as I have mentioned stood in prospect before us. The
end of the war was removed out of sight; and they, who clamored
rather than argued for the continuation of it, contented themselves to affirm, that France was not enough reduced, and that
no peace ought to be made as long as a prince of the house of
Bourbon remained on a Spanish throne. When they would
think France enough reduced, it was impossible to guess.
Whether they intended to join the Imperial and Spanish crowns
on the head of Charles, who had declared his irrevocable resolution to continue the war till the conditions insisted upon at Gertruydenberg were obtained: whether they intended to bestow
Spain and the Indies on some other prince; and how this great
alteration in their own plan should be effected by common consent: how possession should be given to Charles, or any other
prince, not only of Spain but of all Spanish dominions out of
Europe, where the attachment to Philip was at least as strong
as in Castile, and where it would not be so easy, the distance
and extent of these dominions considered, to oblige the Spaniards
to submit to another government: These points, and many more
equally necessary to be determined, and equally difficult to prepare, were neither determined nor prepared; so that we were

reduced to carry on the war, after the death of the emperor Joseph, without any positive scheme agreed to, as the scheme of the future peace, by the allies. That of the grand alliance we had long before renounced. That of the new plan was become ineligible; and, if it had been eligible, it would have been impracticable, because of the division it would have created among the allies themselves: several of whom would not have consented, notwithstanding his irrevocable resolution, that the emperor should be king of Spain. I know not what part the protracters of the war, in the depth of their policy, intended to take. Our nation had contributed, and acted so long under the direction of their councils, for the grandeur of the house of Austria, like one of the hereditary kingdoms usurped by that family, that it is lawful to think their intention might be to unite the Imperial and Spanish crowns. But I rather think they had no very determinate view, beyond that of continuing the war as long as they could. The late Lord Oxford told me, that my Lord Somers being pressed, I know not on what occasion nor by whom, on the unnecessary and ruinous continuation of the war; instead of giving reasons to show the necessity of it, contented himself to reply, that he had been bred up in a hatred of France. This was a strange reply for a wise man: and yet I know not whether he could have given a better then, on whether any of his pupils could give a better now.

The whig party in general acquired great and just popularity, in the reign of our Charles the Second, by the clamor they raised against the conduct of that prince in foreign affairs. They who succeeded to the name rather than the principles of this party, after the revolution, and who have had the administration of the government in their hands with very little interruption ever since, pretending to act on the same principle, have run into an extreme as vicious and as contrary to all the rules of good policy, as that which their predecessors exclaimed against. The old whigs complained of the inglorious figure we made, whilst our court was the bubble, and our king the pensioner of France; and insisted that the growing ambition and power of Louis the Fourteenth should be opposed in time. The modern whigs boasted, and still boast, of the glorious figure we made, whilst we reduced ourselves, by their councils, and under their administrations, to be the bubbles of our pensioners, that is, of our allies: and whilst we measured our efforts in war, and the continuation of them, without any regard to the interests and abilities of our own country, without a just and sober regard, such an one as contemplates objects in their true light and sees them in their true magnitude, to the general system of power in Europe; and, in short, with a principal regard merely to particular interests at home and abroad. I say at home and abroad: because it is not less true, that they have sacrificed the wealth of their country to the forming and maintaining a party at home, than that they have done so to the forming and maintaining, beyond all pretences of necessity, alliances abroad. These general assertions may be easily justified without having recourse to private anecdotes, as your lordship will find when you consider the whole series of our conduct in the two wars; in that which preceded, and that which succeeded immediately the beginning of the present century, but above all in the last of them. In the administrations that preceded the revolution, trade had flourished, and our nation had grown opulent: but the general interest of Europe had been too much neglected by us; and slavery, under the umbrage of prerogative, had been well-nigh established among us. In those that have followed, taxes upon taxes, and debts upon debts, have been perpetually accumulated, till a small number of families have grown into immense wealth, and national beggary has been brought upon us; under the specious pretence of supporting a common cause against France, reducing her exorbitant power, and poising that of Europe more equally in the public balance: laudable designs no doubt, as far as they were real, but such as, being converted into mere pretences, have been productive of much evil; some of which we feel and have long felt, and some will extend its consequences to our latest posterity. The reign of prerogative was short: and the evils and the dangers, to which we were exposed by it, ended with it. But the reign of false and squandering policy has lasted long, it lasts still, and will finally complete our ruin. Beggary has been the consequence of slavery in some countries: slavery will be probably the consequence of beggary in ours; and if it is so, we know at whose door to lay it. If we had finished the war in one thousand seven hundred and six, we should have reconciled, like a wise people, our foreign and our domestic interests as nearly as possible: we should have secured the former sufficiently, and not have sacrificed the latter as entirely as we did by the prosecution of the war afterwards. You will not be able to see without astonishment, how the charge of the war increased yearly upon us from the beginning of it; nor how immense a sum we paid in the course of it to supply the deficiencies of our confederates. Your astonishment, and indignation too, will increase when you come to compare the progress that was made from the year one thousand seven hundred and six exclusively, with the expense of more than thirty millions, I do not exaggerate though I write upon memory, that this progress cost us to the year one thousand seven hundred and eleven inclusively. Upon this view your lordship will be persuaded that it was high time to take the resolution of making peace, when the queen thought fit to change her ministry towards the end of the year one thousand seven hundred and ten. It was high time indeed to save our country from absolute insolvency and bankruptcy, by putting an end to a scheme of conduct, which the prejudices of a party, the whimsy of some particular men, the private interest of more, and the ambition and avarice of our allies, who had been invited as it were to a scramble by the preliminaries of one thousand seven hundred and nine, alone maintained. The persons, therefore, who came into power at this time, hearkened, and they did well to hearken, to the first overtures that were made them. The disposition of their enemies invited them to do so, but that of their friends, and that of a party at home who had nursed, and been nursed by the war, might have deterred them from it; for the difficulties and dangers to which they must be exposed in carrying forward this great work, could escape none of them. In a letter to a friend, it may be allowed me to say, that they did not escape me: and that I foresaw, as contingent but not improbable events, a good part of what has happened to me since. Though it was a duty, therefore, that we owed to our country, to deliver her from the necessity of bearing any longer so unequal a part in so unnecessary a war, yet was there some degree of merit in performing it. I think so strongly in this manner, I am so incorrigible, my lord, that if I could be placed in the same circumstances again, I would take the same resolution, and act the same part. Age and experience might enable me to act with more ability, and greater skill; but all I have suffered since the death of the queen should not hinder me from acting. Notwithstanding this, I shall not be surprised if you think that the peace of Utrecht was not answerable to the success of the war, nor to the efforts made in it. I think so myself, and have always owned, even when it was making and made, that I thought so. Since we had committed a successful folly, we ought to have reaped more advantage from it than we did: and, whether we had left Philip, or placed another prince on the throne of Spain, we ought to have reduced the power of France, and to have strengthened her neighbors much more than we did. We ought to have reduced her power for generations to come, and not to have contented ourselves with a momentary reduction of it. France was exhausted to a great degree of men and money, and her government had no credit: but they, who took this for a sufficient reduction of her power, looked but a little way before them, and reasoned too superficially. Several such there were however; for as it has been said, that there is no extravagancy which some philosopher or other has not maintained, so your experience, young as you are, must have shown you, that there is no absurd extreme, into which our party politicians of Great Britain are not prone to fall, concerning the state and conduct of public affairs. But if France was exhausted, so were we, and so were the Dutch. Famine rendered her condition much more miserable than ours, at one time, in appearance and in reality too. But as soon as this accident, that had distressed the French and frightened Louis the Fourteenth to the utmost degree, and the immediate consequences of it were over; it was obvious to observe, though few made the observation, that whilst we were unable to raise in a year, by some millions at least, the expenses of the year, the French were willing and able to bear the imposition of the tenth, over and above all the other taxes that had been laid upon them. This observation had the weight it deserved; and surely it deserved to have some among those who made it, at the time spoken of, and who did not think that the war was to be continued as long as a parliament could be prevailed on to vote money. But supposing it to have deserved none, supposing the power of France to have been reduced as low as you please, with respect to her inward state, yet still I affirm, that such a reduction could not be permanent, and was not therefore sufficient. Whoever knows the nature of her government, the temper of her people, and the natural advantages she has in commerce over all the nations that surround her, knows that an arbitrary government, and the temper of her people enable her on particular occasions to throw off a load of debt much more easily, and with consequences much less to be feared, than any of her neighbors can: that although in the general course of things, trade be cramped and industry vexed by this arbitrary government, yet neither one nor the other is oppressed; and the temper of the people, and the natural advantages of the country, are such, that how great soever her distress be at any point of time, twenty years of tranquillity suffice to re-establish her affairs, and to enrich her again at the expense of all the nations of Europe. If any one doubts of this, let him consider the condition in which this kingdom was left by Louis the Fourteenth: the strange pranks the late Duke of Orleans played, during his regency and administration, with the system of public revenue, and private property: and then let him tell himself that the revenues of France, the tenth taken off, exceed all the expenses of her government by many millions of livres already, and will exceed them by many more in another year.

Upon the whole matter, my lord, the low and exhausted state to which France was reduced, by the last great war, was but a momentary reduction of her power; and whatever real and more lasting reduction the treaty of Utrecht brought about in some instances, it was not sufficient. The power of France would not have appeared as great as it did, when England and Holland armed themselves and armed all Germany against her, if she had lain as open to the invasions of her enemies, as her enemies lay to hers. Her inward strength was great; but the strength of those frontiers which Louis the Fourteenth was almost forty years in forming, and which the folly of all his neighbors in their turns suffered him to form, made this strength as formidable as it became. The true reduction of the exorbitant power of France, I take no notice of chimerical projects about changing her government, consisted therefore in disarming her frontiers, and fortifying the barriers against her, by the cession and demolition of many more places than she yielded up at Utrecht; but not of more than she might have been obliged to sacrifice to her own immediate relief, and to the future security of her neighbors. That she was not obliged to make these sacrifices, I affirm, was owing solely to those who opposed the peace: and I am willing to put my whole credit with your lordship, and the whole merits of a cause that has been so much contested, on this issue. I say a cause that has been so much contested; for in truth, I think, it is no longer a doubt any where, except in British pamphlets, whether the conduct of those who neither declined treating, as was done in one thousand seven hundred and six; nor pretended to treat without a design of concluding, as was done in one thousand seven hundred and nine and ten, but carried the great work of the peace forward to its consummation; or the conduct of those who opposed this work in every step of its progress, saved the power of France from a greater and a sufficient reduction at the treaty of Utrecht. The very ministers who were employed in this fatal opposition, are obliged to confess this truth. How should they deny it? Those of Vienna may complain that the emperor had not the entire Spanish monarchy, or those of Holland that the States were not made masters directly and indirectly of the whole Low Countries. But neither they, nor any one else that has any sense of shame about him, can deny that the late queen, though she was resolved to treat because she was resolved to finish the war, yet was to the utmost degree desirous to treat in a perfect union with her allies, and to procure them all the reasonable terms they could expect; and much better than those they reduced themselves to the necessity of accepting, by endeavoring to wrest the negotiation out of her hands. The disunion of the allies gave France the advantages she improved. The sole question is, Who caused this disunion? and that will be easily decided by every impartial man, who informs himself carefully of the public anecdotes of that time. If the private anecdotes were to be laid open as well as those, and I think it almost time they should, the whole monstrous scene would appear, and shock the eye of every honest man. I do not intend to descend into many particulars at this time: but whatever I, or any other person as well informed as I, shall descend into a full deduction of such particulars, it will become undeniably evident, that the most violent opposition imaginable, carried on by the Germans and the Dutch in league with a party in Britain, began as soon as the first overtures were made to the queen; before she had so much as begun to treat: and was therefore an opposition not to this or that plan of treaty, but in truth to all treaty; and especially to one wherein Great Britain took the lead, or was to have any particular advantage. That the Imperialists meant no treaty, unless a preliminary and impracticable condition of it was to set the crown of Spain on the emperor's head, will appear from this; that prince Eugene, when he came into England, long after the death of Joseph and elevation of Charles, upon an errand most unworthy of so great a man, treated always on this supposition: and I remember with how much inward impatience I assisted at conferences held with him concerning quotas for renewing the war in Spain, in the very same room, at the Cockpit, where the queen's ministers had been told in plain terms, a little before, by those of other allies, "that their masters would not consent that the Imperial and Spanish crowns should unite on the same head." That the Dutch were not averse to all treaty, but meant none wherein Great Britain was to have any particular advantage, will appear from this; that their minister declared himself ready and authorised to stop the opposition made to the queen's measures, by presenting a memorial, wherein he would declare, "that his masters entered into them, and were resolved not to continue the war for the recovery of Spain, provided the queen would consent that they should garrison Gibraltar and Port Mahon jointly with us, and share equally the Assiento, the South Sea ship, and whatever should be granted by the Spaniards to the queen and her subjects." That the whigs engaged in this league with foreign powers against their country, as well as their queen, and with a phrensy more unaccountable than that which made and maintained the solemn league and covenant formerly, will appear from this; that their attempts were directed not only to wrest the negotiations out of the queen's hands, but to oblige their country to carry on the war, on the same unequal foot that had cost her already about twenty millions more than she ought to have contributed to it. For they not only continued to abet the emperor, whose inability to supply his quota was confessed; but the Dutch likewise, after the States had refused to ratify the treaty their minister signed at London towards the end of the year one thousand seven hundred and eleven, and by which the queen united herself more closely than ever to them; engaging to pursue the war, to conclude the peace, and to guaranty it, when concluded, jointly with them; "provided they would keep the engagements they had taken with her, and the conditions of proportionate expense under which our nation had entered into the war." Upon such schemes as these was the opposition to the treaty of Utrecht carried on: and the means employed, and the means projected to be employed, were worthy of such schemes; open, direct, and indecent defiance of legal authority, secret conspiracies against the state, and base machinations against particular men, who had no other crime than that of endeavoring to conclude a war, under the authority of the queen, which a party in the nation endeavored to prolong against her authority. Had the good policy of concluding the war been doubtful, it was certainly as lawful for those, who thought it good, to advise it, as it had been for those who thought it bad, to advise the contrary: and the decision of the sovereign on the throne ought to have terminated the contest. But he who had judged by the appearances of things on one side, at that time, would have been apt to think, that putting an end to the war, or to Magna Charta, was the same thing; that the queen on the throne had no right to govern independently of her successor; nor any of her subjects a right to administer the government under her, though called to it by her, except those whom she had thought fit to lay aside. Extravagant as these principles are, no other could justify the conduct held at that time by those who opposed the peace: and as I said just now, that the phrensy of this league was more unaccountable than that of the solemn league and covenant, I might have added, that it was not very many degrees less criminal. Some of these, who charged the queen's ministers, after her death, with imaginary treasons, had been guilty during her life of real treasons: and I can compare the folly and violence of the spirit that prevailed at that time, both before the conclusion of the peace, and, under pretence of danger to the succession, after it, to nothing more nearly than to the folly and violence of the spirit that seized the tories soon after the accession of George the First. The latter indeed, which was provoked by unjust and impolitic persecution, broke out in open rebellion. The former might have done so, if the queen had lived a little longer. But to return.

The obstinate adherence of the Dutch to this league, in opposition to the queen, rendered the conferences of Utrecht, when they were opened, no better than mock conferences. Had the men who governed that commonwealth been wise and honest enough to unite, at least then, cordially with the queen, and, since they could not hinder a congress, to act in concert with her in it; we should have been still in time to maintain a sufficient union among the allies, and a sufficient superiority over the French. All the specific demands that the former made, as well as the Dutch themselves, either to incumber the negotiation, or to have in reserve, according to the artifice usually employed on such occasions, certain points from which to depart in the course of it with advantage, would not have been obtained: but all the essential demands, all in particular that were really necessary to secure the barriers in the Low Countries and of the four circles against France, would have been so. For France must have continued, in this case, rather to sue for peace, than to treat on an equal foot. The first dauphin, son of Louis the Fourteenth, died several months before this congress began: the second dauphin, his grandson, and the wife and the eldest son of this prince, died, soon after it began, of the same unknown distemper, and were buried together in the same grave. Such family misfortunes, following a long series of national misfortunes, made the old king, though he bore them with much seeming magnanimity, desirous to get out of the war at any tolerable rate, that he might not run the risk of leaving a child of five years old, the present king, engaged in it. The queen did all that was morally possible, except giving up her honor in the negotiation, and the interests of her subjects in the conditions of peace, to procure this union with the States General. But all she could do was vain; and the same phrensy that had hindered the Dutch from improving to their and to the common advantage the public misfortunes of France, hindered them from improving to the same purposes the private misfortunes of the house of Bourbon. They

continued to flatter themselves that they should force the queen
out of her measures, by their intrigues with the party in Britain
who opposed these measures, and even raise an insurrection
against her. But these intrigues, and those of prince Eugene,
were known and disappointed; and Monsieur Buys had the mortification to be reproached with them publicly, when he came to
take leave of the lords of the council, by the Earl of Oxford; who
entered into many particulars that could not be denied, of the
private transactions of this sort, to which Buys had been a party,
in compliance with his instructions, and, as I believe, much
against his own sense and inclinations. As the season for taking
the field advanced, the league proposed to defeat the success of
the congress by the events of the campaign. But instead of defeating the success of the congress, the events of the campaign
served only to turn this success in favor of France. At the beginning of the year, the queen, and the States, in concert, might
have given the law to friend and foe, with great advantage to
the former; and with such a detriment to the latter, as the causes
of the war rendered just, the events of it reasonable, and the
objects of it necessary. At the end of the year, the allies were
no longer in a state of giving, nor the French of receiving the
law; and the Dutch had recourse to the queen's good offices,
when they could oppose and durst insult her no longer. Even
then, these offices were employed with zeal, and with some effect,
for them.

Thus the war ended, much more favorably to France than
she expected, or they who put an end to it designed. The queen
would have humbled and weakened this power. The allies
who opposed her would have crushed it, and have raised another
as exorbitant on the ruins of it. Neither one nor the other succeeded, and they who meant to ruin the French power, preserved
it, by opposing those who meant to reduce it.

Since I have mentioned the events of the year one thousand
seven hundred and twelve, and the decisive turn they gave to
the negotiations in favor of France, give me leave to say something more on this subject. You will find that I shall do so with
much impartiality. The disastrous events of this campaign in
the Low Countries, and the consequences of them have been
imputed to the separation of the British troops from the army of

the allies. The clamor against this measure was great at that time, and the prejudices which this clamor raised are great still among some men. But as clamor raised these prejudices, other prejudices gave birth to this clamor: and it is no wonder they should do so among persons bent on continuing the war; since I own very freely, that when the first step that led to this separation came to my knowledge, which was not an hour, by the way, before I wrote by the queen's order to the Duke of Ormond, in the very words in which the order was advised and given, "that he should not engage in any siege, nor hazard a battle, till further order," I was surprised and hurt. So much, that if I had had an opportunity of speaking in private to the queen, after I had received Monsieur De Torcy's letter to me on the subject, and before she went into the council, I should have spoken to her, I think, in the first heat, against it. The truth is, however, that the step was justifiable at that point of time in every respect, and therefore that the consequences are to be charged to the account of those who drew them on themselves, not to the account of the queen, nor of the minister who advised her. The step was justifiable to the allies surely, since the queen took no more upon her, no not so much, by far, in making it, as many of them had done by suspending, or endangering, or defeating operations in the heat of the war, when they declined to send their troops, or delayed the march of them, or neglected the preparations they were obliged to make, on the most frivolous pretences. Your lordship will find in the course of your inquiries many particular instances of what is here pointed out in general. But I cannot help descending into some few of those that regard the emperor and the States General, who cried the loudest and with the most effect, though they had the least reason, on account of their own conduct, to complain of the queen's. With what face could the emperor, for instance, presume to complain of the orders sent to the Duke of Ormond? I say nothing of his deficiencies, which were so great, that he had at this very time little more than one regiment that could be said properly to act against France and Spain at his sole charge; as I affirmed to prince Eugene before the lords of the council, and demonstrated upon paper the next day. I say nothing of all that preceded the year one thousand seven hundred and seven, on which I should have much to say.

But I desire your lordship only to consider, what you will find to have passed after the famous year one thousand seven hundred and six. Was it with the queen's approbation, or against her will, that the emperor made the treaty for the evacuation of Lombardy, and let out so great a number of French regiments time enough to recruit themselves at home, to march into Spain, and to destroy the British forces at Almanza? Was it with her approbation, or against her will, that, instead of employing all his forces and all his endeavors, to make the greatest design of the whole war, the enterprise on Toulon, succeed, he detached twelve thousand men to reduce the kingdom of Naples, that must have fallen of course? and that an opportunity of ruining the whole maritime force of France, and of ruining or subduing her provinces on that side, was lost, merely by this unnecessary diversion, and by the conduct of prince Eugene, which left no room to doubt that he gave occasion to this fatal disappointment on purpose, and in concert with the court of Vienna?

Turn your eyes, my lord, on the conduct of the States, and you will find reason to be astonished at the arrogance of the men who governed in them at this time, and who presumed to exclaim against a queen of Great Britain, for doing what their deputies had done more than once in that very country, and in the course of that very war. In the year one thousand seven hundred and twelve, at the latter end of a war, when conferences for treating a peace were opened, when the least sinister event in the field would take off from that superiority which the allies had in the congress, and when the past success of the war had already given them as much of this superiority as they wanted, to obtain a safe, advantageous, honorable, and lasting peace, the queen directed her general to suspend till further order the operations of her troops. In one thousand seven hundred and three, in the beginning of a war, when something was to be risked or no success to be expected, and when the bad situation of affairs in Germany and Italy required, in a particular manner, that efforts should be made in the Low Countries, and that the war should not languish there whilst it was unsuccessful everywhere else; the Duke of Marlborough determined to attack the French, but the Dutch deputies would not suffer their troops to go on; defeated his design in the very moment of its execution, if I remember well, and gave no other reason for their proceeding than that which is a reason against every battle, the possibility of being beaten. The circumstance of proximity to their frontier was urged, I know, and it was said, that their provinces would be exposed to the incursions of the French if they lost the battle. But besides other answers to this vain pretence, it was obvious that they had ventured battles as near home as this would have been fought, and that the way to remove the enemy farther off was by action, not inaction. Upon the whole matter; the Dutch deputies stopped the progress of the confederate army at this time, by exercising an arbitrary and independent authority over the troops of the States. In one thousand seven hundred and five, when the success of the preceding campaign should have given them an entire confidence in the Duke of Marlborough's conduct, when returning from the Moselle to the Low Countries, he began to make himself and the common cause amends, for the disappointment which pique and jealousy in the Prince of Baden, or usual sloth and negligence in the Germans, had occasioned just before, by forcing the French lines; when he was in the full pursuit of this advantage, and when he was marching to attack an enemy half defeated, and more than half dispirited; nay when he had made his dispositions for attacking, and part of his troops had passed the Dyle—the deputies of the States once more tied up his hands, took from him an opportunity too fair to be lost; for these, I think, were some of the terms of his complaint: and in short the confederacy received an affront at least; where we might have obtained a victory. Let this that has been said serve as a specimen of the independency on the queen, her councils, and her generals, with which these powers acted in the course of the war; who were not ashamed to find fault that the queen, once, and at the latter end of it, presumed to suspend the operations of her troops till farther order. But be it that they foresaw what this farther end would be. They foresaw then, that as soon as Dunkirk should be put into the queen's hands, she would consent to a suspension of arms for two months, and invite them to do the same. Neither this foresight, nor the strong declaration which the Bishop of Bristol made by the queen's order at Utrecht, and which showed them that her resolution was taken not to submit to the league into which they had entered against her, could prevail on them to make a right use of these two months, by endeavoring to renew their union and good understanding with the queen; though I can say with the greatest truth, and they could not doubt of it at the time, that she would have gone more than half-way to meet them, and that her ministers would have done their utmost to bring it about. Even then we might have resumed the superiority we began to lose in the congress; for, the queen and the States uniting, the principal allies would have united with them: and, in this case, it would have been so much the interest of France to avoid any chance of seeing the war renewed, that she must, and she would, have made sure of peace, during the suspension, on much worse terms for herself and for Spain, than she made it afterwards. But the prudent and sober states continued to act like forward children, or like men drunk with resentment and passion; and such will the conduct be of the wisest governments in every circumstance, where a spirit of faction and of private interest prevails, among those who are at the head, over reason of state. After laying aside all decency in their behavior towards the queen, they laid aside all caution for themselves. They declared "they would carry on the war without her." Landrecy seemed, in their esteem, of more importance than Dunkirk; and the opportunity of wasting some French provinces, or of putting the whole event of the war on the decision of another battle, preferable to the other measure that lay open to them; that, I mean, of trying, in good earnest, and in an honest concert with the queen, during the suspension of arms, whether such terms of peace, as sought to satisfy them and the other allies, might not be imposed on France.

If the confederate army had broke into France, the campaign before this, or in any former campaign; and if the Germans and the Dutch had exercised then the same inhumanity, as the French had exercised in their provinces in former wars; if they had burnt Versailles, and even Paris, and if they had disturbed the ashes of the dead princes that repose at St. Denis, every good man would have felt the horror, that such cruelties inspire: no man could have said that the retaliation was unjust. But in one thousand seven hundred and twelve, it was too late, in every respect, to meditate such projects. If the French had been unprepared to defend their frontier, either for want of means, or in a vain confidence that the peace would be made, as our king Charles the Second was unprepared to defend his coast at the latter end of his first war with Holland, the allies might have played a sure game in satisfying their vengeance on the French, as the Dutch did on us in one thousand six hundred and sixty-seven; and imposing harder terms on them, than those they offered, or would have accepted. But this was not the case. The French army was, I believe, more numerous than the army of the allies, even before separation, and certainly in a much better condition than two or three years before, when a deluge of blood was spilt to dislodge them, for we did no more, at Malplaquet. Would the Germans and the Dutch have found it more easy to force them at this time, than it was at that? Would not the French have fought with as much obstinacy to save Paris, as they did to save Mons? and, with all the regard due to the Duke of Ormond, and to prince Eugene, was the absence of the Duke of Marlborough of no consequence? Turn this affair every way in your thoughts, my lord, and you will find that the Germans and the Dutch had nothing in theirs, but to break, at any rate, and at any risk, the negotiations that were begun, and to reduce Great Britain to the necessity of continuing, what she had been too long, a province of the confederacy. A province, indeed, and not one of the best treated; since the confederates assumed a right of obliging her to keep her pacts with them, and of dispensing with their obligations to her; of exhausting her, without rule, or proportion, or measure, in the support of a war, to which she alone contributed more than all of them, and in which she had no longer an immediate interest, nor even any remote interest that was not common, or with respect to her, very dubious; and, after all this, of complaining that the queen presumed to hearken to overtures of peace, and to set a negotiation on foot, whilst their humor and ambition required that the war should be prolonged for an indefinite time, and for a purpose that was either bad or indeterminate.

The suspension of arms, that began in the Low Countries, was continued, and extended afterwards by the act I signed at Fontainebleu. The fortune of the war turned at the same time; and all those disgraces followed, which obliged the Dutch to treat, and to desire the assistance of the queen, whom they had set at defiance so lately. The assistance they had, as effectually as it could be given in the circumstances to which they had reduced themselves, and the whole alliance: and the peace of Great Britain, Portugal, Savoy, Prussia, and the States General, was made, without his Imperial majesty's concurrence, in the spring of one thousand seven hundred and thirteen; as it might have been made, much more advantageously for them all, in that of one thousand seven hundred and twelve. Less obstinacy on the part of the states, and perhaps more decisive resolutions on the part of the queen, would have wound up all these divided threads in one, and have finished this great work much sooner and better. I say, perhaps more decisive resolutions on the part of the queen, because although I think that I should have conveyed her orders for signing a treaty of peace with France, before the armies took the field, much more willingly, than I executed them afterwards in signing that of the cessation of arms; yet I do not presume to decide, but shall desire your lordship to do so, on a review of all circumstances, some of which I shall just mention.

The league made for protracting the war having opposed the queen to the utmost of their power, and by means of every sort, from the first appearance of a negotiation; the general effect of this violent opposition, on her and her ministers, was, to make them proceed by slower and more cautious steps; the particular effect of it was, to oblige them to open the eyes of the nation, and to inflame the people with a desire of peace, by showing, in the most public and solemn manner, how unequally we were burdened, and how unfairly we were treated by our allies. The first gave an air of diffidence and timidity to their conduct, which encouraged the league, and gave vigor to the opposition. The second irritated the Dutch particularly; for the emperor and the other allies had the modesty at least not to pretend to bear any proportion in the expense of the war: and thus the two powers, whose union was the most essential, were the most at variance, and the queen was obliged to act in a closer concert with her enemy who desired peace, than she would have done if her allies had been less obstinately bent to protract the war. During these transactions, my Lord Oxford, who had his correspondences apart, and a private thread of negotiation always in his hands, entertained hopes that Philip would be brought to abandon Spain in favor of his father-in-law, and to content himself with the states of that prince, the kingdom of Sicily, and the preservation of his right of succession to the crown of France. Whether my lord had any particular reasons for entertaining these hopes, beside the general reasons founded on the condition of France, on that of the Bourbon family, and on the disposition of Louis the Fourteenth, I doubt very much. That Louis, who sought, and had need of seeking peace, almost at any rate, and who saw that he could not obtain it, even of the queen, unless Philip abandoned immediately the crown of Spain, or abandoned immediately, by renunciation and a solemn act of exclusion, all pretension to that of France; that Louis was desirous of the former, I cannot doubt. That Philip would have abandoned Spain, with the equivalents that have been mentioned, or either of them, I believe likewise, if the present king of France had died, when his father, mother, and eldest brother did; for they all had the same distemper. But Louis would use no violent means to force his grandson; the queen would not continue the war to force him; Philip was too obstinate, and his wife too ambitious, to quit the crown of Spain, when they had discovered our weakness, and felt their own strength in that country, by their success in the campaign of one thousand seven hundred and ten: after which my Lord Stanhope himself was convinced that Spain could not be conquered, nor kept, if it was conquered, without a much greater army than it was possible for us to send thither. In that situation it was wild to imagine, as the Earl of Oxford imagined, or pretended to imagine, that they would quit the crown of Spain, for a remote and uncertain prospect of succeeding to that of France, and content themselves to be, in the mean time, princes of very small dominions. Philip, therefore, after struggling long that he might not be obliged to make his option till the succession of France lay open to him, was obliged to make it, and made it for Spain. Now this, my lord, was the very crisis of the negotiation; and to this point I apply what I said above of the effect of more decisive resolutions on the part of the queen. It was plain, that, if she made the campaign in concert with her allies, she could be no longer mistress of the negotiations, nor have almost a chance for conducting them to the issue she proposed. Our ill success in the field would have rendered the French less tractable in the congress: our good success there would have rendered the allies so. On this principle the queen suspended the operations of her troops, and then concluded the cessation.

Compare now the appearances and effect of this measure, with the appearances and effect that another measure would have had. In order to arrive at any peace, it was necessary to do what the queen did, or to do more: and, in order to arrive at a good one, it was necessary to be prepared to carry on the war, as well as to make a show of it: for she had the hard task upon her, of guarding against her allies, and her enemies both. But in that ferment, when few men considered any thing coolly, the conduct of her general, after he took the field, though he covered the allies in the siege of Quesnoy, corresponded ill, in appearance, with the declarations of carrying on the war vigorously, that had been made, on several occasions, before the campaign opened. It had an air of double dealing; and as such it passed among those, who did not combine in their thoughts all the circumstances of the conjuncture, or who were infatuated with the notional necessity of continuing the war. The clamor could not have been greater, if the queen had signed her peace separately: and, I think, the appearances might have been explained as favorably in one case, as in the other. From the death of the emperor Joseph, it was neither our interest, nor the common interest, well understood, to set the crown of Spain on the present emperor's head. As soon therefore as Philip had made his option, and if she had taken this resolution early, his option would have been sooner made, I presume that the queen might have declared, that she would not continue the war an hour longer to procure Spain for his Imperial majesty; that the engagements, she had taken whilst he was archduke, bound her no more; that, by his accession to the empire, the very nature of them was altered; that she took effectual measures to prevent, in any future time, an union of the crowns of France and Spain, and, upon the same principle, would not consent, much less fight, to bring about an immediate union of the Imperial and Spanish crowns; that they, who insisted to protract the war, intended this union; that they could intend nothing else, since they ventured to break with her, rather than to treat, and were so eager to put the reasonable satisfaction, that they might have in every other case without hazard, on the uncertain events of war; that she would not be imposed on any longer in this manner, and that she had ordered her ministers to sign her treaty with France, on the surrender of Dunkirk into her hands; that she pretended not to prescribe to her allies; but that she had insisted, in their behalf, on certain conditions, that France was obliged to grant to those of them, who should sign their treaties at the same time as she did, or who should consent to an immediate cessation of arms, and during the cessation treat under her mediation. There had been more frankness, and more dignity in this proceeding, and the effect must have been more advantageous. France would have granted more for a separate peace, than for a cessation: and the Dutch would have been more influenced by the prospect of one, than of the other; especially since this proceeding would have been very different from theirs at Munster, and at Nimeguen, where they abandoned their allies, without any other pretence than the particular advantage they found in doing so. A suspension of the operations of the queen's troops, nay a cessation of arms between her and France, was not definitive; and they might, and they did, hope to drag her back under their, and the German yoke. This therefore was not sufficient to check their obstinacy, nor to hinder them from making all the unfortunate haste they did make to get themselves beaten at Denain. But they would possibly have laid aside their vain hopes, if they had seen the queen's ministers ready to sign her treaty of peace, and those of some principal allies ready to sign at the same time; in which case the mischief that followed, had been prevented, and better terms of peace had been obtained for the confederacy: a prince of the house of Bourbon, who could never be king of France, would have sat on the Spanish throne instead of an emperor: the Spanish sceptre would have been weakened in the hands of one, and the Imperial sceptre would have been strengthened in those of the other: France would have had no opportunity of recovering from former blows, nor of finishing a long unsuccessful war by two successful campaigns: her ambition, and her power, would have declined with her old king, and under the minority that followed: one of them at least might have been so reduced by the terms of peace, if the defeat of the allies in one thousand seven hundred and twelve, and the loss of so many towns as the French took in that and the following year, had been prevented, that the other would have been no longer formidable, even supposing it to have continued; whereas I suppose that the tranquility of Europe is more due, at this time, to want of ambition, than to want of power, on the part of France. But, to carry the comparison of these two measures to the end, it may be supposed that the Dutch would have taken the same part, on the queen's declaring a separate peace, as they took on her declaring a cessation. The preparations for the campaign in the Low countries were made; the Dutch, like the other confederates, had a just confidence in their own troops, and an unjust contempt for those of the enemy; they were transported from their usual sobriety and caution by the ambitious prospect of large acquisitions, which had been opened artfully to them; the rest of the confederate army was composed of Imperial and German troops: so that the Dutch, the Imperialists, and the other Germans, having an interest to decide which was no longer the interest of the whole confederacy, they might have united against the queen in one case, as they did in the other; and the mischief that followed to them and the common cause, might not have been prevented. This might have been the case, no doubt. They might have flattered themselves that they should be able to break into France, and to force Philip, by the distress brought on his grandfather, to resign the crown of Spain to the emperor, even after Great Britain, and Portugal, and Savoy too, perhaps, were drawn out of the war; for these princes desired as little, as the queen, to see the Spanish crown on the emperor's head. But, even in this case, though the madness would have been greater, the effect would not have been worse. The queen would have been able to serve these confederates as well by being mediator in the negotiations, as they left it in her power to do, by being a party in them: and Great Britain would have had the advantage of being delivered so much sooner from a burden, which whimsical and wicked politics had imposed, and continued upon her till it was become intolerable. Of these two measures, at the time when we might have taken either, there were persons who thought the last preferable to the former. But it never came into public debate. Indeed it never could; too much time having been lost in waiting for the option of Philip, and the suspension and cessation having been brought before the council rather as a measure taken, than a matter to be debated. If your lordship, or any one else should judge, that, in such circumstances as those of the confederacy in the beginning of one thousand seven hundred and twelve, the latter measure ought to have been taken, and the Gordian knot to have been cut rather than to suffer a mock treaty to languish on, with so much advantage to the French as the disunion of the allies gave them; in short, if slowness, perplexity, inconsistency, and indecision should be objected, in some instances, to the queen's councils at that time; if it should be said particularly, that she did not observe the precise moment when the conduct of the league formed against her, being exposed to mankind, would have justified any part she should have taken (though she declared, soon after the moment was passed, that this conduct had set her free from all engagements) and when she ought to have taken that of drawing, by one bold measure, her allies out of the war, or herself out of the confederacy, before she lost her influence on France: if all this should be objected, yet would the proofs brought to support these objections show, that we were better allies than politicians; that the desire the queen had to treat in concert with her confederates, and the resolution she took not to sign without them, made her bear what no crowned head had ever borne before; and that where she erred, she erred principally by the patience, the compliance, and the condescension she exercised towards them, and towards her own subjects in league with them. Such objections as these may lie to the queen's conduct, in the course of this great affair; as well as objections of human infirmity to that of the persons employed by her in the transactions of it; from which neither those who preceded, nor those who succeeded, have, I presume, been free. But the principles on which they proceeded were honest, the means they used were lawful, and the event they proposed to bring about was just. Whereas the very foundation of all the opposition to the peace was laid in injustice and folly: for what could be more unjust, than the attempts of the Dutch and the Germans, to force the queen to continue a war for their private interest and ambition, the disproportionate expense of which oppressed the commerce of her subjects, and loaded them with debts for ages yet to come? a war, the object of which was so changed, that from the year one thousand seven hundred and eleven she made it not only without any engagement, but against her own, and the common interest? What could be more foolish; you will think that I soften the term too much, and you will be in the right to think so: what could be more foolish, than the attempt of a party in Britain, to protract a war so ruinous to their country, without any reason that they durst avow, except that of wreaking the resentments of Europe on France, and that of uniting the Imperial and Spanish crowns on an Austrian head? one of which was to purchase revenge at a price too dear; and the other was to expose the liberties of Europe to new dangers, by the conclusion of a war which had been made to assert and secure them.

I have dwelt the longer on the conduct of those who promoted, and of those who opposed, the negotiations of the peace made at Utrecht, and on the comparison of the measure pursued by the queen with that which she might have pursued, because the great benefit we ought to reap from the study of history, cannot be reaped unless we accustom ourselves to compare the conduct of different governments, and different parties, in the same conjunctures, and to observe the measures they did pursue, and the measures they might have pursued, with the actual consequences that followed one, and the possible, or probable consequences, that might have followed the other. By this exercise of the mind, the study of history anticipates, as it were, experience, as I have observed in one of the first of these letters, and prepares us for action. If this consideration should not plead a sufficient excuse for my prolixity on this head, I have one more to add that may. A rage of warring possessed a party in our nation till the death of the late queen: a rage of negotiating has possessed the same party of men, ever since. You have seen the consequences of one: you see actually those of the other. The rage of warring confirmed the beggary of our nation, which began as early as the revolution; but then it gave, in the last war, reputation to our arms, and our councils too. For though I think, and must always think, that the principle, on which we acted after departing from that laid down in the grand alliance of one thousand seven hundred and one, was wrong; yet must we confess that it was pursued wisely, as well as boldly. The rage of negotiating has been a chargeable rage likewise, at least as chargeable in its proportion. Far from paying our debts, contracted in war, they continue much the same, after three and twenty years of peace. The taxes that oppress our mercantile interest the most are still in mortgage; and those that oppress the landed interest the most, instead of being laid on extraordinary occasions, are become the ordinary funds for the current service of every year. This is grievous, and the more so to any man, who has the honor of his country, as well as her prosperity at heart, because we have not, in this case, the airy consolation we had in the other. The rage of negotiating began twenty years ago, under pretence of consummating the treaty of Utrecht: and, from that time to this, our ministers have been in one perpetual maze. They have made themselves and us, often, objects of aversion to the powers on the continent: and we are become at last objects of contempt, even to the Spaniards. What other effect could our absurd conduct have? What other return has it deserved? We came exhausted out of long wars and, instead of pursuing the measures necessary to give us means and opportunity to repair our strength and to diminish our burdens, our ministers have acted, from that time to this, like men who sought pretences to keep the nation in the same exhausted condition, and under the same load of debt. This may have been their view perhaps; and we could not be surprised if we heard the same men declare national poverty necessary to support the present government, who have so frequently declared corruption and a standing army to be so. Your good sense, my lord, your virtue, and your love of your country, will always determine you to oppose such vile schemes, and to contribute your utmost towards the cure of both these kinds of rage; the rage of warring, without any proportionable interest of our own, for the ambition of others; and the rage of negotiating, on every occasion, at any rate, without a sufficient call to it, and without any part of that deciding influence which we ought to have. Our nation inhabits an island, and is one of the principal nations of Europe; but to maintain this rank, we must take the advantages of this situation, which have been neglected by us for almost half a century: we must always remember, that we are not part of the continent, but we must never forget that we are neighbors to it. I will conclude, by applying a rule, that Horace gives for the conduct of an epic or dramatic poem, to the part Great Britain ought to take in the affairs of the continent, if you allow me to transform Britannia into a male divinity, as the verse requires.

> Nec Deus intersit nisi dignus vindice nodus
> Inciderit.

If these reflections are just, and I should not have offered them to your lordship had they not appeared both just and important to my best understanding, you will think that I have not spent your time unprofitably in making them, and exciting you by them to examine the true interest of your country relatively to foreign affairs; and to compare it with these principles of conduct, that, I am persuaded, have no other foundation than party designs, prejudices, and habits; the private interest of some men, and the ignorance and rashness of others.

My letter is grown so long that I shall say nothing to your lordship at this time concerning the study of modern history, relatively to the interests of your country in domestic affairs; and I think there will be no need to do so at any other. The History of the rebellion by your great grandfather, and his private memorials, which your lordship has in manuscript, will guide you surely as far as they go: where they leave you, your lordship must not expect any history; for we have more reason to make this complaint, "abest enim historia literis nostris," than Tully had to put it into the mouth of Atticus, his first book of laws. But where history leaves you, it is wanted least: the traditions of this century, and the latter end of the last, are fresh. Many, who were actors in some of these events, are alive; and many who have conversed with those that were actors in others. The public is in possession of several collections and memorials, and several there are in private hands. You will want no materials to form true notions of transactions so recent. Even pamphlets, written on different sides and on different occasions in our party disputes, and histories of no more authority than pamphlets, will help you to come at truth. Read them with suspicion, my lord, for they deserve to be suspected;

pay no regard to the epithets given, nor to the judgments passed; neglect all declamation, weigh the reasoning, and advert to fact. With such precautions, even Burnet's history may be of some use. In a word, your lordship will want no help of mine to discover, by what progression the whole constitution of our country, and even the character of our nation, has been altered: nor how much a worse use, in a national sense, though a better in the sense of party politics, the men called Whigs have made of long wars and new systems of revenue, since the revolution; than the men called tories made, before it, of long peace, and stale prerogative. When you look back three of four generations ago, you will see that the English were a plain, perhaps a rough, but a good-natured hospitable people, jealous of their liberties, and able as well as ready to defend them, with their tongues, their pens, and their swords. The restoration began to turn hospitality into luxury, pleasure into debauch, and country peers and country commoners into courtiers and men of mode. But whilst our luxury was young, it was little more than elegance: the debauch of that age was enlivened with wit, and varnished over with gallantry. The courtiers and the men of mode knew what the constitution was, respected it, and often asserted it. Arts and sciences flourished, and, if we grew more trivial, we were not become either grossly ignorant, or openly profligate. Since the revolution, our kings have been reduced indeed to a seeming annual dependence on parliament; but the business of parliament, which was esteemed in general a duty before, has been exercised in general as a trade since. The trade of parliament, and the trade of funds, have grown universal. Men, who stood forward in the world, have attended to little else. The frequency of parliaments, that increased their importance, and should have increased the respect for them, has taken off from their dignity: and the spirit that prevailed, whilst the service in them was duty, has been debased since it became a trade. Few know, and scarce any respect, the British constitution: that of the Church has been long since derided; that of the State as long neglected; and both have been left at the mercy of men in power, whoever those men were. Thus the Church, at least the hierarchy, however sacred in its origin or wise in its institution, is become a useless burden on the state: and the state is become, under ancient and known forms, a new and undefinable monster; composed of a king without monarchical splendor, a senate of nobles without aristocratical independency, and a senate of commons without democratical freedom. In the mean time, my lord, the very idea of wit, and all that can be called taste, has been lost among the great; arts and sciences are scarce alive; luxury has been increased but not refined; corruption has been established, and is avowed. When governments are worn out, thus it is: the decay appears in every instance. Public and private virtue, public and private spirit, science and wit, decline all together.

That you, my lord, may have a long and glorious share in restoring all these, and in drawing our government back to the true principles of it, I wish most heartily. Whatever errors I may have committed in public life, I have always loved my country: whatever faults may be objected to me in private life, I have always loved my friend; whatever usage I have received from my country, it shall never make me break with her: whatever usage I have received from my friends, I shall never break with one of them, while I think him a friend to my country. These are the sentiments of my heart. I know they are those of your lordship's: and a communion of such sentiments is a tie that will engage me to be, as long as I live,

My lord,

Your most faithful servant.

II
Remarks on the History of England

Letter 1

Sir:

Since the busy scene of the year is over at home, and we may perhaps wait several months before the successful negotiations of France furnish us with new hopes of a general pacification, and give you occasion to carry your speculations forward, it may be proper enough for you to cast your eyes backwards, to reflect on your own conduct, and to call yourself to account before your own tribunal.

I am so much persuaded of the integrity of your intentions, that I do not in the least suspect you will think my advice impertinent; and therefore I shall attempt to lead your thoughts on this subject, by giving you an account of some parts of a conversation, at which I happened to be present very lately.

Several of your papers, and several of those which have been written against you, lay before a company, which often meets, rather to live than to drink together; according to that distinction which Tully makes to the advantage of his own nation over the Greeks. They dispute without strife, and examine as dispassionately the events and the characters of the present age, as they reason about those which are found in history. When I came in, a gentleman was saying, that your victories had been cheaply bought; and that he had not seen one champion, able to break a lance, enter the lists against you, upon which some were ready to observe the inconsistencies of human nature, and how hard it often proves to hire men to avow and defend even that which they are hired to act. Others were willing to hope that corruption had not spread very wide, nor taken root very deep amongst us. All agreed, that if your papers could be suspected to be written in opposition to the present ministers, the feeble and low opposition you have met with would deserve to be looked upon as a very melancholy symptom for them, since it would denote that their cause was deemed universally bad, or that their persons were grown universally odious among men of sense, ingenuity, and knowledge. It would denote their guilt, or their misfortune; perhaps both.

Here one of the company interposed, by observing very prudently, "that any thing so void of probability, as not to fall even under suspicion, was unworthy of farther consideration. But," said he, "whatever particular views Mr. D'Anvers may have had, one general effect, which I cannot approve, has followed from his writings. We must remember that when he began to publish his weekly lucubrations, universal quiet prevailed, if not universal satisfaction; for in what place, or at what time was the last ever found? Few people inquired; fewer grumbled; none clamored; all acquiesced. Now the humor of the nation is altered. Every man inquires with eagerness, and examines with freedom. All orders of men are more intent than I ever observed them to be on the course of public affairs, and deliver their judgments with less reserve upon the most important. From this alteration, for which the Craftsman is chiefly answerable, no good consequence can, I think, proceed; and it is visible that several inconveniences may."

To this many of us could by no means assent. We apprehended that in a country, circumstanced like ours, and under a government constituted like ours, the people had a right to be informed, and to reason about public affairs; that when wise and honest measures are pursued, and the nation reaps the advantage of them, the exercise of this right will always be agreeable to the men in power; that, indeed, if weak and wicked measures are pursued, the men in power might find the exercise of this right disagreeable, inconvenient, and sometimes dangerous to them; but that, even in this case, there would be no pretence for attempting to deprive the people of this right, or for discouraging the exercise of it: and that to forbid men to complain, when they suffer, would be an instance of tyranny but one degree below that which the triumvirs gave, during the slaughter and terror of the proscriptions, when by edict they commanded all men to be merry upon pain of death.

The person from whom we differed, brought us back to the particular case of your writings, Mr. D'Anvers. He endeavored to support what he had said against them in this manner:

"There was no good reason for raising this spirit, which I dislike, in the nation, when the Craftsman began to write, or there was such a reason. If there was none, why has he given so much alarm? If there was one, how has it come to pass that so great an alarm has produced so little effect? Will you say that he had very good reason to rouse this spirit, but that it has hitherto had no opportunity of exerting itself? Or will you say that his reasons were good and the opportunity fair, but that the minds of men, which had been convinced by the former, have not yet been determined to improve the latter? I observe on all these alternatives, that if there was no good and even pressing reason to raise such a spirit in the nation that I dislike (because I expect no national benefit, and I fear much inconveniency from it), Mr. D'Anvers has acted a very wicked part, and is little better than a sower of sedition. If there was such a reason, but no such opportunity, he has acted a very weak part, and is but a shallow politician. If there was such a reason and such an opportunity, but no disposition in the minds of men to follow their conviction, you may excuse your favorite author, perhaps, by alleging that the minds of men are in the power of God alone; but you will represent our national condition to be more desperate than I ever thought it, or am yet willing to believe it. Upon this supposition I affirm that Mr. D'Anvers is not to be excused, if he continues to write; for if he cannot raise this disposition by persuasion, what does he aim at farther? I hope that he and you, who defend him, admire as much as I profess to do that divine saying of Plato: 'We may endeavor to persuade our fellow citizens; but it is not lawful to force them even to that which is best for them.' "

Whilst all this passed, I took notice that an ancient venerable gentleman showed more emotion, and greater impatience than I remembered to have seen him ever express before. As soon as the other had concluded, he broke silence in the following manner:

"You have endeavored to prove, sir, that the Craftsman should not have begun to write; or at least that he is inexcusable for continuing. Now I not only differ from you, but I differ from you upon the very foundation on which you have established that whole argument.

"The face of things was, I agree, as calm as you represent it to have been, when my honest contemporary Caleb took up his pen. They were halcyon days truly. We were not only quiet, but we seemed implicit, and dull uniformity of eternal assent prevailed in every place. I agree that, since that time, things are very much altered. A ferment, or spirit, call it which you please, is raised; but, I bless God, it is not the blind and furious spirit of party. It is a spirit, which springs from information and conviction, that has diffused itself not only to all orders of men, as you observed, but to men of all denominations. Even they who act against it, encourage it. You cannot call it toryism, when such numbers of independent whigs avow it. To call it whigism would be improper likewise, when so many tories concur in it. He, who should call it jacobitism, would be too absurd to deserve an answer. What is it then? It is, I think, a revival of the true old English spirit, which prevailed in the days of our fathers, and which must always be national, since it has no direction but to the national interest; 'est jam una vox omnium;' and I hope we shall never have occasion to add, 'magis odio firmata quam præsidio.'

"This spirit the Craftsman has contributed to raise; and I affirm, in my turn, that supposing him to have no other reason for raising and supporting it, than a general observation of the contrary temper into which the nation had fallen, he deserves the acknowledgments of every honest man in Britain, for the part he has acted. The dispute between us is thus reduced to one single proposition; and if I prove this, all your reasoning, sir, falls of course to the ground."

The other assented; the state of the dispute was fixed; and the old gentleman proceeded in his argument to this effect:

"Give me leave to borrow, upon this occasion, an image which my Lord Bacon employs, in one of his Essays, upon another. A

people, who will maintain their liberties, must pray for the blessing of Judah, to avoid the fate of Issachar, the greatest curse
which can befall them. Far from jogging on silently and tamely,
like the ass between two burthens, such a people must preserve
some of the fierceness of the lion, and even make their roar to
be heard like his, whenever they are injured, or so much as
threatened.

"I do not mean to recommend your seditious, rebellious spirit,
which will create a perpetual scene of tumult and disorder, and
expose every state to frequent and dangerous convulsions.
Neither would I be thought to approve even that popular
peevishness of temper, which sometimes prevails, so as to dis-
compose the harmony of the several orders of government. But
this I assert, that liberty cannot be long secure, in any country,
unless a perpetual jealousy watches over it, and a constant determined resolution protects it in the whole body of the nation.
The principle must be permanent and equal. The exercise of
it ought to be proportioned to the occasions. The hundred eyes
of Argus were not always kept open; but they were never all
closed. The whole body of a nation may be as jealous of their
liberties, as a private man of his honor. They may be, at all
times, animated by a generous resolution of defending these
liberties at any risk; as he may, at all times, feel in his heart the
courage of venturing his life to maintain his honor. But as there
is no necessary consequence from this private character to that
of a quarrelsome bully; so neither is there any necessary consequence from the public character I have recommended to that of
a factious, rebellious people.

"Liberty is a tender plant, which will not flourish unless the
genius of the soil be proper for it; nor will any soil continue to
be so long, which is not cultivated with incessant care. 'Variæ
illudent pestes; mischiefs of various kinds abound;' and there
is no season, in the revolution of the great political year of government, when we can say, with truth, that liberty is entirely
free from immediate or remote danger.

"In every kind of government some powers must be lodged
in particular men, or particular bodies of men, for the good order
and preservation of the whole community. The lines which
circumscribe these powers, are the bounds of separation between

the prerogatives of the prince, or other magistrate, and the privileges of the people. Every step which the prince, or magistrate makes beyond these bounds, is an encroachment on liberty, and every attempt towards making such a step is a danger to liberty.

"Thus we see how great a trust is reposed in those to whom such powers are committed; and if we look into the heart of man, we shall soon discover how great, though unavoidable a temptation is laid in their way. The love of power is natural; it is insatiable; almost constantly whetted, and never cloyed by possession. If therefore all men will endeavor to increase their power, or at least to prolong and secure the enjoyment of it, according to the uncertain measure of their own passions, and not according to the stated proportion of reason and of law; and if neither one nor the other of these can be attempted without a danger to liberty; it follows undeniably that, in the nature of things, the notion of a perpetual danger to liberty is inseparable from the very notion of government.

"That these principles are true, will appear evident from practice and experience, as well as from speculation. All forms of government suppose them to be so; and in such as are not absolute monarchies we find the utmost precautions, which their several institutions admit, taken against this evil; from hence that rotation of employments in commonwealths; the annual or other more frequent elections of magistrates; and all those checks and controls, which the wisdom of legislators, prompted by experience, has invented.

"In perfect democracies these precautions have been taken in the highest degree; and yet even there they have not been always effectual. They were carried so far in the Athenian form of government, that this people seemed more in danger of falling into anarchy than tyranny; and yet one of their magistrates found means to become their tyrant, and to transmit this power to his successors.

"In mixed governments, the danger must still be greater. Such a one we may justly reckon that of Rome, as well during the regal as republican state; and surely no history can be more fruitful in examples of the danger to which liberty stands exposed from the natural, and therefore constant desire of amplifying and maintaining power, than the Roman history is, from the last of the kings to the first of the emperors.

"A monarchy, limited like ours, may be placed, for aught I know, as it has often been represented, just in the middle point; from whence a deviation leads on one hand to tyranny, and on the other to anarchy; but sure I am that if we are situated just in the middle point, the least deviation is the more cautiously to be guarded against. Liberty would be safer, perhaps, if we inclined a little more than we do to the popular side.

"It may be said, and I would anticipate the objection, that if we are thus placed, our care ought to be exerted equally against deviations on either side; and that I am the more in the wrong to appear so apprehensive of those on one side, and so little apprehensive of those on the other; because even our own history might have shown us, that deviations to the popular side have cost us at least as dear as ever those to the other side can be pretended to have done. But let it be considered:

"First, that as far as these national calamities, hinted at in the objection, have been the unavoidable consequences of methods necessary to secure or retrieve liberty, it is infamous to repine at them, whatever they have cost.

"Secondly, that the cases compared together, and supposed in this objection to be equal, are not so. I may safely appeal to every impartial reader of our history, whether any truth he collected from it ever struck him more strongly than this; that when the disputes between the king and the people have been carried to such extremes, as to draw national calamities after them, it has not been owing primarily to the obstinacy and weak management of the court, and is therefore unjustly charged on the just spirit of liberty. In truth a spirit of liberty will never destroy a free constitution; a spirit of faction may. But I appeal again, whether those of our princes, who have had sense and virtue enough to encourage the one, have had any thing to fear from the other.

"Now if experience shows, as I am persuaded it does, that the prerogative and power of a prince will never be in any real danger when he invades, neither openly nor insidiously, the liberties of his people; the same experience will show that the liberties of a people may be in very real danger, when, far from invading the prerogative and power of the prince, they submit to one, and are even so good as to increase the other. The reason of this difference is plain. A spirit of faction alone will be always too weak to cope with the legal power and authority of the crown; and the spirit of liberty, in the whole body of the people, which contradistinguishes this case from the other, may be raised by the fear of losing; but cannot be so raised by the hopes of acquiring. The fear is common to all; the hope can only be particular to a few. The fear, therefore, may become a general principle of union; the hope cannot.

"But if a national spirit cannot be any other than a defensive, and therefore unprovoked, an harmless, inoffensive spirit; that of a prince cannot, without due coercion, be kept within the same bounds; for here the tables are turned; and the hope of acquiring, which can never be a common principle among the multitude, to unite and carry them into action, becomes an almost irresistible motive to the prince; who, by yielding to it, indulges the most powerful passions of the soul; who finds many to share the difficulties and dangers of the enterprise with him; and who shares the prize with none.

"Generally and abstractly speaking, therefore, as public liberty is more exposed under mixed governments, than under perfect democracies; so is it more exposed under limited monarchies than under any form of mixed government.

"What increases the danger to liberty in this case is, that the opportunity of invading it, which lies open to a sovereign prince, suits almost any character. The powers intrusted to other magistrates, as in a commonwalth, are subject to immediate controls, the exercise of them is subject to future revisions, and is limited to a short time; so that if such magistrates invade liberty, with any prospect of success, it can only happen, when they are able to compensate for the disadvantages of their political circumstances, by the greatness of their personal qualifications, by superior understanding and superior courage, by a great, if not a good character, and by the appearance of virtue at least. Few men therefore are fit for such an undertaking.

"But the sovereign prince, who rules in a limited monarchy, has an opportunity open to him for life; and such an opportunity as requires extraordinary personal qualifications. He may possess every vice or weakness, which is opposed to the virtues, or appearances of virtue, requisite in the other case, and yet may destroy the liberty of the bravest people upon earth. The pretences for concealing his designs, and the helps for carrying them on, which his situation affords above that of any magistrate in a commonwealth, will abundantly compensate for the disadvantages arising from his personal character, and will secure his success, if the people are brought, by artifice or accident, to grow remiss in watching over their liberties. Every man is therefore fit for such an undertaking. If these general reflections evince that liberty must always be in some degree of danger under every government; and that this danger must increase in proportion, as the chief powers of the state are intrusted in fewer hands and for longer terms; then liberty is always in some degree of danger; and that not the least, even under our excellent constitution; then the necessity of keeping this jealous spirit, the true guardian of public liberty, always alive and active in this nation, is manifest; then the observation of our being fallen into the contrary temper is alone a sufficient reason to justify Mr. D'Anvers for joining his endeavors to awaken us from our political lethargy; then, sir, my proposition is proved, and your reasoning falls to the ground."

This discourse furnished matter of much reflection to the company; some objections were made; some doubts were proposed; and some explanations asked for. I shall not trouble you with all these particulars, but shall conclude my letter, by relating to you in what manner the old gentleman replied, and by his reply wound up the conversation of the evening.

"I believe, gentlemen," said he, "that we do not differ so much as some of you seem to imagine: for first, though I desire the vessel of the commonwealth may sail safely, yet I desire it may sail smoothly too; and though I must think, till I hear better reasons to the contrary, that public liberty cannot be so easily attacked, and may be more easily defended, in a perfect democracy, or in a mixed republic, than in a limited monarchy; yet will it not follow necessarily from hence, as has been supposed, that I prefer the two first to the last of these forms of government. On either side there are compensations; and if liberty may be better defended in the former, yet still may be defended, and domestic quiet is perhaps better preserved in the latter.

"Secondly, if I agree with the gentlemen who have insisted so much on the little reason which there was in the late reign, or is in the present, to apprehend any encroachments from the crown on the British liberties; these gentlemen must, I think, agree with me likewise that this will not alter the case; subvert what I have endeavored to establish; or derive any blame on those who have endeavored to revive that public spirit of watchfulness over all national interests, which is the proper and true guardian of liberty, in an age when that public spirit has more than begun to sink and die away. I hope there will be always men found to preach this doctrine in season and out of season, as the apostles preached the gospel; because if this spirit is not kept at all times in vigor, it may fail us at some particular time, when we shall want to exert it most. In great and immediate danger, the most sluggish sentinel is alert; but surely they who, in times of apparent security, excite us to be upon our guard, do as real service as they who animate us to our defence when we are actually attacked; and the first is, in my opinion, that kind of service of which we stand the most in need. I confess freely, that I should not apprehend so much danger to liberty in times of suspicion, if I saw that neither power could subdue, nor artifice divert, nor pusillanimity oblige men to abandon this spirit; as I should apprehend in times of apparent security, if I observed it to be lost. In a word, no laws, no order of government can effectually secure liberty any longer than this spirit prevails, and gives them vigor; and therefore you might argue as reasonably for repealing any law, or abolishing any custom, the most advantageous to liberty, and which you cannot be sure of restoring at your pleasure, because you feel no immediate want of it; as you have argued for letting this spirit die away, which you cannot be sure of reviving at your pleasure, because you perceive no immediate occasion for the exercise of it.

"I hope that I have said enough to give me a right to conclude in this manner; and if I was to descend into particular applications, of the general truths which I have advanced, I think that no doubt whatever could remain in any of your minds, upon this subject." After this, our company broke up. If the same subject is resumed when they meet again, or on any other, which I judge proper to be communicated to you, it is highly probable that you will hear again from

Your admirer, friend and servant, &c.

Letter 2

Sir:

The same company hath met, and the same subject hath been resumed; so that I think myself under an obligation of writing to you again.

The person who gave occasion to all that was said in your defence the other day, seemed very desirous that the conversation should be pursued at our last meeting; and therefore as soon as we sat down, he addressed himself thus to the old gentleman who had fought your battle.

"Sir," said he, "I own myself a good deal reconciled to the Craftsman by the discourse you held, when we were last together. That some inconveniences must follow from keeping this spirit of jealousy and watchfulness always alive, seems to me very evident; but I begin to think that this evil may be necessary, in order to secure us against greater. Every system of human invention must be liable to some objections; and it would be chimerical in us to expect a form of government liable to none. Even theocracy was attended by some real inconveniences, according to the Jewish histories; and neither the Divine presence in the tabernacle, nor the ambulant oracle, which the priest carried about with him, could preserve entire purity in religion, or good order in the state. We must be content therefore to bear the disorder I apprehend from that ferment, which a perpetual jealousy of the governors in the governed will keep up, rather than abandon that spirit, the life of which is the life of liberty. When the

163

jealousy happens to be ill-placed, we may hope it will not rise to any great and dangerous height. When it happens to be well grounded, it may have the good effect of destroying a wicked minister, of checking a bad, or of reclaiming a misguided prince.

"You see, sir, that my conversion is pretty far advanced; and if you will please to descend into particular applications of the general doctrines you delivered, as you gave us reason to hope that you would, it is very probable that the few doubts I have still may be removed."

The rest of the company seconded this request. The good old gentleman yielded to our common desires, and spoke to the following effect:

"The general truth I am to prove by particular examples is this: that liberty cannot be preserved long by any people, who do not preserve that watchful and jealous spirit of liberty, on the necessity of which I have insisted. If you are once convinced of this truth, you will know what opinion to entertain of those who endeavor to extinguish this spirit, and those who do all they can to keep it alive.

"There are two other general truths relative to this, which I shall establish likewise by particular examples, as I go along.

"One is this: that the spirit of liberty, far from inspiring that rashness and undistinguishing fury which are peculiar to the spirit of faction, is slow to act even against the worst princes, and exerts itself in favor of the best with more effect than any other spirit whatever.

"The second is this: that how slowly soever the spirit of liberty may act in suspicious times and against encroaching governors; yet if it be kept alive, it will act effectually sooner or later, though under the greatest disadvantages, and against the most powerful opposition; in a word, in the most desperate cases.

"The first of these truths will recommend this spirit to every good prince and honest minister. The other will encourage every man who is a friend to liberty, never to abandon the cause through despondency of success, as long as he sees this spirit prevail, or even subsist.

"Having fixed these principal points of view, let us proceed: and though I would not advise you to admit the works of Machiavel into your canon of political writings; yet since in them, as in other apocryphal books, many excellent things are interspersed, let us begin by improving a hint taken from the discourses of the Italian Secretary on the first decade of Livy.

"He observes that, of all governments, those are the best, which by the natural effect of their original constitutions are frequently renewed or drawn back, as he explains his meaning, to their first principles; and that no government can be of a long duration, where this does not happen from time to time, either from the cause just mentioned, or from some accidental cause.

"The reason is obvious. There must be some good in the first principles of every government, or it could not subsist at all; much less could it make any progress. But this good degenerates, according to the natural course of things; and governments, like other mixed bodies, tend to dissolution by the changes which are wrought in the several parts, and by the unaptness and disproportion, which result from hence throughout the whole composition.

"The most effectual, and indeed the sole method of maintaining their health and prolonging their life, must therefore be to bring them back as near and as frequently as possible to those principles, on which their prosperity, strength and duration were originally founded.

"This change, or renewal of the state, hath been sometimes wrought by external causes, as it happened at Rome, upon the invasion of the Gauls. The Romans had departed from their ancient observances. The ceremonies of religion and the laws of justice were neglected by them. An enemy, whom they despised and provoked, conquered them. The impressions made by this dreadful calamity brought them back to their first institutions and to their primitive spirit. They sprung up from this second original, as Livy calls it, with new vigor, and rose to greater fame, power and dignity than ever.

"But not to dwell on such examples, as point out to us rather the punishment of vice, than the means of reformation, let us observe that this change, or renewal of the state, is oftener and better wrought by internal causes.

"Many excellent institutions were contrived in framing the Roman government, which served to maintain in force the first principles of that political system. Such were the regulations about elections; the laws against bribery; and many other written laws, or confirmed customs. Such again was the constitution of the senate, in whom the majesty of the commonwealth resided, and whose authority controlled the licentiousness of the people. Such was the erection of that sacred, tribunitial power, whose prerogatives served to check the usurpations of the magistrates, and who could arrest with one word, even the proceedings of the senate. Such was the office of the censors, whose inquisitions and lustrations corrected abuses, reformed manners, and purged the senate itself of corrupt and unworthy members.

"These laws, these customs, these different orders, controlling one another, and promoting the general good of the commonwealth, had great effect during some centuries. But this effect could never have followed them at all, if the spirit of liberty, which had enacted these laws, established these customs, and formed these orders, had not continued. The very best laws are a dead letter, nay often a grievance, unless they are strenuously and honestly executed. They never can be so executed, unless the spirit of them possess those to whom the execution of them is committed; and it would be ridiculous to expect to find this spirit in the magistrates, and the several orders of the state, unless it appeared in the body of the people, out of whom these magistrates are chosen, and these orders composed.

"The examples which Machiavel cites to show, that the virtue of particular men among the Romans, did frequently draw that government back to its original principles, are so many proofs that the duration of liberty depends on keeping the spirit of it alive and warm. Such examples were frequent in Rome, whilst this spirit flourished. As it decayed, these examples became more rare, and failed at last entirely. The old laws and customs were, for the most part, still in being. The forms of electing magistrates, and of promulgating laws, were in the main observed. There was still a senate. There were still censors and tribunes. But the spirit of liberty being stifled by that of faction and cabal, and the several orders of the government being tainted by the general corruption, these good laws and customs remained without force, or were suspended, or were abrogated, or were perverted to serve the purposes of private ambition and avarice.

166

"The time-serving flatterers of princes and ministers have no point, amongst all the nauseous drudgery imposed on them, which they are obliged more to labor than that of representing all the effects of a spirit of liberty as so many effects of a spirit of faction. Examples might be found, even without searching long or looking far after them, when this hath been done against the public sense of a whole nation, and sometimes in favor of a cabal, neither numerous nor considerable enough to be called a party. But still it will remain eternally true, that the spirit of liberty and the spirit of faction are not only different, but repugnant and incompatible: so that the life of either is the death of the other.

"We must not imagine that the freedom of the Romans was lost, because one party fought for the maintenance of liberty; another for the establishment of tyranny; and that the latter prevailed. No. The spirit of liberty was dead, and the spirit of faction had taken its place on both sides. As long as the former prevailed, a Roman sacrificed his own, and therefore no doubt every other personal interest, to the interest of the commonwealth. When the latter succeeded, the interest of the commonwealth was considered no otherwise than in subordination to that particular interest which each person had espoused. The principal men, instead of making their grandeur and glory consist, as they formerly had done, in that which the grandeur and glory of the commonwealth reflected on them, considered themselves now as individuals, not as citizens, and each would shine with his own light. To this purpose alone they employed the commands they had of armies, the governments of provinces, and the influence they acquired over the tribes at Rome, and over the allies and subjects of the republic. Upon principles of the same kind, inferior persons attached themselves to these; and that zeal and industry, nay that courage and magnanimity, which had been exerted formerly in the service of the commonwealth, were exerted by the spirit of faction, for Marius, or Sylla; for Cæsar, or Pompey.

"It is plain, that the liberty of Rome would not have been irretrievably lost, though Cæsar had finished the civil war with absolute success, and was settled in power, if the spirit of liberty had not been then lost in the whole body of the people; if the

Romans had not been as ripe for slavery, as the Cappadocians were fond of it; for I think the Cappadocians were the people who desired that a prince might be set over them, and refused to be a free people.

"I cannot believe that those who murdered Cæsar, took such puerile measures as Cicero, who was not let into the secret, pretended that they had taken, when he saw the consequences of their action. But in this they erred. They killed their benefactor; at least, he was such to the greatest part of them; and renewed the civil war, in order to restore liberty to a people, who had lost the spirit of liberty, and who would not take it when it was offered to them. Even in the senate, Octavius had a party; Antony had a party; but the commonwealth had none. In short, the freest people upon earth, by suffering the spirit of liberty to decay, and that of faction to grow up, because slaves to such a succession of monsters, continued with very few exceptions from the reign of Augustus to the destruction of the empire, as God never sent in his wrath to execute vengeance on any other nation.

"Thus I have endeavored to illustrate and confirm the first general proposition laid down, by a summary application of it to the Roman story. I have not explained by what degrees, and by what means one of these spirits gradually decayed, and the other grew up. The subject is fine, and the task would be pleasant; but it is unnecessary to our present purpose. We see enough at this time, if we see that in the greatest revolution of the greatest government in the world, losing the spirit of liberty was the cause, and losing liberty was the effect.

"If now we bring these considerations home, we shall find not only the first general proposition, but the others relative to it, illustrated and confirmed through the whole course of our annals. I shall make a deduction of some of these particulars. To deduce them all would exceed my strength and your patience."

Here one of our company interrupted the old gentleman's discourse, by saying that since we were come to a kind of pause, he desired leave to make an observation, which he thought pertinent and material, on what had been said, before we went into any new matter. "The difference and opposition between a spirit of liberty and a spirit of faction," continued he, "hath been justly stated. A spirit of liberty will be always and wholly concerned about national interests, and very indifferent about personal and private interests. On the contrary, a spirit of faction will be always and wholly concerned about these, and very indifferent about the others. When they appear, therefore, in their proper characters, they are distinguished as easily as light and darkness; and the danger I apprehend is over.

"But faction puts on the mask of liberty; and under this false appearance, disputes her being even with liberty herself. Now here, methinks, a great many dangers arise; the danger of mistaking when it is so hard to distinguish; the danger of being bubbles and tools of faction, whilst we fancy ourselves asserters of public liberty; the danger of continuing under this delusion, till it is too late to prevent such mischiefs as we never intended to bring on our country. The spirit of faction may take, and I doubt not hath often taken possession of numbers, who meant to entertain no other spirit than that of liberty; for numbers have not the discernment of spirits. This possession may continue, and in fact, I believe it hath continued very often, till faction hath accomplished, or secured the accomplishment of her ends. I made this observation, which results naturally from what hath been said, and insist upon it, because if faction could not lie latent under the most specious and popular pretences imaginable, there would be no great need of putting us on our guard against it; and because if it can lie thus latent and concealed, we may be exposed to the dangers I have mentioned, which side soever of the question we take in political disputes. At this time, to speak as I think, the case is so clear on one side, that no man who adheres to it, hath the least pretence left him to say that he pursues the public interest, or is directed in his conduct by the generous, disinterested spirit of liberty.

"I could support my assertion by many proofs, if it was necessary in this company. One I will mention for its singularity; and it is this.

"We have seen and heard, in a nation hitherto free, such maxims avowed and pleaded for, as are inconsistent with all the notions of liberty. Corruption hath been defended, nay recommended, as a proper, a necessary, and therefore a reasonable expedient of government; than which there is not, perhaps, any one proposition more repugnant to the common sense of mankind and to universal experience. Both of these demonstrate corruption to be the last deadly symptom of agonizing liberty. Both of them declare that a people abandoned to it, are abandoned to a reprobate sense, and are lost to all hopes of political salvation.

"The dependence of the legislative on the executive power hath been contended for by the same persons, under the same direction; and yet nothing surely can be more evident than this; that in a constitution like ours, the safety of the whole depends on the balance of the parts, and the balance of the parts on their mutual independency on one another: agreeably to which Thuanus makes Ferdinand say, in answer to the Castilians, who pressed him to take away the independency of the states of Arragon; 'Æquilibrio potentiæ regni regisque salutem publicam contineri; et si contingeret aliquando alterum alteri præponderare, procul dubio alterius aut utriusque ruinam ex eo secuturam; that the public safety depends on the equal balance of the power of the king, and of the power of the kingdom; and that if ever it should happen that one outweighed the other, the ruin of one, or of both, must undoubtedly follow.'

"On one side then the mask is pulled off. The weak may be seduced to concur; the strongest may be forced to submit; but no man can be any longer deceived.

"On the other, it must be acknowledged that the appearances are extremely fair. True notions of liberty and good government are professed and pursued. Our grievances are complained of; our dangers are foretold; not only those which all men feel or see, but those which are more remote from observation. In short, the spirit of liberty, such as it hath been described, seems to breathe from this quarter, and to diffuse its influences over the nation.

"As I am a lover of my country and of liberty, I have rejoiced in this. I rejoice in it still; and yet I confess freely, that I took some umbrage at a paper, which came out not long ago. The design and tendency of it seemed to me to favor the cause of a faction; and of a faction, however contemptible in its present state, always to be guarded against. The paper I mean is Fog's Journal of the 6th of June; where you have seen a ridiculous speech, supposed to be made by General Monk, and translated, as the author says, from Leti's history of Oliver Cromwell.

"If this wretched production had appeared in Mist's Journal, I should have felt neither surprise nor concern. That writer never wore so much as the mask of liberty; and showed his game so plainly, that whatever he got by faction, faction could get nothing by him. But Fog, who writes incomparably better, hath appeared to write with a much better design. Those who are warmest in the national interest, without regard to persons, and independently of all factions, have made this judgment of him; and therefore I was surprised and concerned to find that he exposed himself even once, or in any degree, to the same reproach that was frequently and justly made to his predecessor."

The gentleman's observation gave occasion to much discourse. Our old sage desired it might be remembered that he had not undertaken the defence of every weekly writer, though he had undertaken yours, Mr. D'Anvers. "The paper," continued he, "which hath been so much mentioned, is a very silly paper, to whatever purpose it was designed.

"If it was designed to inspire a horror of those miseries from which the restoration delivered the nation, it was a very superfluous work at this time, when there is no real or pretended difference of opinion upon that head amongst us. Those who do not go to church upon the twenty-ninth of May, nor on any other day, will agree with those who do, in this point, upon better authority than that of Leti, and for better reasons than those which are contained in the foolish declamation attributed to Monk.

"If it was designed to make us commemorate the restoration of the two brothers, Charles and James, as a national blessing in itself, and independently of the other consideration, the project was equally ridiculous. The flattery bestowed upon these princes, whilst they were in exile, might pass, and many things concurred to make it pass. But to talk in the same style to mankind at this time, when they have both sat on our throne, when so many of us remember both what they did, and what they would have done, is contemptible to the last degree.

"If it was designed for more modern application, and to raise a spirit amongst us in favor of the Pretender, the project was too foolish to have been hatched at home. It must have been imported from abroad. What jacobite can be sanguine enough to hope that his cause should revive, when he beholds the heroical king and queen, who fill our throne, auspicious parents of a numerous progeny of young heroes and heroines, rising up to emulate their virtues, and to gladden, like them, the British nation.

"This single consideration might be sufficient to damp the hopes of any jacobite who lives at home, and is a witness of all this glory. But however I shall mention another, which ought to have its weight likewise, and which will have more perhaps amongst some people. The spirit of jacobitism is not only gone, but it will appear to be gone in such a manner as to leave no room to apprehend its return; if we reflect that it hath died away, whilst all that could be done to keep it alive was doing by those who professed it, and by those who valued and recommended themselves on their opposition to all the effects of it; if we consider the numbers of people who have abandoned this interest, notwithstanding the utmost provocations to the contrary.

"In short, I persuade myself that if the Pretender had no rival in the throne, instead of having there one so formidable as our most august monarch, yet his way to the throne would not be more open to him. The whole bulk of the people hath been brought by the revolution, and by the present settlement of the crown, to entertain principles which very few of us defended in my younger days. The safety and welfare of the nation are now the first and principal objects of regard. The regard to persons and to families hath been reduced to the second place; and it holds even that but under the direction of the former. Can any man believe that a people brave enough to dispose of their crown for the greatest national advantage, even when the throne was full, will ever dispose of it as long as the spirit of liberty remains among them, for the greatest national mischief, if the throne should be empty?

"There is but one design more, which I can conceive to have given occasion to this silly paper; but one quarter more, from which it could possibly come: and these guesses, perhaps, will not appear the least probable. Might it not be designed to instil a jealousy of jacobitism, and to prejudice mankind against all writings which those who are offended at them cannot answer? Might it not be designed to furnish the spruce, pert orator, who strewed some of his flowers in the Daily Courant of the eleventh of June, with a hint, which he hath most happily and modestly improved? 'Fog,' says he, 'avows jacobitism; the Crafts-man concurs in the same design; nay, every jacobite in England sinks his master's divine right in the popular topics of debts, taxes and corruption.' So that jacobitism may now be imputed upon this authority, to ninety-nine in a hundred of the whole nation; for ninety-nine in a hundred do complain of debts, taxes and corruption. I am sure there is arrogance and impertinence both in such an insinuation too gross to be denied; whereas the Craftsman may destroy the whole proof brought against him of arrogance, by answering three silly questions in the negative.

"If this was the design, I will be bold, for bold it may justly seem, to say thàt this expedient is, at least, as bungling and likely to prove as ineffectual, as any that have been produced by the same great genius who contrived it; for if we were inclined to believe that the Craftsman, Fog, or any other person, carries on the measures of faction under the mask of liberty; should we be-lieve it on the credit of those who oppose them, and who are notoriously influenced to write, though under specious pretences of promoting loyalty to the king, and an acquiescence in his ma-jesty's measures, yet in reality, for no other service than that of a small number of men; may, strictly speaking, of a single man? With what face can such writers impute faction to any one living or dead?

"Let them be assured that we can examine and judge for our-selves; and that neither the Craftsman nor Fog would be able, if they went about it, to impose upon us, any more than they them-selves have been able to do.

"The pretty author, I just now mentioned, begins his essay with airs of wit, and ends it with airs of wisdom. What pity is it that he should succeed in neither? In his first paragraph he represents the Craftsman, with curious impropriety, as a magi-cian, who conjures up spirits; as a dog, who barks at a distance; as a little insect, who nibbles at a character: and my friend Caleb was all these things, it seems, at the same instant. After this speci-men of writing, we may expect to see him compared, in some other production of the same author, to a bird, and made to fly different ways and in different places at once.

"But let us leave the wit and come to the wisdom; which will bring us back to our subject.

"In the last paragraph of this elaborate piece, the author sets the example of my Lord Falkland and others before our eyes; who strengthened, as he says, the republican party so long, that when they found out their designs and forsook them, it was too late to prevent them. After this, he calls most charitably on several well-meaning persons to take warning; for some, whom he allows to be such, he thinks in danger of being drawn in to favor the purposes of those whom he calls opposers of our government.

"Behold this little Gamaliel in cathedra! Observe the scholars he places at his feet for instruction! 'Risum teneatis amici?' Can the gravest of you forbear laughter?

"When we come to apply the general propositions laid down still more particularly to the English than we have done to the Roman history, I shall show you perhaps that this author, like most other fine men, treasures up in his memory the observations he meets with in history, instead of making his own upon the examination and comparison of the facts and characters he finds there; and that the example he hath chosen will come out against the very purpose he hath applied it to. In the mean time, let us observe that the alarm, which hath been taken by some of this company, and I suppose by others, at the publication of that stupid paper in Fog's Journal, shows how little reason there is to apprehend that those who are actuated by the spirit of liberty, and pursue the national interest, should be imposed upon by the spirit of any faction.

"The spirit of liberty is a jealous spirit; and faction is equally the object of its jealousy, whether the views of faction be directed in favor of the crown, or against it. I make this distinction here, though I shall have occasion to speak more fully upon it hereafter, because I perceive that we are apt to confine our idea of faction to such men and such measures, as are in opposition to the men in power, and to the measures they take; whereas in truth a number of men in power, who exercise it solely for their own private advantage and security, and who treat the nation as their farm, or rather as a country under contribution to them, let them shelter themselves under what authority they please, are as much a faction, as any number of men, who under popular pretences endeavor to ruin, or at least to disturb the government, that they may raise themselves.

"If the spirit of liberty were extinguished, as it is discouraged, the spirit of some faction or other would, no doubt, prevail, but this would not succeed under the mask of liberty. There would be, in such a case, no need of wearing this disguise. Men would avow faction. They would choose that which suited their interest best; and indeed it would be of no great moment which they chose.

"But if the spirit of liberty, which begins to revive in this country, becomes prevalent, there will remain nothing to fear from any faction whatever, whether masked, or unmasked. Whilst it is masked, and the instruments or members of its pursue the national interest, though they intend another, the bad principle is however so far productive of good, and the cause of virtue is so far promoted by vice itself. When it comes to be unmasked, and the instruments or members of it are hurried by indiscretion, or forced by the course of events, as they must be, to show their game, faction is that moment disarmed. The distinction marked, the separation follows of course; and those who espouse the cause of the nation will find themselves doubly strengthened by the assistance which faction gave them at one time, and by the opposition she makes to them at another. In short, gentlemen, the spirit of jacobitism may crawl about and skulk in corners. The spirit of the other faction may roll in gilded spires, and with erected crests in every public place, and hiss and threaten and cast its venom around; but the spirit of liberty, like the divine rod of Aaron, will devour all the serpents of the magicians.

"I see therefore no cause to fear that we may be drawn in to serve the purposes of faction, whilst we pursue the cause of liberty; and if we suffered ourselves to be drawn off from this pursuit by the jealousy which one faction endeavors to give us of another, we should be arrant bubbles indeed. Fog is not to be defended for publishing a paper liable every way to blame, and capable of no excuse; but if he hath hurt any body by it, he hath hurt himself; and the weight which is laid upon it by those on one side, who perhaps wrote it, is as ridiculous as the project of those who thought to advance the jacobite cause by it, if it came from that side."

Here the old gentleman broke off, and though he was pressed to resume the discourse he had begun, when this interruption happened, he desired to be excused, because it was late, and promised to comply with our request upon some other occasion. If he keeps his word, as I am persuaded he will, you shall hear again from,

Sir, yours, &c.

Letter 4

Few nations have gone through more revolutions, few governments have appeared more unsteady, or fluctuated more between prerogative and privilege, than this of Great Britain.

If we are freemen, it is because the spirit of liberty has been never yet quite extinguished among us.

We have been surprised, betrayed, forced, more than once, into situations little better than that of downright slavery. But these usurpations have not become settlements. They have disordered the frame, but not destroyed the principles of a free government. Like cloudy mornings, they have soon passed over, and the sun of liberty has broke out again with double force, and double lustre.

It must be a pleasure to reflect that uniformity of spirit which created, and has constantly preserved or retrieved, the original freedom of the British and Saxon constitutions.

I feel a secret pride in thinking that I was born a Briton; when I consider that the Romans, those masters of the world, maintained their liberty little more than seven centuries; and that Britain, which was a free nation above seventeen hundred years ago, is so at this hour.

However savage our British ancestors may be represented by the Romans, whom the luxury of Greece, and the effeminacy of Asia had already corrupted, they certainly were a people of spirit and of sense; who knew the ends of government, and obliged their governors to pursue those ends.

Cæsar himself acknowledges that they fought boldly for their liberties, when he invaded them; and there is good reason to believe, from his manner of writing, and abrupt way of leaving this island, that they gave him a warmer reception than he is willing to own.

But to speak of them after an author, in whose time they were better known than they were by Cæsar, or even by Tacitus; Dion Cassius, when he is about to relate the expedition of Severus into Britain, says "that they held a great part of the government in their own power."

Their long resistance against the Saxons shows their love of civil liberty.

Their long resistance against the usurpations of the church of Rome, begun by Gregory, that flatterer of Phocas and Brunehault, under pretence of converting the Saxons, shows their love of ecclesiastical liberty.

Though the Saxons submitted to the yoke of Rome, in matters of religion, they were far from giving up the freedom of their Gothic institutions of government.

The Saxon heretoges, that is, public generals, were chosen only to conduct them in war, not to rule over them in war and in peace.

These heretoges, among the German colonies, who settled in the countries they conquered, and founded new governments, became kings, and had trappings enough to set off their majesty, and to enforce their authority; but the supreme power centered in the micklemote, or wittagenmote, composed of the king, the lords, and the Saxon freemen, that original sketch of a British parliament.

Here all important affairs were treated. The conduct of their kings was examined in it, and controlled by it.

The rights of the people in those days, must have been carried to a very great height; since they went hand in hand with those of the church; and since a positive law declared that if the king did not defend both, he should lose even the name of king. "Nec nomen regis in eo constabit, verum nomen regis perdit."

The principles of the Saxon commonwealth were therefore very democratical; and these principles prevailed through all subsequent changes.

The Danes conquered the crown, but they wore it little; and

the liberties of the Saxon freemen they never conquered; nor wrought any alteration in the constitution of the government.

Thus much it was thought necessary to premise, concerning the original constitution of our government. We now come to that period of history, from whence we propose to deduce our following remarks.

William, the Norman, is come down to us in history under the character of a conqueror; and though it may be disputed whether he was strictly so any more than several other princes who have supported their titles by their swords, yet we may confess that he imposed many new laws and customs; that he made very great alterations in the whole model of government; and that he, as well as his two sons, ruled, upon many occasions, like absolute, not limited monarchs.

Yet neither he nor they could destroy the old constitution; because neither he nor they could extinguish the old spirit of liberty.

On the contrary, the Normans and other strangers, who settled here, were soon seized with it themselves, instead of inspiring a spirit of slavery into the Saxons.

They were originally of Celtic,[1] or Gothic extraction, call it which you please, as well as the people they subdued. They came out of the same northern hive; and therefore they naturally resumed the spirit of their ancestors, when they came into a country where it prevailed.

Stephen, the fourth king of this race, owed his crown to the good will of the nation; and he owed this good will to the concessions he made in favor of liberty.

John came to the crown after the death of his father Henry the Second, and his brother Richard the First, by the election of the people. His electors, indeed, found themselves deceived in their expectations; for he governed in the most extravagant manner. But they soon made him feel whose creature he was. The contests between the laity and an ambitious usurping clergy ran very high at this time. John had made his advantage of these

1. We have thought fit to explain the expression in this place, though we know the word Celtic, as well as Scythian, hath been used in the same large and general sense, which is made use of here; and we could show, if such a trifle deserved it, that by the Celtæ antiquity did not always understand the people inhabiting a part of Gaul, notwithstanding the quotations out of Polybius, Diodorus, &c. which have been urged, by way of cavil, against us.

divisions. But the spirit of liberty prevailed, and that of faction vanished before it. Men grew ashamed of being the tools of private ambition, when public safety was at stake. Those of the high church and those of the low church united in one common cause. The king blustered and drew out his army; but it was a British army. No wonder, therefore, if the king submitted, and Magna Charta was signed.

It was signed again by his son and successor, Henry the Third, in full parliament, and with the greatest solemnity. The people however abated nothing of their jealous, watchful spirit; and it was well for liberty they did not. The long reign of this prince was one continual struggle between him and them. The issue of this struggle was favorable to the latter. By exerting their strength, they increased it under Henry the Third. They lost no ground under Edward the First, and they gained a great deal under Edward the Second.

Thus was the present constitution of our government forming itself for about two centuries and a half; a rough building raised out of the demolitions which the Normans had made, and upon the solid foundations laid by the Saxons. The whole fabric was cemented by the blood of our fathers; for the British liberties are not the grants of princes. They are original rights, conditions of original contracts, co-equal with prerogative, and coeval with our government. As such, in the days we speak of, they were claimed; as such they were asserted by force of arms; as such they were acknowledged; and as such they were constantly maintained afterwards by that pertinacious spirit, which no difficulties nor dangers could discourage, nor any authority abate; not even that of the pope, as impudently as it was exercised, and as foolishly as it was revered in those superstitious ages.

Had this spirit relaxed in the course of so many years, our government must have settled in an absolute monarchy, or tyrannical aristocracy.

The Norman kings, of imperious tempers, assumed great power. The barons did the same. The people groaned under the oppression of both. This union was unnatural, and could not last. The barons, enjoying a sort of feudatory sovereignty, were often partners and sometimes rivals of the kings. They had opposite interests, and they soon clashed.

Thus was the opportunity created of re-establishing a more

equal free government than that which had prevailed after the Norman invasion.

The kings, the barons, and the clergy, not less ambitious or avaricious than either of the others, had powerful means of promoting their usurpations. The commonalty had little or no share in the legislature; made no figure in the government; and it is hard to conceive how they could act, as the others might, and certainly did by particular concerts, to the advancement of their particular interests.

All these disadvantages were supplied by that spirit of liberty which diffused itself through the whole mass. Numbers were on the side of the commons. In all disputes, therefore, it was necessary to apply to them. They made the proper use of such conjunctures. Whoever lost, they were sure to be gainers; for so they deemed themselves, when they suffered all the hardships of war, and even laid down their lives in the quarrel, if they left liberty more improved and better secured to their posterity.

By concessions to the commons, our kings maintained and extended their prerogatives over the barons. By espousing the national interest, the barons continued able to cope with the crown, till they broke among themselves. Nay, even the church, notwithstanding that ancient and close alliance between secular and ecclesiastical tyranny, was forced, on some few occasions, to be a friend to the liberties of the people.

The king, the barons and the clergy were all, in reality, enemies to public liberty. Their party were so many factions in the nation; yet they all helped, in their turns, to establish liberty.

So true it is, that every thing, even the vices of mankind, and the misfortunes of a country, will turn to the advantage of liberty, where the spirit of it is maintained in vigor; as every thing, even the good qualities of mankind and the prosperity of a country, may operate a contrary effect, where this spirit is suffered to decline.

As losing the spirit of liberty lost the liberties of Rome, even while the laws and constitutions, made for the preservation of them, remained entire; so we see that our ancestors, by keeping this spirit alive and warm, regained all the advantages of a free government, though a foreign invasion had destroyed them, in great measure, and had imposed a very tyrannical yoke on the nation.

Letter 5

We are now come to the reign of Edward the Third. We must desire our readers to stop here, and at the reign of his successor a little; since no reigns can furnish us with more memorable and pertinent examples, to show how the spirit of liberty exerts itself in favor of good princes; how slow it is to act even against the worst; and yet how effectually it is able to act even in the most desperate cases.

Old Froissart says, that the English had an opinion, grounded on observations made from the days of good king Arthur, that between two valiant and able princes in this nation, there always intervenes a king "moins suffisant de sens et de prouesse; of less sense and courage." I shall not warrant the exact truth of this observation. The proportion, I fear, is much greater on the worst side in all kingdoms. But certainly Edward the Third, whose story gave occasion to Froissart to broach this anecdote, stands between his father Edward the Second, and his grandson Richard the Second, a bright instance of this truth, that "great and good princes are favorers of liberty, and find their account in promoting the spirit of it; whilst the weakest and the worst princes chiefly affect absolute power, and often meet with the fate they deserve for such attempts."

The former know that they have nothing to apprehend from this spirit; and they wisely prefer the generous efforts of good-will and affection to the reluctant compliances of such as obey by force.

The latter, conscious that they are unable to lead, endeavor to drive their people. Unworthy to be kings, they struggle to be tyrants.

Few were the blemishes which may be thought to tarnish the lustre of this reign of Edward the Third. Few and short were the struggles between him and his people; for as he was fierce and terrible to his enemies, he was amiable and indulgent to his subjects. He not only observed the laws, but he made the sense of the nation, in some measure, a law to him. On this principle, in which, to a considering mind, there will appear as much wisdom as goodness, he removed a son, nay a favorite mistress from court.

Henry the Fourth, if I mistake not, did something of the same kind; and which of their successors, after such examples, could presume to think it below his dignity to consult the inclination of his people, and make them the rule of his conduct?

Under this great prince, the constitution of our parliaments, and the whole frame of our government became reduced into a better form. A spirit of liberty breathes in the laws of this glorious king; and the power and duty of parliaments are set forth, in some of them, with such terms as would never have been passed by a prince who had put the least pedantry, or the least foppery, into his notions of kingship.

The spirit of liberty was not idle in this reign, though it had little or no occasion of exercise against the crown. The usurpations of the church were many and grievous. They had been long murmured against; but a false respect for religion had hitherto maintained them. This delusion began now to be removed. Wickliffe arose to dispel this magic charm; to undraw the veil of this pretended sanctuary; and to expose the horrors and trifles which lurked behind it, to public view, indignation and contempt. The axe was now first aimed at the root of popery; and prelates were taught the first lessons of moderation. Parliaments sat and proceeded on business, even on ecclesiastical business, without the intervention of mitres. There was, I believe, one parliament held, to which few or none of the prelates were summoned; in order, perhaps, to teach them how little their concurrence was essential to give due weight to the counsels, or full authority to the acts of parliament.

As this prince loved, instead of hating, as he encouraged, instead of discountenancing, the spirit of liberty in his people; so he was strengthened and supported by it in such a manner, and in such circumstances as cannot be paralleled.

The nation had been miserably harassed by civil wars and oppressions of various kinds, when he came to the crown. The burthen of personal service, and the taxes raised to defend the dominions which his predecessors held on the continent, had exhausted all degrees of people. This mischief was so much resented by them, that foreign interest and foreign counsels may be justly reckoned among the principal causes of all the disputes, and even wars, between them and their former kings.

In this situation, and in this temper of mind was the nation, when Edward the Third, by laying claim to the crown, and undertaking the conquest of France, opened to his subjects the terrible prospect of being worse than ever oppressed by the same grievances; and yet his nobility and commonalty seconded him in all these enterprises, with fewer complaints than could have been expected. These men, so apt to complain of grievances, and so little patient under them, carried him triumphantly through all his wars abroad, though they struggled with want, pestilence and famine at home.

What principle produced this wonderful change? Did higher notions of prerogative prevail? Had the doctrines of a slavish submission at once possessed our ancestors? By no means. It was not the power, it was not the authority of the king, which forced; but it was the character of the man, which invited to those compliances. The spirit of liberty exerted itself in favor of the patron of liberty.

A corrupt parliament, a degenerate nobility, a servile commonalty, will sacrifice anything to any prince; to a Richard the Second or an Edward the Third, equally and discriminately. But a free, a generous, a virtuous people, such as we may boast our ancestors were in those days, will sacrifice everything, except liberty, to a prince like Edward the Third, and liberty is a sacrifice which a prince like him will never require at their hands. To him who would require it, they would sacrifice nothing. Such a people may be well governed with ease; and it ought to be hard to govern them ill. They will do more for a prince whom they love and esteem, than he has a right to expect from them. If they do less for a prince whom they despise or hate, they are surely very excusable.

In order to render this example still stronger and more useful, it may be proper to point out, besides his general character, some of those particulars in the conduct of Edward the Third, which probably induced his people to sacrifice their estates, and their lives too, so cheerfully in a cause, to which, under other princes, they had been so averse.

In the first place, as his father Edward the Second lost his crown and his life, in the most miserable manner, by suffering himself to be governed by his ministers, and protecting them from the resentments of the people; so his son very early exerted his own authority, and freed himself from the guardianship, or rather subjection, of the queen and Mortimer, who had long oppressed the nation, and dishonored the young king by their scandalous conduct.

The next reason seems to have been this: Though he was magnificent in his court, yet he limited, with great care, the exactions of his purveyors, kept a severe hand over them, and suffered no more to be levied on his people, than what the necessary expense of his household required. He saved for his people, not for himself.

Thirdly, the taxes laid in his time, were laid for visible and important services, wherein the honor at least of the nation was concerned; which every man knew and approved.

Fourthly, the expenses were lessened by that double economy, which is so rarely found, or even understood. I mean not only that inferior economy, which consists in the management of the receipts and issues of the public revenue; but that superior economy, which consists in contriving the great schemes of negotiation and action. When the talents for this economy are wanting in those who govern, the public pays for their want of genius; and the prince's, or minister's errors are so many additional taxes on the people. When these talents are wanting, the very reverse happens. The genius of the prince, or minister, comes in aid of the public charge. Much is saved; and art and management supply it all.

Edward the Third began his war against France, in conjunction with German allies. He saw no better expedient at that time. But as soon as fortune and intrigue had procured it for him, he took another, shorter, cheaper, and more effectual method. He supported the Earl of Monfort, competitor with Charles of Blois, for the Duchy of Brittany. "Avecques les Allemans, et les Brabançons," says Froissart, "il n'avoit riens fait, sors despendre grossement; et l'avoit mené et demené les siegneurs de l'empire, qui avoient prints son or et son argent, ainsy qu'ils avoient voulu, et riens fait. Si descendit á la requeste du comte joyeusement," &c. That is, "with the Germans and the Brabançons, all he had been able to do was to spend great sums of money. The princes of the empire, who had taken as much as they would of his gold and his silver, and had done nothing for it, were accustomed to amuse him, and to tire him out. He condescended therefore to the request of the earl very joyfully."

Fifthly, it was not owing to his success that the people had a good opinion of his enterprises, and promised themselves a happy issue, how difficult, or dangerous soever these enterprises might appear. Their confidence was placed, and very justly, in those qualities, and that tenor of conduct, which they observed in their king, and to which his prodigious success was owing. No man contrived, prepared, resolved with more phlegm, or acted with greater fire; the reverse of his successor, who resolved rashly, and executed irresolutely. He waited sometimes for opportunities, but he always improved them when they happened; and those accidents which govern or dictate the measures, and perpetually shift the fluctuating schemes of weak governments, were bent by this great prince to serve the wisest and most steady purposes!

Sixthly, if he drained away some of the national wealth by taxes, he restored it very amply again, by the great care he took of extending and improving trade; by which he opened new mines of treasure; and, for a few temporary contributions, enriched his people to future generations. A prince, who adds to the national stock, has a right to share the advantage he procures, and may demand supplies from his people without blushing. But a prince who lives a rent-charge on the nation he governs, who sits on his throne, like a monstrous drone in the middle of a hive, draining all the combs of their honey, and neither making nor assisting the industrious bees to make any; such a prince, I say, ought to blush at every grant he receives from a people, who never received any benefit from him. The Duke of Gloucester told Richard the Second, on his restoring Brest to the Duke of Brittany, that he should have taken a town by his own valor and conduct, before he resigned what his ancestors had left him. Much to the same purpose might an oppressed people justly answer a craving prince. When you have increased the riches and advanced the prosperity of the nation, you will have some right to make these demands upon us; but till then we shall think that you have none.

Letter 6

The glorious scene of government which displayed itself in the reign of Edward the Third, was strangely altered on the succession of Richard the Second; a violent, haughty, obstinate and weak prince; whose reign, as one of our historians observes, "affords but little matter that may shine in history; and cannot boast of any one great and distinguished captain; any one memorable battle, or important siege; but prorogations of truces, abstinences, sufferances, patiences, tolerances were the language and amusement of the times; and treaties were all the while kept on foot for a perpetual peace; treaties," says he, "hitherto fruitless, illusory and impracticable."

It must be confessed that the reins of government hung pretty loose in the hands of Edward the Third, towards the latter end of his reign; from whence proceeded the growth of those factions which disturbed the beginning of his grandson's reign. Some part of this was owing, very probably, to the abuse of Wickliffe's doctrines: more to the cruel treatment which the inferior part of the commonalty received. The lords grew tyrants, and the commons rebels. But these commotions were soon suppressed by the united force of the rest of the nation; much sooner, and with consequences less fatal than in other countries, where rebellion and popular insurrections seem to have been the epidemical distempers of that age.

Mr. Francklin was taken up for printing this paper and the preceding one, on the reign of Edward the Third; but no farther prosecution hath been yet commenced against him on that account.

If the spirit of faction was soon quelled among the commons, it prevailed openly, scandalously, and dangerously in the court. Something of it might be discerned, perhaps, among the lords, who opposed the court: even in the Duke of Gloucester, the favorite of the people; in the Duke of Lancaster, a wise prince, and who acted long the moderating part; in Arundel and others. Nothing of it was to be observed in the general proceedings of parliament, and in the national conduct.

The justness of the character given before of Richard the Second, discovered itself very early in his actions. He had a brutality, and a good opinion of himself; one of which might have betrayed him into a discovery of what it was his interest to conceal, if the other had not made him capable of doing it, even on reflection. Hence came those famous and foolish sayings of this prince, which history has preserved, and which gave his people timely warning what they had to expect from him. Of his commons he said, "that slaves they were, and slaves they should be." Upon an address from parliament to remove his chancellor and treasurer, his answer was, "that he would not remove, at their request, the meanest scullion out of his kitchen."

However, he found men, as all princes may easily do, who flattered him in his vices and follies; such men, for instance, as Nevil, Vere, Poole, Tressilian, and others; who, to fasten him to themselves, made the nation odious to him, as they made him odious to the nation, by their rapine, their insolence, and by a weak administration, which exposed the kingdom to be invaded by the Scots, and threatened and insulted by the French.

During all this time, parliaments met frequently, and gave necessary supplies; some grievances they redressed, but bore the mal-administration of the court faction till the tenth year of this king, when they prosecuted the favorites with great justice, with temper, and yet with vigor. They spared nothing to provide for the defence of the kingdom by sea and land; and having put the administration, for a time, into the hands of persons chosen by themselves, gave the king such a warning as might have taught him to abandon a faction, and to throw himself on his people—but it proved in vain. His favorite ministers persuaded him that they suffered for his sake; that the aim of their enemies was to dethrone him by disgracing them; and whilst all the troubles of his reign were due to his support of them, they made him believe that they suffered for executing his orders, and maintaining his authority. Nay, they represented to him that, by accusing the counsellors, a man plainly shows that he believes the sovereign incapable of governing; and that the readiest way to discredit a prince is, persuading his subjects that he makes use of ill ministers. These arguments and artifices, ridiculous as they seem, succeeded, and had their effect for some time longer.

The deluded king entered into a closer conjunction than ever with his ministers. He took their iniquities on himself; made their cause his own; was privy to their plots of poisoning their enemies; of packing juries; of corrupting the judges to give opinions against law; and to all that dirty work which they wanted, not he. Nay, by his encouragement they raised troops, and a battle was fought in their quarrel; but they were defeated, and the fourteenth parliament, called the wonder-working parliament, having punished the judges and ministers with proper severity, endeavored to reconcile the king and his people. They gave him great subsidies, and renewed their homage and fealty to him.

Even all this still proved in vain. No experience was sufficient to reclaim Richard the Second. He governed tyrannically at home, and took a wife, and bought a peace from France. It is remarkable, that the peace cost him four hundred thousand pounds, much more than he got by his wife. His favorite ministers had before this time endeavored to persuade him to give up Calais, and purchase the friendship of France, to assist him against the lords and others who opposed him. This is not the last, nor least instance of conducting foreign affairs purely with regard to the interest of ministers, and without any to the honor and interest of the nation.

The factions among the great men were of double advantage to the king for a time.

First, the body of the people, who showed themselves sufficiently animated with a spirit of liberty, grew cool in espousing the quarrels of the lords, after they thought liberty secured by the proceedings of parliament, in the tenth year of this king; and though many particular actions of violence, of treachery, and of cruelty, were committed by Richard the Second, they bore all with the greatest patience for several years.

In the next place these factions among the great men enabled the king to divide them, to play one against the other, and to build up his tyranny on the ruins of both. His uncle, the Duke of Gloucester, was basely betrayed, and barbarously murdered by him. He procured a packed parliament, consisting of men imposed on the shires and towns by the king's authority, wholly managed by court favorites, and which bent all its endeavors to destroy the liberties and privileges of the people. With the help of such a parliament, he wreaked vengeance on those who had opposed him; got his authority exalted above all law, and exercised a most cruel tyranny.

The people still bore, and it is probable that the king, and others as well as he, imagined that they would be obliged to bear on, since the whole legislature united in their oppression. But in this he was deceived. When the parliament took the part of the people, the people followed the motions of parliament. When they had no hopes from parliament, they followed the first standard which was set up against the king. The same spirit of liberty, which had been so slow to act under so many provocations, acted with the greatest vigor when it was least expected. The king, at the head of an army in Ireland, the Duke of York at the head of another in England, and the Earl of Salisbury at the head of a third, could do the king no service. The armies would not fight for the king against their country. The whole nation abandoned him, or acted against him. Some of his ministers were hanged; particularly those who had been the great instruments of taxing and oppressing the people. He was, at length, forced to resign, and to subscribe an instrument with his own hand, by which he confessed himself unworthy to govern the kingdom any longer. This instrument of resignation was not only unanimously approved of in parliament, but articles of accusation were ordered to be drawn up against him, to justify their resolution of deposing him. These articles were thirty-five in number, setting forth the particulars of his misgovernment; two of which are to this effect:

"That he had put the administration of the public affairs in the hands of unexperienced and ill-designing persons, to the great damage of the people, who were loaded with excessive taxes.

"That in his negotiations with foreign princes, he had made use of so many equivocations and sophistries, that none would take his word any more."

It is very observable, that these extremities fell upon Richard the Second, at a time when every thing seemed to contribute to his support, in the exercise of that arbitrary power which he had assumed. Those whom he had most reason to fear, were removed either by violent death, or banishment; and others were secured in his interest by places, or favors at court. The great offices of the crown, and the magistracy of the whole kingdom, were put into such hands as were fit for his designs; besides which, he had a parliament entirely at his devotion: but all these advantageous circumstances served only to prove that a prince can have no real security against the just resentments of an injured and exasperated nation; for, as Rapin observes upon the sad catastrophe of his reign, and that of Edward the Second, "in such governments as that of England, all endeavors used by the king to make himself absolute, are but so many steps towards his own downfall."

It is farther observed by another eminent writer upon this reign, which he justly calls a reign of favorites, "that the king in his distress, saw himself forsaken by those whom he should have forsaken before; the very men, who had so much flattered him with their excessive love and loyalty; and like those mean insects, which live with a little warmth, but shrink at any change of weather, they who had contributed to all his errors in his prosperity, transplanted their zeal into the new sunshine, as soon as his successor demanded the crown."

Letter 7

From the reigns of Edward the Third, and Richard the Second, we shall hasten downwards, as fast as some necessary observations will permit. Those of the princes of York and Lancaster, form a period of more than eighty years, which passed in foreign and civil wars, in frequent revolutions of government, and in all those disorders which usually accompany and follow such revolutions.

The party of Richard the Second, even after the death of that unhappy prince, broke out into open rebellion against Henry the Fourth: but their efforts were vain. He held the crown fast which the parliament had given him; and the chief of his opposers perished in their attempts. Happy had it been, if they alone had suffered; but here we must observe a necessary and cruel consequence of faction. As it oppresseth the whole community, if it succeeds; so it often draws oppression, not on itself alone, but on the whole community, when it fails. The attempts to dethrone Henry the Fourth, justified him, no doubt, in supporting himself by a military force. They excused him likewise; very probably, in the eyes of many, for governing with a severe hand; for doing several illegal and tyrannical actions; for invading the privileges of parliament, at least in the point of elections; and for obtaining, by these means, frequent and heavy taxes on the people: for as all this might appear the harder, because it happened in the reign of a king who had no title to his crown but the good-will of the people, and the free gift of parliament; so it might appear, on the other hand, the less grievous because some part of it was rendered necessary by the opposition which a faction made to a parliamentary establishment; and because the rest of it was represented, perhaps, under that umbrage, to be so likewise, by the court logic of that age.

A people may be persuaded to bear patiently a great deal of oppression, as long as they can be persuaded that they bear it only to defend their own choice, and to maintain their acts; but if they discover this to be nothing more than a pretence, by which such powers are kept up as are unnecessary to their security, and dangerous to their liberty; by which the wealth of the whole nation is drained into the coffers of a few; and by which, in one word, they become exposed to ruin by the very means which they took to avoid it; it cannot be expected that they will be patient very long.

It deserves particular notice, that although Henry the Fourth was willing to show his clemency, at the beginning of his reign, by inflicting a very slight punishment on the wicked and hated ministers of the late king; yet it being alleged in their excuse, that Richard had compelled them to act, the parliament took occasion from thence to pass an act, by which it was declared that, for the future, compulsion should be no legal excuse to justify actions contrary to law. The reasonableness and expediency of this act are very manifest; for it is the indispensable duty of a good minister to dissuade his majesty from all illegal measures; or, if he cannot prevail, to quit his service, rather than suffer himself to be made the instrument of them; and if the commands of the prince were to be allowed a sufficient justification, the prerogative of doing no wrong would be extended to ministers, and nobody would be left accountable for maladministration.

In the short, but triumphant reign of Henry the Fifth, the spirit of faction was awed; and the spirit of liberty had no occasion of exerting itself; at least with struggle and in any signal manner, under a prince just, moderate and pious, according to the religion of those times.

The reign of his son was the reign of faction; and it discloses an horrid scene of iniquity, folly, madness. The scandalous management of public affairs, which brought infinite loss and dis-

194

honor to the nation, gave real occasion, as well as pretence, to commotions and insurrections. The contemptible character of the man who sat on the throne, revived the hopes of the faction of York. The faction of Lancaster took the alarm. Most of the great and active men were attached to one side or to the other, by obligation, by resentment, by hopes, or by fears. The national interest was sunk, to the shame of the nation, in the particular interest of two families.

In the civil wars, which happened a century and a half, or two centuries before this time, the point in dispute was how the people should be governed. In these we are speaking of, the point in dispute was who should govern. The first was worth contending for, and deserved all the blood which was shed in the quarrel. But this cannot be said of the last, which ought always to be looked upon with great indifference; except in cases where it has so immediate and necessary a relation to the first, that securing the first depends, in a great measure, on settling the last. Such cases have happened; and particular instances may be easily found; but the contrary cases, where men have fought for governors without regard to government, are easy to be found likewise; and that was plainly the case of the two factions of York and Lancaster.

The parliaments in those days seemed to be in another temper; very little concerned who was king, and very much to preserve the constitution. In the many revolutions which happened, each side would have the parliament for them. Whatever titles they set up, they were glad to hold the crown by the grant, or by the confirmation of parliament. The parliament wisely complied, whoever prevailed. The chance of war determined who should be king; at one time Henry the Sixth, at another Edward the Fourth, and the parliament accordingly placed them on the throne, and settled their government.

There is another observation which ought to be made, before we leave this period of time. The reigns of Richard the Second and Henry the Fourth had shown the dangerous consequences of that influence which the crown had obtained in the elections of members of parliament. The watchful spirit of liberty was soon alarmed, and prevailed to make such regulations about elections, and about the qualifications of the electors and the elected, as seemed at that time sufficient to prevent this influence for the future. These regulations appear in several laws, made during the reigns of the three Lancastrian princes; and our elections proceed, in a great measure, upon them to this very day. These regulations have required, and must, in the nature of things, require to be altered, as the course of accidents, or the change of national circumstances shall suggest reasons for so doing. But then such alterations have been, and ought always to be contrived so as to adapt them better, and to enforce them more strongly; because the principle on which they are founded, can never vary, and is so essential to the preservation of liberty, that if it be lost, and if a practice in opposition to it should ever prevail, the balance of our government would be that moment lost, and the British constitution left at the mercy of any ambitious prince, or wicked minister.

For this reason Mr. Rapin observes very justly, "that there are but two ways of depriving the English of their liberties; either by laying aside parliaments, or bribing them." And in another place he says, "that the English freedom will be at an end whenever the court invades the free election of parliaments."

It is necessary to insist upon this observation a little; because it hath been ridiculed, though dully, and great pains have been taken to explode the doctrine contained in it, which was laid down in these words. "In a constitution like ours, the safety of the whole depends on the balance of the parts; and the balance of the parts on their mutual independency on each other." These words, it seems, even with those of Thuanus to explain them, convey no idea to the London journalist; but this will be found, as I apprehend, to be his fault, or his defect, not Oldcastle's. A man born without the sense of hearing, or stopping his ears, and determined at any rate not to hear, may be deaf to the voice of Stentor himself.

I shall not enter into any altercations with the London Journalist, nor go out of the road to have the honor of such company. But when I meet him in my way, I shall encounter him frankly, without the least fear of being crushed by the weight of his arguments; or, which is more, by the power of his patron.

To say, like this author, that the "carrying on of business, and maintaining government by powers absolutely distinct, and absolutely independent, is a mere Utopian scheme, must proceed from ignorance or folly." Have not powers, absolutely distinct and independent, been joined by federal unions? Are no such examples to be found, even at this day? Has not this been brought about by the very reason given to prove that it can never happen; because men agree when they see reason for agreement; and they see reason for agreement, when they see their interest in agreeing? Osborne could not be in earnest, when he let such stuff fall from his pen. He meant to elude the argument, and to perplex his readers, or he meant nothing. But this shall not pass. The matter is too important. He shall be talked to as he desires, without a metaphor; and what has been advanced shall be applied to our government.

A king of Great Britain is that supreme magistrate who has a negative voice in the legislature. He is entrusted with the executive power, and several other powers and privileges, which we call prerogatives, are annexed to this trust. The two houses of parliament have their rights and privileges; some of which are common to both, others particular to each. They prepare, they pass bills, or they refuse to pass such as are sent to them. They address, represent, advise, remonstrate. The supreme judicature resides in the lords. The commons are the grand inquest of the nation, and to them it belongs likewise to judge of national expences, and to give supplies accordingly.

If the legislative as well as the executive power, was wholly in the king, as in some countries, he would be absolute; if in the lords, our government would be an aristocracy; if in the commons, a democracy. It is this division of power, these distinct privileges attributed to the king, to the lords, and to the commons, which constitute a limited monarchy.

Again: as they constitute a limited monarchy, so the wisdom of our government has provided, as far as human wisdom can provide for the preservation of it, by this division of power, and by these distinct privileges. If any one part of the three which compose our government, should at any time usurp more power than the law gives, or make an ill use of a legal power, the other two parts may, by uniting their strength, reduce this power into its proper bounds, or correct the abuse of it; nay, if at any time two of these parts should concur in usurping, or abusing power,

197

the weight of the third may, at least, retard the mischief, and give time and chance for preventing it.

This is that balance which has been so much talked of, and this is the use of it. Both are plain to common sense, and to experience; as will appear farther in the course of these remarks, where we shall have occasion to show, how often the proper use of this balance has saved our condition; and to what misfortunes we have been exposed by the neglect, or improper use of it.

Since this division of power, and these distinct privileges constitute and maintain our government, it follows that the confusion of them tends to destroy it. This proposition is therefore true; that, in a constitution like ours, the safety of the whole depends on the balance of the parts. Let us see whether it be true, that the balance of the parts consists in their mutual independency.

To speak again without any metaphor, the power, which the several parts of our government have of controlling and checking one another, may be called a dependency on one another, and may be argued for by those who want to throw darkness round them, as the dependency opposed to the independency mentioned in the proposition. But the fallacy is gross. We have shown that this power of control in each, which results from the division of power amongst all the parts of our government, is necessary to the preservation of it: and thus a sort of constitutional dependency, if I may have leave to express myself in that manner, is created among them; but this mutual dependency cannot be opposed to the independency pleaded for. On the contrary, this mutual dependency cannot subsist without such an independency; for whenever this independency is lost, the mutual dependency is that moment changed into a particular, constant dependency of one part on two; or, which is still more unreasonable, of two parts on one. The constitutional dependency, as I have called it for distinction's sake, consists in this; that the proceedings of each part of the government, when they come forth into action and affect the whole, are liable to be examined and controlled by the other parts. The independency pleaded for consists in this; that the resolutions of each part, which direct these proceedings, be taken independently and without any influence, direct or indirect, on the others. Without the first, each part would be at liberty to attempt destroying the balance, by usurping or abusing power; but without the last, there can be no balance at all. I will illustrate this, by supposing a prince, who claims and exercises a right of levying money without consent of parliament. He could not be opposed effectually, if the two houses of parliament had not a right to oppose him, to call his ministers to account; and to make him feel that, far from being absolute, he was under this constitutional dependency; but he would not be opposed at all, if the two houses of parliament were under his influence, and incapable of directing their proceedings independently of him. One would be ashamed to insist thus much on a point so very clear, if some men were not so hardened to all sense of shame, as to maintain the contrary; and that there are men capable of doing this, is one of those melancholy symptoms which characterise the present age. I could almost appeal to the cool thoughts, and the private reflections of some of these writers, whether any thing can be more scandalous than the task they have undertaken. To screen their patrons, they endeavor to distinguish us out of our greatest national advantages; as was observed in the case of Dunkirk. To reconcile the minds of men to such measures as their patrons may want, and as no honest man will take, they endeavor to demolish the very corner stones on which the whole fabric of liberty rests. Their iniquity, it must be confessed, is very systematical. When they write for corruption, they write for the means. When they write for the dependency of the parliament on the court, they write for the end. Well might Oldcastle say of these writers, their patrons and abettors, "that the mask was pulled off on one side." Let me conjure them, in the name of modesty, to call themselves Whigs no longer. It is time they should lay that appellation aside, since it will not be hard to prove, from the general tenor of their writings, that the maxims they advance, the doctrines they inculcate, and the conduct they recommend, lead to the destruction of civil liberty, as much as the political lessons of Sibthorpe, Manwaring, or archbishop Laud himself. They and their followers declared themselves directly against liberty. To plead for it was almost blasphemy; and to assert it little less than the sin against the Holy Ghost, according to the doctrines taught by those divines. Such absurdities made few converts in those days; and the preachers of them would meet with the utmost contempt in these. But the writers, of whom we now complain, affect to maintain the cause of liberty, whilst they betray it. They assert the principles of liberty in general, and sometimes reason upon them well enough; but when they apply them to particular cases, they prevaricate, evade, and exert all their poor endeavors to turn the cannon of liberty against herself. The others had fænum in cornu. They put mankind on their guard against them, and were the true promoters of all the mischief and confusion which followed, when the nation ran into the utmost extremes, in opposition to them. These men insinuate themselves as friends to liberty. They are looked upon as such by some few persons, who mean well to liberty, even at this time; and yet they are almost wholly employed in promoting that which is destructive of liberty, and inconsistent with it, corruption and dependency. Laud and the others endeavored openly to lop the branches and cut down the tree; but these men are privately poisoning the root of liberty. The power of the court, and the authority of the lawyers could not make the levying ship-money pass for law, nor prevail on the nation to bear it. But if it were possible to suppose a house of commons as dependent as these lawyers (and they would be as dependent, if the doctrines which oppose prevailed amongst them), the nation might then be loaded with taxes, oppressed with debts, and reduced to the greatest misery by law. Our liberties, as well as our estates, might be taken from us. We might be legally undone. These are possible consequences of such doctrines. If they are not probable, we owe no thanks to the weekly preachers of them. The nature of our present settlement, which is built on the foundation of liberty, the interest and honor of the prince now on the throne, as well as of all his illustrious posterity, are our security against these dangers; but still I say, we owe no thanks to the writers on the side of the ministry.

I have dwelt pretty much upon this point, to show what is the real design of these remarks; and I will venture to add that those persons who oppose such doctrines as we have been opposing, will appear at last to be the truest friends to his majesty king George, and the protestant succession; which can subsist only upon those principles upon which it was originally established.

Letter 8

If the reign of Henry the Sixth was a reign of faction, those of the house of York were likewise. The popularity, bravery, cruelty, rashness, uxoriousness, incontinence of Edward the Fourth; in short, his good and his bad qualities worked the different effects of supporting, exasperating and increasing factions. The characters of Henry the Sixth's queen and of the Earl of Warwick, to mention no more of the principal actors on that bloody stage, conspired to maintain and aggravate this national calamity.

In these long continued struggles, the whole nation became involved, and the factions of York and Lancaster growing every day more animated and better disciplined, we are not to wonder that if they fought usque ad internecionem; at least, till the field of battle, the scaffold, and some theatres of clandestine murders had left no man on one side alive, who was in a condition to oppose or give jealousy to the other. But that which may very justly raise our wonder, is that Edward the Fourth, having secured to himself and his family the possession of the throne, by the murder of Henry the Sixth, and his son, and by the total defeat of the whole Lancastrian party, should suffer two new factions to be nursed up, which divided his own party, occasioned the murder of his sons, and by establishing the short-lived tyranny of his brother, brought the Earl of Richmond to the throne, and sunk for ever the house of York in that of Lancaster.

Edward the Fourth's queen was the original cause of all this mischief, and a principal sufferer herself in the course of it. She was resolved to govern at any rate; and Rapin observes

> that as her being queen gave her no manner of title to meddle with the affairs of the public, she knew how to manage that matter another way; namely, by the influence she had over the king. Though Edward often proved false to her, she bore it very patiently, and never showed her uneasiness at it. Edward, charmed to find himself at liberty to pursue his inclinations, without danger of continual reproaches, repaid her moderation with the most obliging and condescending behaviour; of which she knew how to make a good use.

She maintained this ascendant over her husband to the last, and for a little complaisance, which cost her nothing in present, she purchased a degree of power in the state, which cost her dear in consequence, by alienating the affections of the people from her husband during his life, and ruining his family afterwards, as I have hinted before.

"Her aim was," according to Rapin, "to secure her power during the king's life, and in case she survived him, to make sure of the government of the kingdom, in the name of the prince her son, when he should come to be on the throne; but by a fatality, not unusual to the best laid projects, this very thing proved the occasion of her own, and her family's ruin."

I cannot think, as Rapin seems to do, that her project deserved to be ranked amongst those which are the best laid. It appears to be the narrow project of a woman, who had cunning, insinuation, and the spirit of intrigue, with much pride and ambition; but wanted that extensive knowledge, and that superior genius, such as Catharine of Medicis, and our queen Elizabeth possessed, which is necessary to conduct so great a design as her passion prompted her to undertake; for what was her project? Was it to acquire an interest in the nation by deserving well of it? Nothing less. It was singly this; to form a faction at court, by raising her relations and immediate dependents, which should be wholly her own, and into whose hands she might throw all the power and profit which the king had to bestow. She had the good luck to compass this design, and triumphed, no doubt very wisely, in her great success. Surrounded by her creatures, she looked no farther than that circle, and either took no notice of the temper of the nation, or judged of it by the temper of the court. But the rise of this faction immediately formed another, and established the distinction of ancient and new nobility. The former had the true natural strength, which great estates in land and established credit in the nation gave them. The latter had no strength of their own, none but that adventitious strength, which arose from employments and favor at court. They brought nothing to court, which could make the court amends for the envy and discontent which their elevation created. To supply this, two things were done; which served, perhaps, to fortify the queen in her delusion, and thereby made the ruin of her ambitious projects the surer. All those who were not in the good graces of her faction, were disgraced at court, and in effect banished from it. Nay they were persecuted by the power of it; as the Duke of Clarence, the king's own brother, was even to death. The names of the parties of York and Lancaster might subsist and be made use of on proper occasions; but in reality, the being for or against the party of the queen, was the sole distinction which prevailed; and even the friends of the house of York, whom the queen did not affect, were debarred from the king's ear, excepting only three of his old and most faithful servants, who maintained themselves against her and her faction. I mean Stafford Duke of Buckingham, Hastings and Stanley.

Another method which this queen took to strengthen herself and her faction, was by raking up money by illegal and oppressive means; particularly by setting prosecutions on foot against the rich men of the kingdom, several of whom were arraigned for high treason, and encouraging the judges to get them found guilty at any rate. Habington observes, in his history of this king, "that as their wealth was the principal evidence against them, though their persons were acquitted, their estates were found guilty."

The same historian observes farther,

> that the memory of these carriages hithertofore, in a business that concerned the life of a man reputed innocent, drew the world into much fear that he would now decline to rigor. Neither was the king totally excused, although this cruel avarice was laid to the queen, who having a numerous issue and kindred, by favor

raised up to the highest titles, was almost necessitated, for supportance of their honors, to rack the kingdom.

Edward seemed sensible before his death, of the mischievous consequences which this conduct, and the clashing of two factions might produce. He endeavored to prevent them, by "reconciling the two parties; a poor expedient!" Rapin justly observes, "which could not easily produce the effect he expected."

The Duke of Gloucester, who concealed his design till his brother's death, took advantage of these factions. He made his court publicly to the queen, and held a private correspondence with the opposite party. Nay he found means, by fomenting it, to raise a third for himself.

I have dwelt the longer in this place, on the strange turns and cruel effects of faction; because I believe, no example can be produced out of any history, which sets them in a stronger light; and because this period of time affording but small matter to recommend the spirit of liberty, which had little to do in the transactions of it, I imagine that pointing out the fatal consequences of the contrary spirit, which then prevailed, may answer the same end, as exposing of vice is frequently the strongest recommendation of virtue.

But we must not imagine, notwithstanding all the contrary appearances in this period, that the spirit of liberty was absolutely extinguished. Though that flame was lost, for the most part, in the constant glare of faction, yet it was still alive; and by living, preserved the constitution of our government during the whole course of these civil wars.

If we look closely into these scenes of confusion, we may discover many particular instances of the operations of this spirit. Such were the difficulties and delays opposed to the grant of tonnage and poundage, for nine years together; and the many restrictions added to this grant, when it was at last obtained by Edward the Fourth. Other instances to the same purpose might be quoted; but we choose to insist on a more general observation, alrady mentioned by us, which runs through the whole period, and is so strongly vouched by history as to admit of no cavil.

The observation we are going to make, contains a memorable exception to this proposition, which is but too generally true, that the spirit of liberty and the spirit of faction are incompatible, and cannot long subsist together. The virtue of our ancestors made this exception; and if it hath been remembered to their shame, that they sunk the national interest in the particular interest of two families; it ought to be remembered to their honor, that they did so in this single point only, who should reign, and in no other. We took notice, in a former paper, that upon every revolution, each side engaged the parliament for them, and that whoever prevailed, the parliament wisely complied. This conduct, which lasted from Richard the Second down to Richard the Third, preserved our liberties; but it could not have been pursued, nor could our liberties by consequence have been preserved, if the spirit of liberty had not been latent in the hearts of those very men who seem to breathe nothing but faction. How could it have happened that the sole title of conquest was ever established in so many revolutions brought about by the sword, if the actors in them had not been strongly affected with a love and reverence for the free constitution of our government? The princes of York and Lancaster themselves were willing, nay desirous to have a parliamentary confirmation of their titles, real or pretended. But how came they to be so desirous of it? How came they to think it necessary? The case is plain. The temper of their parties and of their armies begot this necessity. The spirit of liberty prevailed enough in the whole body of the nation, out of which these parties and armies were composed, to preserve the principles of public freedom, though not enough to preserve the public peace. Each side contended to have a king of their own party; but neither side would have a tyrant. They sacrificed their lives to faction; but would not give up their liberties. The victorious armies led their kings to the foot of the throne; but carried them no farther.

The author of the Short History of standing armies observes that, "in all the wars of York and Lancaster, whatever party prevailed, we do not find they ever attempted to keep up a standing army. Such was the virtue of those times," says he, "that they would rather run the hazard of forfeiting their heads and estates to the rage of the opposite party, than certainly enslave their country, though they themselves were to be the tyrants." This remark is just, as far as it goes; and it goes as far as that author wanted to carry it; but it is not so full, nor carried so far as history will warrant. That the princes, who obtained the crown by their armies, did not attempt to govern by their armies afterwards, is most true, and may reflect some honor on those princes, and on the heads of their parties. But there is something more than this remarkable in the conduct of those times; for even in the heat of victory, in the raptures of a successful revolution, and before the armies could be disbanded, we see these princes obliged to ascend the steps of the throne in such a manner, and under such conditions, as the parliament thought fit to prescribe, and as were not always agreeable to them. This, I am sure, reflects great honor on the parliaments, who were actors in the last scenes of all these revolutions; and on the armies, who contented themselves to become spectators in such conjunctures. We will take the first example which presents itself in these wars.

The Duke of Lancaster was at the head of an army of sixty thousand men, when he came to the crown. The proclamation which he published the very day he was crowned, showed how very unwilling he was to seem to hold his crown purely by right of election. He would gladly have set up that of conquest; or a title derived from Richard the Second's resignation; or a title by blood; or any title but the true one. Notwithstanding this, he was obliged when nothing could have obliged him but the sense of his own party and army, to submit to as formal an election as ever was made. The two houses took notice of the blind claim of right which he entered. They chose him to be king, upon the question put to them, after having given their negative to the Duke of York, to his sons, and to others, who were severally proposed in the same manner to them. They seem industriously to have contrived and pursued, on this occasion, a method of proceeding as opposite as possible to the views and inclination of this prince, whose army attended him, and whose rival was his prisoner.

Again; to take another example from the latter end of these wars. The battle of Northampton being won, and Henry the Sixth taken, the Duke of York hastens out of Ireland to put himself at the head of his party and his army. The parliament meets. The duke asserts his undoubted right, by descent, to the

crown, which he demands as due to him, without any interposi
tion of parliament. He shows the utmost, and even an indecent
impatience to take possession of it. He is supported by his own
party. He is opposed by others. But the matter is by all submitted to the debate and decision of parliament. The debate
itself must have been grievous enough to a prince so fond of a
crown, and so much warmed with the notion of his hereditary
right. But the decision of this affair must have wounded him to
the quick. So little regard was paid to his right, that he was
forced to content himself with leaving the crown on the head of
Henry the Sixth during that prince's life, and not to have the
prospect of succeeding to it, till after that prince's decease; which,
by the way, was a point of the less value to him, because he was
older than Henry the Sixth, and could not hope to be the better
for it, according to the course of nature. He submitted to all
these mortifications; and a very judicious historian attributes his
submission to his moderation; but I believe those who fully consider his former conduct, and his passionate behavior at this
time, will hardly subscribe to such a judgment. His submission,
like that of Henry the Fourth, in the case before cited, was a
submission, which the temper of his party rendered necessary.
They would not force the resolutions of the two houses; and why
the two houses would go no farther in his favor, at that juncture,
might easily be accounted for, if this were a proper place for that
disquisition. After the battle of Wakefield, where the Duke of
York was killed, and that of St. Albans, where the Earl of Warwick was beaten, the faction of York were determined, by the
dangers they had run, and by the losses they had sustained, to
balance no longer, but to set the crown on the head of the Earl
of March; and yet they proceeded no otherwise than under the
authority of parliament, which had ratified the agreement made
between the late Duke of York and Henry the Sixth. By one
article of this agreement it was stipulated, that if king Henry
broke it in any point, the crown and royal dignity should immediately devolve on the Duke of York, if alive; or, in failure of
him, on his next heir. The Earl of Warwick therefore, in a kind
of military assembly (for a part of the army, at least, was there),
proceeded to the election of Edward the Fourth; but he proceeded on this foundation. The great efforts made to break this

agreement and to defeat the effect of it, by king Henry's queen, and the Lancastrian party, were interpreted, and not without color, as so many infractions of it. By consequence, Edward the Fourth had an immediate right to the crown, by virtue of the act of parliament made in confirmation of this convention, which act and convention were produced by Warwick, who caused them to be publicly read. The proceeding of this assembly, which hath a tumultuous air in history, was therefore in reality a proclamation of a king, made by authority of parliament, and not of an election of a king, without that authority.

Let us conclude, that if the spirit of faction hath, on some occasions, prevailed over the spirit of liberty, so far as to defeat and even pervert the designs of the latter; the spirit of liberty hath likewise revived, in its turn, on other occasions, and prevented the consummation of that misery which faction would naturally and of course have produced. Let us conclude that all standing armies, for whatsoever purpose instituted, or in whatsoever habit clothed, may be easily made the instruments of faction; because a body of men separated, in many respects, from the rest of the nation, constrained to different customs, and in some measure subjected to different laws, may be easily persuaded that they have a different interest. Let us conclude that these casuists in red, are the most dangerous in this respect, that having swords by their sides, they are able at once to cut those gordian knots which others must unite by degrees. But let us conclude, at the same time, that if a spirit of liberty be kept up in a free nation, it will be kept up in the army of that nation; and that when it is thus kept up, though the spirit of faction may do great hurt, it cannot complete the public ruin. We see the truth of this observation exemplified near three centuries ago; and let us remember with gratitude, that the same truth was again confirmed to us no longer ago than two-and-forty years.

Letter 9

One of the historians of Brittany, if I remember right, and I think it is Argentre, says the people of that duchy grew so much tired with the disputes between Charles of Blois and the Monforts, that the two parties agreed, just before a battle, to make an end of the quarrel at once, by taking off that prince, against whom the fortune of the day should declare itself. Our ancestors were very far from following this example; but they seized the opportunity which was presented to them, after Richard the Third had usurped the throne, and murdered his nephews, of abolishing tyranny, and extinguishing faction.

The princes of York and Lancaster butchered one another in such a manner, that the right of the former centered in Elizabeth, eldest daughter of Edward the Fourth, and the pretensions of the latter were allowed, by the whole Lancastrian party, to belong to the Earl of Richmond. This was the state of the families.

The faction of York detested Richard for his usurpation and cruelties. The faction of Lancaster hated him for his name; and neither the great qualities which he really had, nor the good qualities which he affected, could reconcile mankind to his barbarity. This was the temper of the nation.

The opportunity thus formed, was improved by the universal concurrence, which a spirit of liberty and a regard to the public good, independent of party, inspired. The faction of York became willing to receive a king of the house of Lancaster; and the party of Lancaster a queen of the house of York. All parties labored to unite the two roses; and faction itself was bent, in this fortunate conjuncture, to extirpate faction.

The deposition of Richard, and the advancement of the Earl of Richmond to the throne, upon this express condition, that he should marry the Princess Elizabeth, were pursued with success, even when Richard thought himself most secure; when the parliament had been obliged to confirm his usurpation; to declare the children of Edward bastards; and to attaint the Earl of Richmond.

What a scene of national peace and prosperity was opened by this revolution and new settlement! But how soon was it shifted? How soon were the wise and honest views of the many defeated by the cunning and iniquity of the few? Henry the Seventh, a creature of the people, if ever any prince was such, had been raised to the throne, in order to cut up the roots of faction; to restore public tranquility; and to establish a legal government on the ruins of tyranny. He did the very reverse of all this. His reign and that of his son have been two of the severest under which our country hath groaned since the conquest; and yet, in these very reigns, the foundations of liberty were laid much broader and stronger than ever. How this came about, it must be useful, and perhaps it may be entertaining, to consider.

Henry the Seventh, who would have been glad a little before to have assured himself of the crown on any terms, grew difficult as soon as he had obtained it. He durst not avow a title by conquest; but he evaded the appearances of a parliamentary title very industriously, and made the ceremony of his coronation precede the meeting of his parliament. He evaded, in the same manner, the appearances of any communication of right from the Princess Elizabeth, by deferring his marriage till an act had passed to settle the crown on him and his posterity, without any mention of the house of York. In short, his whole skill, credit and power were employed to get the act of settlement so generally and so ambiguously penned, as to leave him room to assert afterwards a right inherent in himself, and independent of the authority of parliament. Nay, he went farther; for, in the bull of confirmation, which he obtained from the pope, and in which he affected to have all sorts of titles enumerated, he took particular care to have that of conquest inserted.

Such a conduct gave sufficient reason for alarm; but we do not find that it was taken. The tyrant was dead, and the new establishment was made. The nation was overjoyed; and the work of liberty was done by halves. The new king found a compliance with all his measures, as new kings generally do. But little reflection was made, perhaps, at that time, on these proceedings of the court; or if a just reflection was made, we may easily believe that it was soon stifled by that adulation, which represents the most necessary precautions, the most just complaints, and the assertion of the clearest rights, as proofs of disaffection.

The whole course of Henry the Seventh's reign was answerable to these beginnings; and he seems to have established himself in the power of pursuing principles of government, evidently repugnant to those upon which he had been raised to the throne, before the nation was well aware of what he intended. He planted faction anew, and was the true cause of all the disturbances which followed from it, and which began even in the first year of his reign. Many of the York party had signalised themselves in his cause. All of them submitted to his government; and that small branch of this party, which had supported Richard the Third, was too inconsiderable to hurt him; but he soon made it considerable, by driving almost the whole York party into that interest. "He had conceived," says Rapin, "so mortal a hatred for the whole house of York, that he let slip no opportunity to humble the Yorkists; behaving always towards them not as a just king, but like the head of a party."

That some of his ministers, of the Lancastrian party, might find their private account in such a measure, and sacrifice to it both the interest of their master and their country, is obvious enough; but how the king, who was certainly an able man, could prefer dividing instead of uniting his people in affection and obedience, would appear very marvellous, if experience had not taught us that men of the greatest genius fall sometimes into the same errors, as men of the least genius would be apt to commit in the same circumstances. How this happens we are not, in this place, to inquire.

Henry the Seventh proceeded as he had been suffered to set out, and established by degrees, and those not slow, a power almost absolute. His jealousy, his pride, and his insatiable sordid avarice had their full swing. He became hated even by his own party, and might very probably have lost his crown, if many circumstances, both at home and abroad, had not conspired in his favor, and if he had not improved them all with the utmost ability of counsel and dexterity of management. The chief of these circumstances, and it well deserves to be remarked, was this—they who ventured their estates and lives in several insurrections against him, and they who privately fomented these insurrections, instead of uniting on a national principle, and bending their endeavors to a reformation of government, united on a principle of faction: for the king's behavior had revived this spirit, as we observed above; but still this spirit, though revived, had not attained its former strength. The nation in general was tired of faction; dreaded a relapse into the consequences of it, and would not engage for a Simnel, a Warbeck, or even a real prince of the house of York. A national coolness on one side, and vigilance and vigor on the king's part, defeated all these enterprises as fast as they were formed. Every one of these defeats gave Henry additional strength and increase of reputation, which is strength in its effects. Thus it happened in this case; and thus it hath happened in many others. By making an ill use of his power, the king was the real author of all the disorders in the state, and of all the attempts against his government; and yet, the better to prevent such disorders, and to resist such attempts, farther powers were intrusted to him. Because he had governed ill, it was put in his power to govern worse; and liberty was undermined, for fear it should be overthrown. It hath fared sometimes with monarchy as with the church of Rome. Both have acquired greater wealth and power by the abuse of what they had, and mankind have been egregiously the bubbles of both.

We must not however conclude that this king made force the sole, though he made it the principal expedient of his government. He was wise enough to consider that his court was not the nation; and that however he might command with a nod in one, he must captivate, at least in some degree, the good-will of mankind, to make himself secure of being long obeyed in the other;

LETTER 9

nay more, that he must make his people some amends for the oppressions which his avarice particularly exposed them to suffer.
For these reasons, as he strained his prerogative on some occasions very high, so he let it down again upon others; and affected
to show to his parliaments much condescension, notwithstanding
his pride, as well as much communication of counsels, notwithstanding his reserve.

To attribute to this Solomon of Great Britain the sole merit of
the laws made in his time, as some have done, seems unreasonable; but it was certainly great merit in him, and we may add rare
merit, instead of opposing, or refusing, constantly to remunerate
his people, by promoting and passing of "good laws, which ever-
more were his retribution for treasure." These are my Lord
Bacon's words, and better than his cannot be found to express
the general character of the laws which the wisdom of those times
produced. "They were deep and not vulgar; not made upon
"the spur of a particular occasion for the present; but out of providence of the future, to make the estate of the people still more
and more happy, after the manner of the legislators in ancient
and heroical times." Husbandry, manufactures, general commerce, and increase of useful people were carefully attended to,
and considerably advanced; so that whilst the weight of taxes
and the vexations of Empson, Dudley, and their subordinate harpies were severely felt, every man felt likewise the particular
benefit which he received in the general advantages procured to
the nation. These drops of manna, which fell from the throne,
softened the murmurs of the people. They could not make the
king beloved, but they made him less hated: and the middle and
lower ranks of men, who felt less the rigor of his government,
felt more immediately the effects of his care and his wisdom.

We will not refine so much as to say that the commons were
patient under the pressures of this reign, because they foresaw
the consequences of those measures which the king took to lessen
the power of his nobility. He did not, perhaps, himself discern
these consequences in their full extent; but surely if this part of
his conduct was polite, it was no less popular at that time; since
the same exorbitant power of the peers, which had been so formidable to the crown, had not been less oppressive to the commons. The weight of personal service had been terribly felt

213

during the wars of York and Lancaster, and the obligation of that tenure had, no doubt, contributed to prolong them. The tenant, therefore, who found this service commuted into a rent, could not but think his condition mended, and be extremely pleased with this alteration, though he did not see the consequences of the other, which, by opening a way to the lords to alienate their lands, opened a way to the commons to increase their property, and consequently their power in the state, as may be very easily observed in the succeeding reigns.

Letter 10

Henry the Eighth came to the crown with very great advantages. Whatever objections had been made to his father's title, there remained no pretence of objecting to his; and if any pretence had remained, the disposition to make use of it would not have been found. The nation was grown weary of faction; fond of tranquility; and every day more and more attentive to the arts of peace. The prerogative had been extended wide and carried high; and the means employed to acquire and maintain this authority, had been established by a reign of twenty-four years. The treasures which Henry the Seventh had accumulated and left to his son, were immense; and in leaving him these treasures he left him that which was more valuable than all of them. He left him an opportunity of gaining the affections of his people, on his accession to the throne, by putting a stop to that public rapine which had been so long exercised, and by disgracing and punishing those who had been the principal instruments of it. Henry the Eighth seized the opportunity and improved it. He confirmed, in the first moments of his reign, that pardon which his father had granted in the last of his life, and when he could hope for no farther profit by not pardoning. He invited, by proclamation, such as had been wronged to complain, and promised them satisfaction.

If Henry the Eighth had been avaricious, or weak enough to prefer wealth to popularity, he would have observed another conduct. He would have thought those men fittest to serve him, who had signalised themselves most in fleecing the people, and without any regard to their ability in playing the game of statesmen, he would have chosen them purely for their skill in packing the cards. Empson and Dudley would have continued in power, and have risen in favor. But he was too wise, or too honestly counselled in these beginnings of his government, to pursue such measures, or to employ such ministers. He kept some in his council, who were of approved abilities; but far from loading his own administration with the principal guilt of the former; far from grieving and provoking his people, by countenancing the most hated, and the most justly hated, men of the whole kingdom, he threw those criminals out of the sanctuary of the court, and exposed them to that national vengeance, under the weight of which they perished. The manner in which their lives were taken away seems liable to great objection, and I would not be thought to approve it; for a spirit of liberty can never approve such proceedings even against the worst and most guilty of men, as may be applied to destroy the best and the most innocent. All I mean to commend is the wisdom of Henry the Eighth, in abandoning these ministers, in gaining the affections of his subjects, and in making such impressions of gratitude on their minds, as lasted long and were of service to him, even when he oppressed the people in his turn.

Vanity and presumption were reigning qualities in the character of this prince. The first betrayed him into continual errors. The last made him persist in them. Pride is observed to defeat its own end, by bringing the man who seeks esteem and reverence into contempt. Vanity, self-sufficiency, presumption, the offspring of pride, have much the same effect; since no one is so liable to be deceived and governed, as he who imagines that he is capable of neither.

The characters of the princes and popes of this age, rendered the scene of foreign affairs very important. Henry the Eighth was happy enough to have no interest of his own abroad worth engaging him in the broils of the continent. He was free from guaranties of foreign dominions, and from all engagements to foreign princes, which could in the least incumber him. In this state he might have kept himself with equal dignity and advantage. He might have increased his strength, whilst other princes wasted theirs. He might have been applied to as the mediator, or arbitrator of the Christian world, and have found his account in all the wars and negotiations, without being a party in them. He did the very contrary. A rose, blessed by the pope, an emperor serving in his army, and taking his pay, a whimsical project of conquests never designed to be made, and impossible to be kept, if they had been made, were sufficient to draw him into the most extravagant engagements, in which he always played gold against counters with allies, who generally played counters against gold. His engagements of this kind became numberless, frequently inconsistent, and so very rash and unadvised, that whilst his aim, or his pretence, was to keep a balance between the great powers of Europe, he more than once assisted the strongest to oppress the weakest. The spring of all this strange conduct lay in the private interests and passions of Wolsey, who became his first minister very early, and was his favorite earlier. If Henry the Eighth negotiated perpetually, and was perpetually the bubble of those with whom and for whom he negotiated, this happened chiefly because he was, in the first place, the bubble of his minister. Wolsey's avarice was fed and his ambition flattered by the emperor, by the court of France, and by that of Rome, in their turns. He supported himself, in great measure, at home, by the opinion of his credit abroad; and his master's favor to him was strengthened by the art of those whom he served at his master's and his country's expense. In short, the success or disappointment of his private schemes were the hinges on which the whole policy of this nation turned for twenty years: and the grossest mismanagement, obstinately pursued, by the minister, in the midst of universal disapprobation, was sanctified by the king.

The king, no doubt, thought himself as infallible in the choice of men as in the choice of measures; and, therefore, when he had once given his confidence to Wolsey, no matter by what inducements, his presumption screened the minister from his suspicion.

It was easy for Wolsey to keep his master from hearkening to particular advice, or to the general voice of the people; because it was easy to persuade him that he wanted no advice; that he could not be deceived, though his people might; and, perhaps, that it was unbecoming a great prince to alter his measures, or withdraw his favor, on the clamors of the public. At the same time, we may fairly suppose (for the monuments of history will justify us in supposing) that the butcher's son was not such a bungler, nor rendered by a low education so void of address, as not to know how to insinuate without the air of advising; and how to receive all his own suggestions back from his master, in the style of orders, with the utmost demonstration of implicit submission to his judgment, and absolute resignation to his will.

But however blind the king might be, the eyes of the people continued to open to his and their true interest. The discontent grew general; and to this general discontent were owing the principal difficulties which Henry the Eighth met with, during the first half of his reign. As much complaisance as he had been used to find in his parliaments, he durst not always demand money of them, for the support of his enterprises. His minister soon put him upon the expedient of raising it by his own authority. But these attempts were resented warmly, and opposed to sturdily, even when the rough name of a tax was changed into the softer sound of a benevolence, that the king was obliged to retract; to compound; to excuse himself; to disavow his minister; and to pardon all those who had been concerned in particular insurrections, from a fear of one which might become universal.

No prince could be more firmly seated on his throne. No prince could be less framed to brook opposition. No prince could be less susceptible to fear. And yet to this point of distress did Henry the Eighth bring himself, by trusting his first minister too much, and regarding the sense of his people too little. All orders of men concurred on these occasions; and the merchants signalised themselves. Neither the flattery, nor the menaces of Wolsey could prevail on them to be silent, when they felt that their own and the national interests were sacrificed or neglected, at every turn. Much less could they be cozened so far as to expose their fortunes in trade, the only fortunes which merchants acquired in those days, in order to conceal the blunder of a minister, or to stop the clamor against him. We find a remarkable instance of this behavior of the merchants in the year 1528; when the commerce of the Low Countries, on which our woollen trade depended principally at that time, was interrupted by a war with the emperor, which evidently took its rise from no other motive than a pique of the minister.

The ill success of these illegal methods, obliged the king to have recourse to his parliament: but his parliament thought like his people; and the opposition given in the house of commons was such as became the representative body of the nation. That which happened in the year 1523, is worthy of particular observation. It was not grounded only on the exorbitancy of the sum demanded, but likewise on the nature of the service for which the demand was made. As high as prerogative was carried at this time, and as undisputed a point as the power of the crown to make war or peace might be; yet it is undeniable that the commons would not give money without knowing how it was to be employed; and that they proportioned their grants to the judgment they made of the reasonableness or unreasonableness of the employment designed. Wolsey, the most insolent minister our nation had seen at that time, was, however, so far from objecting to this method of proceeding in the house of commons, that he opened to that house, in a long discourse, the reasons of the king's measures, as he affected to call his own measures; and endeavored to prove the necessity of supporting them. Nay, when neither his rhetoric could persuade, nor his authority influence, he offered to debate the whole matter, and to answer the objections of those who opposed the king's desires. The house rejected his offer; observed their forms; maintained their dignity. They disapproved a war, wantonly undertaken, and in which the interests of the nation were not concerned. They showed, however, their regard to the king, by giving some part of the subsidy, and their regard to the kingdom, by refusing, to the last, to give the whole.

As for the minister, he received the mortification which he deserved. These frequent oppositions, on the part of the people and the parliament, were really made to the minister. Henry the Eighth seemed, on some occasions, to desire that they should be so understood, even before Wolsey's favor began to be in its wane; and yet we shall have no reason to be surprised, if we consider the true character of this prince, that these very oppositions prepared his mind for receiving those lessons which Wolsey was ready to give him, against liberty, and in favor of arbitrary power. A wicked minister, who neither gains, nor deserves to gain the good-will of a nation, must secure and will endeavor to revenge himself, by persuading his master to neglect it. Force and corruption being the sole means, by which he can maintain his power, and preserve his ill-gotten wealth, it is necessary for him that the prince whom he serves, should look upon those as the sole expedients by which government can be supported. Wolsey pursued this abominable scheme. "He looked upon the king's subjects," says Rapin, "as so many slaves; and unfortunately for them, he inspired the king by degrees with the same principles; and insinuated to him, that he ought to consider the parliament only as an instrument to execute his will." These were the seeds he sowed, which fell on a rank soil, and produced in the latter half of Henry's reign, such bitter fruit as this nation never tasted before, nor since. Wolsey had been the scandal and the scourge of his country, whilst he lived: and he continued to be so even in the grave.

Letter 11

The divorce of Henry the Eighth and Catharine of Arragon begins a new and most memorable era in the general history of England; and indeed of all Europe. It is the beginning likewise of a new period in the particular reign of which we are speaking. A king, who had been till now the greater asserter of the authority of the pope, and the great defender of the doctrine of the church of Rome, undertakes to destroy the former in his dominions, and gives several incurable wounds to the latter. A king, whose whole attention had been employed abroad, and in whose time "there was no treaty and almost conventicle in Christendom, wherein he had not his particular agent and interest," as my Lord Herbert expresses himself, becomes wholly taken up with domestic affairs; and if he looks abroad, during the rest of his life, it is chiefly on account of what passes at home. He, who had connived at seditions and pardoned insurrections, grows impatient of the least contradiction. He, who had often compounded with his parliaments, and submitted to them on many occasions, dictates all their proceedings; and the voice of the law is little else than the echo of the voice of the king. In short, he who had been led, amused, governed by his minister, drives, overbears, tyrannizes; butchers his servants and his wives, his commons and his nobility.

When Henry the Eighth first engaged in the affair of the divorce, he could not foresee the consequences of it; because he certainly did not expect the difficulties which gave occasion to them. He went on during the first two years, in the beaten road, by which so many others had gone before to the same end; and he seemed to have no view besides that of employing the authority of one pope to undo what the authority of another pope had done. Nay, after Cranmer had began to open other views to him, he seemed still to cling to Rome, resolved to succeed any way; but desirous to succeed that way. Happy was it that he took his measures no better, and that he was no better served on this occasion than on many others! He suffered himself to be amused by Clement the Seventh, the least scrupulous man alive; and who would have divorced him, or have done any other pontifical job for him, if the league formed to reduce the emperor's power in Italy had succeeded. But the emperor's power there continuing to prevail, the pope concluded his treaty with this prince on the most advantageous terms. He obtained that favorite point, for which he would have sacrified not only the interests of Henry the Eighth, but even those of the papacy itself. I mean the re-establishment of the family of Medicis on the ruins of the Florentine liberty. The loss of Genoa, the total destruction of the French army in the kingdom of Naples, and several other considerations induced Francis the First to make his peace with the emperor likewise, and to submit to the treaty of Cambray.

Thus did Henry the Eighth find himself at once disappointed in the expectations he had been made to entertain from the court of Rome, and destitute of all foreign assistance; Francis being the only ally, of whom he could avail himself to influence the councils of Rome, in opposition to the emperor.

In this state of affairs, Henry resorted to that which will be always the best and surest reserve of a king of Great Britain; the inclinations and affections of his people. He had not the trouble of disposing them, for he found them already disposed to his purposes. The spirit raised by Wickliffe about two centuries before, against the usurpations of the pope and the clergy, was still alive. The sufferings of the Lollards, as his followers were called, had not abated it. The art of printing had been propagated; and the late success of Luther had encouraged it. There were multitudes, therefore, in all parts of the kingdom, who desired a complete reformation of the church, both in doctrine and in discipline. Others again were content that the papal authority, grievous in its nature, and scandalous in its exercise, as well as the extravagant power and impertinent immunities of the clergy should be taken away. But they meant to go no farther. Many would not go even so far as this; but were still slaves to all their prejudices; and remained in the midst of this defection, attached to the pope as well as to the corrupted doctrine, and the depraved discipline of the church.

Whilst the divorce was solicited at Rome, and the proceedings relating to it were carried on by the direction, and under the authority of the pope, it was the king's affair; it was the affair of his ministers. But when it appeared impracticable in this method, and Henry resolved, in order to accomplish it in another to deliver himself and his people from the yoke of Rome; the affair of the divorce became a national affair, and the cause of the king became the cause of his subjects. As he proceeded in it, he was encouraged to proceed. The concurrence of his people grew every day more general, and he was supported with the greatest warmth. He soon held the clergy at his mercy, and the popish party was broken and terrified, if not entirely crushed.

During this eager pursuit after ecclesiastical liberty, a power very dangerous to civil liberty was erected. We observed before that the prerogative had been carried high, and extended wide in the reign of Henry the Seventh, who obtained much by law, and obtained more by his manner of construing and executing the law. His son, parting with none of his authority, and improving the conjuncture so as to acquire a great deal more, acquired so much at last, that the power of the crown exceeded by far that proportion, which is consistent with the security of public liberty and private property. It is true, indeed, that he always took care to have the law on his side; and would neither venture on the exercise of acts of power against it, or without it. His experience in the former part of his reign, had taught him the danger of such a conduct; and in the latter part, he had no occasion to pursue it. The opinion of the nation went along with him now; and, as exorbitant as his demands frequently were, his parliaments refused him nothing. At one time they gave up to him, in a great degree, the legislative authority: and his proclamations were made, under some restrictions, equivalent to acts of parliament. At another time, they ascribed to him a sort of infallibility; and letters patent, under the great seal, were made necessary to determine the articles of faith, which men were to believe fully, and the doctrines, rites and ceremonies, which they were to observe and practice under several penalties. The suspicious state of affairs abroad was amplified to give a pretence to one of these laws; and the confused state of religion at home, and the clashing of parties about it, might afford some color to the other. The truth is, that any pretence served, at this time to grant whatever the king desired; a stronger instance of which cannot be imagined than that of the subsidy, obtained in the year 1540. Henry had got immense riches by the first and second suppression of monasteries. A principal inducement to the last, which was likewise the greatest, was this; that the king might be enabled, without taxing the people, to defend them against such invasions, as the court had been pleased to suppose; and with the rumors of which the nation had been purposely alarmed. These invasions did not happen. Henry continued in peace with all his neighbors: and yet, the very next year, he not only accepted from the clergy of the province of Canterbury, with the approbation of parliament, a grant of the fifth part of their revenue; but he demanded a subsidy likewise of the house of commons. So extravagant a demand could not but meet with some opposition. The subsidy however was granted in as large a proportion, as if the nation had been engaged in a dangerous war. The reasons for granting it were almost burlesque. It was affirmed, by the king's party, that he had laid out vast sums in securing the coasts; and that the keeping his subjects in peace and plenty cost him more than the most burthensome war. Thus a precedent was made of converting into ordinary aids of the government those heavy taxes, which ought never to be felt by the people, unless upon the most extraordinary occasions. That they ought to be laid in time of war neither was, nor ever could be doubted. That they were equally necessary in time of peace, was now established by the logic of the court; and we may be sure that the argument would have been urged with still more force and effect, if the nation had fallen, by the management of the courtiers in that age, into such a situation as could neither be called properly a state of war, or a state of peace.

The absolute power which Henry the Eighth exercised over the purses, lives, liberties, and consciences of his people, was due to the entire influence which he had gained over the parliament; and this dependency of the two houses on the king did, in effect, establish tyranny by law. If we look for the true cause of this dependency, we shall find it, as Rapin hath very judiciously observed, in those divisions of the nation concerning religion, which I have mentioned above. The party, which opposed all reformation, by a bigoted attachment to the discipline, as well as doctrine of the church of Rome, furnished the king with as many pretences for grasping at power, and squeezing money out of his people, as ambition could wish, or profusion require. The other two parties concurred with the king, and went together to a certain point: that is, to throw off the papal yoke, and to lessen the power of the clergy. But here they separated, and went different ways; one to carry the reformation forward, and the other to stop it where it then stood; whilst the king seemed to keep in a middle way between them both. Sometimes, he seemed to favor those whose principles led them to an entire reformation, and he touched the doctrine, though with a gentler hand than the discipline of the church. Sometimes he appeared zealous for the doctrine, and even for some part of the discipline; and the manner in which he often executed that bloody statute, the law of six articles, would incline one to think that he joined to his political considerations a tincture of religious prejudice on these heads. But however that was, certain it is that the hopes which each of these two parties entertained of the king, and the fears which they entertained of one another, occasioned their continual bidding for him, if I may be allowed to use such an expression. This emulation formed them, what it always must form, the most dangerous conjuncture to which liberty can be exposed. When the motives of contending parties are founded on private ambition and avarice, the danger is great. How much greater must it be, when those motives are founded on religion likewise; when the heads and hearts of both sides are heated even to enthusiasm; when this spirit mingles itself with the spirit of faction; so that some through folly, and some through knavery, are ready to sacrifice public liberty to their particular schemes of religion?

In such circumstances as these was this nation, when Henry the Eighth died; and if he had left a son and successor, of full age, and bold and enterprising like himself, our liberties had been irretrievably lost, according to all appearances. Henry the Eighth, by applying to his parliaments for the extraordinary powers which he exercised, and by taking these powers for such terms, and under such restrictions as the parliament imposed, owned indeed sufficiently that they did not belong of right to the crown. He owned likewise, in effect, more than any prince who went before him, how absolutely the disposition of the crown of England belongs to the people of England, by procuring so many different and opposite settlements of it to be made in parliament, and yet tyranny was actually established. The freedom of our government might flourish in speculation; but certainly it did not subsist in practice. In the case therefore supposed above, our forefathers would very soon have found how fatal it is, in any circumstances, by any means, or under any pretences, to admit encroachments on the constitution; and how vain it is, when these encroachments are once admitted, for the service of some present turn, to prescribe limitations to the exercise or duration of them.

But Providence directed the course of things better, and broke those shackles which we had forged for ourselves. A minority followed this turbulent reign; the government was weak; the governors divided; and the temper of the people such as made it prudent to soothe them. This the Duke of Somerset did out of inclination, and the Duke of Northumberland out of policy. To the former we owe not only the complete establishment of the church of England on the ruins of popery, but the first and great steps which were made to restore a free government. In the very first year of his administration, several acts which had passed in the reign of Henry the Eighth, and in some preceding reigns, grievous to the people, and destructive of liberty, were repealed; and among others that absurd act, which gave to proclamations the force of laws. The law of the six articles was likewise repealed. Others were explained, and several new laws were made in favor of civil, as well as ecclesiastical liberty; both of which got so much strength, in the reign of Edward the Sixth, that they were able to stand the short but violent shock of queen Mary's reign. This princess lived long enough to confirm, not to destroy, our religion by persecution. The ill-concerted insurrection of Wyatt gave strength to the faction which prevailed at court, and discouraged, for some time, all opposition; nay, the methods taken to influence the elections, and to gain by corruption the members who were chosen, were carried on so openly, that the price for which each man sold himself was publicly known. No wonder, then, if the papal authority was restored, and the queen's marriage with Philip the Second approved. But this state of things could not last long, nor was the nation disposed to bear a continual sacrifice of her interest to Rome and Spain.

The parliament, corrupt as it was, began to revolt against the court. The spirit of liberty revived; and that spirit, and the spirit of reformation in religion, had made more progress than was readily perceived. This progress had been made principally among the commons; and therefore, though the authority of the crown, of the council, and of the great lords kept up other appearances, yet there was a secret fire burning, which must and would have broke out. The effects of the causes, laid in the reign of Henry the Seventh, began now to appear. The lands of the nobility were lessened, and those of the commons increased. Trade had been encouraged for several years. We see that some care had been taken of it, even in the troublesome times of Edward the Fourth, and very much was done towards the advancement of it in the reigns of Henry the Seventh and Henry the Eighth. The West Indies had been discovered about half a century before; and part of the immense treasures, which flowed from thence into Europe, began to increase the profits; and, increasing the profits, increase the industry of our merchants. Henry the Eighth had sold a very great part of the church lands at low prices, on purpose to engage the body of the nation in one common interest against the Romish clergy. The commons had made their use of this strain of policy, and had got into very great estates in lands, by these as well as by other means: so that the king, the lords, and the church, who had formerly held so great an overbalance of property in land, had now little more than one-third of the whole belonging to them; the consequences of which were not forseen by queen Mary; neither did she live long enough to feel them in any great degree. They did not escape the penetration of her sister. She foresaw them, and the great glory and happiness of her reign may justly be attributed to this first principle; that she had the wisdom to discern not only the actual alteration, which was already made, but the growing alteration, which would every day increase in the state of property; that she accommodated at once the whole system of her government to this great change; and instead of depending upon expedients, which were now no longer of season, chose the sole expedient that remained, for making herself and her people happy; which was to place the whole strength and security of her government in the affections of her people, and in superior credit with them.

Letter 12

We have now brought these remarks on the English history not only down to times little remote from our own, but to a period, when the monarchy settled on a new foundation; upon which it still continues and rests more firmly than ever at this hour. The observations therefore, which remain to be made, in order to illustrate what hath been advanced, concerning the spirit of liberty and the spirit of faction, will for these reasons be the more apposite, the more affecting, and by consequence the more useful; but, for these very reasons likewise, it is probable that they will become the occasions of louder complaints, and of more impertinent clamor. We shall be sincerely sorry for this; because we look on the alarm, which hath been taken at our endeavors to revive the spirit, and to confirm and propagate the doctrines of liberty, in a country where liberty is still avowed, and under a government established on the principles of liberty, as a most suspicious and melancholy symptom. But the stronger this symptom appears, the more incumbent we shall think it upon us to pursue the honest design, to which we have devoted ourselves with constancy and vigor.

The shameless crew, who write against their country, as they would write against their God, for hire, shall have little regard from us. The scandalous license with which they have presumed to draw odious parallels, and the impudence with which they have imputed these parallels to us, have been abundantly exposed already. The few, the very few things, which they have alleged in point of fact, or argument, have been often answered; perhaps too often, considering how little weight they carried with them, and how little impression they were capable of making on the understanding, even of those, who had other reasons for inclining to that side of the question. The ribaldry which these scribblers employ, hath been and will continue to be despised, not answered. It cannot be expected that we should take notice of every little frivolous, childish declamation, which appears in public, however some persons may demean themselves by pretending to admire them. The menaces affectedly and insolently thrown out on one side; and the flattery, servilely offered on the other, are equally objects of our contempt; and if we take a little notice of the former, once for all, before we proceed any farther in these remarks, it is purely because we cannot understand them to be the language of these writers. When they talk in this style, they speak the language of him who guides their pens, and who is known to reward their labors. To him therefore it may not be improper to address ourselves in the following manner:

"The persons, whom you threaten, sir, neither value your favor, nor fear your anger. Whenever you attempt any act of power against any of them, you shall find that you have to do with men who know they have not offended the law; and therefore trust they have not offended the king; who know they are safe, as long as the laws and liberties of their country are so; and who are so little desirous of being safe any longer, that they would be the first to bury themselves in the ruins of the British constitution, if you, or any minister as desperate as you, should be able to destroy it. But let us ask, on this occasion, what you are, who thus presume to threaten? Are you not one, whose measure of folly and iniquity is full; who can neither hold nor quit his power with impunity; and over whose head the long-gathering cloud of national vengeance is ready to burst? Is it not time for you, sir, instead of threatening to attack others, to consider how soon you may be attacked yourself? How many crimes may be charged upon you and yours, which almost every man can prove; and how many more are ready to start into light, as soon as the power, by which you now conceal them, shall determine? When next you meditate revenge on your adversaries, remember this truth: the laws must be destroyed before they can suffer, or you escape."

Let us now return to our subject. In the early days of our government, after the Norman invasion, the commons of England were rather formidable in their collective, than considerable in their representative body; by their numbers in extraordinary emergencies, rather than by their weight in the ordinary course of government. In later days, they began to acquire some of this weight by degrees. They represented grievances; they gave, or refused subsidies; and they exercised, in a regular, senatorial manner, the powers lodged in them by the constitution; but still they did not obtain the entire weight, till they were wholly emancipated; and they were not so till the great change, which we are speaking of, happened. Before this time, they had too much of the dependency of tenants, and the king, the nobility and the clergy had too much of the superiority of landlords. This dependency of the commons added to that, which the crown frequently found means of creating, either by influencing their elections, or by corrupting their representatives, notwithstanding all the provisions made against it, which we have touched in a former paper,[1] kept this part of the legislature in such a state, as made it unable fully to answer the end of its institution; and the system of our government was by consequence, in this respect, defective.

Could Henry the Seventh have found means, as he reduced the nobility lower, to have hindered the commons from rising higher; could he have opened a way to the diminution of the property of the lords, and have prevented that increase of the same property amongst the commons, to which, on the contrary, he gave occasion, and which time and accidents conspired to bring about; the balance of this government would have been totally lost, though the outward forms of it had been preserved. Our liberty would have been lost by consequence; and our kings, with a house of lords and a house of commons, and all the appearances of limited monarchs, might have been as arbitrary as those princes are, who govern countries, where no such constitu-

1. See the Craftsman, no. 225.

tion prevails. The reason of this will appear plain to those who remember what hath been observed, in some of our former papers, that a dependent exercise of the powers, lodged in the two houses of parliament, will endanger, and may, more effectually than any other expedient, destroy liberty; and that the preservation of our freedom is no way to be secured but by a free and independent exercise of these powers. Now such an exercise could not have continued, much less have been improved, if Henry the Seventh had been able, at the same time, to weaken his nobility, and to keep his commons from acquiring new strength. But this was impracticable. At least, it was not attempted. Henry the Seventh hastened to the cure of that evil which pressed him most, the power of the nobility, as his son soon afterwards effectually reduced the exorbitant power of the clergy; and in pulling down these powers, which, as they were constituted and had been exercised, hurt the crown more than they served the people, these princes, became the instruments of raising another power, which is the best, if not the sole effectual barrier against usurpations of illegal, and abuses of legal prerogatives; and which, at the same time, can never be applied to do any real hurt to the crown, unless in cases where it is bent and forced to do this hurt by the crown itself, in the first place, against the natural tendency and direction of it.

This increase of the property of the commons, by taking off from them a constant dependency of one sort, and by rendering them less obnoxious to an occasional dependency of another, gave greater dignity, and added greater weight in the balance of government, to their representative body. The house of commons became more powerful, without the attribution of any new powers, and purely by the different manner in which their independency, the effect of their property, enabled them to exercise the same powers, which they enjoyed before. A concert with a few great lords, and a few leading prelates, was now no longer sufficient to guide the sense of parliament, and to establish the measures of government; no, not even in cases, where this concert might be extended to some of the commons themselves. Intrigue and cabal became unnecessary, when the national interest was wisely pursued; and ineffectual, when it was not. The way was open to gain the parliament, by gaining the nation; but to impose on the nation, by gaining the parliament was hard; for the weight without doors determined, in those days, the weight within. The same causes, which rendered the house of commons more considerable to the court, to the nobility, to the clergy, to the commons themselves, rendered likewise the whole body of the commons of more importance to those who were chosen to represent them. Besides which, the frequency of new elections, which was deemed an advantage, as long as the service was deemed an honorable burthen, gave the nation frequent opportunities of modelling the representative body, according to the interests and inclinations of the collective body. From hence it followed, that that credit and influence in the nation, which can only be acquired and preserved by adhering to the national interest, became the sole means of maintaining a lasting credit and influence in the house of commons; upon which the harmony of government, and the happiness of prince and people depended more than ever.

Thus were we brought back, in times very distant and in circumstances very different, to the principles of government, which had prevailed amongst our Saxon ancestors, before they left Germany. Whatever particular pre-eminences, or powers, were vested in the principal men, the great affairs of state were directed by the whole body of the nation. De minoribus principes, de majoribus omnes.

Such were the natural effects of this new settlement; and thus our limited monarchy became capable of as much perfection, as wisdom and favorable accidents can communicate to any human institution; for can we raise our ideas of this kind of perfection higher than ordering the distribution of property and power in such a manner, that the privileges of the people and the prerogative of the crown cannot be taken away, unless with their own consent, or by their own fault? Now to this point of perfection was the constitution of our government brought, and farther it could not be brought; because it is impossible to secure either prince or people against themselves, or against the effects of their own conduct.

One part of what hath been said upon this subject, will not, I think, be disputed. The other, perhaps, may seem a paradox; and a settlement, which rendered our government more democratical, will not be readily allowed to have been advantageous to the crown, though it must be allowed to have been so to the people. Let us examine, therefore, whether it was really so or not.

In all limited monarchies, and we are not speaking of any other, the power of preserving these limitations must be placed somewhere. The question therefore is, whether it can be placed more advantageously, even for the crown as well as the people, than in the whole body of the nation.

Whilst the commons had not property enough to have any share in this power, the sole check which could be opposed to the encroachments of the crown was the power of the barons and of the clergy. But these two orders of men had their particular interests, frequently opposite to each other, and to those of the people, as well as to those of the crown; so that they were not only very incapable of forming a secure barrier to liberty, but their power became terrible and dangerous to the crown itself. They slided easily into faction. They often encroached on the prince's authority, whilst they resisted his encroachments, real or pretended, on their own privileges; and under the plausible veil of law, or gospel, private ambition had a greater share than public liberty in their contests. It is true that during these contests Magna Charta was signed and confirmed, and the condition of the people, in point of liberty, very much improved. But this was the accidental effect of the contest between the kings, the barons, and the clergy, as we have remarked, in speaking of those times, and not the natural effect of the property and power lodged in the barons and the clergy. The commons were courted by all sides, because they were wanted by all. Had they been bubbles enough to look on the nobility and clergy as the proper guardians of liberty, and to have adhered to them accordingly, they might indeed have avoided being slaves to their kings, but they would have rendered both their kings and themselves little less than slaves to their temporal and spiritual lords.

After the reigns of Edward the First and Edward the Third, power came to be better poised; and government took a more regular form. The prerogatives of our kings, and the privileges of our nobility, the authority and immunity of the church, and the rights of the people were more ascertained; and yet, after this time, the same observations will hold good in a very great degree.

It is certain that the vast over-balance of property and power, which still continued in the nobility and clergy, instead of preventing, softening, or shortening the calamities which followed, helped to form and maintain those factions, which began, renewed, fomented the civil wars of York and Lancaster, as well as the wicked conduct of Richard the Second, and the weak conduct of Henry the Sixth. Redress of grievances and sufficient security against them for the future might have satisfied the people, if they had been left to themselves; but nothing less than revolutions of government could satisfy the factions, into which the great men were divided, and into which they divided the nation, by their influence over the people, and by the advantages which the ill conduct of the Yorkists and Lancastrians gave to each other.

Thus we see how unsafely for the crown, as well as insecurely for the people, that property and power, which is necessary to preserve the limitations of our monarchy, was placed before the time, when that great change in one and the other happened, which makes the subject of this discourse. But as soon as this change did happen, the crown was no longer exposed to the mischiefs.

When the little power which Henry the Fourth of France had in the town of Rochelle, was objected to him, he made an answer worthy of his heroic spirit. "I do," said he, "all I desire to do there, in doing nothing but what I ought." This moderation of temper is, in all governments, the best; and, in limited monarchies, the only sure durable foundation of power. By preventing jealousy in the people of the prince, it takes away all advantage against his government from faction; and the more watchful the people are over their liberties, the more sensible will they be of this moderation, and the more grateful for it. Faction proceeds always without reason; but it can hardly ever succeed without pretence, and sufficient pretence will hardly be found under such a government.

When a prince, who manifests this moderation of temper, pursues the true interests of his people, and suffers no other interest to come into any degree of competition with it, far from being the object of their jealousy, he will be the principal object of their affection; and if he joins to this character of goodness that of ability, he will be the principal object of their confidence likewise. These are the strongest chains by which a people can be bound to their prince; easier indeed, but far stronger than those of adamant, by which Dionysius the elder boasted that he had secured the tyranny of Syracuse to his son; force, fear, a multitude of troops, and a guard of ten thousand barbarians. A prince, who establishes his government on the principles of affection, hath every thing to hope, and nothing to fear from his people. A prince, who establishes his government on any other principles, acts in contradiction to the very end of his institution. What objection, therefore, could be made, even on the part of the crown, to a settlement of property and power, which put the guardianship of liberty into such hands as never did, nor ever will invade the prerogative and authority of the crown, whilst they are employed to those purposes, for which alone they were entrusted? It is confessed, that if a prince should attempt to establish his government on any other principle than these, if he should choose to depend rather on deceiving, corrupting, or forcing his people, than on gaining their affection and confidence, he might feel the weight of their property and power very heavy in the scale against him. But then it must be confessed likewise, that, in such a case, this opposition of the people would be just; and that the prince, not the people, would be answerable to himself and his family, to God and to man, for all the ill consequences which might follow.

We hope that we have said nothing, in order to show the excellency of our constitution, as it settled about the time of queen Elizabeth, which is not agreeable to reason; and sure we are that the truth of these general propositions will be confirmed by the particular examples which are to follow. The reign of queen Elizabeth will be one continued proof that the power of preserving the limitations of a monarchy cannot be placed better, for a good and wise prince, than in the whole body of the people; and that the spirit of liberty will give greater strength, as well as procure greater ease, to the government of such a prince, than any absolute monarch can hope to find in the most abject spirit, which principles of blind submission and passive obedience are capable of inspiring. The reigns immediately succeeding this, will be one continued proof, that whenever the power of the people hath been exercised against the crown, it hath been owing primarily to the weak management and obstinacy of the court, and to the unhappy choice which those princes made of governing by factions, in opposition to the sense and interest of the nation. From whence it will follow, that the great calamities which befel our country, in the middle of the last century, are unjustly charged on the spirit of liberty, or on the nature of the British constitution of government.

Letter 13

There is no part of our annals, nor perhaps of the annals of any other country, which deserves to be more studied, or to be oftener called to remembrance both by those who govern, and by those who are governed, than the reign of queen Elizabeth. We shall not however descend into all the observations which it affords; nor even into all those which might properly serve to our present purpose.

In some papers[1] we made a few remarks on this reign, and on that of king James the First. We apprehend that the contrast between them appeared very strong on that occasion. This contrast will probably appear still much stronger, and by consequence be the more instructive, when those remarks and these we are going to make come to centre in one single point; to show that the conduct of queen Elizabeth, under great disadvantages, produced all the good effects, which prince or people could desire; because it was wisely suited to the nature of our government: whereas the conduct of king James the First, who had many great advantages which his predecessor wanted, made his reign grievous to the people, uneasy to himself, and accessory to those misfortunes which befel his son; because it was ill-suited to the nature of our government, and founded on principles destructive of liberty.

Few princes, no not even her cotemporary Henry the Fourth of France, have been ever raised to a throne under more disad-

1. See the Craftsman, no. 137, 138, 139.

vantageous circumstances, or have been surrounded in it with more complicated difficulties than queen Elizabeth. Let us take a general survey of them.

The division and animosity of parties had been carried to the height of religious rage. The cruelty of queen Mary's reign, in which much protestant blood had been shed, and even that of her sister with difficulty spared, rendered of course the persecuting side more desperate; and the other more exasperated. It is hard to imagine that queen Elizabeth had been able to cultivate many personal attachments to herself, before she came to the crown; except that of Sir William Cecil, afterwards Lord Burleigh, and perhaps one or two more. Her imprisonment for a time, and the great constraint under which she lived, during her sister's whole reign, gave her little opportunity for it; and the jealous eye, with which Gardiner and other ecclesiastical zealots observed her conduct, made it dangerous to attempt it.

In general, the protestants desired her succession: and the papists feared it. But the former were under oppression, and even a kind of proscription. The latter had the whole authority of the church and the state in their hands, in this kingdom; and that of Ireland, bigotted to popery and prone to rebellion, was at their devotion. The protestants themselves were divided, and those who meant equally a reformation, fell into the utmost asperity against each other, concerning the manner of making it, and the point to which it ought to be carried, on account of religion as well as of policy.

In this divided state, and in the ferment which such divisions must necessarily cause, queen Elizabeth found the people whom she came to govern. Surely, a more nice and perilous state can hardly be imagined; especially for her, who was led by inclination and determined by particular circumstances of interest to establish the reformation; that is, to declare for the weakest, though not the least numerous party.

It is observed, I think by Nathaniel Bacon in his historical and political discourses, that the methods taken by Henry the Seventh to accumulate treasure, made a rich king indeed, but did not enrich the crown. His son had several opportunities of doing both; instead of which he impoverished himself, the crown, and the people, by all the methods which the most wanton profusion could invent. He exhausted the wealth of the nation. He did more. He debased the coin, by mingling it with copper, and loaded the public with debts. These again were considerably increased in the reign of Edward the Sixth. Queen Mary was so far from diminishing them, that one of the principal complaints against her administration, next to the cruelty she exercised, was the great dissipation of the revenue, occasioned by her restitutions to the church, and by her new foundations of monasteries. In this low, incumbered state queen Elizabeth found the revenues of the crown, and the wealth of the nation.

Her situation abroad was still worse than her situation at home. Calais, and the other English possessions in Picardy, had been lost in a quarrel, where the interest of England had no concern. For the sake of Spain, we had war with France. The war with Scotland still continued; and queen Elizabeth had no one ally, on whose assistance she could depend.

Such distressed situations are rare; and when they have happened, they have been often rendered less difficult in reality, than in appearance, by some particular circumstances which have attended them. But when Elizabeth began her reign, no such circumstances existed in her favor. On the contrary, almost every circumstance aggravated her distress. The thrones of France and Spain were filled neither by old men, worn out with age and cares; nor by weak men, unequal to their rank and business; nor by children, under the tuition of regents. Henry the Second reigned in France; Philip the Second in Spain; princes, in the vigor of their age; of great ambition, of great talents; and seconded by the ablest ministers and generals in Europe. The French monarchy had been growing up from the time of Louis the Eleventh, towards that fulness of power and affluence of wealth, at which the Spanish monarchy was already arrived. Both these princes were, by bigotry and by policy, attached to the court of Rome; implacable enemies to the reformation; and such by consequence to queen Elizabeth. Henry the Second had a farther reason for being so. He grasped, in his ambitious views, the crown of England, as well as that of Scotland; and looked on queen Elizabeth as the usurper of a right, belonging to his daughter-in-law. Philip, indeed, kept some faint and affected measures with Elizabeth, as long as he apprehended the union of so many

crowns in the house of Valois: but this apprehension was soon
at an end; and even his shows of friendship with it. Henry the
Second, and his eldest son, Francis the Second, died in about two
years. The deaths of these princes did, perhaps, diminish the
difficulties and dangers to which queen Elizabeth stood exposed
on one hand; but then they increased these difficulties and dangers on the other; since they took off all restraint from Philip in
pursuit of his enterprises against her. His life lasted almost as
long as hers, and his inveterate enmity as long as his life.

Another source, from which difficulties and dangers were in-
cessantly arising to queen Elizabeth, lay in the objections which
the papists made to her title, on a principle of religion; and which
were but too really, though indirectly, abetted by some protestants, on a principle of faction. Whilst disputes about the succession to the crown were confined to England, and turned on
maxims of our own growth, if I may use that expression, we
have seen how little regard was paid to the titles, and to the pretended divine, indefeasible right of princes. But when foreign
nations came to be interested in the succession of our crown, they
reasoned and they proceeded on other notions; not on those
which both custom and law had established here.

The attacks of this kind, made on queen Elizabeth, were the
more grievous to her, because they not only united the Roman
catholic powers against her; but they made the divisions wider
and more irreconcilable at home, where she placed the chief
strength and security of her government.

Mary queen of Scotland, was a pretender, neither abjured in
England, nor disavowed and unsupported in other countries.
Sovereign of one part of the island, she had a powerful party in
the other; wife of the dauphin, and after that queen of France;
encouraged and assisted by her uncles, who possessed more than
regal power in that kingdom; by Spain, and by the whole popish
interest; she was justly formidable to queen Elizabeth, as long
as she lived. Another circumstance made her so still more. The
success of the reformation seemed to increase the zeal of those
who continued in the communion of the church of Rome. The
influence of the court of Rome became consequently stronger at
this point of time. It appeared both in France and in England
too as powerful, though not as successful, here at least, as it had

appeared in the eleventh century, in the days of the brave, but unfortunate emperor, Henry the Fourth, and of that insolent friar, Gregory the Seventh. Even this circumstance may justly seem to have been enforced by another; by the establishment of the order of Jesuits. This order, the offspring of a mad Spaniard, has had the principal honor, though other religious orders have endeavored to share it, of giving to the pope an authority like that which was exercised by the king of the assassins of the old man of the mountain, as he is called by some of the French historians; an authority, which proved fatal to Henry the Third, and Henry the Fourth of France; and which had like to have proved so to queen Elizabeth, and even to her successor.

Such were the difficulties and dangers which encompassed this princess. The situation of England, in her time, resembled that of a town powerfully besieged without, and exposed to treachery and sedition within. That a town in such circumstances, should defend itself, and even force the enemy, by its own strength, to raise the siege, hardly falls within the bounds of probability. But that all this should happen, and the inhabitants feel none of the inconveniences of a long and obstinate siege, nay, that they should grow opulent during the continuance of it, and find themselves at last better able to offend the enemy than they were at first to defend their walls, seems an adventure of some extravagant romance. But it conveys a true image of this reign. Unallied and alone, queen Elizabeth maintained a glorious and successful war against the greatest power and the richest potentate in Europe. She distressed him in the West Indies. She insulted him in Spain. She took from him the empire of the sea. She fixed it in herself. She rendered all the projects of universal monarchy vain; and shook to the foundations the most exorbitant power which ever disturbed the peace, or threatened the liberties of Europe. She supported the oppressed people of the Netherlands, against the tyranny of their prince. She supported the protestant subjects of France, against Catherine of Medicis and her sons, those execrable butchers of their people. She supported the kings of France, Henry the Third and Fourth, against the ambition of the princes of the house of Lorraine, and the rebellious league of their popish subjects. She, who seemed to have every thing to fear in the beginning of her reign, became in the progress of it terrible to her enemies. The Pretender to her crown lost her own. The English, who appeared at first so favorable to the queen of Scotland, became at last as desirous to sacrifice the life of that unfortunate princess to the security of queen Elizabeth. Whilst war, confusion, and the miseries which attend them, raged in the dominions of these who bent their aim at the disturbance of her government, she preserved her subjects in peace and in plenty. Whilst the glory of the nation was carried high by achievements in war, the riches and the strength of it were raised by the arts of peace to such a degree, as former ages had never seen, and as we of this age feel in the consequences. Well, therefore, might my Lord Bacon, speaking of queen Elizabeth, say,[2] "as for her government, I assure myself I shall not exceed, if I do affirm that this part of the island never had forty-five years of better times; and yet not through the calmness of the season, but through the wisdom of her regiment."

Having made these remarks on the difficulties and on the success which attended queen Elizabeth; it is time to consider the cause, which produced the stupendous effects of her reign. Now this cause is, I think, very plain. She was wise enough to see clearly into the nature of that government, at the head of which she was placed; and to know that "the supreme head of such a government owes a supreme service to the whole."[3] She was wise enough to know that to be powerful, she must either usurp on her people, deceive them, or gain them. The first two, she saw, were hard, dangerous and dishonorable. The last, she saw, was easy, safe and glorious. Her head and her heart concurred to determine her choice. She made herself very soon the most popular person in the kingdom. In her reign, the sense of the court, the sense of the parliament and the sense of the people were the same; and whenever she exerted her own strength, she exerted the whole strength of the nation. Nothing she asked was ever refused by parliament; because she asked nothing which would have been refused by the people. She threw herself so entirely on the affections of her subjects, that she seemed to decline all other tenure of the crown. At least, she was not very solicitous about clearing her title to it by descent. An act,

2. Advancement of Learning, lib. i.
3. See Nath. Bacon's Hist. and Pol. Discourse.

declaring her right according to the order of succession settled in parliament thirty-five Henry the Eighth contented her; and she neglected the precaution, which her sister had taken, in getting the act, which excluded them both from the crown, repealed, as far as it related to herself. The particular reasons of her conduct, in this case, might perhaps be guessed at with more probability than they have been; but certainly one general reason outweighed them all in the mind of this heroical princess. She knew that however the subtlety of lawyers and political casuists might influence opinions, nothing but her own conduct could give her the hearts of her people. These she deemed her great security. These she acquired; and the little glosses, which might have been put on her title, she despised. The being not only tied, but knit to her people was her aim; and she pursued this great point of view on all occasions; the least, as well as the greatest; and even on those, where she thought it necessary to refuse or to reprimand. Nature, as well as art, fitted her for this conduct. She had dignity without pride. She was affable, without sinking into low familiarity; and when she courted her people, she courted them like a queen. This popularity was sometimes carried so far, both in her manners, and in her expressions, that her enemies have endeavored to make it pass for gross and fulsome affectation, and for such, indeed, it ought to have passed if it had gone alone. It might have shocked, instead of alluring, if it had not been seconded by every action of her life, and contradicted by none. Let us now consider, therefore, in some instances, what that conduct was, which convinced her people so entirely of her goodness and her wisdom; and which procured her such large returns of gratitude, of duty, of affection and zeal.

Letter 14

A first and essential condition, towards obtaining the love and confidence of a free people, is to be neither feared nor despised by them. Queen Elizabeth was, at no time, in any danger of the latter; and she soon put herself above all the suspicions, which might have exposed her to the former. The only difference between her and her parliament, which carried any passion or unkindness with it, happened in the ninth year of her reign. It was founded on the apprehensions of the dangers which would arise after her death, if the succession was not fixed during her life. But we do not find the least insinuation of any jealousy of her government; though the heat of both houses, at that moment, was too great to have concealed any uneasiness, which had lain at their hearts. That she was fond enough of her prerogative is certain; but then she took care that it should never be grievous; or that if it was so, on some occasions, to particular persons, it should appear, by the occasions themselves, and by the manner of exercising it, specious to the public. The prerogative certainly ran high in those days. Her grandfather had raised it by cunning, and her father by violence. The power of the privy council in civil affairs, and the censorian power of the star-chamber in criminal affairs, as my Lord Bacon very properly styles it, took too much of the pleas of the crown and of the common pleas out of their proper channels, and "served rather to scare men from doing wrong, than to do any man right."[1] But the exercise of

1. Bac. Hist. and Pol. Disc.

these powers having continued in four preceding reigns, the people were accustomed to it; and care being taken to give no flagrant occasion of clamor against it, we are not to wonder if it was born, without opposition or murmur, in a reign as popular as this.

The high-commission court, that we may quote another instance, had no doubt very extraordinary powers. The bishops, who held the principal sway in it, exercised by these means two very great authorities at the same time; one, as ordinaries in their dioceses; the other, as judges in this court; so that they might fine and imprison, as well as excommunicate and deprive. Now, it is not very probable, that the parliament, who thought the first of these powers too much, as may be seen by the attempts made against it, in the twenty-eighth year of this reign, were very well pleased to see the second in the same hands. However, the steadiness of the queen, in maintaining this part of the prerogative, which had been given her, was the less unpopular, on account of the unsettled state of religion at this time; of the great moderation of the bishops in these early days of the reformation; and of the prudent manner, in which the jurisdiction of the high-commission court was executed.

The effects of a bare-faced prerogative are not the most dangerous to liberty, for this reason; because they are open; because the alarm they give is commonly greater than the progress they make; and whilst a particular man or two are crushed by them, a whole nation is put on its guard. The most dangerous attacks on liberty are those which surprise, or undermine; which are owing to powers, given under pretence of some urgent necessity; to powers, popular and reasonable, perhaps, at first; but such as ought not to become settled and confirmed by a long exercise; and yet are rendered perpetual by art and management; and, in a great degree, by the nature of these powers themselves. Examples of this kind might be produced from the Spanish and other histories. But queen Elizabeth was far from setting any such examples. She showed her moderation, in desiring no suspicious powers, as well as in the exercise of her prerogative; and this moderation was the more remarkable, because no prince ever had the pretence of necessity to urge on stronger appearances. Her whole reign may be almost called a state of defensive and offensive war, in England, as well as in Ireland; in the Indies, as well as in Europe. She ventured to go through this state, if it was a venture, without the help of a standing army. The people of England had seen none, from the days of Richard the Second; and this cautious queen might perhaps imagine, that the example of his reign and those of other countries, where standing armies were established, would beget jealousies in the minds of her people, and diminish that affection, which she esteemed and found to be the greatest security of her person, and the greatest strength of her government. Whenever she wanted troops, her subjects flocked to her standard; and her reign affords most illustrious proofs, that all the ends of security, and of glory too, may be answered in this island, without the charge and danger of the expedient just mentioned.

This assertion will not be contradicted by those, who recollect in how many places, and on how many occasions, her forces fought and conquered the best disciplined veteran troops in Europe. Other examples might be brought to show how careful queen Elizabeth was to avoid every thing which might give the least umbrage to her people. But we have said enough on this head. Let us proceed to another.

The conduct she held, with respect to parties, deserves to be remarked; because the moderation, the wisdom, and the equity, which she showed in it, contributed very much to cool the ferment in the beginning of her reign; by which she had time to captivate the good will of her people; to settle her government; to establish her authority; and even to change the national religion, with little contradiction, and without any disturbance.

Notwithstanding all the indignities she had suffered, and all the dangers she had run, before her accession, several persons were restored, and not a man was attainted in her first parliament. The steps I have mentioned being once made, she stood on firmer ground, and had less to fear from the spirit of faction. This clemency once shown, she could, more safely and with greater reason, exercise severity, when the preservation of the public peace made it necessary.

The peace of the kingdom was the standard, to which she proportioned her conduct. She was far from casting herself with precipitation and violence even into that party which she favored, and on which alone she resolved to depend. She was far from inflaming their spirits against the adverse party; and farther still from pushing any sort of men, puritans, and even papists, into despair; or provoking them to deserve punishment, that she might have a pretence to inflict it. She pursued her own scheme steadily; but she pursued it gradually; and accompanied it with all the artful circumstances which could soften the minds of men, and induce those, who were the most adverse to her measures, to bear them, at least patiently. On these principles she proceeded, in the whole course of her reign.

To the papists she used great lenity; till the bull of Pius Quintus, and the rebellion, and other attempts, consequent upon it, obliged her to procure new laws, and execute more rigor. Yet even then she distinguished "papists in conscience from papists in faction."[2] She made the same distinction with regard to the puritans. "Their zeal was not condemned; only their violence was sometimes censured," until they attempted to set up their own discipline, in opposition to that which had been established by national authority; until their motives appeared to be "no more zeal, no more conscience," says secretary Walsingham, "but mere faction and division."

Thus cautious and steady was the conduct of queen Elizabeth towards parties; steady to the principle, and therefore varied in the application, as the behavior of parties towards her government varied; not as success abroad, or the change of servants at home, might have influenced that of a prince of inferior abilities. What has been said relates to parties in the nation; for as to parties at court, the conduct of this queen, though directed to the same general end, seems to have been different. In the nation she chose one party. She rendered the system of that party, the system of the whole. By this establishment the other parties became so many factions; and by the conduct we have described, she defeated and disarmed these factions. At court, she countenanced and perhaps fomented the parties, which different characters and different interests created. But however that was, she found means to attach them all to herself; and she found this benefit by keeping her ear open to them all, that the

2. Walsingham's Letter.

truth could not be concealed from her by the most powerful of her ministers; as we have explained in a former letter on this subject. On her accession to the throne, she retained thirteen of her sister's counsellors, and balanced them by no more than eight of her own religion. "On those, as well as on all others, which she afterwards admitted into the ministry," says Camden, "she bestowed her favors with so much caution, and so little distinction, as to prevent either party from gaining the ascendant over her; whereby she remained mistress of herself, and preserved both their affections and her own power and authority entire."

The favors, by which she distinguished the Earls of Leicester and Essex, are not exceptions, in the course of so long a reign, sufficient to destroy the truth of this general observation. Besides, both these lords felt the weight of her displeasure, nay one of them, the rigor of her justice, when they presumed too much on her favor, and swerved from their duty. The singular confidence which she placed in Cecil and some others of her ministers, cannot be quoted in opposition to it; for if she distinguished them, it was rather by the labors, than the favors she heaped on them. She supported them indeed against their enemies; but then the merit of these men was far from being problematical. Their works testified daily for them, in bold and well-concerted enterprises; in wise and well-conducted negotiations. The people reaped the benefit of their services, as well as the prince. They were justified in the nation, as well as supported at court. In short, by this discernment of spirits, by this skilful management of parties, without the help of military force, unless in actual rebellions, queen Elizabeth preserved her people in tranquility; though there passed not an hour in her whole reign, without some intrigue against her life and the public peace.

This moderation, in assuming and exercising power, might have been illustrated more, and evinced against all the little cavils made, and to be made, if we had not avoided too great prolixity. But it is time to hasten to the consideration of some other parts of her conduct.

Queen Elizabeth was accused of avarice by her enemies; and perhaps she was so by some of her friends. Among that hungry crew, which attends all courts for the loaves and the fishes, she could not escape this charge. But surely the nation had reason to applaud her frugality. Her grandfather hoarded up riches. Her father dissipated them. The consequence under both these princes was, that every slight occasion became a sufficient pretence to ask for subsidies; nay, they were asked and granted too, when even the slightest occasion did not exist. They were asked by Henry the Seventh for wars which he never intended to make; and by Henry the Eighth for resisting invasions which were never designed against him. Thus was the nation equally oppressed by the avarice of one, and by the profusion of the other.

But queen Elizabeth neither hoarded up nor lavished away; and it is justly to be questioned whether any example of prudent economy in private life, can be produced equal to that which she practised in the whole management of her affairs. The famous Burleigh used to say, that "he never cared to see the treasury swell like a disordered spleen, when the other parts of the commonwealth were in a consumption"; and his mistress thought that "money, in the pockets of her subjects, was better placed than in her own exchequer." Surely, these maxims were wise as well as popular. If a prince amasses wealth, to hoard it up like Henry the Seventh, it is useless to himself and lost to the public. If he squanders it away, like Henry the Eighth, he will enrich particular men, and impoverish the state. But whilst these treasures remain in the purse of the subject, they circulate in commerce; they increase the common stock; and they increase by consequence the riches of a princess like queen Elizabeth; for to such a princess this purse will be always open.

As immense as the expenses were, which she found herself obliged to make from the moment she ascended the throne, she received nothing in taxes from her people till the sixth year of her reign. The taxes then given, were given by way of retribution; which was generally the method in her time. In former reigns, the people granted aids, not without a general communication at least of the uses, to which they were to be applied; but often without a sufficient assurance that they should be so applied. In this reign that method of proceeding was inverted.

The prince in the world who deserved to be trusted most, desired to be so the least. The aids which she had from her people were not so properly grants as reimbursements of money advanced for national services. And for what services? For establishing the protestant religion; for defending England; for rescuing Scotland; for carrying on a successful war against an opulent and potent enemy; for assisting the subjects and even the kings of France; for supporting the people of the Netherlands; for refining the debased coin; for paying all the debts, and restoring the credit of the crown; for providing ammunition at home, which before this time we had been always obliged to purchase abroad; for improving both home and foreign trade; for rebuilding and augmenting the navy; and for doing all this, without any burthensome imposition on the people; as the parliament more than once acknowledged.

It was so much a maxim of queen Elizabeth, to save for the public, not for herself; and to measure her riches by the riches of the nation, not by the treasures she had in her coffers; that she refused supplies offered, and remitted payments of supplies granted, when she found that she was able to carry on the public service without them. The two great principles of that economy, which enabled her to do so much for her people, and to oppress them so little, seem to have been these. First, she made the most of her revenues; not by tormenting, and racking her subjects, like Henry the Seventh, but by keeping a strict hand over her officers, and hindering them from enriching themselves, either by direct fraud, or by a clandestine management, which may be justly termed indirect fraud, and is often more pernicious than the other. Secondly, she practised that superior economy, of which we have spoken in a former paper, with the utmost ability. What could be done by wisdom, or courage, she never attempted by money; nor expected that her subjects should buy her out of difficulties. Strong at home, she affected little to lean on foreign help. As her alliance was often courted, and she seldom courted that of others, it was in her power, and she took the advantage, to engage in no expense, but such as the interest of her kingdom rendered immediately necessary. To this interest alone she proportioned her expense. This was the sole rule of her conduct. The Huguenots, whom she assisted in their first war, made their peace without her, and assisted to retake from her the places she had bargained for with them; yet she helped them, in the wars which followed, with her troops, her ships, and her money. The Dutch had given her no cause to complain of their behavior. Yet when France abandoned them at the treaty of Vervins, and they had no support but hers remaining, she made a new bargain with them, and lessened her own charge; bcause she knew they were able, at that time, to supply the deficiency.

In all these expenses, she was careful neither to starve nor overfeed the cause, while it lasted; and she frequently stipulated a repayment; which she might exact afterwards, if she found reason so to do; or which she might remit, and thereby create a second obligation to her, if she found her account in such an instance of generosity. Queen Elizabeth was not only thus frugal for her people, but perpetually attentive to the methods of enriching them. In the very first parliament which she held, amidst the most important affairs; such as the settlement of the crown on her own head; the change of religion, and the establishment of the church, regulations for the improvement of trade, and increase of shipping were not forgot.

We might pursue the same observation through the whole course of her reign, both in parliament, and out of it; and show, in numberless instances, how she rose to the highest, and descended even to the lowest circumstances, which in any degree affected the trade and navigation of her subjects. We might show the advantages she took in these respects, not only of the faults committed by other governments, but of the misfortunes of other countries. In a word, we might show how war itself, one of the greatest public calamities, instead of impoverishing, became a source of riches to this nation, by the manner in which she made it.

But these particulars would carry us beyond the bounds we have prescribed to ourselves. In general, it will not be denied that, beside the spirit of industry, which exercised itself at home, queen Elizabeth raised and pushed to the highest degree, by the protection and encouragement she gave, a spirit of discovering new countries; making new settlements; and opening new veins of trade. The force of this first impression has lasted long amongst us. Commerce has thrived under neglects and discouragement. It has subsisted under oppressions and obstructions; and the spirit of it is not yet extinguished by that of stockjobbing; though the spirit of stockjobbing be to that of trade, what the spirit of faction is to that of liberty. The tendency of both is to advance the interest of a few worthless individuals, at the expense of the whole community. The consequence of both, if ever they prevail to the ruin of trade and liberty, must be, that the harpies will starve in the midst of imaginary wealth; and that the children of faction, like the iron race of Cadmus, will destroy one another.

Before queen Elizabeth's reign, the commerce of England was confined and poor. In her reign, it extended itself over all the known, and even into the unknown parts of the world. We traded to the north, and opened our passage into Muscovy. We carried our merchandise up the Duina, down the Volga, and across the Caspian Sea into Persia.

Our merchants visited the coasts of Africa; all the countries of the Grand Seignior; and following the tracks of the Venetians into the East Indies, they soon followed the Portuguese thither by the Cape of Good Hope. They went thither through the South Sea, and sailed round the world. In the West Indies, they not only traded, but established themselves, in spite of all the power of Spain.

Before queen Elizabeth's reign, the fleet of England was so inconsiderable, that even in the days of her father, if I mistake not, we were forced to borrow, or hire ships of Hamburg, Lubec, Dantzick, and other places.

In her reign, it soon grew to such a number and strength, that it became terrible to the greatest maritime powers of Europe.

On such foundations were the riches and power of this kingdom laid by queen Elizabeth; and these were some of the means she employed to gain the affections of her subjects. Can we be surprised if she succeeded?

Letter 15

Queen Elizabeth succeeded in gaining the affections of her sub-jects, not only by the conduct which she held at home, but by that which she held in the management of the national interest abroad.

We have endeavored to explain some particulars of the former. It remains that we give the least imperfect ideas we are able of the latter, and that we apply the whole great example of this reign, to confirm the doctrines we have advanced.

Queen Elizabeth could not have established and preserved, as she did, the tranquility of her people in the midst of disturbance, nor their security in the midst of danger, if she had not taken some share in the general affairs of Europe. She took therefore such a share as the interest of England necessarily required at that time; and she conducted herself in the management of it with wisdom and address superior to any of her predecessors.

Her sister had been rendered by bigotry an egregious bubble to the court of Rome. Persuaded by her husband, and deceived by her ministers, she was so likewise very fatally in the quarrel, which broke out between France and Spain. The parliament, in assenting to her marriage with a foreign prince, had imposed such conditions, as were judged sufficient to preserve the consti-tution of the government, and the independency of the kingdom.

Philip had sworn to the observation of these conditions. Such of them, as he had not either time, or opportunity, or temptation to break, were observed; but the others proved too weak to hold him. Thus, for instance, we do not find that he enriched himself at the expense of England. He is said, on the contrary, to have brought hither very great treasures; and his father had trusted the distribution of an immense sum to Gardiner: so that if he bribed the nation, it was with his own money, not theirs; but he engaged the nation in a war with France because France broke with Spain; notwithstanding the express condition made by parliament,[1] "that the match should not at all derogate from the league lately concluded betwixt the queen of England and the king of France, but the peace should remain inviolate between the English and the French."

This sacrifice of the national to a foreign interest cost us Calais; a conquest, which the French looked upon as a compensation for near two hundred other places, which they were obliged by the treaty of Cambray, to give up to Philip. Boulogne had been sacrificed in the preceding reign, not to a foreign interest, but to that of the minister, Dudley, Earl of Warwick, afterwards Duke of Northumberland. The people were willing and able to assert their right, and to defend their possession; but the situation of the minister, and the schemes of private interest, which he was carrying on at home, required that he should avoid, at any rate, a war, even a defensive war. In short, Boulogne, for which France had engaged to give two millions, was delivered up for four hundred thousand crowns; and the very same minister, who had opposed with violence all the public considerations, urged by the protector for yielding this place, yielded it to purchase a treaty necessary for himself, detrimental and dishonorable to the nation.

We have said enough, in a former letter, concerning the wild conduct of Henry the Eighth in foreign affairs; and there is no need of going any farther back. These examples are sufficient to show the opposition between that of queen Elizabeth and that of her predecessors. She was neither deceived, like them, by her ministers; nor betrayed by her passions, to serve any other interest at the expense of England.

It would be easy to prove, from many instances, how careful she was to avoid every thing which might even warp the steady

1. Cambden.

tenor of her conduct in this respect. As long as she had no real interest distinct from that of the country she governed, she knew that no fictitious interest could be imposed on her. She kept herself, therefore, clear of any such real interest, and thought that the crown of England deserved her sole, her individual care.

Much has been said of her behavior in all the treaties of marriage proposed to her. We shall not engage in that disquisition. But this, we think, cannot be controverted; that if ever she was in earnest resolved to marry, she was so when the articles of marriage between her and the Duke of Anjou were signed. It is hardly possible, as Rapin observes, to account for her conduct on this occasion by any other principle. Now upon this supposition, what motive could determine her to break this match in so abrupt a manner? The reasons urged by Cambden, and other writers in general, prove too much. They serve rather to prove that she should not have entered into these engagements at all, than to account for her breaking them as she did. But among the reasons, on which Walsingham insisted, when he was sent into France on this occasion, we may observe one in particular, founded on a fact, which happened after the signing of the articles; and which accounts for the queen's conduct in this case agreeably to principles, on which she proceeded in all others. The Duke of Anjou had accepted the sovereignty of the Low Countries. By this step, he had engaged himself in a war with Spain; and the queen would not, on his account, engage her people in it,[2] "desiring nothing more than that by this marriage the realm might be preserved in peace and tranquillity."

She might incline to marry this prince, under all the limitations and reserves contained in the articles, whilst he had no dominions on the Continent; and yet start backwards and resolve to break the match, as soon as she saw him actually possessed of the sovereignty of the Low Countries.

Nay, if we should suppose, against historical probability, that she never designed to consummate her marriage, though she entered into articles, yet there will still remain no reasonable way of accounting for the sudden resolution she took of breaking at this precise point of time; unless we suppose that she thought

2. Cambden.

this reason the strongest and the most unanswerable of all those which could be urged in excuse of a measure liable to several objections, and some very inconvenient contingencies.

There were few things, which she had more at heart than rescuing the Netherlands from the Spanish yoke; and there was nothing in the whole extent of foreign affairs, to which she gave greater attention. Even at this time she supplied the Duke of Anjou with very considerable sums, for the support of his enterprise; and about four years afterwards, she espoused more openly the cause of these provinces, by making a treaty with the states, and by sending an army to their assistance. But as she would not marry a prince who was their sovereign, so she would not accept this sovereignty, when it was offered directly to her. She persisted in avoiding an engagement, which might in its consequence carry her farther than the interest of England required; or oblige her to make greater efforts than were consistent with that easy and flourishing state in which she resolved to preserve her own people.

Much more might be said; but this may suffice to show what the first and fundamental principle was, by which queen Elizabeth governed herself in all foreign affairs. She considered the interest of no kingdom, no state, nor people, no not even the general interest of the reformation, as zealous a protestant as she was, nor the preservation of a balance of power in Europe as great a heroine as she was, in any other light than relatively to the interest of England. She assisted, or opposed, she defended or attacked, just as this interest directed; and the degree to which it was concerned, was the exact and constant measure to which she proportioned her good, and her ill offices, her friendship, and her enmity. She was diverted from this principle of conduct neither by weakness nor strength of mind; neither by fear, nor hope; neither by pusillanimity, nor courage; neither by moderation, nor ambition.

We may conclude this head, by venturing to affirm that, in the whole course of her reign, there was not a penny of English money spent, nor a drop of English blood spilled, except where it was necessary to keep off from this nation some real, visible disadvantage.

Queen Elizabeth's policy was deep; and the means she employed were often very secret; but the ends to which this policy and these means are directed, were never equivocal. Let us now descend into some particular instances of the wisdom and address, with which she pursued this great principle.

These particulars may be reduced properly, we think, under two general heads. The first is this: "she watched the ebbs and flows of the power and interest of Europe; the vicissitudes and fluctuations in the affairs of peace and war." We use the words of a late writer,[3] but shall make a very different application of them.

This uncertain, varied, shifting scene was so far from being the cause of bad measures, or the excuse for bad success, at the time we are speaking of, that it was the very source from whence queen Elizabeth derived those opportunities, which she improved so gloriously. A weaker council than hers might have been puzzled, and weaker heads might have been turned by so confused a state of affairs. Unable to steer steadily through so many difficulties, every current would have carried such men along with it. Every blast of wind would have driven them before it. Perpetually tossed about, at the mercy of every event they must have lived from day to day, or from hour to hour.

If the kingdom had escaped entire destruction in this forlorn condition, it must have been by miracle, and without any merit on the part of those who governed; but this entire destruction would much more probably have followed, after a long series of calamities; without any other excuse on their part, than that of charging the catastrophe to the account of fortune, the common scape-goat of unskilful ministers.

The conduct and the success of queen Elizabeth and her ministers were very different. She managed France, until she had taken such measures, as left her less to fear from Scotland; and she managed Spain, until she had nothing left to fear from France.

She knew what designs Henry the Second built on the pretensions of his daughter-in-law, Mary queen of Scotland; and no one, who considers the history of this time, nay, even as he finds it deduced by Rapin himself, will be of his mind, that she expected

3. Vide Observations on the Writings of the Craftsman.

to "enjoy great tranquillity by the peace," which she made soon after her accession to the throne, with France and Scotland.

But the making this treaty gave her time, which was of the utmost importance to her to gain, abroad as well as at home, in the beginning of her reign. The manner in which she made it, gave her reputation likewise; and she was wise enough to know of what real advantage reputation is, and how much that of a prince depends on the first steps he makes in government.

She practised in this negotiation a rule, which she observed to the last. How much soever Philip resented her proceedings at home, it was plain he could not abandon, at that time, her interests abroad. The point of honor, drawn from the consideration that England had entered into the war for the sake of Spain, did not probably weigh much with him; but the pretensions of France gave him a just alarm; and the same reasons, which are said to have induced him to save her life, when she was princess, stood in force to make him support her, now she was queen, against the power of France. Notwithstanding this plausible consideration, queen Elizabeth revolved to treat for herself, and by herself. "She was of opinion," says Cambden, "that it would not redound to the honor of England, or herself, to be reduced to the necessity of supporting her interests by a dependence on Spain." She exerted the same spirit, and behaved herself with the same dignity, on a very remarkable occasion, and in a very nice conjuncture, at the latter end of her reign; at the treaty of Vervins.

She despised the offers made her by Henry the Fourth. She resolved to continue the war, and to support alone the states of the Low Countries, rather than to suffer the man in the world, who had the greatest obligations to her, to treat for her. True it is, that she had reason to be dissatisfied with his behavior; but besides that, the good understanding between this prince and Philip the Second being promoted by the court of Rome; it is possible queen Elizabeth might think such negotiations, as were devoted to that court, not quite so proper to be trusted with the interests of her kingdom.

As soon as Henry the Second was dead, and his son Francis the Second, a young and in every sense a weak prince, was on the throne of France, she acted with less reserve and caution. The treaty, which had been privately negotiated before with the malcontents of Scotland, was now signed; her army marched to their assistance; the French were driven out of that kingdom; the reformation was solemnly and legally established there, and queen Elizabeth was the avowed defender of the liberties, privileges, and religion of the Scottish nation. Francis the Second lived a very short time, and died without leaving any children. The fear therefore of an union of the crowns of England and Scotland with that of France, terrified Philip the Second no longer. Queen Elizabeth had therefore the more to fear. The court of France had still the same bigotry, and the same hatred to her; though not the same pretensions. The court of Spain could be now no more restrained, by any political consideration, from pursuing those designs against her, even in conjunction with France, which no other consideration had hitherto retarded.

The projects formed and the engagements taken between these powers, at the congress at Bayonne, were not absolute secrets. She felt the effects of them every day, in conspiracies against her government, and even her life. Too weak to defend herself by force on so many sides, she defended herself by stratagem; improved every incident; and took some advantage of every turn. She contented herself to countermine the intrigues of the courts of Rome, of France, and of Spain. With the first she kept no measures, because she could have no war. With the two last she kept all measures to prevent one. Though queen Elizabeth's whole reign was properly a state of war, and there was no point of time in it, where she was free from all attacks, private as well as public, indirect as well as direct; yet the first twenty-five years of her reign may be said, in one sense, to have been neither a state of war, nor a state of peace; because both sides pretended to look on the treaties of peace as subsisting; and either disavowed, or excused the hostilities reciprocally committed, not constantly, but occasionally committed. If she had fallen into this state from that of a settled peace, disentangled from all pretensions, either of her own upon others, or of others upon her, there would be no occasion to admire her conduct. But that she should be able, when she neither had, nor could have a settled secure peace with her neighbors, to stand so long on the slippery verge of war, and avoid the necessity of engaging directly in it, till she was in a condition of doing so with success, is justly matter of the greatest admiration. If she had only aimed to keep off the evil day, it might at last have come upon her with a double weight of misfortune. If she had only gained time to prolong suspense, she might have lost opportunities; wasted her strength; tired, jaded and exhausted her people. But this was far from being the case. She was in this state by good, not by bad policy; and she made the use she designed of it. She disappointed, divided, and weakened her enemies. She prepared the opportunities which she afterwards improved. She united, animated, and enriched her people; and, as difficult as that may seem to be for a prince in such a situation, she maintained her own dignity, and supported the honor of the nation. To exemplify all these particulars, would be to write her history; but it is necessary to say something upon them.

Of the two powers abroad, from whom alone she had any thing to apprehend, and with whom she was principally concerned, France gave her the least and the shortest trouble. Charles the Ninth came a minor to the crown. Two factions, drunk with religious enthusiasm, and headed by men of the most desperate ambition, desolated the kingdom. The queen mother blew up the flames first; and tried in vain afterwards to extinguish them, by a deluge of blood. Queen Elizabeth, who had probably encouraged the famous conspiracy of Amboise, which broke out just before the death of Francis the Second, continued to abet and support the protestant party; but still subordinately to such measures, as her situation, relatively to Scotland, or Ireland, or Spain, obliged her to keep with Charles the Ninth. These measures were sometimes such, and even after the massacre of St. Bartholomew, as the zeal of the Huguenots could hardly forgive her. But she went wisely and steadily on to her own purposes.

Non ponebat enim rumores ante salutem.

When Henry the Third came to the crown, and the league was once formed, the crown of France wanted her assistance, and had it; and as powerful as the princes of the house of Lorraine were, they could give her little open disturbance, unless they prevailed in their wicked, and almost chimerical projects in France. With these princes and their faction, therefore, she never kept any measures—as they never kept any with her. As politic a prince as Philip the Second is esteemed to have been, he was amused by the regard which queen Elizabeth affected sometimes for his person, and always for the treaties subsisting between them; and he lost the opportunity in which he might have attacked her with advantage. The slow councils of Spain, and the slower execution of them, produced opportunities which her sagacity and vigor improved. The support she gave to the Huguenots made the Spaniards afraid of provoking her, by too hasty and direct attacks, to give the same support to the people of the Low Countries. She turned their game against them, and acted in the Low Countries in the same manner as they acted in Ireland, and even in England, but with better effect. From the year 1577 she began to favor this revolt, and in the year 1585 she made a formal treaty with the States. Such of these measures as could be concealed, she concealed. Such of them as could not be concealed, she excused, or endeavored to justify and reconcile with the treaties between Spain and England.

As the time she gained, and the diversion she gave by this management, put it quite out of the power of France, and made Spain less able to hurt her; so they alone put it in her power to settle her government, and to do all the great things at home, of which we have spoken in other papers.[4] We shall not repeat them here; but shall conclude this head by observing, in an example or two, how she maintained her own dignity in other cases, besides that of treating, which is taken notice of above, and how she supported the honor of the nation, and the interests of her subjects.

During the time she was the most careful to avoid a war with Spain, and had the most reason to be so, even in the year 1568, whilst those revolutions, which broke out soon afterwards, were preparing, she would not suffer the least injury to be offered to any of her subjects with impunity. Some vessels and effects, belonging to an English merchant, had been seized by the Spaniards in the West Indies. She did not make war upon this; but she soon found and seized an opportunity of resenting the insult. She laid hands on very great sums of money, claimed indeed by

4. Vide the first seven volumes of the Craftsman, printed for R. Francklin.

Genoese merchants, but sent to the Low Countries, and designed, no doubt, for the Spanish service there. The Duke of Alva seized, in return, the persons and effects of the subjects of England; and she immediately made reprisals on those of the Flemmings. What composition was made with the Genoese, does not, I think, appear; but as the seizure was to the disappointment and loss of Spain, so the composition was probably to the advantage of England; since, at this very time, queen Elizabeth discharged the debts contracted by her father and brother to foreigners. As to the effects of the Netherlands, she returned the overplus of the value, after having repaid to her own subjects the full amount of their losses. She cared for her people; and would not leave it to a dispute, what reparation they should have; much less whether they should have any reparation or not.

Such a conduct as this, which she held, even whilst she kept measures with Spain, and avoided a war, foretold what might be expected from her, and what she actually performed, when she thought it no longer expedient to keep the same measures. But this will come, with other reflections, more properly under the next general head; to which we think that the particular instances of queen Elizabeth's wisdom and address, in the management of foreign affairs, may be reduced.

Letter 16

If queen Elizabeth considered every former interest relatively to the interest of England, she considered likewise every measure to be taken in foreign affairs relatively to the situation of England. This we establish as the second general head, to which the particular instances of her wisdom and address, in the management of foreign affairs, may be properly reduced.

She considered herself as queen of a country cut off from the Continent, and separated by the sea from all other countries, except Scotland. Her conduct, therefore, towards Scotland was very different, in many respects, from that which she held towards every other nation. A due observation of these different principles, on which queen Elizabeth proceeded in the divided state of our island, may serve to set, in a stronger and clearer light, that single principle which remains to be followed in our united state.

The situation of an island affords great advantages, when they are wisely improved; and when they are neglected, as great disadvantages may result from this very situation. The reign, now before us, is a glorious and unanswerable proof that the halcyon days, so much boasted of, and so seldom found, days of prosperity, as well as peace, may be enjoyed in an island, whilst all the neighboring continent is filled with alarms, and even laid waste by war. But our own histories will show us likewise, how an island may approach, as it were, too near the continent, and be fatally drawn into that great vortex. Lest we should ramble too widely in the large field which opens itself, let us confine our reflections to some of those different means and objects, either of defence, or offence, which nature, improved by art, presents to people who inhabit islands, or to people who inhabit the continent, according to their different situations. A powerful navy is of indispensable necessity to the former of these. Without it, they must be poor and exposed. With it, they may be rich and secure. Barriers of fortified towns, and great standing armies are of the same necessity to the latter. Without this security, they lie open to every inroad, and at the mercy of every neighbor. With it, they may be safe from foreign danger, and even terrible to those who live round them. But then, as the sea is a barrier of no expense, and as a maritime force carries no domestic danger along with it, but enriches the community it defends, so a fortified barrier, and a regular army, which are necessary to secure a nation situate on the continent against foreign danger, carry great domestic inconveniencies, and even dangers too, along with them. Both of them, like armor, too heavy to be borne, waste the strength of those who are covered by them; and an army, like a sword, which recoils on the blow, may wound the constitution it was meant to defend. But farther: as particular families, by uniting together, formed larger societies, for their common defence, and gave rise to the kingdoms, and states, which have appeared in the world; so these larger societies have, ever since, found it necessary, or advantageous, to unite together in various manners; sometimes by an entire union, or an incorporation of different people into one body politic; sometimes by a partial, or federal union of distinct states in one common cause; and at all times by alliances, made on particular occasions, and suggested by a real or seeming conformity of interests. This occasional union, by alliances with other states, of which alone we are to speak in this place, is so necessary to all the nations on the continent, that even the most powerful cannot subsist without it; and those who manage it best, are accounted wisest. Their several interests are the objects of their alliances; and as the former are subject to change, the latter must vary with them. Such variations, whether occasioned by the course of accidents, or by the passions of men, though made by a few, will affect many; because there always are, and always must be, systems of alliances subsisting among these nations; and therefore, as a change in some of the parts of one system necessarily requires a change in all the rest; so the alteration of one system necessarily requires an alteration of the others.

Thus are they always tossed from peace to war, and from war to peace. Perpetual negotiation is the life and soul of their governments. Their well-being, nay their safety at home, requires that they should be always busy abroad. It is necessary for them to be mediators, arbitrators, or, which is infinitely worse, guaranties; to be contracting parties in preliminary, provisional, or explanatory treaties; in defensive, or offensive alliances; by which means they get over daily difficulties, by the multiplication of lasting incumbrances.

The interfering and clashing of their rights and pretensions, and the various obligations, by which they stand bound to one another, appear to be and are the immediate causes of all these disputes and contentions. But the principal and remote cause arises from the proximity and other circumstances of their situations. That necessity, or advantage, which gave occasion to the original engagements, has maintained and multiplied them since; and the last would not be reasonable, if the first had not been necessary.

Here then arises an essential difference between those objects, which are proper to the policy of an island, and those which are so to the policy of the continent; a difference greatly to the advantage of the former; the circumstances of whose situation not requiring so constant and intimate an union with other states, either for defence or offence, render unnecessary a great part of the engagements which prove such heavy and lasting incumbrances on the latter.

An island under one government, advantageously situated, rich in itself, richer by its commerce, can have no necessity, in the ordinary course of affairs, to take up the policy of the continent; to enter into the system of alliances we have been speaking of; or, in short, to act any other part than that of a friendly neighbor and a fair trader. If an extraordinary crisis happens on the continent, which may endanger the safety even of those who are separated from it, such as we saw at the beginning of the present century, self-preservation will no doubt determine men, as it ought, to unite by stricter alliances with those powers with whom they are occasionally united by a more immediate interest; but even in this case, neither will self-preservation require, nor good policy suffer, that such a people should enter deep into the quarrels, or involve themselves intricately, much less continually, in the political schemes of the continent. We pass over offensive cases, because it is manifest that the people of an island can have no interest in making foreign acquisitions; and that therefore it would be absurd in them to spend their blood and treasure in acquiring only for others; or to attack any farther than is necessary to defend.

We confine ourselves to the case of defence before mentioned; and upon that we say, a people on the continent may have reason to engage as deeply in defence of another country, as if they defended the walls of their own towns, or the doors of their own houses; because another country may be the sole barrier of their own. But this can never be reasonably done by the people of an island, who have another, and a better barrier than any the continent can form for them. Such a people are to look on their engagements with other countries, as on outworks cast up in haste, which may serve to defeat a weak attack, or to delay and disappoint a strong one. But it would be the height of folly in them, even in one of those extraordinary conjectures, which we now suppose, to lay the whole stress of their defence here; to spend their strength improperly; and to forego those advantages which nature has given them.

The nations on the continent might teach them another lesson. They are careful to employ every advantage of their situations; a river; a lake; a ridge of mountains; and shall the inhabitants of an island neglect the sea? Shall they do by choice all which other nations are obliged to do by necessity? Surely not, and if at any time such a conduct can be proved necessary to certain purposes, we think it will result from this proof, that such purposes should be laid aside, not that such measures should be pursued.

These reflections, with others of the same kind, present themselves naturally to those who consider the conduct of queen Elizabeth, and the events of her reign. We may therefore conclude that they were, at least, some of the principles of her government.

How she formed, or rather how she protected, and aided a party, already formed in Scotland, on principles of religion and liberty, has been observed; as well as the success of this measure, by which the troops of France were driven out of that kingdom, and the influence of France on the government was either removed, or guarded against. To maintain and improve this advantage, was the great affair of her life. England was, with respect to Scotland, like a kingdom on the continent, and queen Elizabeth employed, with respect to Scotland, all the policy of the continent.

We find her busy on that side in almost every page of her history; almost always negotiating, and always intriguing. A friend, an enemy, a mediatrix, an umpire, a guarantee, she played every part, which might keep others from hurting Scotland, and Scotland from hurting her. Her armies were at all times ready to march, and her fleets to sail thither. As strict an economy as she practised everywhere else, she was profuse there; but her profusion turned to account, and therefore deserves another name. There may be such schemes, such management, and such success, as may render even the smallest expense, profusion; but those of queen Elizabeth were sufficient to justify the greatest. The secret service of her reign was private in transaction and public in effect; not equally inscrutable in both.

About the fourteenth year of her reign, she had brought the affairs of Scotland to such a pass, that she seemed to have nothing to fear from that quarter. The plots, in favor of queen Mary, had been discovered; the insurrections defeated; and the Duke of Norfolk executed in England. In Scotland, the same party was broken. The Earl of Morton, a man absolutely devoted to queen Elizabeth, was regent; the castle of Edinburgh was taken; the civil war was finished with complete success, and she enjoyed great tranquility; because according to Rapin's observation, she could now be only attacked by sea; that is, she had now the whole advantage of the island.

This happy state did not continue long without interruption. Morton lost, and reassumed his power, was disgraced, prosecuted, and at last beheaded. King James had taken very young the government of this kingdom; and young, as well as old, was governed by his favorites. The party of his mother in Scotland did not indeed rise again, so as to give queen Elizabeth any umbrage. But his general character, and his behavior on some particular occasions, the character of his favorites, and the intrigues they were known to carry on, obliged her to reassume, if she had ever laid it aside, and to pursue her ancient conduct towards Scotland. She pursued it to the end of her reign: and although king James, when he had more experience, and was better advised, kept such measures with her, as were necessary to secure and to facilitate his succession; yet this wise queen continued to give quite another attention to the affairs of Scotland, than she gave to those of any other country; or would have given to these, if Scotland had been divided from England by the sea.

It is impossible to make these reflections, and not to reflect, at the same time, on that happy change which the union of the two kingdoms has brought about. We are now one nation under one government; and must, therefore, always have one common interest; the same friends, the same foes, the same principles of security, and of danger. It is by consequence now in our power, to take the entire advantage of our situation; an advantage, which would make us ample amends for several which we want, and which some of our neighbors possess; an advantage which, constantly attended to, and wisely improved, would place the British nation in such circumstances of happiness and glory, as the greatest empires could never boast. Far from being alarmed at every motion on the continent; far from being oppressed for the support of foreign schemes; we might enjoy the securest peace, and the most unenvied plenty. Far from courting, or purchasing the alliances of other nations, we might see them suing for ours. Far from being hated or despised, for involving ourselves in all the little wrangles of the continent, we might be loved and respected by all those who maintain the just balance of Europe, and be formidable to those alone who should endeavor to break it.

Having made these few reflections on that part of queen Elizabeth's policy which regarded Scotland, it is necessary that we should say something of that which regarded the nations on the continent. Now with these it is plain she took the fewest engagements she possibly could, and shunned as industriously the occasions of mingling her interests and counsels with theirs, as she sought the occasions of mingling both with those of Scotland.

We believe, upon very good grounds, that periods of four or five years might be pointed out, in which this nation has been a party to more treaties than were made by queen Elizabeth in the course of forty-five years; and yet we presume it will not be easy to show, that this nation had more imminent dangers to avoid and more formidable powers to resist; or that such ends were attained with greater glory and success at these, or any other periods, than in the reign of queen Elizabeth. Let us descend into some particulars.

With the northern crowns she kept in terms of amity, and good correspondence; and had some negotiations with that of Denmark, concerning the interests of her subjects in trade. The same interests drew her into negotiations with the Muscovite, and she found means to conduct them to her great advantage.

The settlement made in Germany, a little before the abdication of Charles the Fifth, continued. The protestants were quiet there, and desirous to remain so. The general interest of religion did not call upon her to look that way; and it is evident, by the whole conduct of her reign, that she thought the particular interests of her kingdom very little concerned in those of the empire.

How attentive soever she might be to penetrate into the councils of the court of Rome, and to trace the intrigues of the Vatican from their source; she bore no part whatever in the affairs of Italy.

In short, as all the measures she took in foreign affairs were considered relatively to the situation of England, she had nothing to do in the much greater part of the business of the continent; and she was so far from entering into engagements by treaty, that she was scarce ever concerned in negotiations about it. In France, Spain, and the Low Countries she had more to do; but even there the part she took was strictly no more than the security and welfare of her own kingdoms required; and she acted it in no other manner than was suitable to the situation of England.

The state of Scotland, of Ireland, and for some time of England itself, gave her just reason to apprehend that the French, or Spaniards, or both, might get footing there. Each of these had, at different times, pretensions of their own to her crown. The cause of Mary queen of Scotland afforded them, for a long time, both pretence and opportunity; and the united force of the Roman catholic party was, at all times, ready to support their enterprises. Spain was the greatest maritime power in Europe, and able to attempt the invasion of England, even when queen Elizabeth had been above thirty years on the throne, and had raised her navy from the low condition in which she found it. In a word, the whole coast, from the strait of Gibraltar almost to Jutland, belonged to France and Spain. Such circumstances formed a conjuncture, wherein these two powers had advantages against her, which they could have had in no other; and if she was obliged to act towards them in a different manner from what she did towards the other powers of the continent, it was because she stood exposed to lose, at least in part, with respect to them, the advantages of her situation.

How she acted towards them, has been observed already. She amused them and eluded their designs, by the most artful series of management. She sought no alliances against them with other nations; and though she did not fail to abet and support the insurrections of their subjects; yet even with these she was cautious of entering into engagements by treaty. She did it with the Huguenots by a treaty signed in 1562, which the vidame of Chartres had negotiated. The success of the treaty, and the ungrateful behavior of the Huguenots to her, confirmed her in the principle of depending little on allies, and much on herself. She chose rather to assist when and where she thought fit, and to assist gratis, than to be tied down to the consequences of constant obligations, for the notional advantage of reciprocal engagements.

In the year 1577 she began to take so intimate a concern in the affairs of the Low Countries, that the most important counsels and resolutions of those states were communicated to her; and she lent them a hundred thousand pounds; yet it does not seem probable, that she entered so soon into a formal alliance with them, though such an alliance be mentioned by Meteren, as well as Cambden, and inserted from the former in the collection of treaties.

In the year 1585 the clouds gathered on every side, and threatened queen Elizabeth with that terrible storm, part of which fell upon her, and part of which she averted. She beheld Philip master of Portugal as well as Spain. She beheld the Duke of Guise growing apace to be master of France. She saw these two princes closely united by principles, which might continue in force long enough to complete her ruin. She saw the Low Countries almost quite reduced by the arms of Spain; and the protestants of France in the utmost danger of being so by the league. Dangers from Ireland, and dangers from Scotland impended over her.

In such a crisis, more terrible, as we apprehend, than any which has threatened this nation since that time, what was the conduct of our heroic queen? Did she immediately prepare to oppose these dangers, by making alliances on the continent? Did she purchase accessions to those alliances? Did she raise armies, and pay subsidies abroad? Did she give guaranties to every prince and state who asked them; and, in order to ward against one danger, sow the seeds of many? By no means. She sent indeed Sir Thomas Bodley, to the king of Denmark, as well as to the landgrave of Hesse, and other Protestant princes of the empire, "to procure a league for defense of their religion," says Cambden. But this league does not appear, nor any other effect of these negotiations. "As she was very saving of her money, it is likely," says Rapin, "that she did not employ the most proper means to bring the princes of Germany into her interests." She secured herself by a great deal of management on the side of Scotland. She assisted the king of Navarre, and the prince of Condé, with money and ships; and the sole treaty she made on the continent was that with the states of the Low Countries, concluded the tenth of August 1585, at Nonesuch. Her chief dependence was upon her own ability and courage; upon the affection and zeal of her people. Neither failed her. Sure of being attacked, she began the attack. Whilst Cavendish pillaged the coasts of Chile and Peru, she sent Drake to the coasts of Spain, with orders to burn all the Spanish ships he should meet. Her orders were executed with the spirit with which they were given. More than a hundred vessels, loaded with provision and ammunition, were burnt at Gibraltar. The Spanish admiral was insulted at the mouth of the Tagus, and the Spaniards were taken, or destroyed, even under his eyes; an infamy so great, that the suffering of it was scarce in example before that time. The riches coming from the Indies to Spain, fell into the hands of the English. The projects of Philip were disappointed in the year 1587; and when the invasion was attempted in the year 1588, his army was blocked up in the ports of the Low Countries, and his invincible armada was beat, scattered, and destroyed.

We have now gone through all we propose to say at this time concerning the conduct of queen Elizabeth, both at home and abroad; concerning that conduct, which, by convincing her people of her goodness and her wisdom, procured from them those large returns of gratitude, of duty, of affection and zeal, the sole foundations on which she rested her authority and her security; and the sole foundations on which they can be rested, suitably to the nature of our government. The limitations, necessary to render monarchy consistent with public liberty, must be many and great; for which reason it has been objected to them, that they took off from that weight of authority, and restrained that fulness of power, which are many times necessary to be exerted, even for the good of the whole community. If this objection was well founded, it would be a sufficient answer to say, that a few accidental inconveniences, which may happen, and which may be recompensed too, in government, deserve not to be prevented, at the expense of leaving liberty perpetually exposed. But the reign of queen Elizabeth proves, beyond contradiction, that a prince like her will enjoy, at the head of the freest people on earth, all the authority, and all the power necessary to promote the joint security, prosperity and glory of prince and people. So that all the objections which can be raised on this side to the British constitution of government, will centre here; that it has not provided for strengthening and enlarging the authority 'and power of a weak or a wicked prince.

A prince who never separates the interests just mentioned, and who pursues them wisely, will have absolute power in the most limited monarchy. A prince who separates these interests, turns government itself into faction; and the spirit of liberty will rise against him. An arbitrary government is suited to any character. A free government requires a great, at least a good one. In the former, all kinds and degrees of power are in the prince, or flow from him. In the latter, his powers are limited and confined. When he wants to increase, or extend them, he must derive the faculty of doing so from his people; and from hence it follows, that as long as such a constitution remains entire and uncorrupted, the prosperity, nay, the ease, and even the security of the government, will depend on the disposition of the people towards the prince—as the disposition of the people will always depend on the behavior of the prince towards the people. Queen Elizabeth saw these truths in all their force. She was both willing and able to proportion her conduct to them. She never felt, therefore, any want of power. She was supported by the spirit of liberty, and she overcame that of faction. Some of her successors either did not see these truths in all their force, or were unable to proportion their conduct to them. These princes, therefore, felt the limitations of our monarchy like shackles upon them. The spirit of liberty either opposed, or did not support them; and they nursed up a spirit of faction to the ruin of themselves, of their families, and almost of the nation.

Letter 17

The scene we are now going to open will appear vastly different from that which we have just closed. Instead of an uninterrupted, pleasing harmony of government, we shall meet with a perpetual, jarring dissonance; instead of success and glory abroad, disappointment and contempt; instead of satisfaction, prosperity and union at home, discontent, distress, and at last civil war, will present themselves to us in all their horrors.

To consider this melancholy change, and to show from whence it proceeded, whether from the prince or from the people, is our present business. That it was brought about and carried on by faction, must not be denied. The sole question will therefore be, which was the factious side? Now to determine this, we need only inquire, which side was for usurping on the other; which was for preserving and which for altering the established constitution of government. On this point the question will turn; for in a country of liberty, in a limited monarchy, whatever some persons may think, or desire to have believed, it is certain that there may be faction for the crown, as well as against the crown. The reason is plain. There may be conspiracies against liberty, as well as against prerogative. Private interest may screen or defend a bad administration, as well as attack or undermine a good one. In short, conspiring against any one part of the constitution in favor of another, or perverting, to the support of national grievances, the very means which were instituted to redress them, are destructive of the whole frame of such a government, and are the proper characteristics of faction.

On which side faction, thus defined, is likely to be found the oftenest, and to act the most effectually, we shall not stay to examine here. They, who have read the first of these letters, may remember what is there said, to show the difference between the motives and the means, which a prince hath of usurping on his people; and those which the people have of encroaching on their prince. We shall only observe, to our present purpose, that as he, who confines his notions of faction to oppositions made to the crown, reasons, in an absolute monarchy, in favor of the constitution; so he, who confines them thus, reasons, in a limited monarchy, against the constitution; is weak enough to deceive himself, or wicked enough to attempt deceiving others; and, in either case, is thus far a betrayer of public liberty. On such principles as these we said, in our last paper, that government itself might be turned into faction; and that some of queen Elizabeth's successors had nursed up a spirit of faction, to the ruin of themselves, of their families, and almost of the nation. We presume that this will appear, in the course of our inquiries, to be undeniably true; and that there will be as little room to doubt whether the factious conduct of the court, in the reigns of king James and king Charles the First, gave a rise to all struggles between them and their people, as there is room to deny that the destruction of our constitution in church and state, was the dreadful consequence of these struggles. The spirit of liberty and the British constitution of government, whose cause we are pleading, and whose cause we are sorry there should be so much occasion to plead, will therefore, we hope, remain clear of all imputations.

We wish that this justice could be done without opening wounds which are hardly yet entirely healed, and without arraigning the the conduct of princes, whose memories have been held in great veneration by many worthy persons: but since this cannot be; nay, since the opening of these wounds may contribute to the more effectual healing of them; and since arraigning the conduct of these princes hath been rendered the more necessary by the accounts which have been given of it, and by the principles on which it hath been defended; we must speak with the same liberty of them, as we have used in speaking of those who reigned before them.

The Ægyptians paid so much respect to their very limited

monarchs, that when they meant to warn these princes against particular vices, they commended them for opposite virtues. We cannot persuade ourselves that this method of reforming, or instructing, by panegyric, the usual and most deadly poison of other princes, had a good effect on those of Ægypt. But however this might be, when these princes were dead, notwithstanding the respect shown to them living,[1] they underwent the same trial as the custom of the kingdom had established for all private persons, and funeral honors were equally denied to them, and to the meanest and most guilty of their subjects, when their memories were condemned, on a solemn and strict examination of the conduct they had held in life.

Though we propose to inquire with all this freedom; and though we are persuaded that the result of these inquiries will be a confirmation of what hath been advanced by us; yet are we very far from admitting many of the objections which have been made to the conduct of king James and king Charles the First. Much less do we approve those cruel insinuations against them, which are to be found in several invectives, not histories, dictated by a spirit of faction, not by the spirit of liberty. The spirit of liberty reflects on the errors of princes with sorrow, not with triumph, and is unwilling to aggravate what it wishes had never happened. In the temper which this spirit inspires therefore, we shall proceed. We shall dwell on no facts, but such as we think uncontroverted; and shall make no reflections, nor draw any consequences from them, but such as arise naturally and without the least force. The truth would not be so evident, as we presume it is in this case, if any thing more was necessary to the illustration of it.

Amongst the many advantages which king James had on his accession to the throne of England, we might very justly reckon the recent example of his predecessor. Her penetration discovered the consequences of that great change in the balance of property, of which we have spoken in letters 11 and 12; and she accommodated at once the whole system of her government to it, as we have there observed. Whatever doubts she might have entertained, concerning the success of her own measures,

1. Diodor. Sic. lib. 2, c. 3.

before she had experienced the happy effects of them, king James could reasonably entertain none. Experience, as well as reason, pointed out to him the sole principle on which he could establish his government with advantage, or even with safety; and queen Elizabeth's reign had every year afforded him fresh proofs that this principle of government, which is easy in the pursuit, is effectual in the end to all the purposes which a good man and a just prince can desire to obtain. But king James paid as little regard to her example as he did to her memory. In the last respect he was indecent; in the other, unwise. He boasted most ridiculously of an influence which he never had over her councils. Happy would it have been for him, for his family, and for this whole nation, if her example had really had a due influence over his conduct; or, at least, if his example had obtained less influence over the conduct of his successor. Fraught with learning, not with knowledge; ignorant of the true principles of government; more a stranger to our constitution by his notions and his habits of thinking, than to our country by his birth; obstinate, though not steady; misled by self-opinion, and confirmed in error by superlative pedantry, king James the First seemed to expect the love, and to demand the obedience of his subjects, purely because the crown had dropped on his head. Whereas queen Elizabeth seemed, both by her declarations and her actions, to think herself entitled to the first, and secure of the last, for no other reason than this; because she wore the crown to the greatest advantage of her people. Her good sense taught her what he had not found in his books; that the ties between prince and people are not the same with those between particular persons in private life. These persons converse and live familiarly together. Natural sympathies, therefore, more easily to be felt than described, may unite them without the motives of gratitude or expectation. Those common good offices, which the heart alone suggests, are often sufficient to maintain such unions; and a man, who is neither a saint nor a hero, may hope to find and keep a friend. But public, or political, or state friendship, by which we mean an intimate and affectionate union between the governors and the governed, cannot be contracted without gratitude, or expectation, nor maintained without both. If it could, if subjects were attached to their prince by a kind of instinct, as hard to be accounted for, and yet as prevalent as the sympathies we have mentioned; the assertors of the divine right of princes, and of the universal obedience due to them, would have had long ago a more plausible argument than they have yet produced in favor of their doctrines. They would have been able to stop the mouths of all gainsayers; even of him who required a miracle to become their convert; and who resolved never to believe that slavery was of divine institution, till he beheld "subjects born with bunches on their backs, like camels, and kings with combs on their heads like cocks;" from which marks it might be collected that the former were designed to labor and to suffer, and the latter to strut and to crow. But till some such miracle is wrought, or the instinct supposed above is born with men, we think it will remain true that the union we speak of, between prince and people, neither can, nor ought to subsist on any other terms, than those of good government on one part, and of gratitude and expectation on the other. This union may be, and hath been maintained by absolute princes with their people; because it is not impossible that an absolute prince should be a wise and good man; and because some such there have been. But here lies a difference. The absolute monarch may exert the whole power of the state. He may govern easily, safely, and with all other advantages, though he neglects to cultivate this union; or, which is worse, though he breaks it. But the case of a limited monarch is not the same, for the reasons which we touched upon at the end of our last letter. It is therefore the immediate, the personal, the highest interest of such a prince, as it is the duty of every prince, to contract this union, and to maintain it inviolate. The wisdom of our constitution hath made it so; and, in making it so, hath imitated that divine wisdom, which appears in the constitution of the moral world. In this, it may be easily proved from a consideration of the circumstances in which we stand as individuals, that the general good of society is the particular interest of every member. Our Creator designed therefore that we should promote this general good. It is by consequence our duty to do so; and every man who believes a wise, all-directing mind, and who knows that proportioning of means to ends is essential to wisdom, must subscribe to this opinion. And yet, determined by false appearances of good, or attracted by the force of immediate objects, men may, and they frequently do, imagine that they pursue their particular and separate interest, whilst they neglect, or act against the general and common interest of society.

In like manner, king James the First, and those princes who have trod in his steps, imagined no doubt that they pursued a particular, separate interest of their own, whilst they neglected an union with their people, and even made such an union impracticable, by transgressing, in pretensions and in fact, the bounds which our constitution prescribed to them. But the mistake is equal in both cases; for in both cases, interest and duty remain indivisibly united, however they may be separated in opinion; and he who sins against one, sins most certainly against the other; though the natural consequences of his actions do not appear immediately, nor on every occasion, to follow.

These consequences followed in a signal and terrible manner upon the occasions which we have mentioned, and into the particulars of which we shall descend some other time. These examples therefore are complete. The causes and the effects come together under one view; and if we carry our observations forward to later times, we shall see causes of the same kind laid again, and producing effects of the same nature; effects always proportionable to them; sometimes jealousy, discontent, tumult; sometimes open resistance and deposition of the prince; for though, in all these cases, the people have suffered, as well as the prince; yet in some, the prince alone hath been undone; and thus, by an equal distribution of justice, the principal share of the common calamity hath fallen on him, without whom no part of it could have happened.

Though these general reflections, which we have premised, may appear long to some of our readers, and may seem too nearly allied to reflections already made; yet we hope for indulgence, on account of the importance of the matter. It must surely be of use to explain very clearly, and very fully, from whence the weakness of our government, at some times, and the disorders and revolutions of it at others, have proceeded since that era, when our liberties became better secured, and our constitution capable of greater improvements, by a new settlement of the balance of property and power. No point hath been more mistaken. None hath been more artfully misrepresented.

Letter 18

We have observed already of how great advantage the example of queen Elizabeth might have been to king James the First. It might have taught him to struggle through the most intricate difficulties. But he had none such to encounter, till he created them by his own management. On the contrary, his accession to the throne of England was accompanied with all the favorable circumstances of ease and security, which were necessary to form a conjuncture proper for him; so that with abilities, much too inferior to those of his predecessors, he might have reigned as gloriously abroad, and as happily at home. Many of the difficulties and dangers which surrounded her, were personal to her. They arose from her birth; from her title; and from that which Mary queen of Scotland pretended. They therefore ceased with her. Many others she had conquered by a wise and steady administration. Many had been worn out by length of time; and many had been so changed by the course of events, that king James was safe, where she was most in danger; and strong, where she was weakest. His title was not contested; nor any opposition, either open or secret, given to his succession. They who had sounded so high the right of his mother, could not refuse to acknowledge the same right in him; and the rest of the nation submitted to it; for how little regard soever many of them might pay to this right in their hearts, or how great suspicion soever of his future conduct might be justly infused into them by his past behavior, the people would have a king, and there was no other prince, in whom the protestant interest could unite at that time. That riddle of a plot, in which Sir Walter Raleigh was involved, does not deserve to be mentioned, as an exception to the national unanimity we speak of. True it is, that, in other respects, the nation was far from being united, either by a conformity of opinion, or by an acquiescence of those who differed from the establishment. It was, no doubt, a severe misfortune, and such it continues to this very hour, that the great and glorious work of the reformation, being carried on at different times, and in different places, was carried on likewise without a general concert. The several churches reformed themselves, according to the different circumstances they were in, and according to the different characters of the few, who led the many in each of them. The separation of them all from the church of Rome was entire; but in some, it was thought proper to reform; in others, to alter the whole model; in some, many things were retained, which had been in practice before the reformation; in others, a total opposition to every instance of conformity with the church of Rome seemed to be the sole standard of Christian purity. This variety of opinions and establishments amongst the reformed was a great evil in itself; but this evil was aggravated by a circumstance of the most fatal consequence. The reformers, and especially those who came latest, as our excellent Mr. Hooker[1] observes, by enforcing too peremptorily their particular modes of reformation, brought the people in many cases to receive and respect, as divine laws, even those orders and that discipline, which expediency or other political motives had suggested. Now, the natural tendency of this persuasion was not only to render all comprehension or reconciliation amongst the reformed churches impracticable; but to make the divisions, in any particular church, incurable. Thus, when queen Elizabeth completed that establishment of a church, which Edward the Sixth had begun, many dissented from it; and the scruples of private conscience were pleaded against submission to the public authority of the state. If regard had been paid to all who petitioned the queen, or admonished the parliament, in the heat of these times, it seems probable that no establishment at all could have been made; and if none had been made, an ecclesiastical anarchy must have

---

1. Eccl. Polity, Pref.

ensued. How far the number of separatists might have been lessened by more compliances with the learned and moderate amongst them, for such there certainly were, we shall neither presume to determine, nor go about to inquire. It is sufficient for our present purpose to observe, that although these seeds of disturbance had been sowed before the accession of king James; yet no disturbance had happened, nor was any likely to happen at that time. The measures which had been pursued, and the temper which had been observed in queen Elizabeth's reign, tended to diminish the religious opposition by a slow, a gentle, and for that very reason an effectual progression; and, in the mean while, to prevent such consequences of it as might disorder or weaken the government. By the laws which were made, the several dissenting sects were discouraged and kept in awe; but by the execution of these laws, they were not exasperated. They were punished, not provoked. They felt the weight of the government, as often as they attempted to disturb it, but they never felt the oppression of party; and when they were treated like factions, they had not the pretence to complain that they were treated so by a faction. Upon this foot there was even room to hope, that when the first fire of these men's zeal was spent, reasonable terms of union with the established church might be accepted by such of them as were not intoxicated with fanaticism. Such as these were friends to order, though they disputed about it, and could have the less pretence to reject with obstinacy that which had been settled by queen Elizabeth, because they knew that their own discipline had been established where it prevailed, as the church of England had been by the supreme authority; that it had been made a law of the country; that the people had been bound by oath to the maintenance of it; and that Calvin himself had been a most rigorous exactor of conformity to it. If such as these had been once incorporated with the established church, the remaining sectaries would have been of little moment, either for numbers, or reputation; and the very means, which were proper to gain these, were likewise the most effectual to hinder the increase of them, and of the other sectaries in the mean time. Upon the whole matter, we think it very plain that king James the First, besides the advantage of coming to the crown, after all the difficulties and dangers of completing the reformation, and establishing a new church were over, had an easy and secure opportunity of preventing any bad consequences, which might be apprehended from the divisions of his protestant subjects; and that the improvement of this opportunity, consisted in giving neither alarm to the well-affected, nor pretence to the factious.

The designs of the Roman catholic party, against the constitution in church and state, were carried on with as much rage, but not with as much strength as ever. The hydra-heads, which sprouted continually out of that body in the former reign, had been lopt so often, that they appeared more rarely; and if the venom of that principle which produced them, was not abated, yet many of the springs, which fed and nourished it, were exhausted. The Guises, Mary queen of Scotland, Philip the Second, were dead. The reformation was established; not only in outward form, but in the hearts of men. It was grown up to be a part, and a favorite part, of the constitution. The spirit of liberty had blended our civil and religious rights together, and was become equally jealous of both. Let us add, for we may add it with great justice, that the church of England was, by the sobriety, wisdom and sanctity of her institution, established on a rock; that this rock was defended by the greatest number of excellent men, which any Christian church could boast of: and from all this let us conclude, that, as she was able to resist the attacks of those sects, which private conceit, mistaken zeal, some enthusiasm, and perhaps some faction had nursed up in her own bosom; so she was better able than any other protestant church to defend herself, and the state too, against the fallacies, the seductions, and the violence of Rome. The policy of this court saw it, and neglected nothing to prevent the consequences. Seminaries had been erected at Doway and other places abroad, for the education of English youth in popery. Gregory the Thirteenth had given the direction of that, which was erected at Rome, to the Jesuits; and upon that occasion these incendiaries crept into England. If we may believe some accounts, they mingled themselves amongst the clergy of the church of England and the puritan ministers. That they took all methods to foment our divisions is probable; and that they were hot men, who would stick at any, may be certainly collected from that account of their conduct here, and of the doctrines they taught, which is contained in the complaints exhibited against them by the rest of the popish clergy.[2]

Thus was the spirit of the church and court of Rome kept up here, even at the time of the accession of king James; a spirit, which might serve to bring about an assassination, or any barbarous and desperate stroke, like that of the gunpowder treason, which a few enthusiasts were capable of executing; but not to subvert the reformation, and introduce popery anew. The efforts of this party now were like the last convulsions of a strong body, mortally wounded; frightful to behold; sufficient to hurt others; but tokens of death, not symptoms of recovery. King James had it therefore in his power to keep down with ease a party, which queen Elizabeth had subdued with pain; and whatever impression the bloody designs they had often formed, and sometimes brought to effect, might make on his mind; certain it was, and the event made that certainty undeniable, that no degree of favor to them, except the utmost, could effectually secure him against their attempts; and that the least degree of favor shown, or encouragement given them, would be productive of the greatest national mischief.

We have dwelt longer on these points of religious divisions, because we think a clear and just notion of them absolutely necessary to fix a right opinion, concerning one of the principal causes which were laid in this reign, of all the national calamities that followed. We shall mention the other advantages which attended king James the First, as briefly as we can; not because they were small, for, on the contrary, they were exceedingly great; but because they are more notorious, and have no need of being so much developed, in order to be made sensible.

Thus, for instance, the different conditions in which he found the navy, the commerce, and the wealth of the nation, as well as the revenues of the crown, from that in which queen Elizabeth had found them all at her accession, is known in general by every one who hath dipped into history. Without entering into more particulars, therefore, than we have done already, we may venture to conclude that he reaped the benefit of her economy, and was a rich, as well as a powerful king. We know very

2. Thuaa. lib. 126.

well that when the session of parliament was opened by commission in 1610, by the Earls of Suffolk and Salisbury, one of the reasons urged, for demanding money of the commons, was grounded on a debt of queen Elizabeth, which was said to have absorbed three hundred and fifty thousand pounds, due on the last subsidies granted to her. If this fact was true, all that resulted from it is, first, that queen Elizabeth left a mortgage on the lands of the crown, and money enough to discharge it; secondly, that king James parted with his money to recover his lands; and we shall not oppose any person who will charitably believe that this prince would have paid the debts of his predecessor, though they had not been thus secured, out of the money she left in her coffers; because to have done otherwise, would have been a manifest violation of all the rules of religion, honor, and common morality. But we much doubt whether even this averment of the lords, who opened the session, will have any great weight when it shall be considered that their whole discourse was too ministerial to be sincere; and that some of the reasons by which they accounted for the king's want of money, such, for instance, as the charge of protecting his wife and children from being robbed on the road to London, were really burlesque.

The advantages which this prince had in the situation of foreign affairs, both at his accession to the throne, and during the greatest part of his reign, were remarkably great; and we doubt whether it is possible to find more than one conjuncture equally favorable since that time. Philip the Third was on the throne of Spain; a prince of small capacity, and less application; governed by his favorite, and his favorite detested by the people. Before the end of king James's reign he died; and Philip the Fourth, his son, succeeded; a youth of sixteen years old, and governed as absolutely by Olivarez as his father had been by the Duke of Lerma. The declension of the Spanish monarchy hastened on apace, under these princes. It is said that Philip the Third refused to support the Roman catholic party, in the beginning of the reign of king James; which is the more probable, on account of the early and precipitate steps made by this prince, towards a peace with Spain. The defeat of Don John d'Aquila in Ireland, and the entire reduction of Tyrone, which happened a little before the death of queen Elizabeth, discouraged the Spaniards from making any more attempts of that kind. They turned their eyes from these islands to the continent; to the Low Countries and to Germany, where they continued, during the course of many years, to consume their remains of strength, in abetting the ambitious projects of that branch of the house of Austria.

As king James had nothing to apprehend from the enmity of Spain, so he was secure of the friendship of France. Henry the Fourth was now established on that throne. He was in peace indeed with Spain, but intended not to be so long. We are very far from believing that this prince could seriously entertain so chimerical a project as that of making an entire new settlement of Europe, by dividing it into fifteen states, which Parefixe and other authors have related, upon the faith of the compilers of Sully's memoirs; but, without doubt, he had great views of checking the ambition, and reducing the power of the house of Austria. It was therefore his interest to live well with the king of Great Britain; and accordingly he sent the Marquis of Rosny, afterwards Duke of Sully, to renew the treaties with king James, as soon almost as this prince was seated on the throne of England. When Henry the Fourth was stabbed by Ravaillac, a minority followed in France, and the counsels of that court were, for many years, chiefly employed about their own affairs: so that nothing could happen on that side, even after this great change, to give the least disturbance to king James.

The states of the Low Countries were no longer in the same distressed condition. Their commonwealth had taken form; their naval force was increasing; and their commerce extending itself every day. Ostend kept the Spanish forces at bay for more than three years; and when Spinola made himself master of that heap of ruins, the Dutch thought themselves sufficiently recompensed by the acquisition which they had made, in the mean time, of Sluyce and other important places. The truce of eight months between Spain and the States was signed in 1607. It was prolonged afterwards; and in the year 1609, the truce of twelve years was concluded at Antwerp; by which the king of Spain was forced to acknowledge the liberty and independency of the United Provinces. Thus was that commonwealth established, to be a great and lasting accession of strength to the protestant

REMARKS ON THE HISTORY OF ENGLAND

interest; and king James might have reaped the benefit of an useful alliance, where queen Elizabeth had no other advantage than that of defending the oppressed, and diverting the forces of a common enemy.

The affairs of the North, indeed, were in great confusion about the same time. The crown of Sweden belonged to Sigismund in course of descent; but Sigismund was a papist, and king of Poland. For both these reasons, he had been excluded, and his uncle Charles preferred to the throne by the states of Sweden; who provided, by the act of settlement, not only that their kings should be of the religion of the country, but that none of the princes of the royal family should accept another crown, nor any foreign dominions. Their experience, it seems, had shown them the necessity of such limitations. This gave occasion to those long and cruel wars, which followed between Sweden and Poland. Others succeeded between Sweden and Denmark; but the scene of them all was so remote, and the interests of this country so absolutely unconcerned in the events of them, that he, who should have advised king James to take any part in them, would have passed, in those days, for a very bad politician.

The indolent Rodolphus slept on the throne of the empire till the year 1614. His brother Matthias succeeded him; and their cousin Ferdinand succeeded Matthias. During the reign of Rodolphus, there were troubles in Hungary, in Transylvania, in Bohemia, and in several parts of the empire. Most of them were caused, all of them were fomented, by religious divisions. During the reign of Matthias, these troubles increased. They grew up to maturity, as the accession of Ferdinand to the empire approached. The Bohemians, long oppressed, and long provoked, took arms at last in 1618. Many causes conspired to render all accommodation impracticable. Amongst the principal were the designs, which all the branches of the house of Austria had laid and begun to execute against liberty and the protestant religion in Germany; the character of Ferdinand, violent, cruel, a bigot, though artful; and, to speak impartially, the ambition of Frederic, elector Palatine. If this ambition had been the sole motive to engage king James in these quarrels, we must think that he could not have answered to his own people the engaging in them, as popular as the Palatine, his wife, and his cause were in England. But these quarrels were of another importance. Frederic lost not only the crown of Bohemia, but his own patrimony. The protestant religion, and the liberty of Germany were well nigh sacrificed to the bigotry and ambition of the emperor; so that the interest of this nation, as well as the king's family interest, was very much concerned to prevent these consequences; and yet, even upon this foot, we must likewise think that it would not have been long popular in those days, when the memory of queen Elizabeth's policy was fresh in the minds of men, to have maintained great armies on the continent, and to have fed with subsidies so many hungry princes, who had, at least in the beginning, nothing less at heart than the common interest.

This difficult and dangerous situation of affairs on the continent, in which we allow that king James ought to have taken some part, may be thought, perhaps, to form an exception to what hath been said, concerning those circumstances of advantage, of ease, and security, which accompanied the reign of this prince; but there will be room to think so no longer, when it shall be considered that king James had time and means to prepare for this critical conjuncture. The distress in foreign affairs began with queen Elizabeth's reign; and she was in danger abroad, before she was settled on her throne at home; but he had reigned near eighteen years before any thing happened on the continent, which could give him a just occasion of acting vigorously in that scene. Besides, when this occasion did happen, he had it in his power to have acted with great glory to himself, and effectually for the service of those whom it was his interest to support, without taking any other part than that which becomes a king of England, in opposition to that which becomes a prince on the continent, and agreeably to the principles of his predecessor's conduct. This will appear evidently true, when we come to consider the part he did take; and we shall insist upon it the rather, because we observe with how much affectation the case we are now speaking of, hath been quoted as parallel to the present situation of affairs; and how impertinently it hath been taken for granted, that king James the First was condemned in his own time, and hath been condemned since, for not doing what these time-serving politicians recommend; that is, for entangling himself in the affairs of the empire, as if he had been a prince of the empire; and for not acting on every appearance of danger, or even of inconveniency to any little state of Germany, in such a manner as is agreeable neither to the interest, nor situation of our island.

What hath been said may be sufficient to show how few the difficulties were, compared with the advantages, which king James had to encounter both at home and abroad; and how fortunate a conjuncture was prepared for him by the wisdom of his predecessor, and by a happy combination of circumstances. What use he made of these advantages, what conduct he held, and what consequences it had, must be the subject of another discourse.

Letter 19

By what hath been said, in former letters, we think it appears, that from the time our constitution settled on the foundation on which it remains still, there hath been not only no possibility of governing this nation with strength and dignity; without the concurrence of the people in their representative body; nor with ease and safety without their concurrence in their collective body; but that this concurrence hath depended, and does and must always depend, on the union of interest and affection between the king and his subjects.

We beg leave to repeat that queen Elizabeth saw this to be a sure, and the only sure principle, on which she could establish her government under such a constitution; that she very wisely took the government on the terms of the constitution, and the constitution as she found it; that instead of struggling through trouble and danger to bend the constitution to any particular notions or views of her own, she accommodated her notions, her views, and her whole character to it. Let us observe, by the way, that this is no more than what every prince ought to do; and what every free people will expect and exact too, if need be, that he should do. He is made for their sakes, not they for his. He is raised to maintain, not to alter the constitution.

Now king James began and continued, through the whole course of his reign, to govern without any regard to this principle; nay, in absolute defiance of it. He chose other expedients of government, and trusted to so many broken reeds. Without any talents to procure the esteem, he awakened the jealousy and never courted the good-will of his people; but, instead of it, endeavored to instil into their minds what was rooted in his own, a very good opinion of himself, and a very mean opinion of them. He endeavored to persuade men, who felt that the balance of property was on their side, and that they held a great share of the supereme power in their hands, that though they had this property, yet they had no right, or a very precarious one, to this power. He meant, by the force of new-fangled opinions, to attach the nation to him, as queen Elizabeth had done by the ties of affection and confidence; or he meant to govern without the concurrence of the nation; or he meant nothing. The first was chimerical, the second was wicked, and the third was stupid. Elizabeth had been jealous of her prerogative, but moderate in the exercise of it. Wiser James imagined that the higher he carried it, and the more rigorously he exerted it, the more strongly he should be seated in his throne. He mistook the weight for the strength of a sceptre; and did not consider that it is never so likely to slip, or to be wrenched out of a prince's hands, as when it is heaviest. He never reflected that prerogative is of the nature of a spring, which by much straining will certainly relax and often break; that in one case it becomes of little, and in the other of no use at all.

As absurd as the notions and principles of government were, by which king James hoped to establish his authority, he found numbers to adopt them; for numbers are at all times liable to be deceived, ready to be tempted, and prone to be corrupted. New systems of law and policy were not only received, but propagated. Some men were heated by opposition. Others were educated in prejudice. The plainest rights of the people were called in question. The least justifiable pretensions of the crown were established as true axioms of government, and certain principles of the English constitution. What Father Paul observes to have happened in the church, happened here in the state. Our court, like that of Rome, by affirming and denying boldly, and by insisting peremptorily, brought many things to be received as certain, which had been never proved, and many others to be looked on as problematical, which had been often demonstrated. Thus were those divisions created, which could alone render the others fatal. Disputes about the use of the surplice, or the cross in baptism, would not have unsheathed all the swords in the nation. Puritanism neither did, nor could make such deadly wounds; but when they were once made, puritanism festered in the sore, and rendered them mortal. King James conjured up, by using trick of government, that storm in which his successor perished. His successor, for we will finish the sketch we have begun, a religious and a just prince, came a party man to the throne. His prejudices, confirmed by habit, fortified by the flattery of his courtiers, and provoked by the opposition which his father and he met with, carried him to continue an invasion of the people's rights, whilst he imagined himself only concerned in the defence of his own. The faction of the court tainted the nation, and gave life and strength, if it did not give being, to the factions in the state. If the spirit of liberty could have prevailed in time against the first, there had been no danger from the others. But the long and obstinate resistance of the first gave time and opportunity, and even assistance to the others to extinguish this spirit. Cavaliers and Roundheads divided the nation; like Yorkists and Lancastrians. No other option was left at last. To reconcile these disputes by treaty became impracticable, when neither side would trust the other. To terminate them by the sword, was to fight, not for preserving the constitution, but for the manner of destroying it. The constitution might have been destroyed, under pretence of prerogative. It was destroyed under pretence of liberty. We might have fallen under absolute monarchy. We fell into absolute anarchy. The sum of all is this. We were destroyed by faction; but faction prevailed at court near forty years before it prevailed amongst the people. It was the original principle on one side. It was an accident on the other. Churchmen and royalists attacked the constitution. Puritans and commonwealthsmen, and, above all, a motley race of precise knaves and enthusiastic madmen ruined it. But the last could never have happened, if the first had not; and whoever will dispassionately trace the causes of that detestable civil war, will find them laid in the conduct of king James the First, as early as his accession to the throne of England.

Having given this general idea of the two reigns which followed that of queen Elizabeth, it is time to examine whether this idea of them can be supported by a series of uncontroverted facts. Let us descend into some particulars.

"A prince that is invited, or comes newly to a kingdom," says Wilson, "must have his chariot wheels smooth shod;" and surely if ever prince had motives and an opportunity to render himself popular, king James had both. Essex, Southampton and others, even Cecil, a principal minister of the late queen had held a correspondence with him, for their own private interest; but the millions who submitted to his accession, submitted to it upon trust, and were determined by the nature of the conjuncture, not by any knowledge of the persons who composed this new royal family. It was not therefore enough for them to be placed in and about the throne. Their true interest required that the hearts of the people should be gained to them; and that popularity should supply that spirit in their favor, which seldom fails to operate in favor of those princes, who are born and bred amongst the people they are to govern. The opportunity of doing this lay fairly before king James. He was received with transports of joy, and all ranks of men made their court to him. If he looked on this national behavior, for so it was, to be the effect of a desire in the people to endear themselves to him, and to unite closely with him, this should have suggested to his mind the ease with which he might acquire popularity, by improving the disposition, and captivate the good-will of a people, so desirous to be pleased with their king. If he looked on this national behavior as the effect of levity, inconstancy and love of change, it should have taught him to apprehend how soon this honey-moon would pass away; how soon the stream of popular favor might turn against him; and how soon they, who seemed to have forgotten queen Elizabeth, might return to regret her. But that which a Scotsman foretold, happened. This behavior of the English spoiled a good king; or made a bad king worse. It was natural for a vain man to believe what his flatterers told him, and what he, his own greatest flatterer, told himself; that these applauses and transports of the people were due to his eminent merit, and were an homage paid for the honor he did them in accepting their crown. He took therefore much state. He did not indeed make his journey, as Henry the Seventh made his entry into London, in a closed chariot; but he forbid by proclamation the concourse of the people to him.[1] "He dispersed them with frowns, that we may not say with curses." Such different turns of thought can vanity inspire. Some will be respected, like eastern monarchs, unseen within the shrine of their court. Others grow fond of public triumphs; delight in noisy acclamations; and are pleased to drive, like Indian pagods, over a prostrate crowd.

As much as king James neglected to gain the public, even at the cheap price of affability, he sunk into low familiarity with his favorites, and was profuse of riches and honors to particular men. He bestowed, at first on a few, and afterwards on one man, that affection which he had promised the whole nation, in some of the plausible, commonplace discourses which he held at certain times. There is no need of mentioning the particular instances of a profusion he acknowledged himself. The estates he gave to his courtiers impoverished the crown; and, as it always happens, the people were forced to pay for those very grants, at which they murmured. Honors he bestowed in so lavish a manner, and with so little distinction, that they ceased, in some sense, to be honors. To know the British nobility, it was become almost necessary to have nomenclators, like those who attended the candidates at Rome, to tell them the names of the citizens. The jest went so far that an advertisement of "an art to help weak memories to a competent knowledge of the names of the nobility,"[2] was pasted up at Paul's.

Thus king James began, and thus he continued his reign. That experience, which he said, in his first speech to his parliament, would teach him not to be so easily and lightly moved in granting, taught him nothing. What a contrast does this conduct make with the affability of queen Elizabeth; with the economy and reserve she used, in disposing of her treasure, and in conferring honors? But king James stood in need of helps, to the want of which she was superior. "A good government," says one of our writers, "makes a good people." When a prince hath turned the spirit of a nation in his favor, he need not be solicitous about gaining particular men; but when he hath turned this spirit against him, he must employ all arts, even the lowest, to detach particular men from the body of the people, and to make them

1. Wilson.
2. Wilson.

295

act by motives of private interest against the public sense. This is faction; and therefore whenever a court is industrious to seduce, to inveigle, to corrupt particular men, we may securely conclude, without waiting for any other sign, that such an administration stands on a factious, not on a national bottom. But to return to king James.

Whilst he neglected the affection and sought the reverence of the public, he lost one, and was disappointed of the other. His private and public character both fell into contempt. Learning was the part upon which he valued himself. This he affected more than became a king, and broached, on every occasion, in such a manner as would have misbecome a schoolmaster. His pedantry was too much even for the age in which he lived. It would be tedious to quote the part he took in the conference at Hampton Court; and in the theological wrangles between the Gomarists and Arminians; or to go about to prove, by some instances, what appeared in all his words and actions; what is universally allowed; and what the unkingly volume he left behind him testifies. Let us only observe, that the ridicule which arose from hence, and which fixed on him, was just; because the merit of a chief governor is wisely to superintend the whole, and not to shine in any inferior class; because different and, in some cases perhaps, opposite talents, both natural and acquired, are necessary to move, and to regulate the movements of the machine of government; in short, because as a good adjutant may make a very bad general, so a great reader, and writer too, may be a very ignorant king.

There are many other circumstances which concurred to lessen this prince in the eyes of his subjects and of all mankind, as we shall have occasion to observe frequently in the course of these remarks. In the mean time, we shall observe here, that the state he affected, and the pompous titles he was fond of, served to render his pusillanimity, which, with his vanity, made up the main of his character, more conspicuous, and his person by consequence more contemptible. The hostilities between the English and Spaniards continued, when queen Elizabeth died. This great queen, not content to have done herself and her subjects justice, on many signal occasions, put it likewise into their power to do themselves justice, by granting letters of reprisal on the subjects of Spain. King James was so fond of peace, that is, so afraid of war, that, without staying to be solicited on this head, or to be complimented on his accession to the throne by the king of Spain, he revoked these letters in a few weeks after he came into England. He disarmed his subjects before he had provided for their better security. He stopped them in the course of doing themselves justice, before he was sure of obtaining reparation for their past losses. The impressions which such a proceeding must make on the minds of a trading people are easily felt. He who had revoked these letters in such a manner, was not likely to grant them on any other occasion. What protection, therefore, and, much less, what encouragement to trade could be expected from a prince who began his reign by sacrificing this, the most valuable interest of his people, to a foreign and hostile nation; to the mean arts of false policy, and even to his fears? Again; one of the first embassies which king James sent abroad, was that of the Earl of Hertford to Brussels. A Dutch man of war meeting the ship which carried the ambassador, refused to strike;[3] and having offered this affront to the united crosses, which had never been offered to that of St. George, went off with impunity. It is said that the ambassador hindered the captain from asserting the

3. N. B. This fact stands in history, as it is here related; but having looked into Sir William Monson's naval tracts, we find it differently told. He says nothing of striking, or not striking the flag; but confesses that an affront was offered by two Dutch men of war. He adds, that he sent for the captains on board his ship; that he threatened to right himself upon them; but that he dismissed them at the entreaty of my Lord Hertford, on their excusing themselves, and promising to punish the offenders. How severely these offenders were punished may be collected from hence. "One of these captains," says Sir William Monson, "was he, who since that time committed a foul murder upon his majesty's subjects in Ireland, that were under protection." If we had no other proofs of the indignities offered to our nation by the Dutch, from the time of the accession of king James the First, than the memorials of this gentleman, they would be sufficient. He complains of these indignities very much, and mentions several. In this very tract he affirms that the Hollanders took and burned our ships, and murdered our men for trading to the ports of Flanders, whilst they suffered their own countrymen, even in our sight, to trade thither. The truth is, that our nation was insulted with impunity, during this pacific reign, not only in Europe, but in every other part of the world; not only by the Dutch, but by other nations; and that our government fell from the highest esteem into the lowest contempt. If, therefore, the instance we have quoted should be disputed, on the representation of this fact by Sir William Monson, an hundred others, and several of them more flagrant, might be soon produced.

honor of the British flag. But two things are certain; one, that queen Elizabeth would have severely punished her officer, and have exacted ample reparation from the States General; the other, that king James did neither. This commonwealth had been raised by queen Elizabeth, and was still in want of the support of England. The sovereignty of her state had not been yet acknowledged by any of the powers of Europe. How much the pacific temper of king James was capable of bearing had not yet become so apparent, as he made it in the course of his reign. From all which it is easy to collect, that if he had demanded satisfaction, he must and would have received it. But the good prince was afraid, where no fear was, and bore dishonorably what he might have resented safely: nay, what he ought to have resented in any circumstances, and at any hazard. We are not to wonder if so poor a conduct as this soon brought king James into contempt, mingled with indignation, amongst a people, eagerly bent on commerce, and in whom high notions of honor and a gallant spirit had been infused, by the example of queen Elizabeth, and encouraged during the whole course of a long reign.

These things, and several others of the same kind, which I omit, might however have been borne. The ridicule might have appeared less in the eyes of men accustomed to it. The other faults might have been excused, or softened at least, by hopes of amendment. But there are some things behind, which no excuse would alleviate, nor any patience endure. We shall now bring them forward, and shall speak of them under three heads. The pretensions set up, and the attempts made against the freedom of this constitution. The management of parties. The conduct of our national interests abroad, against the sense of the nation.

Letter 20

A fundamental principle, on which king James affected to establish his authority, was that of an hereditary right to the crown. This sacred right, according to the political creed which he imposed, was not to be contested, much less to be set aside; and yet this sacred right was a mere chimera; contradicted by the general tenor of custom from the Norman invasion to his time; by the declared sense of his immediate predecessors; by many solemn proceedings of parliament; and by the express terms of law. Two families (for the race of Plantagenet was grafted on the Norman race, and they may be reckoned properly as one) had furnished, indeed, all our kings; but this constituted no hereditary right. When a prince of the royal family, but in a degree remote from the succession, comes to the crown, in prejudice of the next heir, hereditary right is violated as really as it would be, if an absolute stranger to his family succeeded. Such a prince may have another, and we think a beter right; that, for instance, which is derived from a settlement of the crown, made by the authority of parliament; but to say he hath an hereditary right, is the grossest abuse of words imaginable. This we think so plain, that we should be ashamed to go about to prove it; and yet there are men, in this age of paradoxes, either dull enough, or prostitute enough, to assert hereditary right, even in the case above mentioned.

Our kings of the Norman race, were so far from succeeding as next heirs to one another, and in a regular course of descent, that no instance can be produced of the next heir's succeeding, which is not preceded and followed by instances of the next heir's being set aside. Thus Edward the First succeeded his father Henry the Third; but his father Henry the Third and his grandfather John had both been raised to the throne, in plain defiance of hereditary right; the right of Arthur, nephew to John, and the right of Arthur's sister, cousin-german to Henry. Edward the second succeeded his father Edward the First; but Edward the Third deposed Edward the Second; the parliament renounced all allegiance to him; and Edward the Third held the crown by a parliamentary title, as much as William the Third. If we go up higher than this era, or descend lower, we shall find the examples uniform. Examples, sufficient to countenance this pretension of hereditary right to the crown of England, are to be found no where. But we hasten to king James; who raised, or, if you please, revived this pretension, so needlessly for himself, and so very unprofitably for his posterity.

The British race began in Henry the Seventh; and from him alone king James derived that right, which he asserted in such pompous terms; that undoubted right to the throne, as he called it in his first speech to parliament, which God, by birthright and lineal descent, had in fulness of time, provided for him. Now surely, if ever any prince came to the crown without the least color of hereditary right, it was Henry the Seventh. He had no pretence to it, even as heir of the house of Lancaster. His wife might have some, as heir of the house of York; though her hereditary title was not free from objections, which the character of Edward the Fourth rendered probable; but the title of his wife had no regard paid to it either by him, or the parliament, in making this new settlement. He gained the crown by the good will of the people. He kept it by the confirmation of parliament, and by his own ability. The notional union of the two roses was a much better expedient for quiet than foundation of right. It took place in Henry the Eighth; it was continued in his successors; and this nation was willing it should continue in king James and his family. But neither Henry the Eighth, nor his son, Edward the Sixth, who might have done so with much better grace, laid the same stress on hereditary right as king James did. One of them had recourse to parliament on every occasion, where the succession to the crown was concerned; and the other made no scruple of giving the crown by will to his cousin, in prejudice of his sister's right. This right, however, such as it was, prevailed; but the authority of parliament was called in aid by Mary, to remove the objection of illegitimacy, which lay against it. Elizabeth had so little concern about hereditary right, that she neither held, nor desired to hold her crown by any other tenure than the statute of the thirty-fifth of her father's reign. In the thirteenth of her own reign, she declared it by law high treason, during her life, and a præmunire, after her decease, to deny the power of parliament, in limiting and binding the descent and inheritance of the crown, or the claims to it, and whatever private motives there were for putting to death Mary, queen of Scotland, her claiming a right, in opposition to an act of parliament, was the foundation of the public proceedings against her.

Such examples, as we have quoted, ought to have some weight with king James. A prince, who had worn the crown of Scotland, under so many restraints, and in so great penury, might have contented himself, one would think, to hold that of England, whose pensioner he had been, by the same tenure, and to establish his authority on the same principles that had contented the best and greatest of his predecessors; but his designs were as bad as those of the very worst princes who went before him.

Happily for Great Britain, he wanted the capacity of Henry the Seventh; the resolution of Henry the Eighth; and the favorable opportunities which they had the luck to find, or the art to contrive, of raising prerogative, acquiring wealth, and encroaching on liberty.

We observed, in discoursing on the reign of Henry the Seventh, that he had laid the foundations of an exorbitant power, before the nation was well aware of what he intended. King James, on the contrary, showed his whole game from the first. Besides the pleasure, which his vanity found in boasting of an absolute, independent right to the crown, inherent in himself, he imagined that the transition would be easy, and so indeed it proved amongst many, from this to some other useful apophthegms. He hoped to get, and he did get, an act of recognition of his right of succession; for we cannot persuade ourselves, with

Rapin, that he was indifferent on this point: and though this act, as well as the oath of supremacy, which had been established long before, and that of allegiance, which was established soon after, is in itself, as it hath proved in effect, but a feeble prop to support the pretence of hereditary right; yet king James certainly looked on it as an admission of his claim, and meant a real advantage, where the parliament very probably meant nothing more than a compliment. This prince brought with him the true spirit of a missionary; and, by preaching a new doctrine, endeavored to establish a new power. From the notion of independent right was deduced the notion of independent authority; a right superior to law; an authority unbounded by it; a right, which could not be proved; an authority, which might not be defined. The inference from both these was obvious. This independent king must be accountable to God alone. He could not be accountable to man.

If this excellent system of policy could have been generally imposed, his sacred majesty might have battened, with great ease and delight, in the full sunshine of arbitrary power; and that he should succeed in imposing it, his own vanity and the servile flattery of his ministers had made him to expect. True it is, that the language he held was not so plain, nor the efforts he made so direct and violent, in the beginning of his reign, as they grew soon afterwards; but yet, if we consider the multitude of his proclamations; the nature of some; the style of all; the obedience he exacted to them; the cast of power which he exercised; those which he essayed, and many other particulars of his conduct, which, for brevity, we omit; we must of course conclude, that he thought himself sure, at that time, of laying the foundations, since he prepared to erect so great a superstructure. He was deceived. Instead of making his impositions pass on the people, he only awakened their jealousy. He had, in his own age, and he hath, in ours, the demerit of beginning a struggle between prerogative and privilege; and of establishing a sort of warfare between the prince and the people. But the spirit of liberty baffled all his designs. The spirit of liberty was not enervated by luxury in those days. It was not only alive, but vigorous and active. It rose in the nation, as that of faction rose at court. The same principle which complied with queen Elizabeth, resisted king James. The opposition began as soon as the invasion; and tyranny was, at least, nipped in the bud.

King James made one attempt, indeed, in the beginning of his reign, which bid fairer for success than any of those which he made afterwards; and which, if it had succeeded, would have done the great work of his reign, by means more silent and more dangerous; more soft in appearance, and more deadly in effect. We mean the attempt he made on the privileges of the house of commons, in the case of elections. In the proclamation for calling his first parliament, he assumed a new and unjustifiable prerogative, by his manner of prescribing to the electors and to the elected; and by subjecting both to severe penalties, if they failed, not only against the laws and statutes, but against the purport, effect and true meaning of his proclamation. In the course of the session, he endeavored to put this prerogative in execution, by insisting first, that the commons should confer with the lords; and when this was refused, that they should confer with the judges, on the merits of an election and return for the county of Buckingham, which they had already heard and decided. If the king had prevailed in this attempt of garbling the house of commons, he would have prevailed very probably in that which he made some time afterwards, of imprisoning and punishing the members of it. Thus he might have intimidated those by one prerogative, whom he could not exclude by the other. Such an influence as must have resulted from hence, joined to that which the executive power gives unavoidably to every king, would soon have rendered the house of commons as dependent upon him, as the house of lords at that time appeared to be; for if money gets money, which will not, we suppose, he denied in this stockjobbing age, it is no less true, and perhaps no less visible, that influence begets influence. Now we apprehend that, in this case, the barrier of liberty had been totally destroyed, and that king James would have virtually been in possession of arbitrary power; for whether the will of the prince becomes a law, by force of prerogative, and independently of parliament; or whether it is made so, upon every occasion, by the concurrence of parliament, arbitrary power is alike established. The only difference lies here. Every degree of this power, which is obtained without parliament, is obtained against the forms, as well as against the spirit of the constitution; and must therefore be obtained with difficulty, and possessed with danger. Whereas in the other method of obtaining and exercising this power, by and with parliament, if it can be obtained at all, the progress is easy and short; and the possession of it is so far from being dangerous, that liberty is disarmed, as well as oppressed, by this method; that part of the constitution, which was instituted to oppose the encroachments of the crown, the mal-administration of men in power, and every other grievance, being influenced to abet these encroachments, to support this mal-administration, and even to concur in imposing the grievances. National concurrence can be acquired only by a good prince, and for good purposes; because public good alone can be a national motive. But king James was not ignorant that private good may be rendered a superior motive to particular men, and that it is morally possible to make even parliaments subservient to the worst purposes of a court. Richard the Second, by influencing the elections, and queen Mary, by corrupting the members, had created such a dependence of the parliament on the court, that the first had well nigh established, in spite of all other opposition, his absolute power; and that the latter was able to subvert what her father and her brother had done; to govern with the utmost cruelty; and to sacrifice the interests of the nation to those of a husband, whom she took against the general inclination of her people. If therefore king James could have created the same dependence, he might have promised himself the same success. He might have governed in great quiet and safety, with the concurrence of parliament, tyrannically at home, and ignominiously abroad. He might have beggared the nation, as he beggared himself, and have given an absolute dominion over both to one insolent and incapable minister. But this concurrence could not be obtained; because the dependence of parliaments upon the king could not be created. By asserting their privileges, they prevented any direct and open influence of the crown. Had king James been rich, and it was in his power to have been so; had luxury and the offspring of luxury, corruption, both which he introduced, prevailed in the body of the people, an indirect and private influence might have been established; this nation might have been enslaved by the least beloved and most despised of all her kings.

But the king continued poor, and the nation honest; this indirect and private influence was either not attempted, or attempted without effect; and we are persuaded that no advocate for it could have been found, even in this reign, or the next. There were men wicked enough to ascribe such powers to the king, as would have destroyed effectually the powers of parliament; but there was no man absurd, as well as wicked enough, to allow those powers which are given to parliament by the constitution, and to argue for an expedient, which must of course render them ineffectual, or pervert them to purposes opposite to those for which they were instituted. Thus liberty was preserved, by preserving the independency of parliaments. The proceedings of the commons, in the whole course of the affair we have mentioned, were extremely moderate. They went farther, not only in expressions and outward demonstrations of respect and submission, but in real compliances, than could have been expected, or that was perhaps strictly right; and when an expedient was fallen upon to draw the king, with some reputation out of the contest, they gave way to it, although by admitting a writ for the election of a member, in the room of one whose election they had allowed, they suffered a precedent to be established, which might be turned against them. But the spirit of liberty, though easily alarmed, is slow to resent even great provocations, and to act with violence, even against the worst princes. Repeated injuries, imminent and extreme danger can alone bring things to such a pass; and no king of this nation was ever distressed by his people, without receiving frequent warnings, as well as accumulating insupportable grievances. King James felt some part of this distress in process of time. He deserved it perhaps already. The commons however contented themselves in an address to him, to assert their privileges, and to complain of this invasion of them, amongst other grievances. The proceedings of parliament were carried on in subsequent sessions, with the same moderation and temper. In that which followed the discovery of the gunpowder treason, the oath of allegiance was imposed; and this pledge of fidelity, for the future, was the sole hardship, for such the court of Rome and a great number of that communion esteemed it, which the Roman catholic party drew on themselves by so execrable an attempt. The parliament complied, on this occasion, with the king, probably against their own sentiments; since nothing could be more different than his notions and theirs, concerning the conduct to be held with papists, and even concerning popery itself; and since the favor he showed, not to say the court he made to this party, had already created great uneasiness, and began to be a most unpopular part of his government. He had no war on his hands, and his revenues were at least as considerable as those of the late queen. The commons however gave him one of the greatest supplies which had ever been given in parliament; and upon this occasion it may not be improper to observe, in confirmation of what we have advanced already, that the natural bent of the people to live well with their kings, is so strong, that parliaments under no other influence than this, will neglect nothing to gain them; nay, that a prince like king James, disliked, distrusted, despised, may prevail on his parliament, for a time, and till all hopes of gaining him are lost, to do as well as bear in his favor, what would not be attempted in a better reign, nor succeed, perhaps, if it was attempted.

His design of uniting the two kingdoms of England and Scotland failed. It was too great an undertaking for so bad a workman. We must think that the general arguments against it were grounded on prejudice; on false and narrow notions. But there were other reasons, drawn from the jealousies of that time, and from the conduct of the king, who had beforehand declared all the post-nati, or persons born since his accession to the English throne, naturalised in the two kingdoms; and these were, without doubt, the true reasons which prevailed against the union. The next time the parliament assembled, to proceed on business, was in the year 1610, and by that time the general discontent of the nation began to show itself in loud and universal murmurs. Some monopolies, the rigid and impolitic proceedings of the high-commission court and star-chamber, and many other causes, combined to raise them. But no particular grievance either had, or deserved to have, so great an effect as the continual endeavors which were used to establish practices and principles, absolutely destructive of the general constitution of the English government. Such was the attempt made by Bancroft, Archbishop of Canterbury, when he presented the twenty-five articles, commonly called the Articuli cleri, and petitioned the king to grant prohibitions upon them. Such again were the books published by Cowel and Blackwood, asserting that the king is neither bound by the laws, nor by his coronation-oath; that he hath a right to make laws and impose taxes, without the consent of parliament; and that the nation was reduced to a state of slavery by the Norman conquest. Such, to conclude this head, were the many acts which the king himself had done, and the many declarations which he had made; nay, such was the declaration he made in this very parliament, when he affirmed that although "all kings, who are not tyrants, or perjured, will bound themselves within the limits of their laws; yet as it is blasphemy to dispute what God may do, so it is sedition in subjects to dispute what a king may do in the height of his power." These doctrines were new, ungrateful and shocking to English ears; yet the parliament kept in temper, and bore such language from this fearful, bullying prince, as the fiercest of his predecessors, since Richard the Second, had never presumed to hold. They took no notice of Bancroft, nor pursued any farther measures against Cowel and Blackwood, after their libels had been called in by proclamation, and the reading of them had been forbid. Nay, there was a subsidy granted in this very session, with as little pretence as there had been for granting the former. All this temper, submission, and generosity of the parliament were lost on the king. They would not connive at grievances, nor sacrifice liberty; and those were the only terms, upon which an union with him was to be obtained. From the year 1610 to 1614, he held no parliament; and it is evident, that he would never have called another, if his ministers could have supplied his profusion by all the illegal and oppressive means, which they used to raise money on the people, and which we forbear to enumerate, because the most partial writers, who have endeavored to excuse them, have not presumed to deny them. Even under this necessity, he did not take the resolution of calling a new parliament, till he was prevailed on by his favorite, Somerset, who had formed a scheme for influencing the elections, and, at the head of several other undertakers, flattered himself and his master, that he could get such members chosen, "as should comply solely to the king's desires."[1] But this project proved abortive. "The English freedom cannot be lost," says Wilson; and may his saying prove true to all future generations! "by a few base and tame spirits, that would unmake themselves and their posterity, to aggrandise one man." It happened to king James, as it happened to his son. Disgrace at court proved a recommendation in the country; and the faces which appeared in this new parliament, made the countenance of the court to droop.

From this time began that conduct, on the part of the court, and on the part of the parliament, which continued to be held, with very fatal uniformity, till it ended in a civil war. That the people had reason to be jealous of the designs of the court, hath appeared, and will appear still more flagrantly in the sequel; but that the court had at this time, nay even in the month of May 1640, when king Charles dissolved the last parliament he had it in his power to dissolve, any reason to be jealous of the parliament, or the people, we deny; and are able to justify our denial by fact and authority; even the authority of my Lord Clarendon. But the father and the son, and especially the former, having no end in calling their parliaments but to get money from their people, and to evade rather than refuse the redress of grievances; the art of the court was constantly employed, under the pretence of the urgency of affairs, and in the parliament of 1614, without any pretence at all, to get the subsidies first despatched. The commons, on the other side, who knew for what they were called together, and who expected that little time would be allowed them to inquire into mal-administration and to represent grievances, when they had once given the money, insisted for the most part, for there happened occasions, in which they did not insist, that the consideration of grievances should precede, or at least go an equal pace with that of the supply. This was the rock on which so many parliaments split. This alone occasioned the dissolution of that we are speaking of, and made king James resolve, though he could not support his resolution to the end of his reign, to govern by his prerogative alone, and without the assistance of his parliament; that is, to avow absolute power.

1. Wilson.

Letter 21

In our last discourse, concerning the pretensions set up, and the attempts made by king James against the freedom of the English constitution, we carried these remarks down to the year 1614. We chose to stop there, because it seems to be the very diametrical point of opposition, or a point very near to that, between the government of this prince and the government of queen Elizabeth, which we have so largely insisted upon. The distrust between him and his people was now entirely formed. His offensive and their defensive pretensions were now fully explained. A union of affection between him and his people, which the latter still desired and had long courted, was now grown desperate. A union, unworthy of a free people, a factious union between the parliament and the court, founded in the dependence and submission of the former, and so much affected by the latter, was after many trials become evidently impracticable. The king, as he had managed affairs, could never govern with parliament, nor without it; and whose powers, which are designed to be mutual helps, were turned to be mutual clogs on one another; not by any deviation on the side of the people, or of their representatives, from the true line of government; but by a manifest and almost continual deviation from it, on the side of the crown.

Thus were those great disorders in government and that national confusion raised, which in a few years more destroyed the whole constitution. In short, that melancholy scene, which had been preparing ever since the accession of king James, was opened about this time, and continued open with a few variations, every one of which was for the worse, till that tragedy began, wherein the noblest as well as the meanest blood in the nation was shed so profusely, and with the beginning of which we purpose to conclude these remarks.

We have charged the whole, and we think very justly, to the account of king James; who attempted to govern England by foreign, not by English maxims; nay, by such as he was unable to govern his own country. Sure we are, that no part of it can be laid to the constitution, or people of England. The constitution was the same in his time as in the time of queen Elizabeth; and the people claimed under him, no other privileges, nor powers, than they had enjoyed under her. It was his fault, not theirs, if by treading in the same path, which had kept them united with her, they were divided from him. These are points, on which we think it proper to insist a little more in this place, in order to cast a greater light on the particulars which follow, and to avoid any prolix repetitions, when we come to wind up the whole.

King James had opened the parliament, which met in 1614, by asking money for the portion and other expenses of his daughter's marriage to the elector Palatine, and promised the commons leave and leisure to inquire into grievances, when they had complied with this demand; but distrust, the bane of all harmony, prevailed amongst them, as it is plain even from this conditional promise that it prevailed with him, and they resolved to begin the work of the session by a representation of grievances.

A principal article in this roll was the growth of popery, encouraged no doubt by several passages in the conduct of king James, and particularly by two; his employing not only suspected, but known Roman catholics, in offices of the highest trust and consequence; and his avowed design of marrying his son to some princess of that religion. Shall we say, in the style of king James, that it was presumption in the commons to meddle in such deep matters of state? Shall we not rather think it was presumption in the prince to determine a matter of this importance to the public welfare, to the present and to future generations, without the advice, nay against the opinion of the great council of the nation? Shall we not rather applaud the wisdom and foresight, as well as the virtue of those men, who discovered the fruit in the seed; whose minds foreboded all the mischievous consequences of such an alliance, and who did their utmost to prevent the true, original cause of our greatest misfortunes?

Under another head of grievances, complained of at this time, were the monopolies, and many illegal exactions of money from the people. The parliament had the more reason to lose no time, and to spare no endeavors in putting a stop to these encroachments on liberty, because the longer they lasted, the more familiar they grew. The court improved in the practice of them. The people, who submitted to them by force, might have been brought to submit to them by custom, and the king might become able in time to supply his wants without the assistance of parliament; a case almost as desperate as that of his being able to supply them when, in what manner, and in what proportions he thought fit, by the assistance of parliament. We say almost as desperate, on the principles touched in our last letter; for, in the first place, if king James could have supplied his wants without parliaments, he would certainly have called none, and the condition of this nation had been worse than that of Spain, of France, and of other nations, whose examples have been absurdly enough quoted, to justify these arbitrary methods of raising money, and to induce mankind to submit to them. In France, for instance, the people must suffer; but they may complain. Their mouths are open; that is, their parliaments may represent, and even remonstrate; nay, they have gone so far as to refuse with success to register and give the necessary forms of a law to an edict of the prince, which they judged oppressive to the people. But if king James had prevailed, he would have governed without even these shadows of a parliament. The people must have suffered, and could not have complained. Their sole mouth, the mouth of parliament, would have been stopped, and redress of grievances being no longer attainable by the applications of their representative body, which would no longer have existed, they must have submitted tamely and silently, or have sought a remedy in their collective body, which can only act by resistance and force. This situation would have been bad enough, God knows; yet not so bad as the other; for, in the second place, if the parliament had been made dependent on the crown, no matter by what kind of influence; whether by the distribution of honors, the translation of bishops, the corrupting the electors and the elected, or the other methods king James took, the mouth of the people had not been stopped indeed; but it had been formed to speak another language than that of the heart. The people must have suffered, and the parliament must have rejoiced. If they had felt an increasing load of debt, the parliament must have testified great satisfaction at the diminution of it. If they had felt the decay of trade, and the growth of national poverty, the parliament must have boasted of the wealth and flourishing stage of the kingdom. If they had seen the interest and honor of the nation, as they saw it too often, neglected or sacrificed, the parliament must have exulted in the triumphs of both. In short, such a depending parliament must not only have connived at the grievances of their country, but have sanctified them too. They must not only have borne the rod, but have kissed it too; not only the rod of their prince; but the rod of some upstart minister, who owed his elevation to his dishonor, and his favor to his shame. But as the integrity of parliament secured the nation from any danger of this kind; so the necessities of the king were the great security against any danger of the other. Was the parliament therefore to blame, who opposed strenuously every innovation set on foot, to lessen this security?

A third grievance, which the parliament desired to have redressed, was that incredible waste, which king James made of the revenues of the crown. These revenues were, at that time, so much more than sufficient for all the ordinary occasions of the government, that queen Elizabeth, who had so many extraordinary occasions of expense, who paid so many old debts, without contracting new, and achieved such glorious enterprises abroad, as well as at home, did not receive in grants from her people above four millions[1] in more than forty years. If king James,

---

1. We do not want to be told that the value of money was very different at that time from what it is now; but though we admit of the highest calculations, this sum will appear surprisingly small for so many years when compared with the profusion and extravagance of some later reigns.

who had no extraordinary occasions of expense, who paid no
debts, who achieved no glorious enterprises any where, had
neither asked money, nor raised it without asking, the squandering his revenue had not probably come under debate in parliament; but, since he expected that the people should provide for
his debts, and supply his necessities, it was just that the representatives of the people should examine how they were contracted. The immense estates, which were made in these days
at court, the known corruption not only of inferior agents, but of
principal ministers, and even of those who were at the head of
the treasury, made such an examination the more necessary, and
provoked and excited the more to it. The house of commons
would have thought that they had betrayed their trust, if they
had neglected so important a part of it. By the proceedings, as
well as declarations of the parliaments in these times, it is plain
that they thought they had not an arbitrary, but only a conditional power, over the purse of the nation, though the strings of
it were in their hands; that they were to tax the people in no
greater proportion than was strictly necessary to support the
honor and interest of the nation, and the dignity of the crown;
that they could make no judgment concerning this proportion, if
they had not a full communication of the nature of the service,
for which extraordinary aids were demanded; and if they did
not examine before they granted these aids, how the ordinary
revenues and any precedent extraordinary grants had been applied. Such maxims as these will not be condemned, we presume. They have been always professed and frequently pursued,
from the time we speak of, down to the age in which we
live. Since the reign of king William the Third, our princes
have indeed stood on a different foot. They have had a distinct
revenue assigned to them for their particular use. The annual
expenses and the debts of the nation have been separately provided for by parliament; and yet not only the management and
application of these annual grants, but also the immense property
of the creditors of the public have been left to the crown, as the
management and application of those revenues were, which belonged properly to the crown, and by deficiencies, on which the
crown, not the nation, was immediately affected. It is no wonder therefore if our parliaments have thought themselves obliged,

since this great alteration, sometimes by committees, and sometimes by extraordinary commissions, to inspect more narrowly into revenues, which are still managed by the officers of the crown, though they make no longer any part of the estate of the crown; and we persuade ourselves that no honest man would be sorry, if the wisdom of our present representatives should think fit to make any inquisitions of the same nature; but even before this alteration, before the settlement of a civil list, and when our princes stood on the same foot as king James the First, with respect to their private and public revenue, the maxims we speak of were pursued on many occasions, and always with the universal applause of the people. In the reign of king Charles the Second, for instance, our whig patriots endeavored not only to detect and punish frauds and abuses, by inquiries into the management of the public money, but to prevent them likewise, by appropriating what they gave to the uses for which it was given; and thus much we think may suffice, to clear the conduct of the parliament of 1614 from any imputations on this head.

Let us mention, in this place, one grievance more, which we have touched upon in another. A former parliament had taken some notice of it, and this parliament would probably have taken more, if the king had allowed them time. The doctrines which established the unbounded and ineffable prerogative of the king; which reduced the privileges of parliament to be no longer an ancient and undoubted right and inheritance, but derived from the permission and toleration of the crown, and declared them liable to be retrenched at the will of the prince; and which by necessary consequence changed at once the nature of the English constitution, from that of a free to that of an arbitrary government, all these doctrines, we say, or the principles, on which they were established, had been already publicly and frequently asserted by king James. They were the language of the court; and a party had been formed in the nation, who made profession of them. They were maintained in conversation. They were pleaded for in print; and they became soon afterwards the disgrace and profanation of the pulpit.

We have sometimes compared, in our thoughts, these usurpations of king James over the privileges of his people to those of the popes, which gave that prince so much offence, over the rights of the emperors, and indeed over the civil rights of mankind. Charlemagne had made these priests princes. They continued for about two hundred and sixty years, to submit, in the main, to those rules, which the imperial constitutions and ecclesiastical customs had established; after which they started, at once, out of these bounds. They would be limited pontiffs no longer, but arbitrary high priests, like the dairo of Japan, something more than human, and civil as well as ecclesiastical tyrants. They scorned to go to tyranny by degrees, but carried their usurpations at one leap to the utmost pitch of extravagance. Alexander the Second denied the right of the emperors to choose, or to confirm the election of a pope. His successor took the investitures from them. Henry the Fourth asserted the imperial rights, in opposition to this invasion; but Gregory the Seventh asserted, in opposition to him, that Rome was the capital of the world; that the pope was independent of all powers on earth; that kings and emperors were liable to be deposed by the plenitude of his authority. The pope was believed by many, on his word; and there were more, who found their private account in seeming to believe him. Factions were raised to maintain these principles. They were consecrated by the church. The prevailed in those days. More than five centuries were not sufficient to abolish the practice, and more than six have not been sufficient to extirpate the principle. True it is, that these popes had several advantages, which king James had not; and amongst others, the minority of Henry the Fourth, at the time when they began this monstrous usurpation; whereas when king James set up his pretensions, and talked, and wrote of prerogative, in terms as ridiculous and full of as much bombast as those which the briefs and other public acts of Hildebrand contained, the commons of England were grown up to a full maturity of property and power. Shall we condemn them for endeavoring to preserve the principles of liberty, that they might preserve the spirit of it; and by preserving the spirit, deserve and secure the continuance of so great a blessing? Should an English parliament have sat quiet and silent, in humble dependence on the prince, whilst slavery in speculation, as well as practice, was making such large advances; whilst the laws of the land, the laws of nature, and those of God himself were perverted to impose a yoke of base and servile prejudices on the understandings and consciences of mankind? We think not. Sure we are that our parliaments have been always watchful to censure and explode, in time, such doctrines as might, even by induction and consequence, weaken the foundation of liberty. The instances of this kind are so well known, and some of them so recent, that we need not quote them. But, in order to justify still farther the sense and conduct of our forefathers, let us appeal even to the present sense of mankind. We all know that there are mercenary and abandoned wretches amongst us, who have dared to plead for a dependence of the parliament on the crown; not for that dependence of the several parts of the government on one another, which our constitution hath formed, and on the preservation of which the freedom of our government entirely rests; but for the most indirect, the most iniquitous, as well as dangerous dependence imaginable; for a dependence, to be created by corruption, which must always produce effects as infamous as its cause. Corruption, we say, hath been defended, nay, recommended, for we will repeat the assertion, as a necessary expedient of government. The representation of the country by the independent gentlemen of the country, hath been saucily and awkwardly ridiculed; as if a bill, to prevent all persons, who have neither places nor pensions, from sitting in parliament, was proper to be passed, and those salutary laws, which are in force for preventing persons who have places and pensions from sitting there, were as proper to be repealed. Nay, these incendiaries, who go about to destroy our constitution, have not blushed in the same breath to admit, that standing armies have been generally the instruments of overturning free governments, and to affirm that a standing army is necessary to be kept up in ours; if you ask them against whom, they answer you very frankly, against the people; if you ask them why, they answer you with the same frankness, because of the levity and inconstancy of the people. This is the evil; an army is the remedy. Our army is not designed, according to these doctors of slavery, against the enemies of the nation, but against the nation. We are confident that the present army is incapable of being employed to such purposes, and abhors an imputation, which might have been justly cast on Cromwell's army, but is very unjustly insinuated against the present.

Now let us suppose that the time was come, when the parliament should think fit to censure and put a stop to the influence of such writings as these; would any honest man, if he laid his hand upon his heart, disapprove their proceedings? On the contrary, would not every man, who wished that the constitution of this government might be preserved, applaud such measures and bless the representatives of his country for their zeal against the betrayers of it?

Upon the whole matter, we think it very plain that the alarm, which was taken at the propagation of those infamous doctrines, in the reign of king James the First, is abundantly justified not only by the examples of other parliaments, but by the general sense of mankind in all ages.

Whenever the fundamentals of a free government are attacked, or any other schemes, ruinous to the general interest of a nation, are pursued; the best service that can be done to such a nation, and even to the prince, is to commence an early and vigorous opposition to them; for the event will always show, as we shall soon see in the present case, that those who form an opposition in this manner, are the truest friends to both, however they may be stigmatised at first with odious names, which belong more properly to those who throw the dirt at them.

If the opposition begin late, or be carried on more faintly, than the exigency requires, the evil will grow; nay it will grow the more by such an opposition, till it becomes at length too inveterate for the ordinary methods of cure; and whenever that happens; whenever usurpations on natural liberty are grown too strong to be checked by these ordinary methods, the people are reduced to this alternative: they must either submit to slavery and beggary, the worst of all political evils; or they must endeavor to prevent the impending mischief by open force and resistance, which is an evil but one degree less eligible than the other. But when the opposition is begun early and carried on vigorously, there is time to obtain redress of grievances, and put a stop to such usurpations by those gentle and safe methods, which their constitution hath provided; methods, which may and have often proved fatal to wicked ministers, but can never prove fatal to the prince himself. He is never in danger but when these methods, which all arbitrary courts dislike, are too long delayed.

The most plausible objection to such proceedings, and by which well-meaning men are frequently made the bubbles of those who have the worst designs, arises from a notion of moderation. True political moderation consists in not opposing the measures of government, except when great and national interests are at stake; and when that is the case, in opposing them with such a degree of warmth, as is adequate to the nature of the evil, to the circumstances of danger attending it, and even to those of opportunity. To oppose upon any other foot; to oppose things which are not blame-worthy, or which are of no material consequence to the national interest, with such violence as may disorder the harmony of government, is certainly faction; but it is likewise faction, and faction of the worst kind, either not to oppose at all, or not to oppose in earnest, when points of the greatest importance to the nation are concerned.

The truth of all this reasoning will be confirmed by what remains to be said of king James and king Charles the First. If there had not been an early and honest opposition, in defence of national liberty, against king James, his reign would have sufficed to establish him in the seat of arbitrary power. If the opposition had been more generally backed with the weight of the nation in due time; if the court had not been able to divide men against their general interest, upon principles of prerogative and liberty, king James must have complied in time; the constitution would have been preserved; all our national calamities would have been prevented; and the sins of the court might have been expiated by the punishment of one or two of the ministers. But a prerogative party having been nursed up from the beginning, and gained strength in the whole course of king James's reign, the strength of the nation was divided, and the contest continued so long between the king and the people, that resentment and passion and prejudice and faction took place on all sides. The soft and gentle methods of cure, which our constitution had provided, became impracticable. A provoked people sought their remedy in resistance. A civil war followed. The English government was subverted, instead of being reformed.

What hath been said will serve to justify the conduct of the parliament, as well as the general alarm, which the nation had taken in 1614. These were the crimes, the heinous, unpardonable crimes, for which king James dissolved this parliament, with so much indignation, after they had sat but a few weeks, and had not time given them to pass even one law. These were the crimes, for which he confined to the Tower and other prisons, and punished in other ways, so many of the most active members. Lastly, these were the crimes which made him resolve, what he had before attempted, to govern without parliament. The particular consequences of these measures will appear in our next letter, when we come to consider his conduct of our national interests abroad, against the sense of the nation; in which period of time, the foreign affairs are so intermixed with parliamentary and domestic affairs, that we shall not divide them, but speak of them together, having first very briefly made our observations on his management of parties.

Letter 22

In letter 18, we have spoken of the state of parties at the accession of king James. We are now to make our observations on his management of them. It is necessary we should do this, in order to give a complete and just idea of his government; and yet so much hath been said on the subject by writers of all denominations, and even by ourselves, that there remains but very little to be added, either for curiosity or instruction.

We might observe how he drew himself into some trouble, if not danger, and exposed himself to the necessity of shedding some blood, in the very first months of his reign, by espousing the passions of a party; by disgracing and proscribing men, who had no crime at that time towards him but their attachment to the late queen; by avowing the cause of the Earl of Essex, whose designs had been, no doubt, as treasonable, at least, and as chimerical too, as those into which he drove Grey, Cobham, and Raleigh, or which were imputed to them.

Several other anecdotes, concerning factions at court and parties in the nation, might be collected and remarked upon. But we shall pass them over, and confine ourselves to observe, in a very few instances, how he adapted his particular management of parties to the general and main design of his policy; what strength he acquired; what strength he lost by this conduct; and what contests he entailed on posterity.

There were no parties, at this time, in the nation, but such as were formed on religious differences; and it had been a great object of the policy of queen Elizabeth, to keep all parties within these bounds. We know the maxims on which she proceeded, by a letter of Sir Francis Walsingham, wrote expressly on this subject. She thought that "consciences were not to be forced, but won and reduced by truth, time, instruction and persuasion; and that causes of conscience lose their nature, when they exceed their bounds and grow matter of faction." By keeping to these maxims, she succeeded. The parties in the church made none in the state. They were obliged to live in due subjection to laws, wisely made and moderately exercised. They were never punished, whilst they continued in this subjection, much less were they provoked or encouraged to go out of it. The powers of the church were applied to the support of the establishment, not rendered subservient to any factious designs of the court; and ecclesiastical violence was restrained from confirming the obstinacy of those who dissented, by persecution of them, or from increasing their numbers, by persecution of others.

Directly opposite to this conduct was that of king James. In haste to show his parts, he had a conference between the bishops and the puritan ministers at Hampton Court, in a few months after his accession; where he made himself a principal party in the dispute. His courtiers flattered him, and Archbishop Whitgift, who died soon afterwards, and probably doated then, declared himself "verily persuaded that the king spake by the spirit of God." But surely such a confidence, however it might frighten and silence, could neither instruct nor persuade; and the king was so far from trusting, like his predecessor, to the force of truth and the aid of time, that in this very conference he threatened to employ another kind of force, if he did not meet with compliance in a time to be limited. The bishops were at first to admonish paternally and to confer amicably; but lest they should not succeed by preaching, writing and living men into conformity, the sole means they ought to desire; or, if they desired others, the sole means they ought to be suffered to employ, they were to have recourse to compulsion afterwards. The same spirit reigned in the first speech which this prince made to his parliament; for there he not only massed together, imprudently as well as unjustly, all the dissenters from the established church, under the general denomination of puritans and novelists, but he declared them all "insufferable in any well-governed commonwealth:" so that he put them all out of his protection, even though they confined themselves within those bounds, to which causes of conscience may reasonably extend, and proscribed them for their opinions, not their practices.

On these principles he proceeded, and what we have said here may suffice, upon this head, for his whole reign. The consequence of this conduct was that those sects, who were not dangerous at first, became so at last. They became so, in some degree, from the moment the declarations we have mentioned were made: for nothing is found more true in nature and experience than this, that they who are oppressed by governments, will endeavor to change them; and that he who makes himself terrible to multitudes, will have multitudes to fear. But this was not all. As he made these sects his enemies, so he gave them great advantages of popularity and strength. The first of these advantages which we shall take notice of, arose from the great indulgence he showed to the Roman catholics, and the favorable sentiments of that religion, which he expressed on all private and many public occasions. We need not descend into the particular instances; for though we give little credit to Deageant's memoirs in general, and none to what he says of a letter, written by king James to the pope, acknowledging him vicar of Christ and head of the church; yet there is a multitude of other proofs, too notorious and too well supported to be denied. We think it plain, upon the whole matter, that several passages in his conduct, both before and after his coming into England, were unworthy of a protestant king at any time, and were equally impolitic at this time, when the zeal of papists to attack, and of protestants to defend the reformation was at the highest pitch; and when even the least condescension on either side, would have been thought little less than apostacy. Fear for his person, and little notions of policy, were probably the motives which determined this part of his conduct; but whatever the motives were, the effect was certainly this. He made the cause of the court to pass amongst many for the cause of popery; and it was not hard by consequence for the puritans, who were oppressed by the court, to make their cause pass for that of the reformation. We are far from thinking that this was properly the case on

322

either side; but the appearances were strong enough to fix such prejudices in the minds of men, already prepared by jealousy and suspicion. This advantage, so foolishly given, operated strongly against the court, both in this reign and the next. In this it was applied to no ill purposes. In the next, it was very wickedly improved; but they who gave it first, and who continued to give it afterwards, are justly to be reputed the accomplices of those who improved it so wickedly, how much soever they stood in opposition to one another.

A second advantage of popularity and strength, which king James gave to the puritans, was this: He ranked amongst their party, nay he drove into that party, as much as he was able by severe usage, all those who stood up in defence even of civil liberty. The aversion which he expressed to the puritans, formed a kind of league between him and the warmest of the established clergy; and when these were once become a court party, we are not to wonder if others grew as warm as these, and if the greatest part of that body of men united in a cause which flattered their passions, and opened the road of preferment to them. No king no bishop, was the language of the court. No bishop no king, was that of the church. Had the monarchy and the hierarchy been attacked, this united zeal in a common cause would have been commendable and successful too; for the nation was not now, nor for a long time afterwards, so distempered, that any faction could raise its head with effect against the just prerogative of the crown and the established rights of the church. But the truth requires we should say, that this union was formed to offend and invade, and to extend both beyond the bounds prescribed to them by the English constitution. It was great blindness in the clergy not to see that to enlarge the bottom of the court, they narrowed their own; that they fixed a centre of union, wherein all their divided enemies would meet and unite with many, who were then friends to the church, but might come, as it happened afterwards, from being against the clergy to be against the church itself. It was a great misfortune to the nation, that the clergy did not see these truths in time; since, if they had seen them, they might have been happy instruments of preventing that mischief which followed soon after the time we speak of, and that division of interests between the crown and the people, which was created by king

James, and hath proved so fatal to his posterity. But to return. By a contrary conduct, by espousing and sanctifying the principles and by promoting the measures of king James, the clergy became part of the faction of the court, and shared very unjustly the imputation of favoring popery, but very justly that of advancing tyranny. This was a second advantage, which king James gave to the puritans. He varnished their cause with popularity, and he increased their numbers. He made puritans in his time, as Jansenists have been since made in France, in Jacobites in Britain, by calling men so and by treating them as such. They must have been sharp-sighted, indeed, of whom my Lord Clarendon speaks, and who could discern "the rebellion contriving from, if not before, the death of queen Elizabeth"; but they must be quite blind, who do not discern the seeds of rebellion sowing in every part of the conduct of king James, and particularly in this which we have now touched, the management of parties.

These evils were aggravated, and the consequences of them were precipitated by his conducting our national interests abroad against the sense of the nation.

During the first period, into which we divide this reign, that is, to the year 1614, king James meddled little, and, to say the truth, had little occasion to meddle in foreign affairs. The treaty which he made with Spain in 1604, had been much censured, and Sir C. Cornwallis, in a letter to the Lord Cranburne, asserts "that England never lost such an opportunity of winning honor and wealth unto it, as by relinquishing the war against an exhausted kingdom and a prince held in little veneration for suffering himself to be wholly governed by a man generally hated." This treaty, however, was not probably so bad as it had been represented, and the commerce opened with Spain became a source of inexhaustible riches to our nation; but still there was something preposterous and mean in the conduct of king James abroad, even whilst he had so little to do there, and so safe a part to act. He courted that very power, the power of Spain, whom queen Elizabeth had broke, and who would have courted him, if he had known how to put so much as dignity in his proceedings. He disobliged the Dutch, whose power had been raised by queen Elizabeth, and who must have continued to depend on him, if he had known how to be either a friend or an enemy; and yet he bore most ignominiously from this very people the greatest injuries and affronts imaginable. He had neither the courage to chastise this infant state, nor the sense to protect it. Their treaty with their old masters, the Spaniards, began in the year 1607; was continued in 1608; and ended in 1609, in a truce of twelve years. During the whole course of this long negotiation, king James showed his partiality in favor of the Spaniards; and though he signed, about this time, two treaties with the states as sovereigns; yet he made no scruple, upon some occasions, of declaring them rebels. The death of the Duke of Cleves, and the disputes about that succession, presented to Henry the Fourth an opportunity he waited for; and he was ready, when Ravaillac stabbed him, to attack the house of Austria, whose power in Germany began once more to give umbrage, though Rodolphus the Second was still on the imperial throne. King James left his troops with the Dutch, notwithstanding the truce. They were employed in this quarrel; and we cannot think him to blame for taking no farther part in the hostilities. His views were, and they ought to have been, at this time, and in this respect, very different from those of that heroical king of France. But in the new scene of German affairs, which opened a few years afterwards, and which continued, during the last period of his reign, that is, from the year 1614, nothing could be more scandalous than his taking no part at all, except his taking the part he did take. That he should have made himself a principal in that terrible war, which broke out in Germany in 1618, and which lasted thirty years, we cannot persuade ourselves; neither do we believe that any man, who does not take up his opinions on trust, but examines this intricate and perplexed part of the history of the last century with care, will be of another mind; and yet king James must have made himself a principal in this war, if he had engaged in it, as he was advised by some to engage, and as he hath been blamed by many for not engaging. The censures, under which he hath passed on this occasion, would have been juster, if those who have made them, had distinguished better between the patrimony of his children, by defending the Palatinate, and promoting their grandeur, by seconding their ambition; between contributing to support the protestant interest abroad, and taking on his shoulders a load which it was neither reasonable nor possible that he should bear; between that conduct, which he ought to have held, as king of this island, and that which he might have been obliged to hold, if his dominions had laid on the continent. Our writings will not pass, we believe, for apologies in favor of king James; and yet we shall explain this point a little less to his disadvantage, perhaps, than it hath been usually taken.

If king James had followed the advice of those who would have had him enter into an immediate war to maintain the elector Palatine on the throne of Bohemia, he must have exhausted and ruined this nation to support it. He must have furnished subsidies to Bethlehem Gabor and the prince of Anspach; he must have fed the war in Hungary; fomented the revolt in Austria; paid the army of the princes of the union; opposed the Duke of Bavaria in Bohemia, and Spinola in the Palatinate. Let us consider in opposition to whom, and in concert with whom, he must have carried on this vast undertaking. On one side, the whole popish interest in the empire was closely united, and the cause of Ferdinand was the common cause of the party. The popish interest out of the empire conspired in the same cause. The king of Poland assisted the emperor in Hungary. Troops from Italy and a great army from the Netherlands acted for him in Germany. The purse of the pope and that of the king of Spain were open to him. Even France, who ought in good policy to have opposed the house of Austria, was induced, by the bigotry of her court, and, perhaps, by the private interest of Luines, to declare for the emperor against the king of Bohemia. On the other side, the protestant interest in the empire was far from being closely united, and farther still from making the cause of Frederic the common cause of the party. Even the princes of the union had different views; many of them leaned to the emperor; none of them could be entirely depended upon; and the elector of Saxony, the most powerful of the protestant princes of the empire, was so far from uniting with the others, that he was first privately, and afterwards openly, but all along very steadily on the side of Ferdinand. Out of the empire, some assistance might have been expected from the king of Denmark and the Dutch; but even their accession must have been purchased; at least, it must have been made useful at the expense of Britain. What other allies could king James have hoped for; and who can see, without smiling, in that goodly prelate, Archbishop Abbot's letter to Sir Robert Naunton, the name of the Duke of Bouillon, together with Tremouille, a rich prince in France, mentioned upon such an occasion? Short and imperfect as the account we have given is, those who know the state of Europe at the time we speak of, know that it is true; and if we were to look no farther than the representations made by Juliana of Nassau to her son, against his accepting the crown of Bohemia, we should discover in them, with the true and fatal reasons why king James did not assist Frederic at all, unanswerable reasons why he ought not to have taken upon him the Bohemian quarrel, in the manner he must have taken it, if he had taken it upon him at that time. That king James should have prepared for this storm, which was long in gathering, that he should have labored to unite and fortify the protestants of Germany before it happened, and to comfort, and succor, and protect them, after it happened; that he had many fair opportunities of doing this, without engaging farther than the interest of Britain allowed, and that he neglected them all, we admit, and are able to show. He might have put himself on such a foot in Europe, as to have mediated at least, which was the only part he attempted to act, successfully for the Bohemians, and to have screened his son-in-law from the vengeance of the emperor, and the ambition of the Duke of Bavaria. But he put himself on such a foot, and he acquired such a character, that he had no credit among the protestants, nor much influence over his son-in-law, and that the Roman catholic party, sure of amusing him, neglected and despised him. He might have declined taking the Bohemian quarrel upon him, and yet not have made his court to the emperor and the king of Spain, by disavowing and condemning Frederic, and even by suffering them not only to drive this prince out of Bohemia, but to take the Palatinate from him and his family, and give a wound, almost mortal, to the whole protestant cause in Germany. Nay, he did worse. By foolish embassies and ridiculous negotiations, he gave time and furnished advantages, which could not have been had without his assistance to the popish party. By the same means he checked, he weakened, he discouraged, and more than once disarmed the protestant party. In short, not only the principles of his conduct were wrong, but the measures of it composed such a series of blunders as we seldom find in history; because it is hardly possible, in the course of nature, that such characters, in such situations, should appear above once in a century.

It may be objected, perhaps, by some of the writers, who adorn and instruct the present age, that king James was universally and justly condemned for not taking the Bohemian quarrel upon him, as well as for not defending the Palatinate; and that he must have pursued, in the last case, the same measures as we think him justified for not pursuing in the former. We shall not refute this objection by showing, as it would be easy for us to do, in various particulars, the prodigious difference between the two cases; the insuperable difficulties he would have encountered in one, and the many facilities he would have had in the other. The deduction would be too long and extensive for the narrow limits of these essays. But we shall content ourselves with making two observations, sufficient to satisfy any reasonable man, and which will show, at the same time, what different notions of the part of this nation ought to take in foreign affairs, were entertained by our forefathers, from those which we, their wiser offspring, have pursued. When king James took the resolution of calling the parliament, which sat in 1621, the battle of Prague was lost, and Bohemia too with it. The affections[1] of the people were raised, but it was for the recovery of the Palatinate; and in this point the sense of the parliament went along with the affections of the people. On the other point, the sense of the parliament had not been expressed, there having been no parliament held from the year 1614 till this time. But what this sense would have been, may be easily collected, from the advice given in the petition and remonstrance of the commons at this time. As zealous as they were to engage even in a war, for recovering the Palatinate, they were not enough transported by their zeal, or enough biassed in favor of any foreign interest, to forget the true interest of Britain. They advised the king to a war; but they advised him not to rest upon a war in those parts only which would consume his treasure and discourage his people. They advised that the bent of this war might be against

1. See Rush. Coll.

that prince, the king of Spain, whose armies and treasures had first diverted and since maintained the war in the Palatinate. On which side now was the sense of the nation; and how impertinent are they who have quoted this sense, to authorise our taking part in every German quarrel, by paying subsidies, maintaining armies, and involving ourselves in all the affairs of the continent? How monstrous is the absurdity and impudence[2] of those who have asserted that the case of the people of the Palatinate, invaded by a powerful enemy, who pretended to nothing less than the conquest of them, is parallel to that of the people of Hanover, invaded by no body, and over whom no foreign power pretends to any dominion! The parliament pointed out to king James a measure effectual for supporting the protestant interest abroad; but such a measure as this nation might pursue by exerting her natural strength. The power of Spain supported the emperor and the popish league; an army of Spain conquered the Palatinate; and yet the artifices of that court deluded king James to such a degree, that he dreamed of recovering the patrimony of his children by the good offices of the Spaniards, and was incapable of pursuing in earnest any other measure, even at the time when Spinola was stripping them of this patrimony, and reducing them to seek their bread in another country. To this dependence in Spain he sacrificed not only them, but his own honor, the affection of his subjects, the prosperity of his kingdoms, and the security of the protestant religion. It was this magic charm which the parliament endeavored in vain to dissolve, by pressing him to a war with Spain, which his maritime force could have carried on principally; which would have stopped that source from whence the popish party in Germany derived so many supplies; and which would have rendered the protestant party, by consequence, a more equal match for the emperor. But this was not the sole wise and honest view which the parliament proposed, by pointing out and insisting on this measure. There was another, which touched them more nearly, and which they had more at heart. We shall mention it in our next discourse, and it will lead us from our observations on this reign to those few on the next, with which we intend to close, at least for the present, all our remarks on the history of England.

2. See Observations on the Present State of Affairs.

Letter 23

Another object besides recovering the Palatinate, which the parliament had in view when they pressed king James to break with Spain, was preventing the marriage of the Prince of Wales to the Infanta. He had been bantered and abused by the Spaniards, when he treated of a marriage between his eldest son, Prince Henry and Anne of Austria; and yet no sooner did the Duke of Lerma, in the year 1616, make some overtures of marrying the Infanta Mary, second daughter of Philip the Third, to Prince Charles, but this Solomon of ours caught at the bait which was thrown out to him, and hung fast on the hook for seven years together.

The scheme of farther usurpations in Germany was already laid by the house of Austria; and the character of Ferdinand, who was to succeed Matthias, and who did succeed him three years afterwards, gave hopes of pushing these usurpations with vigor and advantage. The part of Spain had been great in promoting these designs. It was essential to their success that it should be so likewise in the execution of them. No opposition of any moment was to be apprehended from France, where the principles of despotism and of bigot-popery prevailed more than ever, and who had concluded, in the year 1615, a double marriage with Spain. The truce of twelve years, made with the Dutch in 1609, would enable the Spaniards to support the popish league from the Low Countries, as in all cases they might do from Italy; and if they could keep the king of Great Britain from

330

diverting the forces of Spain in the mean time, there was reason to hope that these united powers might conquer both the Palatinates, as well as Bohemia, and break the force of the protestant league in Germany, before the expiration of the truce and the renewal of the war with the united provinces of the Low Countries should create another diversion. This was a principal part of the plan laid by the house of Austria and the other Roman catholic princes, for oppressing the protestants and invading the liberties of Germany. To the eternal infamy of king James, it succeeded even beyond the hopes of those who laid it. The hints which Digby gave him in the very beginning of this negotiation, might have put him on his guard, and a thousand things which happened in the course of it, would have undeceived, provoked and determined any other man. His presumption, his fear, and, above all, his perverse system of policy prevented any effects of these kinds. We forbear entering into the particulars of what he did for Spain; of what he suffered Spain to do; and of all the indignities which he received from every branch of the house of Austria, during these transactions. Most of them have been observed, and are sufficiently known; and it would be an unnecessary work to point out some few instances more, which have not been, perhaps, taken notice of, or explained as much as they deserved. We shall spare ourselves and our readers this disagreeable recollection, and only observe in general the plan upon which king James appears to have acted; as we have observed what the plan was of those who made so fatal a use of his weakness. His silly pride could not be satisfied, unless he matched his son with a daughter of Spain, or France. He had been disappointed formerly on that side, and lately on this. He was resolved at any rate not to be disappointed a third time. The immense sum which had been promised for the Infanta's portion tempted him the more, because for several years he would call no parliament to grant him supplies, and he found it hard to raise them, even in small proportions, without a parliament. He imagined vainly that this alliance with Spain would give him great consideration abroad; and wickedly, that it would afford him means of raising and extending his prerogative at home. He saw the mischiefs which accrued to the protestant interest abroad, either as immediate, or as remote effects of his conduct; either in consequence of what he did, or in consequence of what he neglected; and we are willing to believe that he felt, in some degree, those which fell on the family into which he had married his daughter. But the interest of the protestants in general touched him little. Abroad, as well as at home, he chose rather by condescensions and submissions to court his enemies, than to unite his friends among one another, and to attach them to himself. In his zeal for the imaginary rights of princes, he could not forgive the elector Palatinate for taking arms against the emperor; and whilst he looked on him as a rebel, forgot that he was his son. If he remembered it at any time, and felt any concern, the sentiment was surely very faint; since we find that the distant and uncertain prospect of making some tolerable composition for this unhappy prince, by the intercession of Spain, was always sufficient to calm his paternal solicitude. He saw, without doubt, at least during the life of Philip the Third, who did not die till the year 1621, that Spain was not much in earnest to give him the Infanta; but he seemed resolved to overcome all difficulties, and to determine the councils of Spain, and even of Rome, in his favor, by dint of concessions. The truth is, he went so far in his concessions at last, that these councils seemed to be determined. Those of Spain, at least, were so most certainly in the year 1623, even before the voyage of the prince into Spain; and the articles sworn to both by him when he was there, and by his father here, amounted to little less than a direct establishment of popery. That this charge is just will, we think, appear evident, when it shall be remembered, without entering into more particulars, that by these articles the king and Prince of Wales engaged for the suspension, and even abrogation of all laws made against Roman catholics; that they engaged never to consent to the making any new laws of the same kind; and that, as the children to be born of this marriage were to be educated by their mother, till ten years of age, in compliance with the king of Spain's demands; so the prince was prevailed on to promise that he would lengthen this term till twelve years, according to the desire of the pope.

Thus was king James amused till the beginning of the year 1623, when the Upper Palatinate and the dignity of elector were taken from Frederic and conferred on the Duke of Bavaria, by the diet of Ratisbon: or, to speak more properly, by the prerogative of Ferdinand, who acted in the diet as dogmatically and as absolutely as king James endeavored to act in his parliaments. When this point was gained by amusing king James, and the protestant interest was broken in Germany; the next point was to be carried by concluding with him and making the match on such terms, as might secure an immediate toleration, and open the prospect of a future establishment of popery in this kingdom. The parliament of 1621, beheld part of this scene, and apprehended, upon very just grounds, the sequel. They saw the fatal consequences of the negotiation, whilst it was in suspense, and they dreaded those which would follow the conclusion of it. To stop the first, and to prevent the last, there was but one expedient; the forcing king James into a war, for recovering the Palatinate. This they endeavored with all their might; but he meant nothing less, and had called a parliament purely to get money from his people, on the pretence of a war he was resolved not to make. Some money he got by this trick; but when he had it squandered away in trifling negotiations and a ridiculous show of war, he could get no more: so that this parliament ended as others had done, and even with greater dissatisfaction between the king and the people, both on account of his conducting foreign affairs against the interest and sense of the nation, and of his attacking more openly than ever the privileges of parliament. The parliament remonstrated, petitioned, protested. The king dissolved the parliament in a rage; imprisoned several members of the house of commons, and even some of the house of lords. He resumed his project of governing without parliaments, since he could not govern as ill as he had a mind to govern with them. But this project was not pursued above two years; for what his parliament could not obtain from him an unworthy favorite did obtain. Motives of private interest, and, perhaps, of a worse nature, made that great turn in affairs, which so many motives of a public nature and of national interest had never been able to make. In short, a cabal at court prevailed on this prince to alter his conduct in those very points, on which the parliament, seconded by the clamors of the whole nation, had been never able to prevail. We shall not attempt to guess, as many have done, at the secret reasons, which determined Buckingham, nor at those by which he determined the Prince of Wales to undertake the romantic and, in every light, ridiculous journey into Spain, to carry the treaty of marriage to a conclusion; then to break it off again in so abrupt and ungracious a manner; and to become so earnest for engaging in a war with Spain. Whatever these reasons were, the reason given for breaking the match was not the true one. The restitution of the Palatinate had been very coolly pressed, not to say neglected, even whilst the prince was at Madrid; and yet after he came from thence, the king of Spain had signed an act, by which he engaged for this restitution: so that on the principles on which this negotiation had been conducted, there seemed to be no reason for breaking it off given by Spain at the time when it was broken. But the parliament which king James called upon this occasion, proceeded like the last, on other principles than the court had done, and was therefore, very consistently with these principles, ready to seize the opportunity offered, by advising the king to break the match, and enter into a war for recovering the Palatinate, and by giving him very large supplies for this purpose. We cannot, upon this occasion, subscribe to the censure passed by my Lord Clarendon, how much soever we esteem his history, and honor the memory of that noble historian; for in the first place, the supplies given by this last parliament of king James, were not only very large, as we have just now said, but they were such as the king was contented with, and thanked the parliament for, in his answer to the speaker of the house of commons. Secondly, we cannot agree that it was the parliament, properly speaking, who prevailed on the king, and engaged him in the war. The parliament advised him to it indeed; but nothing can be more manifest than this, even by my Lord Clarendon's own account, that the measure was resolved on before, and that it was the measure of the prince and of Buckingham, which the king, however unwillingly, adopted. The parliament in truth did no more than advise him to break the treaty which he had already broken; and those who reflect on precedent passages, will easily concur with us, that if this had not been the case, it would not have been in the power of the parliament to break the match; much less to engage the king in the war. Thirdly, if subsequent parliaments did not support those mountains of promises, as they are called, which this parliament raised, we shall venture to affirm that it was the fault of the court, not of the parliament.

This last article requires to be set in a very clear light, because it opens to us a source of causes, from whence a great part of the mischiefs, which followed in the next reign, arose; or by which, at least, they were aggravated and precipitated. First, therefore, we observe that the measures of the court were so foolishly taken for pushing the war, that if parliaments had given by millions, and given with as little stint in those days, as they have given since, their grants must have been ineffectual to any good purpose. Just before the death of king James, an army had been raised for the Palatinate war, under the command of the famous Mansfeldt. The French first and the Dutch afterwards refused passage to these troops, or even to suffer them to land. The cry of the court was loud against the perfidy of France, as it had been against the emperor and Spain in their turns. This will be always the case, when silly ministers bungle themselves into difficulties, of which others make their profit; or when they knavishly engage a national quarrel for some private, indirect interest, and inflame the people to resent imaginary injuries. But the truth is, that king James had nobody to blame but himself, when he took general and ambiguous answers for sufficient engagements, and did not see that France would refuse passage to these troops for the same reasons as made her decline entering, at that time, into a league against the house of Austria.

Another blunder committed about the same time, by this wise king, and that wise minister, his scholar, Buckingham, must be mentioned. He was to take possession of Frankendal, which had been deposited in the hands of the Infanta Isabella. The Infanta agreed to yield the palace to him, and to give passage to his troops, who were to compose the garrison, according to her engagements; but refused to answer for their passage over the lands of the empire, to which she was not engaged. Then, and not till then, he made this discovery in geography, that his troops must march over the lands of the empire to get from the Low Countries into the Palatinate. Such blunders as these were sufficient to disgust the parliaments of that age, and to make them backward in supplying a war thus managed. Much more reason had they to be so, when they saw the same managers and the same management continue in the next reign. This disgust at the management of the war, however, would not have produced so many fatal consequences, if it had stood alone. But we observe, in the second place, that the parliaments, which met after the accession of king Charles, became incensed, as they discovered more and more that the account given by the Duke of Buckingham, in the reign of king James, and on which the resolutions of that parliament had been taken, was false in almost every point. A system of lies dressed up to deceive the nation, and imposed on the parliament, could neither remain undiscovered nor escape the resentment and indignation it deserved, when discovered. Besides, that parliament and the nation too, when they expressed so much joy at the breach with Spain, flattered themselves that, by preventing the marriage with the Infanta, they had prevented all the dangers, which they apprehended from that marriage; whereas it appeared soon afterwards that they stood exposed to the very same dangers by the marriage concluded with France; nay, to greater; since the education of the children by the mother, that is in popery, had been confined to ten years by the former treaty, and was extended to thirteen by the latter. In short, it cannot be denied, and my Lord Clarendon owns, that as the insolence of Buckingham caused the war with Spain, so his lust and his vanity alone threw the nation into another with France. Spain was courted first without reason, and affronted afterwards without provocation. Ships were lent to the king of France against his protestant subjects; and the persecution of his protestant subjects was made the pretence of a rupture with him. Thus was the nation led from one extravagant project to another, at an immense charge, with great diminution of honor and infinite loss to trade, by the ignorance, private interest, and passion of one man. The conduct therefore of the parliament, who attacked this man, was perfectly consistent with the conduct of that parliament, who had so much applauded him; and one cannot observe without astonishment the slip made by the noble historian we have just quoted, when he affirms that the same men who had applauded him, attacked him, without imputing the least crime to him, that was not as much known when they applauded him, as when they attacked him. Now it is plain that many of the crimes imputed to him, in the reign of king Charles, when he was attacked, could not be known, and that many others had not been even committed in the reign of king James, when he was, upon one single occasion, applauded.

To the disgusts taken at the management of foreign affairs, must be added those which were daily given by the court in the management of domestic affairs. Real, not imaginary, grievances arose and were continued in every part of the administration. Some of these king Charles, like his father, was obstinately bent to maintain, and his right of imposing them was asserted. Others were disguised and excused rather than defended; but in redressing even these, he showed such a reluctance, that he complied without obliging, and increased the disgust of his people, even whilst he granted their requests. We have said in a former discourse, that king Charles came a party man to the throne, and that he continued an invasion on the people's rights, whilst he imagined himself only concerned in the defence of his own. In advancing this proposition, we were far from meaning a compliment at the expense of truth. We avow it as an opinion we have formed on reading the relations published on all sides, and to which, it seems to us, that all the authentic anecdotes of those times may be reconciled. This prince had sucked in with his milk those absurd principles of government, which his father was so industrious and, unhappily for king and people, so successful in propagating. He found them espoused, as true principles both of religion and policy, by a whole party in the nation, whom he esteemed friends to the constitution in church and state. He found them opposed by a party, whom he looked on indiscriminately as enemies to the church and to monarchy. Can we wonder that he grew zealous in a cause, which he understood to concern him so nearly, and in which he saw so many men, who had not the same interest, and might therefore be supposed to act on a principle of conscience, equally zealous? Let any one, who hath been deeply and long engaged in the contests of party, ask himself on cool reflection, whether prejudices concerning men and things, have not grown up and strengthened with him, and obtained an uncontrolable influence over his conduct. We dare appeal to the inward sentiments of every such person. With this habitual bias upon him king Charles came to the throne; and, to complete the misfortune, he had given all his confidence to a mad man. An honest minister might have shown him how wrong his measures were; a wise one how ill-timed. Buckingham was incapable of either. The violence and haughtiness of his temper confirmed his master in the pursuit of these measures; and the character of the first minister became that of the administration. Other circumstances, which often happen, happened likewise in this case. The minister was universally hated; the king was not. To support the minister, it was necessary that the prerogative should be strained, and violent and unpopular means should be employed. To support the government, nothing of this sort was necessary. Nay, the very contrary measures were necessary to reconcile the king to his people, and to stop in time that alienation of their minds from him; which began even then to appear. In this difference of interests, those of the crown were sacrificed to those of the minister. King Charles, who had encouraged parliamentary prosecutions, in his father's reign, would not suffer them in his own. He dissolved his parliaments, and broke almost all the few ties of union, which remained between himself and the nation, that he might screen some of the most unworthy men who ever disserved a prince, or dishonored a court. Before the death of Buckingham, irreparable mischief was done. "The distemper of the nation was so universal," according to my Lord Clarendon, "that all wise men looked upon it as the prediction of the destruction and dissolution that would follow." This prediction was soon verified. The king executed what he had often threatened. Parliaments were laid aside. The very mention of them was forbid; and he continued to govern without any for twelve years. During this interval, the distemper lurked indeed; but it grew more malignant; and if a national serenity appeared about the time when the king went into Scotland, it appeared just when the poison worked most effectually and began to seize the heart. Jealousies about religion and liberty were now at their height. The former, as far as they affected the king and his protestant ministers, were illfounded; but for that very reason, it would have been easy to cure them; and if they had been cured in time, as we think, on my Lord Clarendon's authority, that nothing could have led the Scotch nation into rebellion, so are we persuaded that a great motive and spur to the rebellion in England would have been taken away. The latter were certainly but too well founded. The king had, in a manner, renounced the constitution; and instead of governing with the assistance and concurrence of a parliament, he governed by illegal acts of power, which the council, the star-chamber and the high commission exercised. There was something still more dangerous to liberty in practice. Not only the government was carried on without law, or against law, but the judges were become the instruments of arbitrary power, and that law, which should have been the protection of property, was rendered, by their corrupt interpretations of it, so great a grievance that "the foundations of right were, to the apprehension and understanding of wise men," says my Lord Clarendon, "never more in danger to be destroyed."

Whilst things were in this situation here, king Charles lighted up another fire in Scotland, by resuming the project of modelling that church, which king James had begun. Archbishop Laud, who had neither temper nor knowledge of the world enough to be intrusted with the government of a private college, conducted this enterprise and precipitated the public ruin. The puritans of England soon united in a common cause with the puritans of Scotland; and the army, which the latter had raised, marched into England. Many of those who had appeared against the court, and even some of those who were on the side of the court, favored, in different manners, the Scots, and hoped to apply this force and to improve this incident so as to restrain the prerogative within known, perhaps narrower bounds, and to strengthen the barriers of public liberty. That this might have been brought about, and that the civil war which followed, might have been prevented, appeared very manifestly in the temper and proceedings of the parliament, which met in April 1640, when all had been done, which could be done, to destroy the constitution; for if the king had been able to continue to govern without parliaments, the constitution had been destroyed; and when calling a parliament was visibly the effect of necessity and fear, not choice, the parliament, which was called, showed wonderful order and sobriety in their whole behavior. If some passion had appeared in their debates, it might have been well excused in a house of commons assembled at such a time; and yet scarce an angry word was thrown out. The few, that escaped from some, were either silently disliked, or openly disapproved. The king, even in this crisis of affairs, preserved the same carriage he had formerly used towards them, and showed too plainly that he regarded them only as tax-layers. In a word, about a month after their meeting, he dissolved them, and as soon as he had dissolved them, he repented, but he repented too late, of his rashness. Well might he repent; for the vessel was now full, and this last drop made the waters of bitterness overflow. Here we draw the curtain, and put an end to our remarks, by observing, first, that if the spirit of liberty had once relaxed in the space of almost forty years, liberty must have been swallowed up by prerogative; secondly, that after these long contests between the king and the people, and when the latter had received the utmost provocations, the spirit of liberty was not transported into any excess; determined to defend the people, but unwilling to offend the king. The king, and he alone could have done it, forced the affairs of the nation, as he had put his own long before, into the hands of a faction. The true friends of the constitution were divided; and divided, were too weak to prevail on either side. The spirit of faction, not the spirit of liberty, is answerable for all which followed; and who is answerable for reducing the contest on both sides, to be the contest of faction may, we think, be sufficiently collected from what hath been said in these discourses.

Index

Adams, John, xi
Alary, Pierre Joseph (Abbé), xxxii, xxxiii, xl
Anne (queen of England), xii, 56, 139, 144, 145

Bacon, Francis, xxi, xxii, xxviii, 22, 77, 87, 91, 156, 243, 245
Balance of power, 99–140, 254–267
Bayle, Pierre, xxviii, xxix, xxxi, xxxvi, xxxvii, xxxix, 51
Biblical history, 35–48, 72–77
Bodin, Jean, 29, 30, 57
Bolingbroke, works: *The Crafts-man*, xiii, xviii, xxxix, xl, xliv, l, 154, 155, 156, 163; *Dissertation upon Parties*, xiii, xlv, l; *The Idea of a Patriot King*, xiii, l, li, lii; *Letters on the Study and Use of History*, xiii, xiv, xv, xix, xxii, xxiii, xxvii, xxxii, xxxv, xxxviii, xlvi, xlix, 2–152; *Philosophical Fragments*, xiv, xxii; *Remarks on the History of England*, xiii, xl, xli, xliii, xlv, 153–340; *Substance of Some Letters to M. de Pouilly*, xxxviii
Boulainvilliers, Henry, xxiii, xxvi

Brady, Robert, xli, xlii, xliii, xliv, xlv
Brumfitt, J. H., xxvi, xxxv
Buckingham, first duke of (George Villiers), 334–39
Burgh, James, xix
Burke, Edmund, xi

Carr, E. H., xxxix
Charles I (king of England), 276, 308, 318, 337–39
Charles II (king of England), 19, 96, 314
Charles V (Holy Roman Emperor), 99–101
Cicero, xvii, xix, xxiv, 11, 12, 18, 60, 68, 147, 153
Clarendon, first earl of (Edward Hyde), 77, 308, 334, 338–39
Cranmer, Thomas (archbishop), 222
Cromwell, Oliver, xlvi, 20

Daily Courant, xl
Daily Gazetteer, xliii
Diodorus Siculus, xvii, xxiii, xxxii, 18, 35
Dionysius of Halicarnassus, xvi, xvii, 9, 67

Douglas, D. C., xxiv, xxv, xxviii, xxix
Dugdale, William, xxv, xlii

Edward III (king of England), 182–88, 234
Edward IV (king of England), 201–4, 208
Edward VI (king of England), 226–27, 300
Elizabeth I (queen of England), xlvi, xlix, 96, 202, 236–74, 277–79, 281–83, 291–92, 294, 301, 321

Fénelon, François de Salignac de La Mothe, xxvi
Filmer, Robert, xlii
Fontenelle, Bernard le Bovier de, xxvi, xxx
Frederick (Prince of Wales), xiii

Gay, John, xi, xlix
George I (king of England), xii
Gibbon, Edward, xlviii
Glorious Revolution, the, xliv, xlix, 21, 125, 148, 313
Guicciardini, 27, 57, 70, 91

Harley, Robert, xii, 124, 139
Harrington, James, xliv, xlix, l, li
Hellanicus, 33, 34, 64
Henry IV (king of England), 183–84, 193–95
Henry V (king of England), 194
Henry VI (king of England), 194–95, 201–2, 207, 208, 235
Henry VII (king of England), xliv, 89–92, 210–14, 231–32, 300
Henry VIII (king of England), 85, 90, 215–28, 300
Herodotus, 33, 34, 66
Hume, David, xx, xxxviii
Hyde, Baron (Viscount Corn-
bury), xix, xxvii, xxviii, xlviii, 3

Jacobites, 171–73
James I (king of England), 20, 96, 238, 268–69, 276–337
James II (king of England), 19, 20
Jefferson, Thomas, xi
Johnson, Samuel, xiv, xxix, xxxvi
Josephus, 22, 32, 34, 35, 37, 38, 39, 43, 51
Julius Africanus, 5, 32, 35

La Mothe le Vayer, xxx, 11, 59
Laud, William (archbishop), 200–201, 339
Le Moyne, Pierre, xviii
Levesque de Pouilly, xxxii, xxxiii
Livy, xxiv, 61, 65, 67, 70, 165
Locke, John, xxii, xxviii, 29
London Journal, xl, xliii, 196
Louis XIV (king of France), xii, 111, 121, 124, 128–33
Lucian of Samosata, xvii, 56

Machiavelli, xix, xx, xxii, xxxii, xlv, l, li, 26, 60, 165, 166
Magna Charta, xlii, xliii, 234
Mallet, David, xiv
Marlborough, first duke of (John Churchill), 13, 103, 104, 121, 135–36
Marsham, John, 5, 6
Mary (queen of England), 227–28, 239, 240, 304
Mary (queen of Scotland), 241–42, 254, 258, 281
Mirror for Magistrates, xviii, xix, xxv
Montaigne, Michael Eyquemde, 56, 57, 61
Montesquieu, Charles de Secondat, Baron de, xii, xlviii

Nadel, George, xvi, xvii, xxi, xxiii, xxxv

Pitt, William, xiv
Plutarch, 31, 35, 57, 61, 65
Pocock, J. G. A., xxiv, xxv, xxxv,
   xli, xlviii
Polybius, xvii, xix, xx, xxi, xxxii,
   xlvii, 16, 24, 67
Pope, Alexander, xi, xiii, xxxii,
   xlix, 60, 62
Puritans, 321, 323, 324
Pyrrhonism, 50–51, 55, 57

Rapin de Thoyras, xviii, xxiii,
   196, 202–3, 213, 220, 225,
   258, 302
Richard II (king of England),
   188–96, 235, 304

St. Evremond, Charles de Marque-
   tel de Saint-Denis, xxx
St. Jerome, 36, 43
Sallust, xxiv, 12, 67
Saxon Constitution, xl–xlv, 177–
   80, 231, 233, 299–300
Seneca, 9–10, 30, 60, 63
Simon, Richard, xxxi, 39
Spelman, Henry, xxv, xlii
Stanhope, Philip D. (earl of Ches-
   terfield), xii

Swift, Jonathan, xi, xii, xiii, xxxii,
   xlix

Tacitus, xvii, xxi, xxxii, 9, 18,
   57, 67
Taylor, Brook, xxxiii
Thucydides, xxxii, 66, 70
Torrey, Norman, xxxiv
Trevor-Roper, H. R., xlviii

Utrecht, Treaty of, xii, 56, 106,
   129–33, 145

Voltaire, F. M. Arouet, xii, xv, xxvi,
   xxix, xxxi, xxxiv, xxxv, xxxviii,
   xlviii

Walpole, Horace, xiv, xxxvi
Walpole, Robert, xi, xiii, xiv,
   xxviii, xxxix, xlii, xliii, xliv,
   xlv, xlvi, xlix, l
William I (king of England), xlii,
   xliii, 179
William III (king of England),
   13, 21, 101–4, 313
Wolsey, Thomas (cardinal), 217–
   20

Xenophon, 11, 33, 66, 67